MAKING SENSE OF TANTRIC BUDDHISM

SOUTH ASIA ACROSS THE DISCIPLINES

SOUTH ASIA ACROSS THE DISCIPLINES

◈ ◈ ◈

EDITED BY DIPESH CHAKRABARTY, SHELDON POLLOCK, AND SANJAY SUBRAHMANYAM

Funded by a grant from the Andrew W. Mellon Foundation, and jointly published by the University of California Press, the University of Chicago Press, and Columbia University Press.

Extreme Poetry: The South Asian Movement of Simultaneous Narration by Yigal Bronner (Columbia)

The Social Space of Language: Vernacular Culture in British Colonial Punjab by Farina Mir (California)

Unifying Hinduism: Philosophy and Identity in Indian Intellectual History by Andrew J. Nicholson (Columbia)

Everyday Healing: Hindus and Others in an Ambiguously Islamic Place by Carla Bellamy (California)

The Millennial Sovereign: Sacred Kingship and Sainthood in Islam by A. Azfar Moin (Columbia)

South Asia Across the Disciplines is a series devoted to publishing first books across a wide range of South Asian studies, including art, history, philology or textual studies, philosophy, religion, and the interpretive social sciences. Series authors all share the goal of opening up new archives and suggesting new methods and approaches, while demonstrating that South Asian scholarship can be at once deep in expertise and broad in appeal.

MAKING SENSE OF TANTRIC BUDDHISM

HISTORY, SEMIOLOGY, AND TRANSGRESSION IN THE INDIAN TRADITIONS

Christian K. Wedemeyer

COLUMBIA UNIVERSITY PRESS *NEW YORK*

Columbia University Press
Publishers Since 1893
New York Chichester, West Sussex
cup.columbia.edu
Copyright © 2013 Columbia University Press
Paperback edition, 2014
All rights reserved

Library of Congress Cataloging-in-Publication Data

Wedemeyer, Christian K.
Making sense of Tantric Buddhism : history, semiology, and transgression in the Indian traditions / Christian K. Wedemeyer.
pages cm—(South Asia across the disciplines)
Includes bibliographical references and index.
ISBN 978-0-231-16240-1 (cloth : alk. paper)—ISBN 978-0-231-16241-8 (pbk. : alk. paper)—
ISBN 978-0-231-53095-8 (e-book)
1. Tantric Buddhism—India. I. Title.
BQ8912.9.I5W43 2013
294.3′925—dc23
2012006168

Columbia University Press books are printed on permanent and durable acid-free paper.
This book was printed on paper with recycled content.
Printed in the United States of America

Cover image: Accession #851, *Rajshahi Museum, Rajshahi, Bangladesh.*
Photographed by John C. and Susan L. Huntington, June 1994.
Cover design: Katie Poe

References to Internet Web sites (URLs) were accurate at the time of writing. Neither the author nor Columbia University Press is responsible for URLs that may have expired or changed since the manuscript was prepared.

For

Josie,

who gave so much to so many,

and

Gita,

who waited so patiently for me to write a “real book”

◈ ◈ ◈

For the scholar of comparative religions,
Tantrism must represent the ultimate challenge.

—Michel Strickmann

CONTENTS

List of Figures and Tables xiii

Preface and Acknowledgments xv

List of Abbreviations xix

INTRODUCTION: MAKING SENSE IN AND OF THE HUMAN SCIENCES 1

PART I: HISTORIOGRAPHY

1. ORIGINS, RELIGION, AND THE ORIGINS OF TANTRISM 17

Understanding Tantric Buddhism Through Its Origins 18

The Quest for Origins as Method in the History of Religions 32

2. NARRATING TANTRIC BUDDHISM 37

The Poetics of Historiography 38

Tantra as End: The Decline and Fall of Indian Buddhism 43

Tantra as Beginning: The Primordial Undercurrent 51

Tantra as Middle: Medieval Esotericism 58

Historical Narrative and Ideological Implication 66

3. GOING NATIVE: TRADITIONAL HISTORIOGRAPHY OF TANTRIC BUDDHISM 68

Historiography and Cosmology in Exoteric Buddhism 71

Historiography and Cosmology in Esoteric Buddhism 79

Observations on Structure, Function, and Historiography 95

PART II: INTERPRETATION

4. THE SEMIOLOGY OF TRANSGRESSION 105

The Literal and the Figurative in Tantric Hermeneutics 107

Connotative Semiotics as Exegetical Method 113

Connotative Semiotics in Tantric Ritual 117

Connotative Semiotics in Tantric Scripture 125

5. THE PRACTICE OF INDIAN TANTRIC BUDDHISM 133

Interpreting the Practice Observance I: Irony and Inversion 144

Interpreting the Practice Observance II: Prerequisites and Temporal Frame 149

Interpreting the Practice Observance III: Śaiva Parallels 152

6. TANTRIC BUDDHIST TRANSGRESSION IN CONTEXT 170

The Social Location of Esoteric Buddhism as an Interpretative Problem 171

Contriving Marginality 173

The Common Repertoire of Buddhist Professionals 175

Carnivalesque or Rituals of Rebellion? 188

But . . . Did They Really Do It?! 192

CONCLUSION: NO TWO "WAYS" ABOUT IT 200

APPENDIX I: THE INDRABHŪTI STORY ACCORDING TO PAD MA DKAR PO (CA. 1575) 207

APPENDIX II: CHAPTER NINE OF THE *BUDDHAKAPĀLA TANTRA*, THE "PRACTICE" (*CARYĀPAṬALA*) 209

Notes 211

Bibliography 267

Index 301

FIGURES AND TABLES

Figure 2.1	Definitions of the medieval period in India	60
Figure 4.1	Structure of the linguistic sign according to F. de Saussure	113
Figure 4.2	Structure of metalanguage	114
Figure 4.3	Structure of connotative semiotics	114
Figure 4.4	Barthes' first example	115
Figure 4.5	Barthes' second example	116
Figure 4.6	Suggested semiology of antinomian discourse in the Mahāyoga Tantras	121

Table 2.1	Conceptual binaries of rhetoric of Tantra as beginning	56
Table 2.2	Conceptual binaries of rhetoric of the medieval	62
Table 5.1	Central and related terms	137
Table 5.2	Sites of practice	139
Table 5.3	Dress/accoutrements for practice	141
Table 5.4	Behaviors prescribed in practice	142
Table 5.5	Behaviors proscribed in practice	143
Table 5.6	Qualifications/prerequisites for practice	151
Table 5.7	Duration of practice	153

PREFACE AND ACKNOWLEDGMENTS

THE INTERPRETATION of Indian Tantric Buddhism presented in this book has developed over many years (ca. 1998–2010), and I have benefitted enormously from the thinking and assistance of numerous friends, family, and colleagues over this time. Parts of the argument may be traced back to my 1999 doctoral dissertation, when I first began to look more critically at the rhetorics structuring modern accounts of Asian history. Instrumental in shaping my approach to these questions was the inspiration and guidance of Ted Riccardi, who urged me to revisit the work of Hayden White and suggested that I pay close attention to "how people write about India." I have endeavored to put that advice into practice here and have also taken a run at how Indians have written about and for themselves.

In many ways, the discussions I had with Ted advanced longstanding questions of method and theory first posed to me by my undergraduate advisor in religion, J. H. Stone II. Although Professor Stone did not actually introduce me to the work of Roland Barthes (that was a fortuitous result of a sale at a New York City bookstore in the early 2000s), he had planted the seed long before. The challenging approach to the study of religions that he exemplified then has impelled me in the decades since to follow up on the many similar pregnant hints he was so good at dropping.

Writing and thinking, in my experience, are highly context-dependent; this book could not have been what it has become were it not for the climate of constant stimulation and challenge offered at the University of Chicago. Colleagues both within and outside the Divinity School have served in general as examples of the very best critical scholarship and have also offered concrete encouragement and criticism as I ventured the various essays that coalesced in this volume. Thanks in particular are due to Wendy Doniger, Matthew Kapstein, and Bruce Lincoln of the History of Religions; Divinity faculty Dan Arnold, Catherine Breckus, Clark Gilpin, Margaret Mitchell, Willemien Otten, Richard Rosengarten, Kathryn Tanner; South Asianists Muzaffar Alam, Yigal Bronner, Steven Collins, Whitney Cox, and Gary Tubb; East Asianists Paul Copp and Jim Ketelaar; and Assyriologist Seth Richardson.

Outside the University of Chicago, I have benefitted immensely from discussions and assistance from many scholars of South Asian religions and civilizations, of whom particular mention should be made: Ashok Aklujkar, Yael Bentor, David Drewes, David Gray, Janet Gyatso, Charlie Hallisey, Shaman Hatley, Roger Jackson, Karen Lang, Rob Linrothe, Dan Martin, Robert Mayer, Poornima Paidipaty, Peter Skilling, Jan-Ulrich Sobisch, Robert Thurman, and Vesna Wallace. Allan D. Megill and Marina Bollinger offered much appreciated help with Paul Veyne. Many others have helped with obtaining the textual resources required for this type of study: Jim Nye, Beth Bidlack, and the staff of the interlibrary loan office at the University of Chicago libraries; the staff of the Newberry Library; and the National Archives of Nepal. The digital Sanskrit manuscript collection of the University of Tokyo has been absolutely invaluable for my work. Leonard van der Kuijp was most generous in sharing with me both his own writings and copies of rare Tibetan historical manuscripts. Various research assistants have been invaluable over the years: Brad Aaron, Erin Burke, Amanda Huffer, Karin Meyers, and Susan Zakin. Likewise, my secretary Judy Lawrence has also been invaluable. Justin Henry was most kind in offering help with the Sinhala *Nikayasamgrahawa*. Larry Rosansky and Ted Arnold gave very kind feedback on the draft manuscript.

Very special and heartfelt thanks are due to Ronald M. Davidson, who, for almost two decades now, has been a remarkably generous, tolerant, and unfailingly learned interlocutor. Although we continue to disagree on numerous issues of method and interpretation, Ron has shown remarkable goodwill in indulging my compulsion to follow out my intuitions, however contrary they may be to his own. His 2002 *Indian Esoteric Buddhism* fundamentally reset the standard for scholarly works on Tantric Buddhism, raising the bar rather dramatically. Had it not been for his work, I could barely have conceived of the projects that took shape herein. All scholars working in this field owe him an immense debt of gratitude.

The arguments that developed into chapter 2 were first crafted into a publishable form during a fruitful research stay at New College of Florida, for which I thank Bob Schiffman, Darilyn Avery, and the late Roland Heiser. Chuck Matthews and the anonymous reviewers of the *Journal of the American Academy of Religion* challenged me to refine elements of what became chapter 4. Many universities and learned societies were kind enough to invite or allow me to present parts of these arguments in their presence. Thanks are due in this regard to the American Academy of Religion, the American Oriental Society, the Columbia University Seminar on Buddhist Studies, the Cornell University South Asia Series, the Harvard University Buddhist Studies Forum, the International Association of Buddhist Studies, the University of Chicago Divinity School, and the University of Toronto Department of Religion.

I am likewise indebted (fortunately, not literally) for the financial support that I have received over the years from a variety of sources. University of Chicago Divinity School deans Richard A. Rosengarten and Margaret M. Mitchell have been unfailingly supportive of my work in a variety of ways, lavish in both their financial support and their intellectual critique. Likewise, the Committee on Southern Asian Studies provided ongoing research support and opportunities for travel to archives and institutions in South Asia. The final stages of writing were supported by a National Endowment for the Humanities Fellowship, although it is important to emphasize that any views, findings, conclusions, or recommendations expressed in this publication do not necessarily reflect those of the National Endowment for the Humanities.

Preliminary versions of some chapters have appeared previously in various journals, and I am grateful both for this and for the chance to revisit them here. Elements of chapter 2 appeared as "Tropes, Typologies, and Turnarounds: A Brief Genealogy of the Historiography of Tantric Buddhism," *History of Religions*, vol. 40, no. 3 (February 2001), 223–259 (© 2001 by the University of Chicago; all rights reserved). The central argument of chapter 4 first saw publication as "Beef, Dog, and Other Mythologies: Connotative Semiotics in Mahāyoga Tantra Ritual and Scripture," *Journal of the American Academy of Religion*, vol. 75, no. 2 (June 2007), 383–417. The central argument in chapter 5 was first articulated in "Locating Tantric Antinomianism: An Essay Toward an Intellectual History of the 'Practices/Practice Observance' (caryā/*caryāvrata*)," *Journal of the International Association of Buddhist Studies*, vol. 34 (2011). Thanks are due to the University of Chicago, the American Academy of Religion, and the International Association of Buddhist Studies for the opportunity to include them here. I am grateful as well to the editorial board of the South Asia Across the

Disciplines series for believing in this project and including it among the wonderful books in this series; and to Susan, John, and Eric Huntington for providing the cover image.

Finally, as always, my family deserves highest praise and eternal gratitude for their support: my parents, Anne Wedemeyer and Phillips Wedemeyer; my stepmothers, Josephine Wedemeyer and Jeanne Hanchett; my nanny, Margarete Wiener; my sisters, Hope and Willow; and all my wonderful stepsisters and brothers, cousins, aunts, uncles, nieces, and nephews. The late Gen. Albert C. Wedemeyer took an early interest in my education and travels in Asia, and I belatedly acknowledge his kindness here. My many friends and acquaintances—a kind of family themselves—bring warmth and cheer to my world, making this kind of thing possible. Most of all, though, my deepest gratitude goes to my wife, Gita, and my two amazing girls, Maitreya and Isolde, for giving me three unsurpassable and compelling reasons to love, live, and strive.

Christian K. Wedemeyer
Chicago, Illinois

ABBREVIATIONS

AVP40:	*Atharvaveda Pariśiṣṭā* 40
BK:	*Buddhakapāla Tantra*
BY/PM:	*Brahmayāmala/Picumata*
CMP:	*Caryāmelāpakapradīpa* of Āryadeva
CMT:	*Caṇḍamahāroṣaṇa Tantra*
CPAMA:	*Catuṣpīṭhākhyāta-mantrāṃśa*
DN:	*Dīghanikāya*
DP:	*Dhammapada*
Grk.:	Greek
GS:	*Guhyasiddhi* of Padmavajra
GST:	*Guhyasamāja Tantra*
HA:	*Herukābhidhāna*
HT:	*Hevajra Tantra*
JS:	*Jñānasiddhi* of Indrabhūti
KKP:	*Kālīkulapañcaśataka*
KMT:	*Kubjikāmatatantra*
LS:	*Laghusaṃvara*
MK:	*Mahākāla Tantra*
MMK:	*Mañjuśrīmūlakalpa*
MNS:	*Mañjuśrīnāmasaṃgīti*
MS(s):	manuscript(s)
MVT:	*Mahāvairocana Tantra*
PU:	*Pradīpoddyotana* of Candrakīrtī
Skt.:	Sanskrit
SU:	*Saṃvarodaya Tantra*
ST:	*Saṃpuṭa Tantra*

STTS:	*Sarvatathāgatatattvasaṃgraha*
SU:	*Saṃvarodaya Tantra*
SYM:	*Siddhayogeśvarīmata(tantra)*
TD:	*Tattvadaśaka* of Advayavajra
Tib.:	Tibetan
VĀ:	*Vajrāralli Tantra*
YRM:	*Yogaratnamālā* of Kāṇha
YS:	*Yoginīsaṃcāra Tantra*

MAKING SENSE OF TANTRIC BUDDHISM

INTRODUCTION

MAKING SENSE IN AND OF THE HUMAN SCIENCES

śvā-kharoṣṭra-gajādy-asṛk pītvā māṃsena bhojanaṃ nityam || iṣṭaṃ sarva-viśeṣa-rakta-vilipta-mahāmāṃsaṃ samasta-kutsita-māṃsaṃ prāṇaka-śata-lakṣa-saṃyuktaṃ divyam | vairocanenâtipūṭaṃ kīṭa-śataiḥ simisimāyamānaṃ śvāna-nara-cchardita-miśram māṃsaṃ vajrāmbu-marjikā-yuktam | vairocana-saṃmiśraṃ bhoktavyaṃ yoginotsāhaiḥ |

Having drunk dog, donkey, camel, and elephant blood, one should regularly feed on their flesh. Human flesh smeared with the blood of all species of animals is beloved. Entirely vile meat full of millions of worms is divine. Meat rendered putrid by shit, seething with hundreds of maggots, mixed with dog and human vomit, with a coating of piss—mixed with shit it should be eaten by the yogin with gusto.[1]

—Saṃpuṭa Tantra

TANTRIC BUDDHISM presents to the historian of religions an interpretative conundrum. It is, to all appearances, a significant branch of a major world religion—one whose scriptures and practices spread from India across Asia, capturing the minds, voices, and purses of millions in Nepal, Tibet, Bhutan, Mongolia, Sri Lanka, Bali, Cambodia, China, and Japan. More recently, these traditions have begun to take root in regions as far-flung as Russia, the United Kingdom, South Africa, and Brazil. On the other hand, their widespread popularity seems virtually incomprehensible in light of the highly objectionable features of certain of their scriptures and rituals. The citation from the *Saṃpuṭa Tantra* is a clear case in point: It is difficult to imagine a more disgusting and degraded vision of spiritual practice, yet this passage is found in one of the most respected scriptures of the esoteric Buddhist Adamantine Way (Vajrayāna). What sense can one make of a religious tradition that seems to advocate behaviors that most sane human beings would consider aberrant (at best), if not criminal or pathological?

This precise question was in fact raised over a century ago as modern studies of Tantric Buddhism were just beginning. The eminent scholar of Sanskrit literature, Rajendralal Mitra, was understandably troubled by similar statements found in the even more highly-revered *Guhyasamāja* (*Esoteric Community*) *Tantra*. Finding these "at once the most revolting and horrible that human depravity could think of," Mitra empathized with the many among his readers who might consider that such teachings "would, doubtless, be best treated as the ravings of madmen." He cautioned, however, that following this particular interpretative avenue—as attractive and instinctual as it might at first appear—may be premature insofar as this same text "is reckoned to be the sacred scripture of millions of intelligent human beings."[2]

Although much important work has been done in the field of Tantric studies since these words were first written, scholars continue to struggle with and offer conflicting resolutions to what we might call "Mitra's quandary."[3] Attempts in this direction are complicated by the fact that all would-be interpreters of Tantric Buddhism in India must negotiate a fundamental methodological challenge. Statements such as those quoted here from the *Saṃpuṭa Tantra* appear in texts that are historically disconnected from the cultural milieu that created and sustained them. Scholars of the history of Tantric Buddhism, therefore, must themselves reconstruct a cultural context within which to interpret the discourses and practices found in its literature. Without an informing context, it is not at all clear what such scriptural statements might mean. For instance, a stated injunction to (pardon my French) "eat shit" effectively means quite distinct things in different contexts. It might, for instance, be spoken by a government operative engaged in torturing a prisoner, forcing feces into his mouth in an effort to demean and disgust him and thus break his spirit. On the other hand, it might be spoken by one starving castaway to another, helpfully, suggesting a desperate means to stave off hunger in the absence of other sustenance. In addition to these more literal—albeit quite different—usages, the same words might also be spoken metaphorically (e.g., by one frustrated driver to another, expressing the anger and hatred of "road rage"). Just as easily, it may be spoken by one friend to another in jest, in the course of playful mutual teasing.

When confronted with Tantric Buddhist scriptures that say "eat shit," the responsible interpreter is likewise not immediately certain how those words are to be taken. It is necessary first to determine the cultural milieu in which these scriptures and their associated rituals were created and used. This, however, presents another challenge to scholarly method. There is virtually no evidence beyond textual accounts to determine when, where, why, or by whom these discourses were used in late first-millennium India. In order adequately to interpret these scriptures, the historical contexts of their articulation must be reconstructed. In so doing, however, scholars must rely primarily on the corpus of scriptures themselves. Thus, as in all historical inquiry, the interpretation of Tantric Buddhism in India unavoidably involves a complex dialectic of content and context: The transgressive statements of the Tantras are interpreted on the basis of an imagined context, yet that context is itself the result of prior interpretation of the statements. To call it a dialectic is therefore to be rather charitable, for such methods run great risk of committing the fallacy *circulus in probando*, or circular reasoning.

Even though, ultimately, any solution will inevitably be subject to some such element of circularity—bound as all interpreters are in the hermeneutic circle—there are, I believe, methods of analysis that provide greater purchase on the nature of the significations that occur in this complex corpus of literature. In particular, I believe that the methods offered by semiology have tremendous promise for studies in this area. This is so for two reasons. On the one hand, semiological perspectives in general allow greater insight into the nature of discursive signs and the complex uses to which they are put in a variety of social contexts. Semiology, that is, is devoted to—and thus excels at—demonstrating how it is that (as J. L. Austin put it) people "do things with words."[4] Furthermore, semiological analysis—insofar as it tends to focus attention on macroscopic patterns of signification across entire texts or larger corpora—allows a much more reliable and nuanced approach to interpretation than the more intuitive, microscopic avenue that attempts to generalize directly from interpretations of expressions taken individually. By comparing usages across texts and corpora and analyzing their relations, semiology allows a greater and more sensitive attention to the contexts of particular expressions than is possible with a less systematic approach.[5]

Before these methods may be fruitfully applied to the project of advancing an alternative reconstruction of the meanings and contexts of Indian Tantric Buddhism, however, a certain amount of preparatory work is required in order to clear the ground. In particular, critical attention needs first to be paid to the interpretative models that have been advanced in previous scholarship, so that a new approach may proceed free of encumbering assumptions that have so strongly marked earlier accounts. This is necessary insofar as there has developed over the course of two centuries of research a consistent, hegemonic, effectively autonomous, and self-sustaining network of scholarly discourses on Tantric Buddhism that authorizes and reinforces certain ways of speaking about and otherwise representing it. In this respect, modern discourses about Buddhist Tantrism are similar to the phenomenon of "Orientalism" as discussed by Edward Said. In his work, Said was concerned to illustrate inter alia the remarkable "internal consistency of Orientalism and its ideas about the Orient . . . despite or beyond any correspondence, or lack thereof, with a 'real' Orient."[6] That is, once certain rhetorical tropes by which the East may be represented had become familiar to European audiences, they developed a certain authority. They sounded plausible—all the more so because they drew upon and redeployed well-trodden and familiar themes in the European historical and cultural imagination. Likewise, the discourses used by modern scholars in reading the literature of and reconstructing the nature and history of Tantric Buddhism display much the same internal, tautological consistency. The same limited stock of ideas—often couched in nearly identical language—recurs decade after decade in new publications and is rarely subjected to critical analysis of its own genealogy.

Of primary concern in this regard is not merely scholarly repetition or redundancy, but what might be called methodological solipsism: a kind of "emperor's new clothes" effect. The discourses that circulate in the secondary literature condition what people see in the primary sources. Scholars read the secondary literature before they read the primary literature and, having thus been prepared by the discursive community to see the emperor's clothes, are thereafter predisposed—socialized—to see the data in light of those models and to replicate them in their writings. There is, as Said indicated, a "complex dialectic of reinforcement" by which prior discourses condition what we experience of the data presented to us, which interpretations then further reinforce our commitment to those very discourses.[7] Predictably, then, once the path was blazed, the road of academic representations of India and Indian Buddhism quickly developed significant discursive "ruts." Just as ruts in real roads constrain the choices of drivers, discursive ruts confront authors with a choice: Either follow the ruts, and accept the sometimes problematical interpretative ride they offer, or risk "breaking one's axle" (in the form of incomprehension of the texts or, worse, loss of academic recognition and prestige) in seeking to travel outside of them.

Chapters 1 and 2 are thus devoted to critically reassessing the historiography of Indian Tantric Buddhism, identifying and engaging key "ruts" in these discursive practices. This focus on the models and intellectual structures that inform the writing of history is necessary insofar as it is precisely via the discourses of history that scholars have sought to resolve Mitra's quandary—to "make sense" of Tantric Buddhism. There recur throughout the scholarly literature stylized modes of discourse concerning the origins and history of esoteric Buddhism. These various scholarly constructs—although cast in historical idioms—are essentially interpretative: In one way or another, they all function to account for the transgressive discourses and practices found in the Tantras. All of the most common models for representing the history of Tantric Buddhism exist as attempts to make sense of the radical, transgressive features of these traditions. They all do so, furthermore, by suggesting (implicitly or explicitly) a social context within which these developments are thought to be comprehensible. That is, the rhetorics of the origins of Tantrism and narratives of its history are fundamentally driven by the need to provide an interpretative framework for cultural analysis and they do this by arguing indirectly for the social context within which these practices are to have taken place.

Historiography of whatever sort—etiological or narrative—always involves making sense of its object. As Marc Bloch has observed, "The nature of our intelligence is such that it is stimulated far less by the will to know than by the will to understand."[8] The production of mere antiquarian data is not in itself a fully scholarly (or intellectually satisfying) project. Human beings seek to understand—to make sense of—their world. It is precisely the purpose of historiography to take a set of data and lend it meaning and coherence. Historiography is always an act of making sense insofar as it brings order and (consequently) meaning to events.[9] As Roland Barthes writes:

> The historian is not so much a collector of facts as a collector and relater of signifiers; that is to say, he organizes them with the purpose of establishing a positive meaning and filling the vacuum of pure, meaningless series.[10]

It is impossible for a proper history not to interpret its subject—not to make it into something—to transform isolated events through an act of imaginative creation into a process that can be grasped by the reader as a coherent object of understanding.

This crucial act is accomplished through what historians call conceptualization—the bringing of coherence to the historical archive by identifying an organizing principle or theme. This, of course, involves using rhetoric to juxtapose two or more things, with the aim of illuminating the subject matter through comparison, employing, as Nietzsche put it, "a movable host of metaphors, metonymies, [and] anthropomorphisms."[11] This is accomplished by that aspect of scholarly writing that Ronald Inden has termed the "commentative"—that which, above and beyond the description of texts and their contexts, represents "its subject-matter *as* something."[12] Thus, to write a history is always to interpret a cultural practice and, thus, always to transform the subject, representing the unknown as or in the form of something known.

In interpreting the Tantric traditions, modern scholars have put forward a number of such conceptualizations. The form these reconstructions have generally taken is an attempt to discern the origins and/or to construct a narrative of Tantric Buddhism that situates it within a historical process. All of the solutions offered, however, have one crucial feature in common: They all concur that, ultimately, transgression in Indian esoteric Buddhism does not in fact make sense. They do so by locating antinomian practices and discourses (historically) in social contexts wherein they appear as expressions of either animal impulses, primitive mentality/superstition, or merely slavish imitation. That is, Tantric transgression is ascribed to irrational or arational impulses, for which further explanation is neither necessary nor possible. Such an adjudication thus serves to absolve scholars of the responsibility to confront the difficult challenges of cultural interpretation: Once it has been made, interrogation ceases. Mitra's quandary is resolved by a half-measure—not the ravings of madmen perhaps, but in the end those of the ignorant, the semi-civilized, or the mimic/ape.

Contrariwise, I believe it is both possible and necessary to make sense of the transgressive discourses of the Buddhist Tantras, and that this can be accomplished by employing semiological methods. As mentioned earlier, semiology is uniquely well-placed to facilitate this advance, insofar as it is the science dedicated to understanding linguistic signs in their social aspect;[13] and, further, (in its structural form) such analysis is especially attuned to the challenges of interpreting the use of signs across large corpora of documents (such as the Buddhist Tantras). Rather than interpreting statements considered separately—and thus confined to the level of their ostensive or immediately manifest content—structural analysis of patterns of usage discernible across a substantial corpus of literature may be of inestimable aid in reconstructing the meanings of particular signs within the larger system(s) of shared conventions within which they become meaningful. Using these methods in concert, the task of reconstructing the cultural contexts of Tantric transgression may then proceed on a more secure footing.

Roland Barthes, who contributed so mightily to our understanding of rhetoric, its uses and connotations, has written of structural analysis that its "constant aim [is] to master the infinity of utterances [*paroles*] by describing the 'language' ['*langue*'] of which they are the products and from which they can be generated."[14] That is to say, behind the diversity of individual utterances (*paroles*), there are discernible patterns of rhetoric that are susceptible to analysis and that allow us to get some purchase on the larger system of signification (*langue*) in which those utterances make sense.[15] Once the general system is grasped, this then further informs our understanding of the complex significations that take place in each individual instance of communication, allowing a richer analysis. Grammar is a simple example of this. By describing the patterns of linguistic usage, general rules may be abstracted. By identifying how those rules play out in individual expressions, a more complete analysis of the specific instance becomes possible. Grammar is, of course, only the most basic of such systems. Semiology takes as its object the larger and intersecting systems of signification that take place simultaneously with grammatical reference or simple denotation. In addition to the *langue* of language itself there are *langues* proper to various domains of cultural practice: types of discourses or networks of articulation that become habituated over time which are susceptible to semiotical analysis.

In a sense, the two parts of this book seek to apply such analysis to two distinct corpora of literature. The essays in part I interrogate the corpora of modern and traditional discourses on the origins and history of Tantric Buddhism (qua *paroles*) in an attempt to discern the larger contours, or *langue*, from which they have been generated and that lend them coherence. They analyze the ways in which modern scholars have attempted to make sense of these traditions through speculations as to their origins and through narrating their history. This investigation will demonstrate what is really at stake in such modern historiography, by situating scholarship on Tantric Buddhism within the larger context of modern discourses on cultural origins and history (chapters 1 and 2) and by further comparing these modern practices with the historiographical practice of the Buddhist Tantric traditions themselves (chapter 3).

Part II shifts attention to the semiological patterns of the ritual practices and scriptural discourses of Tantric Buddhism itself in order similarly to discern the subtending structure within which these transgressive statements and practices themselves make sense. These chapters demonstrate that, through semiological and structural analysis, one can make sense of that aspect of the Buddhist Tantras that has proven most intractable for modern writers—the antinomian discourses (chapter 4) and practices (chapter 5) of the Mahāyoga and Yoginī Tantras—offering new answers to the question of how one makes sense of a religious tradition that has seemed at least puzzling, if not downright nonsensical, primitive, and/or irrational. Such an interpretative realignment invites and enables a further reassessment of the larger issue of the social location of these traditions (chapter 6).

The double entendre of *Making Sense of Tantric Buddhism* thus reflects what might be called the book's implicit methodological or (after Collingwood's usage) philosophical project. An approach that "never simply thinks about an object," but "always, while thinking about any object, thinks also about its own thought about that object."[16] The aim is to consider not merely the object itself (Indian Tantric Buddhism), or solely the theoretical frameworks by which scholars come to understand it, but to grapple with these two in their mutual relation. By so doing, the goal is to make both a critical intervention into scholarly method and a constructive contribution to the interpretation of its object.

In a sense, this method of critical attention to the structure of rhetoric—in terms of the subject and the object of scholarly research—represents a practical solution to the challenge raised by some contemporary critics in the human sciences. That is, many advocates of contemporary critical theory, when confronted with systemic problems of cultural interpretation—structuring presuppositions, reading in of one's own cultural expectations (what has been called isogesis[17]), Orientalism, and the like—recommend as a way forward that scholars exercise a critical self-awareness of their own presuppositions. This can be rather a challenging task, however. To extract and abstract one's own subjectivity from the intentional state(s) in which it is embedded is not and has never been an easy task. Were it so, we would all be objective, or at least much more so.

In place of the somewhat impractical and imprecise openness or critical self-consciousness often advocated,[18] I would suggest that there is a clear, concrete step that scholars can take to cultivate a more critical perspective: One that is implied in prior studies, but which has not (to my knowledge) itself been abstracted as such. Bound as we are in networks of rhetoric, we cannot easily inventory our own presuppositions and ideological blinders, casting them off and purifying our perspective.[19] We may, however, through structural reading of the discourses in which we participate, inventory our predecessors' presuppositions and so come to have critical distance on our own through comparison. That is to say, by understanding the patterns of scholarly discourse (*langue*), out of which our individual research (*paroles*) is generated, we can better understand the histories we compose and the interpretations we advance.

Structural semiological analysis is thus a critical tool for both poles of the interpretative dialectic. On the one hand, it allows one to discern the consistency and perpetual replication of modern scholarly discourses on Tantric Buddhism and so to problematize and denaturalize them, recognizing their distortions and aporia. On the other, these methods also may be used to demonstrate a clear semiotical structure organizing the transgressive elements in the Buddhist Tantras. Working from this basis, further analysis opens up novel approaches to the vexed question of the actual practice of these transgressions. The results of these inquiries, in turn, suggest a fundamental revision of certain modern idées fixes concerning the social contexts of Tantric Buddhism in India.

Before proceeding, it may be helpful to say a word or two about the nomenclature that will be used in this book. As the term will be used in what follows, Tantric Buddhism comprehends those forms of esoteric Buddhism that are nondualist in their conceptualization of ritual purity and pollution and are, accordingly, antinomian or transgressive in their ritual praxis and scriptural discourses. What, then, is esoteric Buddhism? This expression distinguishes those forms of Buddhism that require a special initiation ritual to authorize their central practice (excluding those not so initiated from access to ritual and doctrine) and are thus *esoteric*: "Designed for, or appropriate to, an inner circle of advanced or privileged disciples; communicated to, or intelligible by, the initiated exclusively."[20] The esoteric Buddhist traditions encompassed a variety of different submovements and doctrinal and ritual innovations within (primarily

Mahāyāna, or bodhisattva-oriented) Buddhism, beginning in the early-mid first millennium.[21]

Within esoteric Buddhism, there are discernible, clear divergences regarding at least two forms of dualism: that between the divine and the practitioner and that between the pure and the impure. Some forms of esoteric Buddhism maintain a doubly dualistic ritual and doctrinal platform in which, on the one hand, substantial attention is paid to the maintenance of ritual purity regarding conduct within and without the rites, and, on the other, the practitioner relates to the divine as petitioner, interlocutor, or invoker, but is never identified with the divine itself. Other forms of esoteric Buddhism break down the dualism between the practitioner and the divine—allowing the practitioner to adopt the identity of a divinity or divinities in ritual/meditative practice—yet nonetheless lay relatively marked stress upon the maintenance of rules of ritual purity.

Finally, other forms of esoteric Buddhism—those that form the primary subject matter of this book—are thoroughly nondualistic insofar as they ritually collapse the distinction between the divine and the human and that between the pure and the impure. The sacred scriptures of these latter traditions come to be called the Mahāyoga ("Great Yoga") or Yoginī ("Female Yoga Practitioner") Tantras; and (as is evident in our epigram from the *Saṃpuṭa Tantra*) advocate the deliberate transgression not only of the entire gamut of purity strictures found in the dualistic traditions of esoteric Buddhism, but of all the most central dictates of Buddhism in its entirety. In thus inciting violation of established rules (Greek, *nomoi*), these traditions are accordingly described as antinomian. Though other forms of esoteric Buddhism also feature texts called Tantras among their scriptures, because contemporary usage has already conspired to stress the transgressive aspects of these traditions, they will herein be designated Tantric Buddhism.

Over the course of six chapters, this book will address five major topics on which scholars have advanced divergent views concerning Tantric Buddhism: its origins, history, textual interpretation, religious practice, and social context(s). Part I, (Historiography) analyzes the discourses used to reconstruct the origins and history of Tantric Buddhism, in modernity and in traditional India. Chapter 1 argues that there has been a consistent and overweening concern in modern scholarship with locating the origins of Buddhist Tantrism, and that this putative originary moment has then been made to serve as the key to subsequent interpretation of these traditions and their transgressive discourses. Three variant origin tales are abstracted: That Tantric Buddhism is the product of a degeneration of Buddhist morality, that it preserves primordial or primitive religious practices, or that it is entirely borrowed from contemporaneous Śaivism. Each of these models will be tested against the available evidence and the inadequacy of each account will be demonstrated. More tellingly, it will be argued that all are essentially attempts to explain transgression by constructing a social context within which antinomian statements make sense.

Etiological historiography that seeks explanatory purchase through appeal to origins, however, is not the only method of historical explanation used in this regard. Narrative historiography is another mode of historical explanation, and we turn to these discourses in chapter 2. This chapter addresses Tantric Buddhism in its historical development, taking a metahistorical perspective on modern historiography, its rhetoric, and its ideology. Drawing on insights of Hayden White on the role of stock story forms in the construction of historical accounts, this chapter analyzes the three predominant modes of narrating the history of Tantric Buddhism—as the conclusion of Indian Buddhism, as a primordial beginning of Indian religions, and as a medieval midpoint in a larger historical process. All such narratives are, I suggest, underdetermined by the historical data they serve to organize: They are fictive, contingent, and inescapably ideological products of the intellectual practice of modern scholarship that appeal to commonly available models from the European literary imagination to offer an interpretative context for Tantric transgression. The structure of these rhetorics will be analyzed, along with their relationship to the modes of ideological implication that they encode: that is, their implicit "prescriptions for taking a position in the present world of social praxis and acting upon it."[22]

Chapter 3 takes the historiographical discussion further, reorienting the critique by analyzing the historical models used by indigenous authors in interpreting the history of their own traditions. The historical discourses of Tantric Buddhists will be shown to be much more complex than typically understood, encompassing a number of stylized historical motifs and distinctive narratives far beyond a simple assertion that the Buddha taught them. These various indigenous historiographical forms are likewise given a metahistorical analysis, situating them in larger patterns of discursive practice within Buddhism and the broader context of contemporaneous Indian culture. Such a perspective demonstrates that, like modern historiography, traditional historiography of esoteric

Buddhism aims to negotiate interpretative quandaries through historical explanation.

Part II advances over the course of three chapters a new interpretation of Indian Tantric Buddhism and its transgressive antinomianism, bringing novel modes of analysis and fresh philological spade work to bear. Chapter 4 offers a reading of the antinomian discourses of Tantric Buddhist ritual and scripture, demonstrating that these are neither fully literal nor truly figurative, as has previously been claimed. Applying methods outlined by Roland Barthes to a comprehensive analysis of the *Guhyasamāja Tantra*, I argue that the transgressions of Tantric ritual and scripture constitute a form of connotative semiotics. In this mode of communication, a complete sign in natural language (in this case, the signifier–signified complex of transgression and ritual pollution) functions as a signifier in a higher order cultural discourse. At this higher, performative level, the signified is the attainment of the goal of advanced Tantric practice: nondual gnosis (*advayajñāna*). This approach provides a new lens for appreciating the sophisticated systems of signification functioning in esoteric scripture and ritual, and a rather different framework for representing Tantric antinomianism.

Chapter 5 advances the semiotical discussion through another mode of textual criticism: a quantitative, structural analysis of the contexts of transgression across a broad range of antinomian Buddhist literature. This chapter indexes and analyzes the dress and accoutrements, prescribed and proscribed behaviors, sites, and prerequisites of a central ritual observance as presented in over twenty Tantric scriptures, Buddhist and non-Buddhist. The results demonstrate a remarkable fact about the term *caryā* (practice) in Tantric literature, in which context the vast proportion of the antinomianism of the Tantric scriptures occurs. Far from representing esoteric practice broadly construed—as it has uniformly been taken by modern interpreters—structural analysis reveals that *caryā* is in fact a term of art in Tantric Buddhism, referring to a very specific and highly managed and contextualized ritual observance (*vrata*), a rarified discipline reserved for a sacerdotal elite.

Chapter 6 broadens the issue of interpretation and practice further, raising the question of the social context(s) within which Tantric Buddhism flourished. This chapter argues that, although the rhetorical divergence of dualist (nontransgressive, "institutional") and nondualist (transgressive, "siddha") Tantric traditions has been explained by postulating two independent communities, there is no good reason to infer a sociological cleavage based on a rhetorical one. In fact, the available evidence clearly suggests to the contrary that it was precisely the cultural milieu of the conservative monastic institutions from which these radical movements emerged. That is, the transgressive practices were by and large the métier not of marginal figures, but of professional Buddhists with mainstream concerns, educations, and institutional locations. The social context and function of these transgressions require, therefore, to be reinterpreted, for which the work of Max Gluckman on rituals of rebellion suggests a suitable framework.

In conclusion, it will be recalled that—although the shift in interpretation suggested herein runs against the grain of most modern scholarship on Tantric Buddhism—a very similar reorientation has, in fact, also taken place in contemporary scholarship on the exoteric Buddhist traditions of the Mahāyāna. These, too, were originally imagined as separate, breakaway communities of lay people outside the hegemony of the monastic institutions. New, more critical studies, however, suggest that the radical new Mahāyāna teachings similarly developed in conservative Buddhist centers. Five points of comparison between these two models will be articulated and a revised appraisal of Tantric Buddhism suggested accordingly.

I

HISTORIOGRAPHY

{1} ORIGINS, RELIGION, AND THE ORIGINS OF TANTRISM

Science deals with relations, not with origins and essences.

—E. E. Evans-Pritchard

The mode in which the genesis of a thing is explained is the candid expression of opinion, of sentiment respecting it.

—L. Feuerbach

Les origines sont rarement belles.

—Paul Veyne

In seeking to make sense of Tantric Buddhism, scholars have often looked to its origins as a way of explaining its most basic nature and causes, identifying it, and thus accounting for it. This method has been common throughout humanistic and historical studies of culture, and the study of Buddhism is no exception. Like other scholarly discourses, this one has its own coherency and structure in which a limited number of rhetorical modes recur consistently. In fact, the various accounts of the origination of Tantric Buddhism comprise a highly delimited set of possible representations.

This chapter will explore the rhetoric of the origins of Tantrism and its modern history, observing its basic modes and its range of variants. Having surveyed the discursive terrain, the discussion will then turn to the cogency of these various models taken on their own terms, and argue that each of them contains fatal flaws of logic and evidence. Particular attention will be paid to two currently popular accounts that ascribe the origins of Tantric Buddhism to either tribal religions or Śaivism.

The discussion will conclude with a more fundamental critique of the search for origins as a method in the human sciences, and of the approach to historical interpretation of cultural forms that it subtends and enables.

UNDERSTANDING TANTRIC BUDDHISM THROUGH ITS ORIGINS

Readers of historical literature will be quite familiar with discussions of origins as a mode of locating and interpreting figures or movements. This approach has, in fact, a very respectable pedigree in the human sciences. No less a thinker than Emile Durkheim stressed the need to trace one's scholarly subjects from their origins and only then through the course of their subsequent existence. Historical objects, Durkheim argued, are shaped by and irrevocably linked with the circumstances of their birth:

> Every time that we undertake to explain something human, taken at a given moment in history—be it a religious belief, a moral precept, a legal principle, an aesthetic style or an economic system—it is necessary to commence by going back to its most primitive and simple form, to try to account for the characteristics by which it was marked at that time, and then to show how it developed and became complicated little by little.[1]

In the study of Tantric Buddhism, this method has been extremely popular. Throughout the scholarly literature, one finds chapters and subchapters with titles such as "Tantric Buddhism: Its Characteristics and Origins"[2] (L. de La Vallée Poussin 1898), "Origin of Buddhist Magic: Rise of Vajrayāna" (B. Bhattacharyya 1931), "The Genesis of Vajrayāna"[3] (H. von Glasenapp, 1936), "Origin and Development of Tantric Buddhism" (S. Dasgupta 1946), "Origins" (D. Snellgrove 1959), "The Seventh-Century Beginning" (R. Davidson 2002), and so on. An entire volume on *The Origins of Yoga and Tantra* (G. Samuel) appeared as recently as 2008. Even among those authors who do not explicitly use the language of origins, recourse to this mode of explanation is frequent.

How then have we moderns discussed the origins of Tantric Buddhism? There seem to be three primary modalities.[4] According to some, Buddhist Tantrism emerged as an outlet for transgressive or degenerate impulses by monks. Others discern its roots deep in the religious primordium of India. Yet others refer the rise of Tantric Buddhism to a wholesale borrowing from the traditions of its Śaiva compatriots. In a certain sense, each of these imputed origins is keyed to a particular narrative account of the history of esoteric Buddhism. That issue will be set aside for the moment, as it will form a part of the discussion in chapter 2. For now, let us get a sense of the variety of rhetoric that has been employed in discussing the origins of Tantric Buddhism and the interpretative work that these conceptions perform.

One of the original causes to which scholars have turned in accounting for the rise of Buddhist Tantrism is a lack of moral rigor in the flourishing Buddhist monasteries of the first millennium. One of the most influential advocates of this etiology is Benoytosh Bhattacharyya. This influential Bengali scholar rightly observes that "it is very doubtful whether we will ever be in a position to trace the origin of the Tantra in the most precise manner possible."[5] He nonetheless felt that an adequate account of its principal causes could be produced. In several of his published works, Bhattacharyya attributes authorship of the Tantric movement to the influence of degenerate monks and a need to accommodate these tendencies. Observing that sources relate that many monks either left on their own or were expelled from the Buddhist monastic community because they were unable to practice the strict morality required of them by the Discipline (Vinaya), Bhattacharyya speculates that

> there were many others who were not bold enough to proclaim a war against the rules imposed on them, but violated them in secret. It is thus very natural to expect that there arose secret conclaves of Buddhists who, though professing to be monks, violated all the rules of morality and secretly practiced things that were considered by others to be revolting. After the death of the Buddha, such secret conclaves must have grown in number in every province, until they formed into a big organization. If we add to this the *yoga* practices and the practice of mantras, we get a picture of the Tāntrika cult at its early stage.[6]

Here, the inspiration for the development of the Tantric traditions is attributed to a moral turpitude alleged to have been widespread even in the time of the Buddha himself, to which period Bhattacharyya locates the earliest esoteric communities. There are some unexplained gaps in this account. For one, the argument is largely based upon speculative assumptions ("it is very natural to expect . . ."), which premises are implicit rather than acknowledged. Furthermore, while one can certainly understand that monks may desire pleasures prohibited them, it is more difficult to understand why they would necessarily gravitate toward the revolting. (Presumably, Bhattacharyya has in mind here the ritual consumption of polluting substances, with which this book began—a topic that will be discussed in detail in chapter 4.)

The rise of Tantric Buddhist literature is described in similar terms in Bhattacharyya's works. "Those monks who saw salvation only in leading a natural life went on devising plans and probably by writing what we call the original Tantras which were secretly handed down through their trusted disciples who could practice the rites only in secret."[7] The notion invoked here—of a "natural life"—is central to this hypothesis. For Bhattacharyya, the monastic regulations were composed largely of "unnatural rules of discipline,"[8] which he also calls "unnatural and strict rules."[9] Here, "natural life" means enjoying pleasures,[10] a habit that is attributed to the Buddha himself who, the reader is told, "took food and nourishment in a natural way."[11] As the monastic discipline asked Buddhists to go against their most basic human nature, it could only be expected that there would arise an impulse to circumvent the rules that frustrated the realization of such a "natural life." This impulse, Bhattacharyya insisted, found expression in the Tantric scriptures, wherein "everywhere any casual reader can detect a desire on the part of the authors to thwart all unnatural rules and regulation forcibly chained on to the followers of Buddhism."[12] In short, Bhattacharyya maintained that the Tantras were composed in order that unregenerate monks might enjoy the pleasures of life with Buddha's imprimatur, thus giving rise to a long tradition of Buddhist thought and practice dedicated to the realization of this goal.[13]

Another influential account of the origins of Tantric Buddhism maintained that the Tantras could be traced back to the most remote antiquity in India. Tantrism, that is, has no discernible origins per se but rather represents the oldest indigenous religious tradition of the Indian subcontinent. These traditions are here regarded as "pre-Āryan"—belonging to the culture of India that preceded the alleged advent of Central Asian immigrants who brought the Vedic revelations southeast into new territories. The great art historian Stella Kramrisch wrote in 1929 that Śāktism (the worship of the female element, often considered the sine qua non of "Tantra") had "its roots in the most remote antiquity."[14] Indologist E. J. Thomas made much the same claim in 1933, commenting that "Tantrism as a form of religion is of unknown origin, and may possibly have arisen among some indigenous and non-Aryan people."[15] This view too has continued to have its proponents. In 1962, R. O. Meisezahl wrote that "the Tantra, whether Hindu or Buddhist . . . consists essentially of religious methods and practices which were current in India from times immemorial."[16] The French Indologist André Bareau similarly claimed in 1966 that "the origins of the Tantric movement go back rather far in time and seem allied with ancient magical and religious beliefs that remain as alive in India as elsewhere."[17]

Sinologist Robert van Gulik, in a monograph on the esoteric Buddhist divinity Hayagrīva, provides a more thorough elaboration of this idea:

> The roots of this curious system may be traced back to very old, probably even pre-Indo-Aryan days. The belief in the power of the magic formulae . . . seems to be particularly rooted in the propensity towards magic existing among the ancient aboriginal tribes of India. Many of these ancient conceptions were adopted by the Indo-Aryan conquerors and made an integrant part of their own conceptions.

Van Gulik's account incorporates a related but distinct claim that characterizes much of contemporary thought about the origin of the Tantras. This is the notion that—even after the ascendency of the Vedic cultural model—primordial, pre-Āryan religious currents continued to be practiced among "marginal" communities that included primitive groups such as India's so-called "tribal" population. Van Gulik continues:

> In different parts of India, however, situated outside the centra of Indo-Aryan culture, where the aboriginal population was better able to preserve its own character, the native usages of magic and witchcraft maintained themselves in a form more closely resembling the pristine.[18]

Vedic culture, it is claimed, adopted some of the magical rites of the aboriginal population of India in the ancient period in the form of the Atharvavedic rituals. The original rites, however, lived on pristine among primitive aboriginal communities, from which they were subsequently incorporated into the later Tantric literature. This same link between primordial Indian religion and the timeless tribal cultures is made by Cintaharan Chakravarty in his article "The Antiquity of Tantrism," although he characterizes the ancient inheritance differently. Rather than merely magic, for Chakravarty Tantra represents the "sex-magic" of primitive peoples that "seem[s] to have come down from primitive times and [is] known to be prevalent even in the present days among people with a primitive culture."[19]

This "aboriginal/tribal" theory of origins continued to flourish in the late twentieth century. Miranda Shaw, in her 1994 book *Passionate Enlightenment*, claims that "practices that had great antiquity in India's forests, mountains, and rural areas, among tribal peoples, villagers, and the lower classes, were embraced and redirected to Buddhist ends."[20] Geoffrey Samuel too has claimed that "much of both Tantric vocabulary and Tantric techniques . . . seems to have derived from 'tribal' or folk shamans."[21] This view has continued to attract advocates into the twenty-first century, in which Ronald Davidson has argued for the tribal origins of many Tantric Buddhist practices and divinities.[22]

Others argue that Buddhist Tantrism came entirely by way of borrowing from contemporaneous Śaiva literature and practices. Occasionally, this appears as a variant on the "pre-Āryan" theme, since Śiva has frequently (if *very* tenuously) been associated with the ithyphallic, horned god on the famous Harappan seal 420.[23] However, the theory that the origins of Tantra are specifically Śaiva and that it was from these traditions that some Buddhists ultimately adopted it, has its own rhetorical density as a theory of origins and deserves separate treatment.

The association, even equation, of Tantrism and Śaivism appears quite early on in the study of Buddhism. Indeed, E. Burnouf himself thought it "likely" that the Buddhist Tantras were propagated by "Buddhists who, while entirely preserving their beliefs and their philosophy, consent to practice certain Śaiva rites that promise them success in this world."[24] As is frequently the case in Burnouf's work, he is following the lead of a British researcher based in South Asia. In this context, he echoes the views of Horace Hayman Wilson, who had written that in the Buddhist Tantras of Nepal "the worship of SIVA, and *Tantra* rites, are . . . widely blended with the practices and notions of the *Bauddhists*."[25]

This conception of the origins of Tantric Buddhism has likewise had a long career and has recently experienced a vigorous resurgence. In 1911, Louis de La Vallée Poussin categorically claimed that "Buddhist tāntrism is practically Buddhist Hinduism, Hinduism or Śaivism in Buddhist garb."[26] In 1987, David Snellgrove replicated exactly Burnouf's model of two kinds of Buddhist Tantra: those that share more features in common with the Mahāyāna sūtras and those "with Non-Buddhist Associations,"[27] by which he means Śaiva associations. More recently, a specialist in Śaiva traditions, Alexis Sanderson, has made an expansive case, arguing that the rise of Tantric Buddhism "had been achieved by absorbing and adapting non-Buddhist practices," specifically Śaiva practices.[28]

Thus, over the course of decades of research on Tantric Buddhism, the best scholars of several generations have provided a number of competing (and sometimes intersecting) accounts by which they claim to locate the origins of these traditions. Nearly all theories offered, however, replicate one or the other of a rather limited stock of origin concepts. One thing all of these scholars have in common, however, is the presupposition that it is in fact important that historical studies locate the origins of religious traditions, insofar as doing so is thought to provide a privileged perspective on the tradition's most essential nature, providing a key by which the meaning of its discourses and practices may be best interpreted. The conclusion of this chapter will be devoted to evaluating the cogency of this shared presupposition. Before turning to the larger interpretative context of these claims, however, it may be of some use first to evaluate these models on their merits. Bracketing for the moment the larger explanatory arguments of which they provide key propositions, or the more subtle question of whether or not it is in fact explanatorily useful or important to identify the origins of religious traditions, it is worth considering at least briefly whether or not the scholarly accounts commonly advanced are actually supported by the available evidence.

The notion that Tantric Buddhism was created to accommodate degenerate tendencies in the Buddhist monastic community, whose members sought pleasures of the flesh prohibited them by the disciplinary rules of the order, is perhaps the easiest to dismiss. It is, after all, an example of the clumsiest sort of origin tale: a "just so" story. Much like the account of how the elephant got his nose (or the tiger his stripes) or other such folk etiologies, there is no real evidence for this view at all. It is entirely speculative, based upon a series of assumptions about men, their desires, and their behavior.[29] Indeed, insofar as some have sought to found it more solidly upon literary evidence, this is limited to farcical, bawdy representations in Sanskrit satires, such as the *Mattavilāsaprahasana*, or tendentious allegories, such as the *Prabodhacandrodaya*.[30]

Whatever the desires of first-millennium Indian Buddhist monks may have been, the cogency of this account also hangs critically on the question of whether Tantric practice was, in fact, primarily pleasurable. Alex Wayman questioned this basic presumption when he noted that

> to be practical, it is passing strange that anyone would bother with the Tantra to justify his "degenerate" practice, for who so bent among worldly persons would divert his energies by muttering a *mantra* a hundred thousand times at dawn, noon, sunset, and midnight, with fasting and other inhibitions, to engage in a "degenerate" practice, when, as we know so well, people at large engage in degenerate practices without bothering to mortify themselves at dawn, noon, sunset, and midnight![31]

Wayman suspects that the contrived sexuality of Tantric ritual would not have been much fun—or, at least, not so much that it would be worth executing all the elaborate rites accompanying it. Of course, both Wayman's view and the one he rejects are entirely speculative, based merely upon the authors' intuitions as to what would or would not have been pleasurable to a late first-millennium Indian Buddhist. Whether or not it was due to an awareness of this fact, this model has largely been abandoned. Yet something of its influence continues to operate at a more subtle level. In a widely praised 2002 work, the composition of Tantric scriptures is attributed to a desire by Buddhist monks to have scriptural warrant for their lusts for "drinking wine and making love to nubile women."[32]

While this account is quite easily discounted, the other two models have been more durable and thus call for more detailed treatment. There do remain a few retrograde writers who continue to maintain that, for instance, the presence of large-breasted female terracotta figurines in the prehistoric sites of the Harappan civilization are evidence of the antiquity of Śāktism and Śākta tendencies in pre-Āryan Indian society; however, virtually no serious scholar of today would advocate this view.[33] The notions of Tantrism as a primordial tradition of matriarchal mother worship, magic, and sex rites—or as representing a perennial "pre-Āryan" religion of India—are largely defunct.[34] On the other hand, more historically and anthropologically savvy writers continue to maintain that these rites and traditions must have come from similarly primitive tribal communities in India. This view consequently continues to attract considerable attention and assent in contemporary scholarly accounts.

To ascribe the origins of Tantrism to tribal groups, however, is no less problematic than the other variants on this theme; and it is clearly a variant, not an independent, account, for the operative concept in this interpretation is similarly the notion that it must be simple, primitive societies, in which "magic" held sway, from which the Tantras derive.[35] Underpinning this view is the notion that India is host to tribal groups that have continued to practice primitive religious traditions, alongside but independent of the Indian mainstream. The anthropologist C. von Fürer-Haimendorf, for instance, has written that these tribes "persist in an economic and social organization that elsewhere fell into desuetude at the end of the neolithic era."[36] Thus, via the medium of India's tribes, the primordial, primitive rituals made their way into the religious mainstream in the form of the Tantric traditions.

Geoffrey Samuel and Ronald Davidson—among the more influential scholars of esoteric Buddhism in recent decades—maintain variants of this view. However, very little at all is clear concerning any communities that might be called "tribal" in the late first-millennium. There are no primary source documents or monuments upon which scholars might draw in order to understand these cultures in their own right. The only sources available are inscriptions and literary works of mainstream Indian society that make reference to them, and the latter do not give uniform or detailed accounts of the religions of these cultures. In general, these sources merely make derogatory remarks that highlight their alterity, much like British accounts of Indians in the nineteenth century, who similarly considered their subjects "backward." The very notion of what might constitute a "tribe" is itself quite vague in modern scholarship on the Tantras. Samuel himself notes that "it is difficult to know quite what 'tribal' might mean at this period," since "'tribal' in the modern sense . . . is the product of a long-term relationship between the populations which we now label tribal and those which we now term caste Hindu" who "may well have separated out from an initially more uniform population."[37]

Thus, while there seems to be some good evidence that there did exist communities in the late first millennium with distinctive names—Doms, Gonds, Śibis, Niṣādas, and the like—that were considered "other" than the Brahmanical communities of the time, very little is known of their cultures, how they were distinctive, or even if they were truly distinctive. These tribal peoples, furthermore, were not enclaves of autochthonous peoples living in a primitive state of social organization. Sources indicate that at least some of these groups migrated within India, such that these "autochthonous tribes" were often centered far from their alleged homelands.[38] In terms of social formation, insofar as we know from inscriptional sources, many tribal communities were well-established states that carried on high-level cultural and diplomatic intercourse with neighboring Brahmanical polities.[39] Nor is it clear, as it has been claimed (if not assumed), that their religious practices centered on devotion to local nature deities (such as were allegedly later incorporated as Tantric divinities). In the ninth century, for instance, a "tribal chief" Pulindarāja (king of the Pulinda "tribe") "prevailed upon a Bhaumakara ruler in Orissa to grant land for the maintenance of a Śaiva temple and Śaiva ascetics."[40] In fact, it has been observed that in the Tantric period many of these "tribes" were "champions of neo-brāhmaṇism" or Hinduism.[41] The Niṣādas, a famous tribal group considered to be "marginal" and a subject of scorn in Brahmanical sources—and thus precisely the sort of community to which the source of Tantrism is ascribed—are known from early first-millennium literature to be a settled people, who engaged in unobjectionable rites such as offering *caru* (a dairy offering common in mainstream Hindu ceremonies,) and even performed orthodox Vedic fire offerings.[42]

Furthermore, what very little evidence we have for the direction of transmission of Tantric culture suggests unmistakably that the tribal or marginal communities were in fact the *targets* of Tantric transmission, not the source. Alexis Sanderson, for instance, has drawn attention to a passage in the Buddhist *Guhyasiddhi* that advocates Buddhist Tantric yogins traveling among untouchable communities, giving initiation and teaching Tantric scriptures *to* them.[43] Likewise, where there is clear evidence of local (and thus marginal, if not necessarily tribal) deities in Tantric traditions—far from constituting the main focus of these cults, bringing with them well-formed tribal ritual programs—they are found instead incorporated into already well-established, pan-Indian esoteric systems such as Buddhism and Śaivism. For instance, certain Kashmiri Śaiva ritual manuals (*paddhati*), based on pan-Indian Āgamic sources such as the *Netra* and *Svacchanda Tantras*, were at a very late date "elaborated through the insertion of the worship of numerous subsidiary deities drawn from various sources, some of them local goddesses . . . and others drawn from mainstream traditions."[44]

More importantly—and this point is central to the overarching thesis of this book—the critique of the theory of the tribal origins of Tantrism does not stand or fall on whether or not such communities existed or what they were like (although I think the evidence to this effect rather seriously weakens, if not destroys, the case).[45] Rather, the notion that Tantrism derives from tribal traditions is largely the result of a widespread tendency by modern scholars to read the rhetoric of the Tantras hyperliterally. As a consequence of this interpretative choice, the occurrence of (allegedly) tribal terms is taken as evidence of tribal provenance and, thus, of the social location, origins, and interpretative context proper to Buddhist Tantrism. A clear example of the general trend may be seen in the logic employed by the historian R. S. Sharma, in making the case for the tribal origins of Tantrism:

> [The goddess] Śakti is known as Mātaṅgī, which shows that originally the goddess belonged to the Mātaṅga tribe. She is also called Caṇḍālī, which indicates that she was a goddess of the Caṇḍālas. According to the *Kulārṇava Tantra*, a *caṇḍālī, carmakārī, māgadhī, pukkasī, śvapacī, khaṭṭakī, kaivartī, vaiśyayoṣitaḥ, śastrajīvinī, kauñcikī* (or *kandukī*), *Śauṇḍikī, rañjakī, gāyakī, rajakī, śilpinī*, or *kaulikī* . . . is to be worshipped as Śakti . . . . Obviously the list contains the names of mostly śūdra and untouchable women, generally of tribal origin.[46]

One can very clearly discern the theoretical assumptions that underlie this interpretation. The first two claims are both based upon the premise that when well-known tribal ethnonyms are employed as names of divinities, this necessarily implies that the divinity in question had its origins in that community. However, this interpretation is based on a fundamental misunderstanding of the semiological system at play in the use of these terms, taking them as instances of primary reference or denotation. In another example of the same error, Sharma asserts that the *Mataṅgapārameśvara Tantra* (an influential scripture of the Śaiva Siddhānta) "was evidently composed to serve the needs of the [tribal] Mātaṅgas living in eastern Madhya Pradesh and Andhra."[47] However, even the most casual perusal of this latter work will reveal that it takes its name from the legend that it was taught by Śrīkaṇṭha [Śiva] to the sage (*muni*) Mataṅga.[48] There is nothing in the description of this sage to suggest that he is of tribal ancestry, or that his background is anything but mainstream Brahmanical. He is described as outstanding in his gnosis (*jñāna*) and meditation (*samādhi*)—key terms in Brahmanical religious discourse—such that he is described as a "preeminent lion of sages" (*munīnāṃ śārdūlaḥ siṃhaḥ*).[49] In this regard, comparison might be made to the "Śabara Commentary" (*Śabarabhāṣya*) on the famous *Mīmāṃsāsūtra* of Jaimini. No one in their right mind would ever speculate that it was written for (tribal) śabaras or that its author Śabarasvamin was a tribal. Indeed, a ritually impure śabara would never have been allowed near the hyper-Brahmanical *Mīmāṃsāsūtra*. Yet, due to an idée fixe that has become established from early studies of Buddhism, this logic is deemed compelling in the Tantric case.

The reference to Śakti as Mātaṅgī and Caṇḍālī—both of which are untouchable caste names—is clearly an outgrowth of the semiological system that informs the list given in the latter part of Sharma's argument. Contrary to Sharma's view, these women are not at all "generally of tribal origin." In fact, of the sixteen types of women advocated as *śakti* in this passage from the *Kulārṇava*, there is only one that is arguably an ethnonym: Māgadhī ("woman from Magadha"). Of the others, twelve of them are occupations despised within the Brahmanical system: leatherworker (*carmakārī*), two types of dyer (*pukkasī*, *rañjakī*), butcher (*kaṭṭikī*), fisherwoman (*kaivartī*), mercenary (*śastrajīvinī*), barber (*kandukī*), liquor-dealer (*śauṇḍikī*), singer (*gāyakī*), washerwoman (*rajakī*), craftswoman (*śilpinī*), and weaver (*kaulikī*). The three remaining are caste names: one a cliché for the lowest of untouchables (*caṇḍālī*), another a stylized, derogatory term for the alien subaltern (*śvapacī*, or "dog-cooker"), and the last, not tribal, but twice-born Hindu women of the "merchant" caste (*vaiśya-yoṣitaḥ*).

Even the one ethnonym, Māgadhī, does not hold up as a reference to a woman of tribal origin. Magadha is a toponym that refers to the "central land" of Buddhism, around the older royal capital Rājagṛha and the later imperial capital of Aśoka, Pāṭaliputra (modern Patna). It is listed by the *Āpastamba Śrautasūtra* as an outlying region, others being Kaliṅga (Orissa) and Gandhāra[50]—the latter the location of the stereotypical center of lettered learning in Pāli literature, Takṣaśila (Taxila). Thus, Māgadhīs are not mentioned as examples of primitive, tribal womanhood. Rather, the relevance of the term here derives from the fact that the Indian Dharma literature considers people from this region to be of mixed caste and, thus, impure.[51]

This list becomes even more coherent when one notes that the term "merchant women" (*vaiśya-yoṣitaḥ*) is a very unlikely reading. The editor of the *Kulārṇava* reports *vaiśya-* as attested in two of five manuscripts but relegates it to the textual apparatus. The preferred reading of the editor, Tārānātha Vidyāratna, which fits the context perfectly, was not *vaiśya-yoṣitaḥ*, but *viśva-yoṣitaḥ*: "everyone's women" or prostitutes.[52] Indeed, it is strongly to be suspected that the true reading of the variant texts is not *vaiśya-yoṣitaḥ*, but *veśya-yoṣitaḥ*: quite literally "prostitute women."[53]

The structure that lends coherence to this otherwise heterogeneous list may be found in the fact that these terms *all* refer to occupations or castes that are considered low and/or polluting by the orthodox Indian socio-religious order. The women suggested as objects of Śākta worship in this

Tantra (and in other, similar lists elsewhere in the Tantric literature) are uniformly those who are considered to be the most ritually impure persons. Although my full argument for this position will not be presented until chapter 4, it is sufficient to say here that this list has nothing to do with tribals and should not be construed as evidence for tribal origins of the traditions of the *Kulārṇava*. This is merely the ostensive content of the discourse. Structural analysis reveals that it is the expression of a pervasive discourse of ritual purity and pollution in dialog with mainstream Brahmanical Hinduism, not an external reference to marginal communities or to tribal societies. This same hermeneutical principle also accounts for Śakti being given the names Mātaṅgī and Caṇḍālī: Neither of these names occurs here as an ethnonym; they appear rather as metonyms for ritual impurity, which Śakti (it is thereby communicated) transcends.

The same interpretation recurs throughout modern analyses. References to (allegedly) tribal groups are read as directly referring to those groups, whereas a close, critical attention to those terms indicates that they occur in clusters of semiotically related words that reference concepts of purity and pollution. It is as if one were to read contemporary advertising and conclude that Ivory Soap was derived from elephantine communities or, at least, their byproducts. Of course, anyone cognizant of the semiotical community that produced these ads would know that "Ivory" refers to the whiteness of the soap (and, thus, its [99.44 percent] purity), not its derivation or ingredients. To read references to tribal or outcaste ethnonyms as evidence for the origins of the Tantric traditions within these communities is similarly and fundamentally to misconstrue the meaning of the terms in context.

This notion of the tribal origins of Tantrism has, however, developed tremendous authority through continual repetition in the scholarly literature. So strong has this presumption become that scholars have begun to see tribalism where there is none. For instance, in a section on "[Tantric] Siddhas in the Tribal Landscape," Ronald Davidson makes the strong claim—central to his argument—that "we find . . . canonical and exegetical references to tribal . . . peoples almost at every turn."[54] Consulting the footnote that will presumably detail these abundant references to tribals, the reader is directed to two passages: one from the *Guhyasamāja Tantra* (and its commentary, the *Pradīpoddyotana*) and another from the *Kṛṣṇayamāri Tantra*.[55] These passages in the Tantras both employ the term *mahāṭavīpradeśa*, which Davidson translates as "domains of the great forest tribes."[56] However, *aṭavī* does not mean "forest tribe." It merely refers to a forest.[57] The *Kṛṣṇayamāri* verse is the first of a passage that describes the special practice (*caryā*—the subject of chapter 5) that typically takes place in liminal or remote places such as forests. The *Guhyasamāja* passage speaks of religious practice taking place "on a remote mountain, in great forest regions provided with fruits, flowers, and the like."[58] The commentary, which Davidson also cites as evidence of tribal provenance, glosses *mahāṭavīpradeśeṣu* as *mahāṭavyāḥ pradeśeṣu* "in regions of great forests," which, the commentator further notes, means "in excellent places" (*prakṛṣṭeṣu deśeṣu*), their excellence due to the fact that they are "delightful [on account of having] ponds and so forth" (*jalāśayādimanoharatvāt*). Thus, there is nothing in any of these passages that suggests anything about "forest tribes."[59] The "references . . . at every turn" turn out to be a chimera of a long-standing scholarly rhetoric and testify to the remarkable durability of habitual ways of thinking and speaking about Tantric Buddhism inherited from (and consecrated by) more than a century of scholarly repetition. This is a clear example of the manner in which theories concerning the social context of Tantric Buddhism markedly structure and reinforce the interpretations contemporary scholars advance concerning Tantric Buddhist literature. The list is "about" tribals and thus was probably composed by tribals, which in turn accounts for why the list and the transgressive practices it describes "appear to us so meaningless and puerile."[60]

This assumption operates in concert with another important, structuring scholarly axiom, one that undergirds the second major account still active in contemporary scholarship. This is the notion that Tantric Buddhism is not in fact Buddhism at all and, thus, must have originated somewhere else. There is an extensive academic literature arguing for the foreignness of the Tantric movements, locating them either to the west of India among the "Magi priests of the Scythians,"[61] or to the east in Chinese Daoist circles.[62] More recently, this foreign source has been identified with Śaiva groups that were the neighbors and compatriots of the esoteric Buddhist communities. This notion continues to be very influential in shaping scholarly discussions, although Louis de La Vallée Poussin critiqued it as early as 1898:

> One commonly regards idolatrous and superstitious Tantrism as "no longer Buddhism;" one forgets that Buddhism is not separable from Buddhists, and that the Indian Buddhists (*les Hindous bouddhistes*) were willingly idolatrous, superstitious or metaphysicians.[63]

I do not mean to suggest that there is no trace of interaction with esoteric Śaivism in the Buddhist Tantric traditions. To adequately address the issue of Śaiva influence on esoteric Buddhism would require a monograph in itself. (In fact, Alexis Sanderson has recently devoted a monograph-length essay to exactly this topic.[64]) Suffice it to say that, unlike theories of tribal origins, there is substantial evidence of sustained and intense interaction between contemporaneous esoteric Śaiva and Buddhist communities. That said, it seems equally clear that the influence was mutual, with each tradition leaving significant traces of their own thought and practice on currents in the other.[65]

Consequently, it is not cogent to speak of esoteric Buddhism having "originated" in esoteric Śaivism. Just as Śaivism and Buddhism interacted in the preceding millennium (ca. 450 B.C.–A.D. 550)—sharing the same social spaces, political structures (that generally patronized religious orders eclectically), and economy, as well as a common spatial and temporal framework for religious activity, those communities centered around various Śivas, Viṣṇus, Buddhas, and (Jaina) Tīrthaṅkaras in the late first millennium (A.D.) participated mutually in a pan-Indian religious culture, most of whose structuring assumptions were the same and in which a variety of ritual forms were shared and developed across traditions.[66] The only way in which esoteric elements *tout court* can be considered to have originated in Śaivism is if one reifies these traditions as having been not only institutionally but also intellectually, socially, and ritually isolated from one another at the beginning of the Tantric period. That is to say, the only way that it is cogent to speak of esoteric Buddhism having originated from Śaivism is if one begins with an already fully-formed notion of Buddhism that does not include Tantric elements. Yet the only way to do so is to adopt a normative position on what "real" Buddhism is. We will return to this issue in a moment.

Before moving on to the larger methodological question, lest there be any doubt that these same old chestnuts about the origins of Tantra are alive and well today, consider this passage from a recent (2006) undergraduate textbook issued by the British academic publisher Routledge:

> Tantra derives from a wide constellation of beliefs and practices that mostly belonged to the non-Vedic religious traditions of the Indian subcontinent. Tantra may date back to the period of the Indus Valley Civilization which, together with the religions of chthonic tribes, form part of its source. . . . [Later,] beliefs and practices of these once marginalized groups

> began to bleed into the Sanskritic tradition. . . . The content of the Buddhist Tantras appears to have Hindu, especially Śaiva, origins.[67]

This summary may unfortunately be said to represent the current, mainstream consensus on the origins of the Tantric traditions: The theory of decline has dropped out, leaving a synthetic account—a bricolage of the prehistoric, tribal, and Śaiva models.

THE QUEST FOR ORIGINS AS METHOD IN THE HISTORY OF RELIGIONS

As noted previously, the method of locating the origins of a historical object and tracing its development thereafter is a widely practiced and well-pedigreed method in the human and social sciences. In the nineteenth century, and well into the twentieth, it was considered a fundamental approach to historical scholarship. As Eric Sharpe has observed of late nineteenth-century intellectual currents:

> Virtually every philologist, every historian, every archaeologist would at this time have been able to subscribe to what Jane Harrison had written in 1885 in her *Introductory Studies in Greek Art*, that "The historical instinct is wide awake among us now. We seek with a new-won earnestness to know the genesis, the *origines* of whatever we study . . ."[68]

That is, the quest for origins was considered in this period to be not merely a, but *the*, primary tool of history (*and* an epitome of fashionable French theory[69]). This is important to grasp; without this insight, the many claims made by, for example, phenomenologists of religion to study their subject "historically," are incomprehensible. What is very often meant by historical scholarship in religious studies well into the twentieth century is essentially to identify the identity or core nature of a tradition by reference to its origins and to trace the fortunes of this (self-consistent) object over time.[70]

As Paul Harrison observed in 1995, this approach is very much alive in contemporary studies on Buddhism:

> The fascination with origins, beginnings or sources does appear to be a kind of scholarly universal. Part of this—and this much is clear enough—is the idea that if we can understand the beginnings of something, we are better

> placed to understand the whole thing, as if its essential character were somehow fixed and readable in the genetic encoding of its conception.[71]

This notion that the origins of a thing determine its fundamental nature has a longer history but was perhaps most clearly articulated in the early eighteenth century by the Italian scholar Giambattista Vico. In his *Scienza Nuova* (*New Science*), Vico distilled the essence of this method, summed up in the equation of nature (*natura*) and origin (*nascimento*). This appears as the fifteenth axiom of his historical method:

> The inseparable properties of things must be due to the mode or fashion in which they are born. By these properties we may therefore tell that the nature or birth (*natura o nascimento*) was thus and not otherwise.[72]

That is, historical things have essential (or inseparable) qualities that are fundamentally conditioned by the circumstances of their origin—that the birth of a historical thing brings forth a "quiddity" that makes the thing what it is and no other.

This is an element of the "new science" that is stubbornly entrenched in academic research. Historian Marc Bloch describes an obsession with origins as "the idol of the historian tribe" and even as an intellectual "hypnosis."[73] More recently, historian of religions Daniel Dubuisson has remarked on what he sees as a pervasive "mythic imagination" in the human sciences "where origins are considered by many—and often—in an almost spontaneous way as the locus of perfection, of initial fullness and simplicity."[74] This is perhaps especially true in scholarship on religions. No matter how much training is given in historical method (and in most religious studies departments, this is practically none), a seemingly basic human impulse to grasp things through their origins continues to function.[75]

There is, furthermore, an observable and intriguing codependence between the acts of defining a historical entity and identifying its origins. For example, it is only through the intellectual operation of *defining* esoteric Buddhism as one thing and not another that an origin can be constructed in the first place. One can only identify the origins of a thing if one has already defined what that thing most essentially is; and, conversely, identifying the most essential nature of a historical thing is generally made with reference to its origins. It is only, for instance, by identifying Tantrism as essentially the worship of women that one can claim to locate its origins in the prehistoric world of buxom terracotta figurines; by identifying it as pursuit of pleasure that one can point to derivation from monastic unrest; or by identifying it as essentially Śaiva (or un-Buddhist) that one finds its origins in Śaivism.

A consistent appeal to origins would (and, in fact, practically does) make the study of Tantric Buddhism impossible. This is so because the various definitions involved (and the structuring assumptions that undergird them) render the very term "Tantric Buddhism" an oxymoron. Insofar as any religious phenomenon is truly judged "Tantric," and thus fundamentally tribal/marginal/Śaiva, it is thereby rendered non-Buddhist—a foreign growth grafted onto the Buddhist tree. Conversely, insofar as texts, artifacts, or practices are considered "Buddhist," for much of the scholarly community they become ipso facto non-Tantric, since "real" Tantrism (we all "know") is not the "semanticized" and "bowdlerized" version practiced by the Buddhists but rather the tribal, marginal, Śaiva variety. In a bizarre fashion, Tantric Buddhism finds itself an awkward stepchild of studies of both Tantrism and Buddhism.

Accounts of origins, then, are fundamentally the product of the historian (of religion)'s constructive activity in identifying a most central aspect of the tradition.[76] Dubuisson, in fact, argues that a scholarly focus on the origins of things is fundamentally mythical, not scientific, for "the typical and almost exclusive question posed by myths is that of origins" and "the fascination that the human sciences have for such simple, 'theological' explanations [that reduce the infinite diversity of reality to a principle or to a unique, ontologically homogenous cause] probably represents the greatest obstacle that they have to overturn and overcome."[77]

Analogies can easily be found in the human sciences. Clothing, for instance, is likewise not susceptible to a monocausal account of origins that serves as a totalizing interpretative key to its historical meanings. It very well may have been originally crafted for the purpose of warmth, but if clothing as a human phenomenon is consistently interpreted in light of this it will introduce major distortions. A tremendous amount of the cultural life of societies is devoted to clothing without much, if any, reference to its actual pragmatic value. If a scholar were to define its origins and to attune her cultural interpretations accordingly, she could not in fact be said to understand clothing in any but the most superficial and ahistorical sense. Much the same can be said of the Tantric Buddhist traditions. Were one to find a satisfactory account of its origins—and, as I have endeavored already to show, this has not successfully been accomplished to date—one will certainly "make sense," but one would still be no closer to understanding Tantric Buddhism. Scholars, consequently, would be best served by getting out of the origins business.

More importantly for our purposes, however, in identifying its origins (and thus, essential nature), the scholar simultaneously (if surreptitiously) constructs an ideal social context for Tantric Buddhism that then serves as an interpretative frame within which to make sense of transgressive discourses and practices. What Hayden White has said of historical works in a narrative mode (a topic to which we will proceed shortly) is as true of historical models in an etiological mode, insofar as both purport to be "a model, or icon, of past structures and processes in the interest of *explaining what they were by representing them*."[78] By locating an origin, these approaches seek to "make sense" of Tantric transgression by ascribing them to an historical agent or agency. That is, by depicting transgressive discourses and practices as being expressions of a particular *kind* of actor, they thereby become assimilated to known *types* of transgression, and thus meaningful (or, at least, comprehensibly meaningless).

Thus, for instance, when the Tantric traditions become owned by rebellious, pleasure-seeking (ex-)monks, the motives and meaning of their transgressions are thereby also communicated. Why do they advocate breaking all the rules? Obviously, since they are boys subject to "unnatural rules of restraint" and they "naturally" seek to transgress them. By attributing them to primordial or contemporary primitive tribal peoples, their motives may be less clear, but the explanation is nonetheless transparent: these are strange rites of unfamiliar people with "marginal" ideas about the power of sex and natural forces they do not fully understand. No further explanation is needed, since Tantric transgression thereby becomes an expression of the "primitive mind: superstitious, childlike, incapable of either critical or sustained thought."[79] The popularity of this mode of explanation may perhaps be attributable to such longstanding modern associations as, for instance (as Bruce Lincoln has indicated), the association of "episodes of incest and cannibalism" with "irrationalities that reveal the childhood of human thought."[80] By ascribing Tantric practices to imitation of the Śaiva traditions, the meaningfulness is displaced, and thus deferred. The rites do not need to make sense (in and of themselves they can be perfectly meaningless)—one only needs to account for why the Buddhists imitated them, for which patronage jealousy is a ready-made and common attribution.

Therefore, it should be clear that the construction of etiological histories of Tantric Buddhism are driven fundamentally by—and their most palpable effect is in potentiating—the project of making sense of the transgressive aspects of these traditions. As Mitra made clear, we cannot merely write them off as the "ravings of madmen;" but, through imaging their origins (and, correlatively, the social location in which these practices *paradigmatically* take place), they can be accounted for adequately, if patronizingly. These are practices, one concludes, driven either by animal impulses of the sexual drive, primitive superstitions, or slavish imitation. All are, ultimately, explanatory paradigms, which is precisely what the etiological mode of historiography is meant to provide. By identifying its "true" meaning in and by a scenario of origination, interpretation may proceed and be fixed, whereby—wonder of wonders—Tantric Buddhism "makes sense."

[2] NARRATING TANTRIC BUDDHISM

[The] goal [of historical research] is less to tell new stories than to retell familiar ones.

—Philippe Carrard

IN ADDRESSING issues of cultural understanding and interpretation, there is perhaps no discipline more crucial than history. In the past two centuries, for better or worse, history has become a dominant (perhaps *the* dominant) mode of understanding the world and ourselves. It is the privileged medium for expressing ideas and values, and for signifying meaning in the human sciences. There are other discourses, of course, by which persons, ideas, and institutions may be represented, associated, and evaluated; but when it comes to understanding dynamic processes of change, the language of power—the effective language—is history. It is thus to be expected that modern scholars would endeavor to make sense of Tantric Buddhism through the medium of narrative historiography. Telling the story of a religious tradition allows the scholar (and her reader) some purchase on its development—how it changed over time and was influenced by various circumstances. In allowing a diachronic perspective, the writing of narratives is generally thought today to be a more truly historical approach to the study of religions than that allowed by the search for origins. It is to the modern historiography of these traditions, its rhetoric, and the structure thereof that we shall now turn our attention.

Narrative structure is fundamental to history as it is understood today. This is what distinguishes histories from mere annals or chronicles.[1] Historical narratives make sense of an otherwise meaningless series of events, and are a fundamental mode of human understanding. Narratives communicate a logic of change, a connection between events, and they situate historical actors in comprehensible contexts with discernible lines of development. It is, first and foremost, through casting events and actors in narratives that the otherwise nonsignifying (if not insignificant) flow of events is rendered sensible. In what follows, I will consider briefly the poetics of narrative representation. I will touch on the structure of the historical imagination and the role of narrative form in making historical sense. Subsequently, I will outline the three major modes in which the history of Indian Tantric Buddhism has been narrativized and the subtending structures (*langues*) that inform these various articulations (*paroles*).

THE POETICS OF HISTORIOGRAPHY

In coming to understand the rhetoric employed in the historiography of Indian Buddhism, it is necessary first to consider the nature of historiography itself. Hayden White, one of the leading lights of modern historiographical thinking, has observed, "It is often said that history is a mixture of science and art. But, while recent analytical philosophers have succeeded in clarifying the extent to which history may be regarded as a kind of science, very little attention has been given to its artistic components."[2] It is in this latter area that White's own work has made an invaluable contribution. In his research, White draws attention to the fictive, contingent nature of the rhetorics that structure and inform historical writing. Following his lead, historians have begun to take more seriously the fundamental fact that narrative forms are in principle independent of the evidence they serve to organize.[3] Rather, they are the result of an imaginative process by which the historian constructs them as a story—a set of events with a narrative arc.

Historical accounts thus consist of at least two elements—a factive aspect and a fictive one. That is, histories consist of certain factual elements or data (which themselves may be more or less independent of a subtending interpretative framework) that are organized and given meaning by a fundamentally fictive,[4] narrative structure. Once a phenomenon has been constituted as an object of historical discourse—itself an act of imaginative construction—a range of rhetorical moves are potentiated. The phenomenon in question can then be conceived as having an origin, a development, and a resolution—that is, it now can become, in the Aristotelian sense, a story to be told.[5]

Louis Mink, whose marvelous essays on the *Historical Understanding* were much admired by White, has described a widespread (albeit naive) attitude in historiography that claims (implicitly) that "the historian . . . finds the story already hidden in what his data are evidence for; he is creative in the invention of research techniques to expose it, not in the art of narrative construction."[6] Mink, quite rightly, finds this view highly problematical. It is the historian, after all, who imparts identity, meaning, and narrative function to the data at her disposal. The narrative role and, thus, the historical meaning of any historical fact are in themselves indeterminate. Any event may be cast in a variety of narrative contexts and serve a variety of narrative functions, while remaining entirely faithful to the historical record. At the most basic level, events may be cast as either a beginning, a middle, or an end: the three fundamental elements of narrative according to Aristotle. However, while Aristotle seems to have believed that events were naturally and necessarily so structured,[7] such is demonstrably not the case.

One example from (relatively) recent history should suffice: the independence of India. One can easily see that its narrative role is underdetermined. At midnight on the 15th of August 1947, certain events seem definitely to have taken place—new pieces of colored cloth were raised on poles at Lal Qila and elsewhere, words were spoken, new authorities were vested, festivities undertaken, while, at the same time, a certain Mohandas Karamchand Gandhi slept (perhaps uneasily) in Calcutta. Yet, in what way do these disparate events cohere in a unified narrative? Did these events constitute, for instance, the end of British rule of the subcontinent? Were they instead a median point in larger processes of social and political change taking place in South Asia? Or were they the beginning—the dawning—of a new age and a new order? It is all, I would say, and none, and more than these. To use a Buddhist idiom, these are *saṃvṛtisatya*, not *paramārthasatya*: Each is a reality conjured forth by the consensual agreement of a signifying community, not realities that exist in and of themselves. Each are possible ways of *interpreting* those events; each serves the aims of a certain set of embodied interests; but there is no independent, epistemic criterion by which we may privilege one over the others as a more true presentation of the realities they represent.

The appropriate question in discussing narrative emplotments of historical events is therefore not which is true. Rather, the key issues are (a) what is the semiotical logic or structure that informs each narrative? And, (b) what ideological ends does each serve? White's *Metahistory* advanced this discussion by highlighting the mechanics of the modes of emplotment, explanation, and ideological implication that structure modern historiography. Drawing on the work of Northrop Frye, White explored the manner in which identical series of events could be rhetorically cast in either comedic, tragic, romantic, or satiric modes. For instance, the history of any given phenomenon could be told as an instance of the triumph of good over evil (romance), a transitory triumph (comedy), a momentary defeat (tragedy), or as a failure to master a world that is captive to death and the specter of meaninglessness (satire).[8] What is important to note about these choices is the irreducibly imaginative element in them. The narrative form is nowhere found *in* the data itself. Indeed, both Mink and White are concerned to elucidate the extent to which "histories" are not ultimately the product of the facts that inspire them, but of the poetical imagination of the historian who "emplots" them—an imagination which, in short, situates these facts within one of several conventional narrative structures.

The availability of historical narratives is thus largely independent of the data that they emplot. Moreover, the variety of narratives available to a historian is (like theories of origins) limited. There are only a handful of narrative forms available in any cultural idiom, with a limited range of distinctive varieties of story structures based upon them, and these latter are by no means universal. They are rooted in the narrative traditions of specific cultures. As White noted, the historian brings "to his consideration of the historical record . . . general notions of the kinds of stories that might be found there." These notions are provided by the culture(s) into which the historian has been socialized. For instance, with regard to nineteenth-century historiography, White observed that "the normally educated historian of the nineteenth century would have been raised on a staple of classical and Christian literature. The *mythoi* contained in this literature would have provided him with a fund of story forms on which he could have drawn for narrative purposes."[9] A skillful historian draws on the stories best-known, best-loved, by her audience. By retelling these stories using data drawn from the period she is describing, a historian is able to tell a persuasive tale. These stories are those that seem "natural" and obvious within the culture. They are familiar and, thus, seemingly self-evident.

The range of interpretative models available and persuasive within a culture in part predetermines the interpretations found by the historian. One sees what one knows—what one has been accustomed to seeing. The manner in which the historical imagination shapes our understandings of history and the range of possibilities within the historical field is another of the important implications of contemporary, critical historiography. Not only are historical narratives fundamentally fictive and based on precritical choices, but the range of historical imagination within a cultural-linguistic group also limits the types of emplotment available and, thus, the data deemed relevant to that group. Cultural habits of historiography can serve as methodological blinders or, as suggested in the introduction, "ruts" in the avenues of scholarly research.

A third important contribution of this type of analysis is the manner in which it highlights the ideological implications that the various story forms entail. Ideology, in this context, is defined by White as "a set of presuppositions for taking a position in the present world of social praxis and acting upon it."[10] By emplotting events in a certain way, one implies a valuation of those events and, concurrently, consequences that understanding has for current actions and attitudes. History is not merely, as some have suggested, "written by the winners." The services of a skillful historian, or historical mythologist, are a necessary precondition for *being* a winner. Effective leaders or visionaries are those who can craft (or commission) compelling narratives, such that others find it sensible to interpret their own experience and activity within the same narrative framework.[11]

To return to our example of Indian independence, it may be emplotted in a variety of ways with very different ideological implications.[12] For instance, independence as a beginning seems to correspond to a romantic or comedic mode of emplotment. Beginnings carry a load of imaginative baggage: dawning, freshness, light, and promise. Here, independence means the nascence of a new political and social order, wherein "young India"[13] embarks on fulfilling its destiny and taking its rightful place among the family of nations. Yet, for others, it may be emplotted as an ending—a sunset, portending darkness and dismay. This mode of emplotment foregrounds the demise of British rule in India, which had brought such glories and achievements as political unification of the subcontinent, the railway system, the Delhi Golf Club, punch, and the like. Here, one constructs this event as a tragedy: a death to be mourned, as some—British and Indian alike—still do. For others, it is a fulcrum point—an ethically neutral shift of power between two equally loathsome, equally corrupt legions of bureaucrats—one foreign, one native, yet cut of the same cloth. In this case, one sees an ironic or satiric mode of emplotment.

None of these narratives, it should be clear, is unqualifiedly true. They all shape (and by shaping distort) the limitless complexity of the event, with its manifold actors, ambivalent or polyvalent motivations, and interacting social, political, cultural, religious, linguistic, and economic currents. Likewise, they all have palpable ideological implications. Such valuations are not some extrinsic element of bias that may be systematically eliminated by the scientific historian. Benedetto Croce, for instance, observed that "historical affirmation is the quintessence of judgment, indeed is the only true judgment; . . . historical works are a web of narrative appraisals."[14] Histories make sense, not truth; and sense is always for someone or someones.[15] One is reminded of Alex Wayman's observation that the measure of an adequate study of esoteric Buddhism is precisely that it enables the reader to come to a judgment about it.[16] Croce was a more subtle thinker than Wayman; he was well aware that good historiography does not traffic in petty tribunals by which one may become (as Wayman put it) "genuinely for [or] against it." Rather, by staking out an interpretative context (plot, characters, etc.) and locating her subject therein, the historian inevitably and unavoidably communicates a relationship between the reader and the subject(s) of the history, simultaneously indicating the appropriate normative stance with regard to the subject(s). Historical judgment sheds light and "opens the way," writes Croce, on "the struggle of good against bad, useful against harmful, beautiful against ugly, true against false, in a word, value against non-value."[17]

With these considerations in mind, let us turn our attention to the various narratives that have informed the writing of the history of Tantric Buddhism in India. What modes of emplotment have typically been used in representing these traditions? What implicit explanatory logics or cultural associations inform the rhetorics used in each? And what do they indicate to the reader concerning the proper interpretative stance to take with regard to Tantric Buddhism in "the struggle of good against bad, useful against harmful, beautiful against ugly, true against false, in a word, value against non-value?" What sense do these narratives make of Indian esoteric Buddhism? Like Indian independence, the narratives that have been used to structure histories of Tantric Buddhism follow three basic models, each of which corresponds to one of the three most fundamental narrative termini. That is to say, one may read of Tantric Buddhism as the end of a prior process (the history of Indian Buddhism as a whole), or as the ancient beginnings of Indian religion, or as a medieval waypoint.

TANTRA AS END: THE DECLINE AND FALL OF INDIAN BUDDHISM

Anyone who has read even a modicum of the scholarly literature on the history of esoteric Buddhism cannot help but be struck by how frequently narratives link these traditions inseparably with the decline and disappearance of Buddhism in India. The narrative of decline was undeniably the single most popular motif used to structure the history of Buddhism in the years 1820–1930. Even as late as 1975, Per Kværne could write that "to regard tantricism as a 'degeneration' of earlier Buddhism has been—and in many circles still is—extremely widespread."[18] Again, titles of book chapters clearly attest to how prevalent this model has been. The relevant chapter in William Theodore de Bary's sourcebook *The Buddhist Tradition* (1969), penned by eminent Indologist A. L. Basham, is frankly titled "Tantricism and the Decline of Buddhism in India."[19] The conceptual linkage of Tantric Buddhism and the end of Indian Buddhism was well-established considerably before this and was so taken for granted in the early twentieth century that Louis de La Vallée Poussin, in "Notes de Bibliographie Bouddhique"—a running series of bibliographical notices—treated Tantric Buddhism and the disappearance of Buddhism as one unified rubric: "44. Tantrisme, disparition du bouddhisme."[20]

Seen from a certain perspective, Tantric Buddhism as a historical endpoint seems to make a good deal of intuitive sense, insofar as the flourishing of these traditions coincided with the last centuries (the end of the timeline) of the flourishing of Indian Buddhism itself. This observation, however, hardly begins to account for the prevalence of this narrative in the modern historiography of Buddhist Tantrism. As in all three of the narrative forms we will explore, there is a clear "semio-logic" that structures these discourses: a deep structure of the modern historical imagination. Underpinning the various individual articulations of narratives of decline is one of the most popular and recurrent poetic models, both East and West: the metaphor of organic development.

To structure narratives according to stages of organic life has been extremely common not only in the historiography of Buddhism, but equally so in historiography generally. Its use can be traced from hoary antiquity through the present, having been the model of choice among discerning authors from the very advent of Western historiography. It has been utilized by writers such as Homer, Hesiod, Plato, Vico, Hegel, and Marx, to name only a few. In brief, this archetype conceives that, just as plants and animals are seen to go through a process of birth, growth, maturity, decline, and death, so other (even all) phenomena can be traced across this same trajectory. Thus, cities, nations, schools of thought, political parties, and even religions, have been conceptualized in these terms, and the events of their histories interpreted accordingly. We must insist, nevertheless, on the *metaphorical* nature of this model. While we may, for instance, quite genuinely speak of the childhood, adulthood, decline, and death of individual men (although even here there is frequently an element of metaphorical comparison), we are speaking in a poetic mode when we talk of the childhood of Man.

This metaphorical emplotment became codified and objectified by Vico, when his *New Science* posited universal cycles of organic development in human history.[21] In Vico's historiography, we see a model of historical development in which civilizations follow a regular cycle of eras—a divine period, a heroic period, and a human period portending a decline into barbarism. R. G. Collingwood describes a further analysis into six periods:

> First, the guiding principle of history is brute strength; then valiant or heroic strength; then valiant justice; then brilliant originality; then constructive reflection; and lastly a kind of spendthrift and wasteful opulence which destroys what has been constructed.[22]

Although it became the foundation for much of the modern practice of history, this vision of a determinate and regular succession of eras—eras that end in decline—was not a novel creation of modernity. It is merely a refinement of the ancient mythopoeic vision of the successive ages of civilization: the Golden, Silver, Bronze, and Iron Ages, in which the nature of humanity progressively declines. This trope is operative too in the similar theory of the four ages in India: the Kṛta, Dvāpara, Tretā, and Kali Yugas, wherein living beings become by stages less and less intelligent, ethical, and vital. We find a similar series of four stages, ending in decadence, in the sociohistorical theories of Ibn Khaldûn.[23] In more recent memory, one finds Rousseau, in a strangely Buddhistic moment, commenting that "the body politic, like the human body, begins to die from the very moment of its birth, and carries within itself the causes of its destruction."[24]

Clearly, this metaphorical reading of historical processes as conforming to the pattern of the individual organic life cycle has been endemic to historiographical practice throughout its history. The early nineteenth century, in which the historiography of Buddhism was initiated, marked the zenith of popularity for this vision. History became a quest to find the stories waiting "out there" in the data. Of these stories, at least one thing was certain: They would follow, with law-like regularity, a cycle of organic development. "Hegel," says White, "broke down the history of any given civilization and civilization as a whole into four phases: the period of birth and original growth, that of maturity, that of 'old age,' and that of dissolution and death."[25] For Hegel, not only the total structure of civilizational development, but all the microcosmic histories within it (in fractal fashion), traverse the selfsame four historical moments—moments that correlate to his vision of the successive transformations of human consciousness.

In light of this narrative structure, so characteristic of European historiographical practice, consider the following comment made by Cecil Bendall (professor of Sanskrit at Cambridge) wherein, with acute clarity, the model of organic development is used to structure the history of Buddhism:

> Much . . . has been written about the glorious and vigorous youth of Indian Buddhism; something about its middle age of scholasticism and philosophy; but next to nothing about its decay, decrepitude and dotage, as shown in the Tantra-literature.[26]

In line with this model, the following common version of Buddhist history is constructed. First there was Śākyamuni Buddha, the original propounder of Buddhism, (of whom most reputable scholars will admit that we really have no reliable data). The first period of Buddhism per se, then, is said to be that of the so-called Hīnayāna/Theravāda. Here we see the traditions and the literature of Theravāda Buddhism, the currently-dominant school of Buddhism in most of Southeast Asia, defined as functionally equivalent to original Buddhism. This Buddhism, while not quite as "pure" as that taught by Śākyamuni (and certainly not in its contemporary form in colonial Ceylon), is fairly faithful to the source. Then, the story goes, the literature of the Mahāyāna began to emerge. At this point, after the pure ethical teachings of the early Buddhist schools (which, one is cautioned, were a philosophy or a way of life, not a religion), Indians were no longer able to follow the dictates of such a lofty path. They began to rationalize their instinctive, plebian bowing and scraping to idols as orthodox Buddhist practice. At the end of this process, Buddhism finally goes off the deep end. After being continually eroded by the slothful, sensual tendencies natural to Indians (and other natives of warm climes), the Buddhist tradition finally decided to give free license to do whatever one wanted and to call it Buddhist practice. To this end, however, it was thought necessary to fabricate apocryphal scriptures (Tantras) in which such sensual indulgences could be passed off as orthodox practice, sanctioned by the Buddha.

This is clearly the view ascribed to by Monier Williams, Boden Professor of Sanskrit at Oxford, in his volume on *Buddhism*. All of the foregoing models are brought together in this influential work. "The tendency of every religious movement," claims Williams, "is towards deterioration and disintegration."[27] After the Buddha's death, he claims, "the eternal instincts of humanity . . . insisted on making themselves felt notwithstanding the unnatural restraint to which the Buddha had subjected them"[28] and Buddhists quickly began to give up the celibacy, ethics, and other teachings enjoined by the Buddha. Then, he claims:

> The Protean system called Mahā-yāna arose, and *grew, by the operation of the usual laws*, . . . into a congeries of heterogeneous doctrines, including the worship of Bodhi-sattvas, deified saints, and personal gods.[29]

Yet, "far worse than this, Buddhism ultimately allied itself with Tāntrism or the worship of the female principle (śakti), and under its sanction encouraged the grossest violations of decency and the worst forms of profligacy."[30]

Substantially the same narrative is found in Louis de La Vallée Poussin's later work:

> Criticism can admit this tripartite division: a Buddhism undevotional and exclusively monastic, or the Little Vehicle, *which goes back without doubt* [!!] *to the founder*; a Buddhism much more composite, monastic and secular, devotional, polytheistic, at times monotheistic, highly commingled with pure philosophy and gnosticism (*gnose*): this is the Great Vehicle . . . ; finally, the *degraded* and *denatured* Buddhism of the Tantras, attested since the VIIth Christian century.[31]

Repeatedly, the same story appears in the standard works on the history of Buddhism. There is no need to multiply examples—anyone who has read works on Buddhist history has come across this story or one very much like it. The question this poses for the critical historiographer is how, with a variety of narrative forms available, did this one so quickly become dominant?

The answer may be found by attending to patterns observable in the use of historical narrative and historical explanation in European literature. The narrative of civilizational decline following upon moral (especially sexual) degeneracy was well-established in the classical historical tradition—and was thus readily available to the historical imagination of early scholars of Buddhism, whose education was founded in large part on the study of classical literature.[32] Perhaps the paradigmatic example is the tale of the Etruscan decline. Here, in a significant and popular historical episode of Roman history, the fall of Etruria—a powerful neighbor of early Rome (subsequently incorporated into the empire)—is attributed to their moral degeneracy.[33] R. A. L. Fell states in his work on *Etruria and Rome*:

> The decline of the Etruscan people is often ascribed to the nature of their religion, and the depravation of their morals. Greek writers have much to tell us of the luxury and the vices of the Etruscans, of their elaborate feasts and flowery coverlets, silver vessels and numerous attendants, and the Roman poets echo the taunt.[34]

It is worth noting that this trope is later co-opted by Christian historians—developing from the Roman intellectual tradition—to explain the fall of Rome itself. The decrepit civilization of paganism with its Neros and Caligulas, phallic cults and games, they claimed, must necessarily give way to the vigorous, youthful moral power of Christianity.[35] It is clear here from whence Vico derived his final phase of "spendthrift and wasteful opulence."

It was precisely this historical archetype that informed the fashioning of the history of Tantric Buddhism. Given the basic datum so strikingly evident to writers of British India—the absence of a Buddhist presence and, hence, the ostensible disappearance of Indian Buddhism—one needed to account for this fact historically. For many, Tantrism fit the exigencies of narrative quite nicely, providing a familiar and easily-digestible account. The idea most commonly associated with Tantra from the outset (and still widespread today) was sex;[36] and sex, of course, was associated with decadence. Inevitably, this conception of the Tantric traditions suggested to the narrative imagination of the nineteenth century the classical archetype of the decline and fall. The resulting tale, it should be apparent, is a familiar one, recapitulating that of Etruria: A once strong and vital culture becomes seduced by pleasure and renounces its earlier commitment to purity and virtue. In particular, the lure of the pleasures of the flesh—so difficult to keep in check—overcomes the people and society becomes decadent. The ultimate outcome is the death of the once-great society.

Of course, this choice of fictive emplotment is predicated upon two prior interpretative choices: For one, it foregrounds a theory of civilizational decline due to moral degeneracy and, second, it identifies the Tantric traditions primarily with moral failings. The arbitrary and essentially fictive element of these choices becomes strikingly apparent when one considers alternative narratives based on alternative interpretative choices. Alexander Cunningham, for instance, although well aware of the existence of Tantric Buddhism, gives the following variant account of the Buddhist decline:

> Buddhism had in fact become an old and worn-out creed, whose mendicant monks no longer begged their bread, but were supported by lands long since appropriated to the monasteries. The Srāmanas and Bhikshus were not like those of ancient days, the learned and the wise, whose bodily abstinence and contemplative devotion, combined with practical exhortations and holy example, excited the wonder of the people. The modern Buddhists had relapsed into an indolent and corrupt body, who were content to spend a passive existence in the monotonous routine of monastic life. . . . there were still the same outward signs of religion; but there was no fervent enthusiasm in the lifeless performance of such monotonous routine.[37]

Cunningham invokes another popular archetype of the nineteenth century historian's arsenal. In this account we hear—not the echoes of the classical tale of the Etrurian debauches—but rather the strains of the (neo-classical) tale of the Reformation (and Enlightenment). Here, the relevant connection is not sex, but ritual. Late Buddhism is homologized with Romish religion, as opposed to the pure sermons of the Son of God. We see yet another clergy that has become pampered and luxurious, content to defraud the populace with their "priestly mummery."[38] The invocation of this narrative model bears witness to Cunningham's place among the heirs of the Renaissance, the Reformation, and the Enlightenment. It is not, however, convincing witness to actual events in India. This emplotment too is a fundamentally fictive account that crafts a unified understanding of a complex process. While making sense of the same evidence, it stands in direct competition with those who would account for the putative decline of Indian Buddhism in terms sexual and moral, rather than ritual and ecclesiastical.[39]

In this regard, we may note the following, extremely illuminating, statement of T. W. Rhys Davids that reveals how the exigencies of plot structure can far outweigh (and even supplant) the testimony of concrete evidence. Starting from the premise of the putative decline and fall of Buddhism, Rhys Davids leaves the reader of his *Buddhist India* with the following considerations:

> Gibbon has shown us, in his great masterpiece, how interesting and instructive the story of such a decline and fall can be made. And it is not unreasonable to hope that, when the authorities, especially the Buddhist Sanskrit texts, *shall have been* made accessible, and the sites *shall have been* explored, the materials *will* be available from which some historian of the future will be able to piece together a story, equally interesting and equally instructive, of the decline and fall of Buddhism in India.[40]

In case there had been any doubt about the fundamental, formative influence of precritical, fictive, theoretical models on the construction of Indian Buddhist history, here there can be no question. Rhys Davids indicates in essence that, before scholars have even collected the evidence available from literary and archaeological remains, they can a priori assume a narrative structure along the lines of Gibbon's *Decline and Fall of the Roman Empire*. Gibbon's masterwork had allowed a new way of making sense of the fall of a hugely successful enterprise (Rome); some such account was seemingly needed to understand India's loss of Buddhism as well.

At times, then, narratives of the fall of Buddhism were crafted on the model of the classical story of decline through sexual degeneracy. At others, the decline is attributed to an alleged disconnection of scholastic Buddhism and its ritually-oriented priesthood from the needs of the laity—reflecting the popular Enlightenment/Protestant narrative of the decline of Catholicism. In very recent work too one finds echoes of this rhetoric of degeneration, of the decline and loss experienced by Buddhist communities in the Tantric period.[41] One may be excused a sense of déjà vu when one reads in such works that yet another culprit was responsible, since skeptical Centrist (Madhyamaka) thought "constructed the ideal justification for the morally indolent to buttress their unwillingness to adhere to the precepts. Such indolence was ever lurking in the background . . . *the history of Buddhist monasticism is a narrative about the extended testing of preceptorial boundaries by the morally challenged*." Even the media are called to account in this contemporary rendition of the decline and fall of Buddhism, insofar as they featured "erotized compositions of the Sanskrit and Prakrit poets."[42]

What is most striking among these various discourses is that regardless of whether an author blames sex, or scholasticism, skepticism, indolence, titillation by the literary media, or a combination of all of these, the fundamental narrative remains the same. The ideological implications of these narratives—their "prescriptions for taking a position in the present world of social praxis and acting upon it"[43]—are abundantly clear. Narratives of decline never entail a positive assessment. They are meant, rather, as object lessons in what to avoid. In casting Tantric Buddhism in the role of a conclusion, these traditions are made to appear as destructive and dangerous—causes for the erosion of quality and goodness.

The same is true of the inverse of this model—the similarly teleological trope of triumph. Such narratives merely represent the ideological inverse of the supercilious scolding of the decline model, serving to valorize and advocate for the traditions. For those with an opposite ideological agenda—drawing on an alternative theory of cultural history—a narrative of Buddhist Tantrism as an end may be cast in a progressive mode, wherein the Buddhist traditions would have been cut down at their height within the flourishing artistic, intellectual, and political culture of Pāla period Bengal. In practice, such narratives are rather rare in scholarly literature; however, an interesting example of this may be found in Miranda Shaw's *Passionate Enlightenment*, wherein Tantric Buddhism is depicted as "the crowning cultural achievement of Pāla period India."[44] It is noteworthy that, although her narrative promotes an opposing normative agenda, the various data Shaw cites to argue for her narrative of progress (e.g., various emoluments offered to successful scholar-monks) are precisely those cited by Davidson to justify his narrative of decline. The two differ only in their choice of interpretative model.

TANTRA AS BEGINNING: THE PRIMORDIAL UNDERCURRENT

In the early twentieth century, with the narrative of decline firmly established in scholarly discourses, a second historical model emerged that told a very different story of the history of Tantric Buddhism. This new rhetoric seems originally to have been the product largely of Indian (chiefly Bengali) scholars but was quickly taken up and amplified by the more Romantically-inclined interpreters of the West. The core idea of this narrative is that the Tantric traditions represent the primordial religion of the Indian subcontinent that was driven underground by the invading Āryans whose patriarchal, Vedic religion established itself on top of this earlier, matriarchal tradition, which was dominated thereafter but never entirely extinguished. As in the case of the trope of decline, what is most worthy of notice is the consistent structure of the rhetoric across its many iterations. In this case, throughout the many works that employ this narrative, there appears a set of hierarchical, binary oppositions that lend meaning and coherence (and ideological valency) to the discourse. These core binaries are below/above and past/present—the Tantric traditions are a cultural *under*current that derives from the most ancient *past*. Yet these basic dualities ramify throughout the literature, articulating in turn not merely a spatial and temporal difference, but an entire network of such hierarchical binaries, including that of gender.

Both of the valences of this discourse—the spatial and the temporal—appear quite clearly in Giuseppe Tucci's influential 1949 essay on Vajrayāna Buddhism. Tantric Buddhist rites

> show the gradual ascent to the *surface*, the invasion and the spread, of older intuitions, which dig their roots deep into India's spiritual and religious *bedrock* and hand down from it primitive, sometimes barbarous, ideas.[45]

The historical emergence of the Tantric Buddhist traditions in the mid-late first millennium, then, may be explained as an occasion in which—like Jed Clampett's black gold, bubbling up from the ground—"the old bedrock again came to the surface." Tucci considered this bedrock to consist in "the inexhaustible fund of Indian folklore."[46]

The language of spatial hierarchy is pervasive in this narrative. George Elder, writing in 1978, echoes Tucci, claiming that "the [Tantric] cults may have been a hidden force within India from pre-Aryan times" and that the rise of Buddhist esoterism in the first millennium represented "a sudden and even violent eruption of pre-Aryan religious life never really conquered by chariot or fire sacrifice but seething more or less underground for many centuries."[47] That is, the Tantras come down from ancient (pre-Āryan) times, were suppressed (but not conquered) by the culture of the Āryans, and later erupted to the surface from underground. It is also noteworthy that the ambiguity of the word primitive (meaning both first and/or crude) is very much in play in this discourse. For his part, Elder sees these pre-Aryan religions as existing in primitive fertility rites of ancient days.

As was not uncommon in scholarship of this period, three very different constituencies were incorporated within a unified academic discourse about ancient Tantrism: early peoples, contemporary primitives, and contemporary lower classes. The cultural forms of the lower social orders were considered to be of ancient provenance (folklore), providing a conceptual (and historical) link between the past and the provincial.[48] Similarly, as Johannes Fabian has so clearly demonstrated, there was a pervasive anthropological conflation of ancient societies and contemporary cultures possessed of simple (primitive) technology.[49] Thus, in Tucci's analysis, the bedrock of folklore may inevitably be found among provincial peoples insofar as "in the literary descriptions of the Vajrayāna pantheon late though it be, prehistorical Indian religion survives, with its old deities of the tribes and villages."[50]

Shashibhusan Dasgupta uses much the same rhetoric when he asserts that "Tāntricism seems to be a religious under-current, originally independent of any abstruse metaphysical speculation, flowing on from an obscure point of time in the religious history of India."[51] Here again, one sees a rhetoric in which temporal priority and spatial and intellectual/cultural inferiority are unified. Dasgupta stresses the important role of the laity as a force in leading Buddhist communities to move toward Tantric ideas, insofar as he considers Tantricism both as reflecting the mass-mind and as being aboriginal (again conflating early and/or primitive peoples and contemporary commoners).[52] A. L. Basham likewise describes a historical scenario in which ancient Tantricism was practiced among the "*lower* social orders" before (presumably) rising to appear in the literature of the elite.[53]

In the writings of Edward Conze one can see a further elaboration of this discourse. The beginnings of Buddhist Tantrism, he writes, "go back to the dawn of human history, when an agricultural society was pervaded by magic and witchcraft, human sacrifice and the cult of the mother goddess, fertility rites and chthonic deities. The Tantra was not really a new creation, but the result of an absorption of primitive beliefs by the literary tradition."[54] As in Tucci's work, these ancient peoples are identified as those indigenous (autochthonous) populations that inhabited India before the coming of the Āryans—here identified with the Dravidian peoples of the South:

> The erotic mysticism and the stress on the female principle owed much to the Dravidian stratum of Indian culture which, in the cult of the Village Goddess had kept alive the matriarchal traditions about the Mother Goddess to a greater extent than the Vedic religion had done.[55]

Note that another, related hierarchy is here articulated: that of gender. Shiníchi Tsuda, in an extremely influential 1978 article, likewise invokes a hierarchy associating the female and the provincial when he describes the Tantric practices of the charnel ground as "prevalent among the lowest strata of rural, matriarchal community of the time."[56]

Historian of religions Mircea Eliade brought practically all of the various parameters of this discourse of binary oppositions together when he represented Tantrism as a "great *underground* current of *autochthonous* and *popular* spirituality." "Tantrism," Eliade tells us, "developed in the *provinces* . . . where the spiritual counteroffensive of the *aboriginal* inhabitants was in full force." And, further, that "here we recognize the 'religion of the *Mother*' that in ancient times reigned over an immense Aegeo-Afrasiatic territory and which was always the chief form of devotion among the autochthonous peoples of India. In this sense, the irresistible tantric advance also implies a new victory for the *pre-Āryan* popular strata."[57] It should be noted that this discourse continues to circulate in contemporary scholarly accounts, as in *The World's Religions*, published in 1988:

> Historically speaking, it seems possible to explain the literary emergence of esoteric material by reference to the changed social and cultural circumstances in northern India after the collapse of the Gupta Empire. A "normative" and intellectual superstructure collapsed which made it possible for religious *undercurrents to rise to the surface* and find literary expression.[58]

Likewise, in 2002:

> The religions of the Āryans, from the very beginning of their expansion, had been compelled to tolerate and even to assimilate the popular cults of the masses, including primitive erotic fertility rites and animistic beliefs. These folk cults in their canonized forms lived on through the ages under the shadow of the Āryan religions, to become overwhelmingly powerful again in the medieval period of India when Āryan culture began to wane.[59]

In the light of the evident density of this discourse, its remarkable consistency, and its utter lack of any but the most tenuous evidentiary foundation, the critical reader will be bound to wonder: From where does this extraordinary univocality derive? And, why was (and is) this historical vision considered so compelling by so many modern interpreters? I believe there are two explanations—one historical and one structural.

Historically speaking, this model was—like that of the decline of Etruria and Rome—very much available to modern interpreters in the late-nineteenth and early-twentieth-century context in which it emerged. This period witnessed a tremendous amount of scholarly activity concerning what was called *Mutterrecht und Urreligion*: Mother Right and Primordial Religion. This was the title of a 1926 collection of the most essential writings of the German classicist and scholar of ancient myth, Johann Jakob Bachofen, originally penned in the mid-nineteenth century. The most influential of Bachofen's writings was his 1861 monograph *Mother Right: An Investigation of Matriarchy in the Ancient World in its Religious and Juridical Character*.[60] In this highly regarded work, Bachofen set out his theory of *Mutterrecht*—"mother-power"—arguing that in all societies there was a cultural stage preceding the rise of patriarchy in which social power was located in the mother, society was organized around matrilineal descent, and the very semiotics of its cultures and its values were oriented toward what Bachofen considered the characteristically feminine. *Mutterrecht*, in essence, was "the law of the material-corporeal, not of higher spiritual life . . . a product of the maternal-tellurian, not of the paternal-uranian."[61] These cultures, moreover, were to be found "among peoples who never achieved the level of classical culture" who followed "a more primitive way of life."[62] Where would one find such cultural forms? They "are to be observed chiefly among the *pre-Hellenic* peoples and are an essential component of this archaic culture" that "began to decline only with the victorious development of the paternal system."[63]

If the reader is beginning once again to experience a sense of déjà vu, she will be perfectly entitled to feel so. It is, after all, transparently obvious that the elaboration of the narrative of Tantric Buddhism as an archaic and primitive religious formation, deriving from a matriarchal culture associated with the earth and the body—a culture that was pre-classical and declined due to the victory of a later, classical, patriarchal people—is precisely predicated on this vision of the universal existence of archaic matriarchal cultures elaborated by Bachofen and the many he influenced.[64] Historically speaking, this narrative—like that of decline—derived from one of a limited stock of story forms circulating in the contemporaneous intellectual culture of Europe. In this case, it was not a narrative derived from classical antiquity,[65] but one that had its source in nineteenth-century scholarly interpretation of the classical cultures of the Mediterranean basin.

This historical reason for the widespread plausibility of this narrative as an explanation of the trajectory of Tantric Buddhism is further reinforced by the highly structured and cohesive intellectual perspective that underlies and finds expression in this model. As mentioned previously, all of these various narratives—in each of its distinctive articulations—are structured around a series of conceptual binaries. The range and coherency of these binaries have been schematized in table 2.1. As previously noted, the primary binaries are spatial and temporal: The Tantric traditions are phenomena of *below* (bedrock, undercurrent, etc.) and *before* (prehistorical, old, ancient). These basic binaries are supplemented by a series of further conceptual pairs clustered around gender, center/periphery, and other polarities; and all of these stand in relationship to the putative opposite of the Tantric traditions. Thus, Tantric Buddhism is not only temporally, but culturally then (primitive), not now (civilized). It is signified as subordinate in gender (mother/female vs. father/male, etc.) and ontology (body rather than mind). It is socially exterior (villages, provinces, agricultural), rather than interior (cities, center, mercantile). It is *inferior* in terms of class (lower), intelligence (mass-mind), and religion (magic/witchcraft). All of these binaries correlate conceptually and are linked historically with a quasi-racial classification (Āryan/pre-Āryan).

None of these polarities will be terribly surprising: They are the classic binaries of patriarchal, literate, urban societies, such as those inhabited by most modern scholars. They are all indisputably hierarchical; and Tantrism finds itself consistently cast as the inferior pole in this regime. This binary schematization by which the Tantric traditions are conceptualized

TABLE 2.1 Conceptual binaries of rhetoric of Tantra as beginning

CATEGORY	TANTRA	NON-TANTRA
Hierarchical metaphors	Depth/underground	Surface
	Under	Over
Temporal metaphors	Prehistory	History
	Ancient	(Modern?)
	Aboriginal	(Contemporary)
	Pre-Aryan/Dravidian	Aryan
	Autochthonous	(Metropolitan)
	Primitive	(Advanced)
	Barbarous	Civilized
Gender metaphors	Mother	Father
	Matriarchy	Patriarchy
	Female	Male
	Body	Mind ("abstruse metaphysical speculation")
	Mass-mind	Individuated mind
Other metaphorical hierarchies	Lay (amateur)	Monastic (professional)
	Tribes	(Developed societies)
	Villages	Cities
	Provinces	Center
	Popular/folk	(Cosmopolitan)
	Agricultural	(Trade)
	Magic/witchcraft	(Religion)
Related (implied?) semioses	(Nature)	(Culture)
	(Animal)	(Human)

is precisely that found in Bachofen's theory of archaic matriarchal societies. This cultural stage (note the hierarchy implicit here as well) is marked by a conceptual consistency, Bachofen insists: There was a "homogeneity of a dominant idea" in the ancient matriarchal cultures, consisting of a thorough-going privileging of the mother, the female, the left, the passive, the body, earth, the moon, and so on.[66]

These binaries are by their very nature hierarchical, and encode an overarching system of valuation marked by either thoroughgoing derision or valorization. Of course, the predominant valuation in most cultures (past and contemporary) has been that which privileges the patriarchal pole of the binary. These discourses function to devalue Tantric Buddhism: infantilizing it, feminizing it, casting it as marginal and obsolete. The good is the Hellenic/Āryan rather than the pre-Hellenic/pre-Āryan, the male/patriarchy rather than the female/matriarchy, religion rather than magic, the elite rather than the mass, individual rather than group, civilized rather than barbarous, (developed) societies rather than (primitive) tribes, the present rather than the past, and so on. Ultimately, of course, these articulated binaries betray a tendency that terminates in considering one pole culture and the other nature, or even one (fully) human and the other sub-human or animal.

A whole cottage industry of critical theory developed in the late twentieth century around an attempt to erode the ideological hegemony of this network of associations—evidence itself for how hegemonic this ideology has been. Once again, then, the dominant form of this narrative is one that devalues Tantric Buddhism as an inferior cultural form: a "survival" or obsolete vestige of a stage of cultural development long since past. However, in this case, there has been more room for ideological ambivalence in the treatment of the narrative. That is, historically speaking, unlike the model of decline, a positive evaluative interpretation of this conceptualization has had some play in Western intellectual culture. In response to this (Enlightenment) conceptual structure, there arose as well a (Romantic) counter-narrative. As often happens in the case of such hegemonic ideologies, however, the counterculture accepted the basic premises of their opponents' perspective. They did not challenge the temporal and cultural binaries themselves, but merely inverted their valuation—valorizing the ancient and the primitive (though rarely the feminine). Mircea Eliade is a prime example of this type of thinking—an author who held up archaic thinking as a spiritual salve for a world wounded by the excesses of modern ideology and saw wisdom, not ignorance, in the culture of the peasantry of the villages.[67] Yet, these voices were very much a minority and—given that, in making their case, they had acceded to the fundamental dualistic conceptualization of Tantrism that undergirded the ideology of its detractors—theirs was rather a lost cause. In the end, then, this narrative too is the product of a mode of cultural imagination popular in the late nineteenth and early twentieth centuries, not the product of evidence and sustained argument. It is a projection of a culturally available narrative onto a new sphere of cultural history, based on little more than a superficial resemblance of Tantric worship of the feminine with alleged matriarchal tendencies in ancient Mediterranean societies.

TANTRA AS MIDDLE: MEDIEVAL ESOTERICISM

Alongside these two, a third rhetorical model (representing the last of Aristotle's major plot elements) has emerged recently as the dominant narrative of Tantric Buddhist history. In this mode, Tantric Buddhism is cast as a midpoint in a larger historical movement—in a word, a "medieval" phenomenon. This discourse has had a remarkable surge in popularity over the last decade or two. One measure of this can be taken from the relative frequency of usage of the word medieval in the treatments of Tantric Buddhism across the five editions of *The Buddhist Religion*, originally authored by Richard Robinson and arguably the most popular introductory textbook on Buddhism in the United States since its first publication in 1970.[68] The first edition contains no references to Tantra as medieval, although it does make four references to witches and/or covens (terms often associated with the medieval). The second and third editions (1977 and 1982) are yet more circumspect: While they do mention wizards and medieval (each once), these are in reference to pre-Tantric Buddhist saints and Theresa of Avila, respectively. The rhetoric begins to shift by the fourth edition (1997), which features three references to the medieval or middle ages, and one each to feudatory and fiefdoms. A major swing is evident in the fifth edition (2005), however. Therein, one not only gets scattered references to wizards (once), and feudalism (thrice), but the word medieval is used no less than thirteen times in the sections on late Indian Buddhism![69]

While this rhetoric of the medieval is experiencing (as it were) a major renaissance at present, its use in the historical representation of esoteric Buddhism is by no means a recent phenomenon. Monier Monier-Williams uses this term in his 1885 book on *Hinduism*, describing Tantricism as the "last and worst stage of medieval development."[70] This style of representation draws in part on the association of the medieval period with magic. As Helmut Hoffman put it, "many of the texts of the so-called Diamond Vehicle . . . [show] a strange relationship with similar hokus-pokus popular in Europe in the Middle Ages."[71] This usage was further reinforced by its use in David Snellgrove's influential 1987 work, *Indo-Tibetan Buddhism*, in which he explicitly defends his use of this idiom. According to Snellgrove, "the resemblance between much of that superstition and magic [of the Middle Ages] with tantric rites aiming at magical powers of a mundane kind cannot be denied."[72] In line with this thinking, Snellgrove further advocates translating mantra as spell. However, the recent, marked increase in this type of rhetoric is doubtless attributable to the influence of Ronald M. Davidson's *Indian Esoteric Buddhism*. In this work, Davidson consistently uses the term to describe the Tantric period; he further employs a constellation of related key terms (feudalism, etc.) that constitute the essential elements of the imagination of the medieval in modern cultures.

Like the two previous modes of narration, here too we see a model widespread in contemporaneous Western thought serving to structure the historical representation of Tantric Buddhism. The idea of an intermediate period in European history appears as early as the fifteenth century, but the historical model of three periods—classical, middle, and modern—is only fully attested rather later, from about the late sixteenth century.[73] "Medieval" itself is primarily a nineteenth-century usage.[74] Accordingly, this schema was imported into the periodization of Indian history in the late nineteenth century.

There are, as one might imagine, a number of problematical issues surrounding the use of this periodization in tracing the history of India. Not the least of these is the remarkable inconsistency observable in its application to Indian chronology. Typically, those who employ this term to describe the history of Tantric Buddhism mark the beginning of the medieval period by the decline of the Gupta Empire—metaphorically equating the Guptas with the Romans as the keepers of the classical civilization which is alleged (by definition) to have declined in the medieval period. In a similar vein, the *Annual Bibliography of Indian Archaeology for the Year 1933* conceives of the medieval period precisely as falling between the Guptas and the Delhi Sultanate, insofar as they categorize numismatic researches thus: "a. Early Indian Coins, b. Indo-Scythian and Kushān, c. Guptas, d. Medieval, e. Moslem."[75] This usage is by no means the norm, however.

FIGURE 2.1 Definitions of the medieval period in India

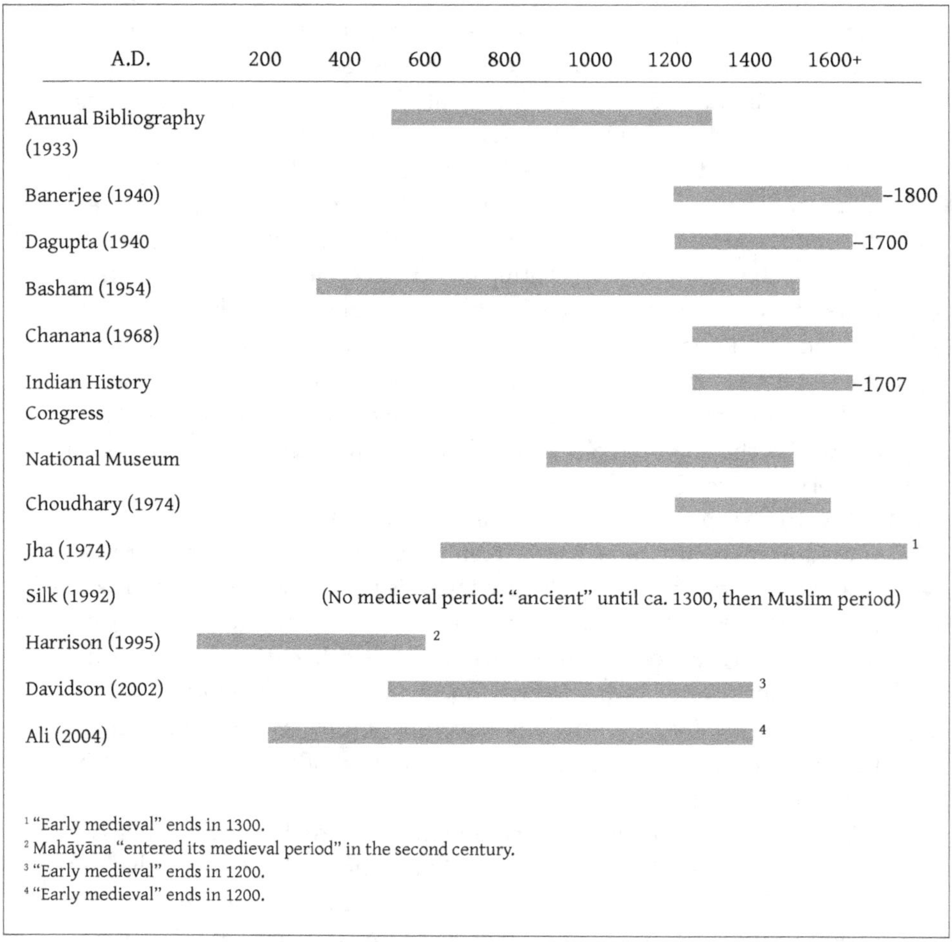

As can be seen in figure 2.1, some authors use this term to refer to periods as early as A.D. 200, while numerous others (perhaps most historians of India) consider the medieval period to have begun in A.D. 1200 or even later. That is, while some consider the medieval (or early medieval) to end with establishment of Islamic hegemony, others consider it to begin therewith. In this latter, very common usage, medieval refers essentially to the period of Islamic rule of India.[76] The Indian History Congress in fact "formally adopted 1206 C.E. as the date when 'ancient India' ended and 'medieval India' began."[77] Other authors see no utility in distinguishing a medieval period at all. Jonathan Silk, for example, uses the term "Ancient India" to refer to the entire period before the Muslim hegemony.[78] Thus, there is little uniformity observable in the application of this periodization to Indian history. What there is tends on the whole to define the period as not beginning until after the era in which Tantric Buddhism flourished in India.

In fact, the use of this periodization seems little more consistent with regard to the European histories it was developed to account for. There one likewise finds considerable disagreement among professional historians concerning the proper application of this term (if any).[79] In a presidential address to the Medieval Academy of America, Fred C. Robinson, after noting the wildly divergent periods considered medieval, is forced to conclude that "in light of all this disagreement . . . perhaps we should content ourselves with saying that our period extends from the close of the classical period to the beginning of the Renaissance."[80] This point is crucial to understand: The medieval period is not an absolute construction, but entirely relational or structural. Its core semantic function is to facilitate drawing a contrast between this period, an earlier classical, and a later modern era.[81]

Thus, although some have characterized the notion of a medieval period as an "ultimately meaningless generalization,"[82] the consistent, contrastive use of these terms indicates that, to the contrary, they are far from "meaningless." They are in fact redolent with well-established meanings—meanings that are encoded in the structural relationship of these three terms. In particular, the asymmetry of authority in the series classical, medieval, modern should be transparent—as should be the fact that this periodization is precisely about authority. Much like the discourses that construe Tantrism as a narrative beginning, there is a clear binary (or ternary) that structures discourse on the medieval.

I have attempted to schematize this in table 2.2. What is clear is that the positive poles of the ternary are the classical and the modern. The medieval represents a regrettable lapse in cultural quality. We have seen the association of Tantra, magic, and the medieval earlier. One primary contrast of this discourse is thus that between religion (characteristic of the classics and moderns) and the magic or superstition of the medieval. This latter is associated with unreason, another key duality insofar as the classical and modern periods are associated with reason. Similarly, the

TABLE 2.2 Conceptual binaries of rhetoric of the medieval

MEDIEVAL	CLASSICAL	MODERN
Magic	Religion	
Superstition	Reason	Reason (reborn)
Irrational	Rational	
Violent	Non-violent	?!
Catholic	Evangelical	Protestant
Ritual	Doctrine	
Body	Mind	
Spawned	Born	
Bloated (medieval-sized implements)	(Normal)	
Inhuman (medieval torture)	Human	
Obsolete	Relevant	

medieval (and, in recent works, Tantric Buddhism) is associated with another aspect of unreason: violence (allegedly the province of the irrational). Violence is further associated with the *body* and the latter (in terms of religion) with ritual; ritual, in turn, has well-established negative religious associations insofar as it is correlated with unreason, and (further) with the allegedly rational, doctrinal nature of evangelical (classical) and Protestant (modern) Christianity.

Fred Robinson, president of the Medieval Academy, himself notes that "*medieval* is most often used in Modern English simply as a vague pejorative term meaning 'outmoded,' 'hopelessly antiquated,' or even simply 'bad.' Renaissance and classical . . . are never used in this pejorative way."[83]

Robinson further enumerates the variety of alternative names for what came to be called the Middle Ages—what he calls a "host of also-rans like *Barbarous Age(s)*, *Dark Age(s)*, *Obscure Age(s)*, *Leaden Age(s)*, *Monkish Ages*, *Muddy Ages*, and of course the eighteenth-century favorite, *Gothic Period*."[84] The negative connotations of the first six should be evident. Lest the last should appear less pejorative than the others, one may recall that—as an early-nineteenth-century commentator noted—Gothic was "used at first contemptuously, and in derision . . . deprecating the old Medieval style, which they termed Gothic, as synonymous with everything that was barbarous and rude."[85] Nor is this usage limited to English. Rather, the same connotation is to be found throughout European languages: It is integral to the concept itself.[86]

Some scholars—European medievalists, in particular[87]—may here object that terms that have negative connotations in conventional discourse may be used nonetheless in scientific writing. For instance, the use of the term "cult" in studies on religions is an example of a word with negative connotations in the colloquial language, used (generally) responsibly in professional literature. In matter of fact, Indologist André Wink and Buddhologist Ronald Davidson both maintain that the term "medieval" is not so compromised and stress that legitimate scholarly use can be made of this periodization in the context of Indian history. Both scholars moreover are critical of some uses of the term. Davidson, for instance, echoing similar remarks made by Wink, notes that the word "comes with much baggage and can become a tool for dubious strategies."[88] Wink similarly stressed the methodological problems that arise, insofar as the use of this historical analogy has (in his view) frequently driven the interpretation of the evidence, rather than the reverse.[89] On the other hand, while criticizing its ideological use by "Indianist historians," Wink himself claims to use the term in an "innocent" way as a "purely neutral denominator" of "particular clusters of centuries."[90] Davidson likewise claims to be able to use the category of the medieval in an ideologically-neutral fashion, asserting that "we employ the nomenclature of periodization as a convenient rubric—and nothing more."[91]

However, at least in the case of Davidson, this disavowal is belied by clear patterns of usage discernible in the rhetoric he employs. Throughout his work, one finds clusters of terms connotatively related to the medieval—such as chivalry and feudalism—being invoked to describe the culture of esoteric Buddhism. His discourse is further peppered with tongue-in-cheek comments about violence as "the standard medieval mode of settling disputes"[92] and the "medieval-sized" (i.e., presumably bloated or otherwise grotesque) implements wielded by esoteric monks.[93] Whether intentional or not, this "convenient rubric" sets in motion networks of interrelated rhetorics, such that—much as Wink said of the Indianist historians—the interpretation of the evidence seems to proceed in service of the metaphor, rather than the reverse.[94] The association of the medieval with violence, for instance, reflects precisely a metaphorical understanding, expressed (among other places) in the recent American usage "to get medieval"—defined in the *Oxford English Dictionary* as "to use violence or extreme measures on, to become aggressive."[95]

That the negative connotations of Davidson's rhetoric are not lost on his scholarly readers—and are understood as being entirely of a piece with his interpretation of Tantric Buddhism—may be observed in the manner in which his conclusions have been read, understood, and recast by others.[96] One very well-regarded scholar, in summarizing the scholarly contribution of *Indian Esoteric Buddhism*, states that it establishes that the Tantric scriptures were "spawned by medieval Indian sāmanta feudalism."[97] However innocent or well-meaning this reader—and whether or not it was consciously registered by him—it is clear that the trend of Davidson's rhetoric has had a distinctive and predictable effect. For one, we again see connotatively interrelated terms ("medieval" and "feudalism") foregrounded[98]—in short, the predictable constellation of associations with the European Middle Ages.

Perhaps more notably, however, in recasting Davidson's message this author revealingly uses the word "spawn" to refer to its mode of production. Needless to say, this is not a discursively innocent term, and I believe it reflects a cogent reading of Davidson's prose, which frequently drips with contempt for its subject. Twice in the *Oxford English Dictionary*'s definitions of spawn as a verb, the meaning involves an attitude of condescension toward the object: that is, "in contemptuous use, to give birth to" and "in contemptuous use with reference to literary work, utterances, etc." (precisely the usage found in this passage). Similarly, in its use as a noun spawn denotes "a person contemptuously regarded as the offspring of some parent or stock." Furthermore, being spawned is typically correlated with teeming or swarming (neither a flattering term). In case there is any further doubt about its connotations, consider the objects typically spawned in the OED's many quotations illustrating the historical usage of the word. These include fish and fungi (the primary metaphors for the broader usage) and, metaphorically (as in our passage), tornadoes, hurricanes, flash floods, "a race obscene," "ill ones," falsehoods, "seeds of sinne," "cursed spawne of serpents," "mischiefs and outrages," apostates (a "spawn of Beelzebub"), those who "practice the frauds of courts," "wretched Heretics," heresies, libels, atheism, "monstrous and misbegotten fantasies," and evil.[99]

Paraphrasing Richard King's observations about the mystical, the following might consequently be said:

> Defining the medieval then is never a "purely academic" activity (in the sense in which one means "of no real consequence"), nor can it ever be completely divorced from the historical remains of past definitions of the term.[100]

Rather, the scholarly usage of medieval in reference to Tantric Buddhism trades precisely on these negative connotations. When James H. Sanford describes the antinomian, left-handed practices as "the more *baroque* forms of tantrism,"[101] it is abundantly clear that we are dealing not with an innocent temporal periodization—a convenient rubric—but rather with a thematics of style intimately interwoven with an elaborate network of associations within the Western historical imagination, whose applicability to Buddhist Tantrism is based on little more than the most tenuous of historical analogies.

A central element of the semiology of this term (as noted by Robinson) is that the medieval is *obsolete*.[102] While the ancient may be recovered (in a renaissance) for the benefit of the modern, the medieval cannot (or should not) be. It is merely to be transcended (or, at best, regarded as quaint). One may further observe that—although some do speak of ancient India and even of classical India—one never encounters the expression Renaissance India. Given that the idea of the Middle Ages in the Western historical imagination is inextricable from that of the Renaissance—without that contrast, its use in the European context is meaningless[103]—one may have legitimate doubts about the coherency of speaking of medieval India.[104] That this asymmetry is integral to its Indian application is made abundantly clear in the remarkable (and by no means uncommon) historiography found in James Fergusson's influential *Tree and Serpent Worship* (1873):

> Three hundred years after Buddha Aśoka did for Buddhism exactly what Constantine did for Christianity. . . . Six hundred years after Buddha, Nâgârjuna and Kanishka did for the eastern faith what St. Benedict and Gregory the Great did for the western, . . . We must go on further still for four centuries more . . . before we find our Mediæval churches quite complete . . . In the sixteenth century after Christ came the reformation, and with it the restoration of Evangelical Christianity. In the sixteenth century after Buddha came a reformation, but it was one of extermination of the faith, so far as India was concerned. . . . Whatever may have been the abuses and corruptions that had crept into Buddhism in the eighth

> and tenth centuries of our era, they were replaced by a faith much less pure, and far fuller of idolatrous absurdities than that which it superseded. What the western reformers aimed at, was to restore the Christian Hînayâna. In the east this was not thought of, hence the different fate of the two faiths. In Europe Christianity was invigorated by the struggle, in India Buddhism perished altogether.[105]

In a significant respect, then, the narrative of the medieval as it is used to describe Indian history—lacking as it does any redeeming renaissance or reformation—ultimately appears as merely a more subtle (and more plausibly objective) version of the model of decay. Like the models of decline and primordial undercurrents, it is one of a limited fund of stock narratives that recur in modern historiography; and the choice of this over either of the others is essentially arbitrary.

HISTORICAL NARRATIVE AND IDEOLOGICAL IMPLICATION

What, then, remains of the project of making sense of Indian Tantric Buddhism through narrative historiography? Paraphrasing Richard Evans, Davidson claims that historians who take structuralist or postmodern discussions seriously, "sometimes . . . demonstrate a confusion between their theories, on the one hand, and method and evidence, on the other."[106] It should be abundantly clear, however, that as long as several narratives can account for established events, there is no method or evidence that can serve as a valid criterion for preferring one among several plausible alternative narratives over others. As noted earlier, there is an irreducibly ideological element in the construction of historical narrative; all the posturing about rigorous historical method in the world will not impact that fact in the least.

The move from historical evidence to historical narrative is one that is essentially and inescapably characterized by a precritical (or, at least, arbitrary) choice among available narrative forms. Such a choice is not ultimately generated from the data themselves, but is rather a product of the theoretical framework within which authors have already chosen to interpret that data. As White puts it, "the best grounds for choosing one perspective on history rather than another are ultimately æsthetic or moral rather than epistemological."[107] That is, whether one casts the history of Tantric Buddhism as a sad decline into a moral cesspool (end, bad), or the story of the tragic loss of a glorious religious civilization at the peak of its creativity (end, good), as a sinister and primal religious undercurrent (beginning, bad), as the survival of the pure religious intuitions of the early days of mankind (beginning, good), or as a violent and superstitious interlude in the passage from the glories of classical times to the achievements of modernity (medieval, almost always bad[108]): ultimately, this choice has little or nothing to do with the raw historical record, and everything to do with the normative posture the historian has chosen to adopt in interpreting that data *as data*.

The employment of familiar narratives from European historical imagination—and of analogies between historical events and figures (as seen in the passage from Ferguson)—allows these discourses to appear as natural and unproblematical. To readers socialized into communities in which these narratives are canonical, that is, the modern West and those educated in its regimes, such stories do not seem contrived. These narratives are part of the architecture of our understanding; their use in structuring histories of unknown cultures like that of Tantric Buddhism intuitively make sense. Or, rather, they do so until one sees them juxtaposed one with others such that the deep structure of the modern historical imagination and its role in shaping historical narrative is exposed. This is precisely what I have attempted to do in this analysis.

It may be hoped that, by developing a greater awareness of the literary and rhetorical elements that structure their work, historians of religions may contribute to liberating their imaginations from the ruts of the easy, seemingly natural narratives that have been deployed to interpret the history of Tantric Buddhism. It may not be possible to escape narrative altogether, but at least we can endeavor to avoid the coarse, analogical models that only allow us to see the same thing over and over again. History, it might be said, does not repeat itself; historians repeat themselves. In advancing this project, however, there is another perspective that is worth considering: Modern scholars are neither the only nor the first to craft narratives by which to identify and interpret the esoteric traditions. Long before the first scholars in the nineteenth century articulated narratives to make sense of Tantric Buddhism for themselves and their contemporaries, this task was undertaken by the authors of the esoteric Buddhist traditions themselves. A comparative look at the structure and function of these narratives may thus allow the critical historian greater purchase on the project of narrative historiography across cultures.

[3] GOING NATIVE

TRADITIONAL HISTORIOGRAPHY OF TANTRIC BUDDHISM

MODERN SCHOLARS have only recently begun to devote attention to the question of how indigenous sources understand and depict the origins and history of their traditions, although this question figures prominently in esoteric Buddhist literature. Virtually none of the standard scholarly works on Indian Buddhism devote any attention whatsoever to the question of how the community that holds them sacred understood the history of these texts, but merely pass over the question in silence.[1] What little comment one does encounter on occasion is largely confined to depicting the indigenous view as reducible to the claim that the Tantras were taught by the (historical) Buddha himself, centuries before the Christian era—a fantasy clearly beneath the dignity of modern historical science even to entertain.[2] We have previously seen how Benoytosh Bhattacharyya at times maintained (although not without substantial self-contradiction) that such Tantras as the *Mañjuśrīmūlakalpa*[3] derive "probably from the time of the Buddha himself."[4] In more cautious moments, though, Bhattacharyya brackets this as the native view; that is, he claims that the historiographical conceit of the esoteric Buddhists was to "introduce their doctrines into Buddhism by the composition of a new Saṅgīti or collection of verses, all of which were to be taken to have been delivered by the Buddha in an assembly of the faithful."[5]

As we shall see, there are indeed passages in the Tantras and in the indigenous narratives of the history of esoteric Buddhism that assert that these scriptures were taught by Śākyamuni himself.[6] However, it is important to understand that there is considerably more to indigenous historiography of esoteric Buddhism than merely a baldly-stated anachronism. We will, accordingly, begin by considering the range of narratives crafted by Tantric Buddhists through which they conceived of the innovative ritual and cultural forms that united their communities as entirely of a piece with the older Buddhist traditions. To do so is not only essential to understanding the attitude adopted by esoteric Buddhist groups toward cultural innovation, but provides an invaluable perspective on their most fundamental self-understanding. The narratives of the revelation and spread of esoteric Buddhist teachings constitute an essential resource in reconstructing the "distinctively human world, [the] 'second environment'"[7] of Indian esoteric Buddhists—the shared world of meaning in which they imagined themselves and into which they socialized new members. Much as Georges Dreyfus has argued regarding the role of scholastic treatises such as the *Abhisamayālaṃkāra* in contemporary Tibetan monastic communities,[8] the frame stories of Buddhist scriptures serve to locate those revelations (and their target audience) in meaningful contexts—contexts that reinforce communal identity and within which the various semiotical transactions that constitute the religious and social life of the group are understood as reasonable.[9] That is, just as we have noted in chapter 2 that the use of historical narrative in modernity reveals more of the contours of the modern cultural imagination than information about events in the past, so too does the use of narratives by Tantric Buddhists gives us insight—beyond their own ostensive claims—into the subtending historical imagination of religious communities in late first-millennium India.

Our primary focus of critical attention begins to shift here from the scholarly subject to its object. The introduction and the preceding two chapters were largely devoted to the task of "what Victor Shklovsky termed 'defamiliarization'—*making the familiar seem strange in order to enhance our perception of the familiar*."[10] That is, we took as the object of our rhetorical analysis the very discourses used to represent Tantric Buddhism in order to demonstrate that the models taken for granted in modern academic research are themselves not only contingent and historical, but reflect rather more of the constitutive imagination[11] of the modern interpreter than of the object they purport to explain. In so doing, the aim was to identify and warn of ruts in the scholarly road, so we can be free to follow new approaches. The task for the rest of the book is to bring an equally acute analysis of rhetoric to the study of Tantric Buddhism itself as an object. Accordingly, we must take up the other challenge in the analytical dialectic of the history of religions: to make the strange seem familiar, in order to enhance our understanding of the strange.

Until rather recently, the study of the indigenous historiography of Indian Buddhism has not been marked either by its sophistication or its hermeneutical generosity.[12] It might be said (albeit uncharitably) that it has often been undertaken with the attitude of an adolescent toward parents: Get what resources you can from them, but contradict (or deride) them whenever possible. Yet, there is significantly more to be garnered from these documents than merely lineage lists or other nuggets of historical data that can be freed from the dross of their narrative contexts. These narratives are themselves a crucial subject of inquiry in their own right. Just as the modern narratives analyzed here contribute to constructing and maintaining a meaningful world for their readers within which to situate and interpret Tantric Buddhism, so too do the traditional narratives perform much the same function for their own intended audience. True, they invoke divine and semidivine agents and heavenly locations that the modern critic cannot countenance as real. The mere presence of the miraculous, the divine, or the transcendent in these accounts does not, however, ipso facto set them beyond the appropriate range of serious scholarly attention.[13] As Bruce Lincoln has observed:

> Processes of authorization that invoke the divine or transcendent at some crucial point of their operation seem typical of societies in which the foundational assumptions . . . made normative by the European Enlightenment have not acquired hegemonic status. It would be foolish—not to say presumptuous and ethnocentric—for those of us who stand on one side of this divide to underestimate the complexity, seriousness, efficacy, and importance of the differing ideological styles more commonly employed by our counterparts located on the other.[14]

Although the constitutive imagination of modern historical research does not countenance the divine or the miraculous, that of the esoteric Buddhist communities of the late first millennium clearly did. The ideological style thus constituted is, as we shall observe, by no means as simple as a claim that "Buddha really did say it"; and the "complexity, seriousness, efficacy, and importance" of these strategies in the documents of Indian esoteric Buddhist communities have a significant role to play in the scholarly reconstruction of these traditions and their relationship to other contemporaneous Indian knowledge systems.

In this chapter, we will survey a range of primary sources that bear on the indigenous historiography of the Buddhist Tantras. We will begin by reviewing the conceptions of history and scripture shared commonly by Indian Buddhist communities before attending to the particular innovations of the early Mahāyāna. Against this background, we will examine the historical indications to be found within the esoteric scriptures themselves, noting their general ideological consonance with the preexisting Buddhist symbolic order. Subsequently, we will turn to the more developed and individualized narratives to be found in the parallel corpus of esoteric Buddhist literature not considered to have been revealed by buddhas.[15] As the national literatures of the countries to which esoteric Buddhism was exported in this period—China, Tibet, Japan—also contain similar narratives, these too will be explored for their insights into the structure of esoteric Buddhist historiography. These observations will form the basis for reflection on trends in Indic historiography more broadly, and the socio-epistemic role of such discursive practices in the formation and maintenance of the traditional sciences. Continuities between the intellectual practices of the ancient Indians and Greeks, and those of modernity, will be discussed in light of the overarching problematics of history and cultural interpretation.

HISTORIOGRAPHY AND COSMOLOGY IN EXOTERIC BUDDHISM

In order properly to comprehend the indigenous historiography of esoteric Buddhism, it is necessary first to grasp the cosmological, "buddhalogical," and historiographical realignments effected by the early Mahāyāna movements.[16] The conceptualization of the situation of suffering humanity in the cosmos underwent at their hands a major spatial and temporal realignment that deeply conditioned the subsequent course of the tradition. However, one must also be careful not to exaggerate the degree of innovation in the Mahāyāna cosmos. The remarkable innovations in Buddhist historiography witnessed in the years ca. 200 B.C.–A.D. 500 took shape in the context of an already well-established program adopted by several currents within the early communities.

According to some trends in early Buddhism, prior buddhas—including Gautama after his passing—were in general unavailable for further spiritual assistance. The incredible salvific power attributed to the Buddha—such that the liberation of beings from the endless round of suffering was frequently thought to have been occasioned by his mere presence—was considered (with few exceptions) confined to the short window of his limited sojourn of eighty years in his final incarnation. After his passing, this power was thought to persist in an attenuated fashion in his bodily relics, speech relics (in the form of the teachings of dharma), and (for a few generations at least) those considered liberated saints in his community (*saṅgha*). All of these, it was thought, would fade in the course of some centuries, leaving the world a spiritual wasteland until the coming of the next buddha, Maitreya.[17] Such enlightened beings, however, were believed to come only when the fluctuating lifespan of humanity was one hundred years: a circumstance that was thought to transpire at most every thousand years.[18] Thus, the Buddhist communities who adopted this perspective considered themselves as living in a world between buddhas, preserving the precious few, remaining fragments of Gautama Buddha's legacy in text and monument, and seeking to emulate his ideal of moral discipline and mental development for the good of self and other, so as to prepare themselves for the advent of Maitreya in some future life.

This particular form of Buddhist cosmological historiography contains implicit assumptions regarding the relationship of the faithful to the divine and the nature of the canon of revealed word (*buddha-vacana*) considered authoritative by the community. This latter was in principle conceived of as a closed corpus of those teachings given by the Buddha during his lifetime and remembered by reliable sources, as signaled in the expression found at the beginning of all scriptures "thus have I heard" (*evaṃ mayā śrutam*). Likewise, in the absence of a living buddha between the passing of Gautama and the arrival of Maitreya, Buddhist communities were led to focus their efforts on presencing the departed Buddha through media such as corporeal images, production and recitation of texts, and construction of reliquary shrines (*stūpa, caitya*). Through interaction with these mediated forms of the enlightened presence, it was claimed, one could obtain "welfare and happiness for a long time" or "birth in a happy state or a heavenly world."[19]

However, these perspectives were by no means universally held by early Buddhist communities.[20] In terms of authoritative scripture, for instance, a number of exceptions were admitted. Whether or not anything in any of the extant collections was actually taught by the person alleged to have initiated the Buddhist traditions ("the Buddha") is an open and ultimately insoluble question for modern scholars.[21] Significant disputes existed even among the early communities. However, there were also clear cases in which these communities agreed to include in the developing corpus of Buddhist literature teachings that were not even alleged to have been spoken by the Buddha. In fact, a considerable degree of flexibility was allowed in this regard. For instance, in the *Saṃyutta Nikāya* of the Theravāda canon (*pāli*),[22] numerous teachings are cast narratively as having been given by worldly divinities—even on such elevated subjects as the proper practice of the monk (*bhikkhu*), how the properly religious (here called the brahmin) should conduct himself, and the nature of the enlightened saint (*arahant*). Similarly, in the *Dīgha Nikāya*, a powerful spell of protection to be used by monks meditating in the forest is given *to* the Buddha by four kings of the gods.[23] Consequently, as Paul Harrison has noted "even the Mainstream canons contained teachings believed to have been preached by deities, but nevertheless accepted as *buddhavacana* [Buddha Word]."[24] Etienne Lamotte has likewise noted a universal acceptance in literature of the Buddhist monastic discipline (*vinaya*) of authentic dharma being taught by a wide range of special beings other than the Buddha.[25]

The Buddhist communities of the waning centuries of the first millennium B.C. also witnessed a major revolution in scriptural thought, in which a large corpus of much later materials was incorporated into the Buddhist canonical collections. I am referring, of course, to the Abhidharma, the writings that systematized the sometimes diffuse teachings of the sūtras into a uniform vocabulary and intellectual framework. Although clearly a later synthetic product, most Buddhist communities came to accept these works as (in some sense, at least) authentically the word of the Buddha, and they were incorporated conceptually as a third "basket" of scriptures placed on a position of equal (or even greater) authority to the sūtras and vinaya.[26] Thus was born the concept of the Tripiṭaka ("Three Baskets" of scripture) we know today, which superseded the older twofold Buddhist corpus of Dharma-Vinaya ("Teaching-Discipline"). Accordingly, as Peter Skilling has observed:

> If we examine the history of the transmission of the Abhidhamma closely, we see a process in which a set of texts was gradually naturalized and canonized . . . This is only one example of the inadequacy of the "very idea" of canonicity as a primary tool of analysis in the historical study of Buddhist literature. "Canons" were continually redefined, refreshed, and reinvented. Yesterday's apocryphon becomes today's canonical text.[27]

Notably, the Theravāda tradition took a unique course in rationalizing their acceptance of this corpus. Alone among the early traditions, the

Mahāvihāravāsins (whose texts comprise virtually the whole of the contemporary Theravāda canon) innovated a remarkable narrative of revelation for their Abhidhamma in which the Buddha was said to have taught these scriptures in the heavenly realm of Trayastriṃśa while visiting his late mother there.[28] In so doing, they joined other communities in creating a distinctive narrative by which to conceive of the intervention of the Buddha in the world. That is, his salvific power was not confined merely to the forty-five years of his teaching career in the quotidian human world, but could also reach Buddhist communities through the mediation of divine realms. The narrative is careful, however, to link this intervention with (and situate it in the accepted teaching career of) the Buddha.

In addition to accepting a more expansive conception of the pedagogical reach of the Buddha than typically assumed, early Buddhist communities were likewise not uniformly as buddhalogically parsimonious as the common ideal-typical characterization would suggest. All the Buddhist communities of which we know allowed for the existence of a number of buddhas other than Gautama. In fact, in the view of many early Buddhist schools (with the notable exception of the Mahāvihāravāsin branch that came to dominate later Theravāda), buddhas were considered "infinite in both space and time"[29]—a view that became normative for the later Mahāyāna movements. However, even among contemporary Theravāda communities—who only admit of one buddha of the present—the following verse appears in widely recited liturgies:

> The buddhas of the past, and those yet to come,
> Those [pl.] of the present, too—[to these] I pay homage always![30]

All of which suggests that throughout the course of history, by far the majority of Buddhist communities considered themselves to inhabit a world in which there were multiple buddhas not only in the past and future, but also in the present.

With the rise of the cultural currents that coalesced into the Mahāyāna movement, both of these aspects of the early traditions became central components of an evolving perspective. On the one hand, the conceptual architecture of their cosmology considered the universe (made up of numerous worlds) to be inhabited by countless buddhas and aspiring buddhas (bodhisattvas)—all active in teaching, disciplining, and liberating beings. They were also notably prolific in the creation of new scriptural materials: So much so, that at least one contemporary scholar has characterized the Mahāyāna as consisting at its core primarily in the production of new scriptures.[31] In so doing, the authors of the Mahāyāna accounted for this efflorescence of scriptural composition as the product of processes of ex post facto (yet authoritative) revelation similar to those we have seen here. Some, for instance, emulated the Mahāvihāravāsins in attributing new scriptures to revelation in a heaven. The scripture called the "Chapter on Trayastriṃśa" (*Trayastriṃśatparivarta*) is a classic instance of this. This work locates its own revelation during the very same journey of the Buddha to teach his late mother in heaven. In terms of content, however, it presents a distinctively Mahāyāna perspective on the teachings the Buddha gave at that time, attributing lectures on voidness and the perfection of wisdom to this occasion.[32]

There were, very likely, Mahāyāna communities that claimed that their scriptures had come to them through conventional channels, having been taught by the Buddha during his lifetime, then learned, compiled, and transmitted. However, it would seem as if this model—which we may call the "bare historical" model—was not the predominant narrative created to account for the Mahāyāna, its communities, and the revelation of its scriptures. It is important to recognize in this regard that not all narratives that feature teaching by the Buddha Śākyamuni reflect an identical historical perspective. That is, the mere assertion that groups considered their teachings to be "taught by the Buddha" does not evince an adequate level of critical analysis. As we have seen here, both Śrāvaka and Mahāyāna apocrypha had had recourse to the notion of miraculous teachings by gods or in heavens to account for scriptural innovation. However, even in cases in which the teaching is said to have taken place on Earth (Jambudvīpa)—and thus conform spatially to the conventional narrative—the temporal parameters of the Mahāyāna narratives are shifted in such a way as to fundamentally reconfigure their meaning.

In line with their greatly expanded vision of the cosmos and their equally ramified buddhalogy, the burgeoning corpus of Mahāyāna literature added a number of new features to the world presupposed by their narratives. Essentially, these authors incorporated into these new works a substantially refigured metanarrative of revelation, in which Śākyamuni's Śrāvakayāna teaching—although still accorded great respect—is decentered in such a way as to provincialize the conventional life of the Buddha as a site of scriptural revelation.[33] That is, the primary focal point of revelation is no longer merely the forty-five-year teaching career of the Buddha Śākyamuni. Rather, the locus of articulation of the dharma is reconfigured to encompass all the many buddhas of past, present, and future. For instance, in the *Śūraṃgamasamādhi Scripture*, a divine being is said to arrive from another world, the Abhirati Universe of the Buddha Akṣobhya. In characterizing that world for his disciple, the Buddha observes that "there, [Akṣobhya] always expounds the *Śūraṃgamasamādhi*. O Dṛḍhamati, all buddhas without exception expound the *Śūraṃgamasamādhi*."[34]

That is, the true dharma (*saddharma*) is being constantly taught by buddhas in an array of universes. Śākyamuni, in this perspective, is merely a local—and somewhat peripheral—transmitter of this teaching. Further, this true dharma consists of the teachings of the way of the bodhisattvas (*bodhisattvayāna*), not the mainstream teachings of the way of the śrāvakas (*śrāvakayāna*). These latter, in contrast, *are* depicted as the unique teachings of Śākyamuni, the expression of his distinctive pedagogical genius, devised for the limited and unimaginative beings of his especially recalcitrant buddhafield.[35] The *Scripture of the Lotus Blossom of the True Dharma* (*Saddharmapuṇḍarīka Sūtra*; the "Lotus Sūtra") is exemplary in this regard. It contains a variety of Mahāyāna narratives that speak of new scriptures as having always been taught, or (at least) as having been taught long ago by the great buddhas of the past.[36]

The widely (and rightly) praised work of Paul Harrison has drawn attention to the remarkable contribution of the *Scripture of the Samādhi of Face-to-Face Confrontation with the Buddhas of the Present (Pratyutpannabuddha-saṃmukhāvasthita-samādhi-sūtra)* to the Mahāyāna articulation of the source of new scriptures.[37] This work makes similar claims about being the eternal teaching of all the buddhas.[38] Its novel contribution, however, consists in the fact that this relatively early Mahāyāna scripture[39] provides a systematic presentation of two modes of revelation that may be used to rationalize novel scriptures. On the one hand, as its title indicates, it contains a meditational method by which a practitioner may invoke the presence of a buddha, receive teachings, and return with them to the ordinary world.[40] If practitioners who are well-disciplined "concentrate their thoughts with undistracted minds on the Tathāgata Amitāyus for seven days and nights, then, when a full seven days and nights have elapsed, they will see the Lord and Tathāgata Amitāyus."[41] This is presented as a real and direct encounter with that buddha, for it specifies that if that practitioner does not meet the buddha they are invoking that day, they will receive a dream vision at night. This concentration notably claims the specific benefit of providing new teachings, for they

> see that Lord and Tathāgata Amitāyus . . . and also hear the Dharma. And they retain, master and preserve those dharmas after hearing them expounded. . . . [O]n emerging from that samādhi the bodhisattvas expound at length to others those dharmas, just as they have heard, retained, and mastered them.[42]

The *Samādhi of Face-to-Face Confrontation* also speaks of scriptures being sequestered in caves or other secret places to be extracted and revealed to the world in later times by bodhisattvas who have pledged to reincarnate then for that purpose. In particular, it is worth noting that the sūtra describes its text as being placed inside a stūpa after the death of the Buddha, to be guarded by gods and snake-spirits (*nāga*) until the time arrives for them to be re-revealed by the predestined bodhisattvas.[43]

In the course of the development of this new cosmo-historical perspective, the degree of flexibility allowed in the visionary revelation of new scripture at times reached extremes. For instance, the *Dharmasaṃgīti Scripture* says:

> For the one whose spiritual inclination is perfect, Lord, if there are no buddhas, the sound of the Dharma issues from the vault of the sky and from walls [and] trees. For the bodhisattva whose spiritual inclination is pure all instructions and precepts issue from his own internal dialogue.[44]

That is, ultimately speaking, because from a fully-developed Mahāyāna perspective—such as is adopted throughout the esoteric Buddhist traditions—the entire fabric of reality is made of buddhas (*buddhamaya*), reality is only mind (*cittamātra*), and the minds of all beings are ultimately enlightened (possessed of *tathāgatagarbha*), the power of the enlightened ones need not be mediated through so-called "historical buddhas." It radiates from the very substance of a world that is mind and buddha.

This conception of the omnipresence and omni-availability of divine revelation may be found expressed throughout various esoteric ritual practices. The vast preponderance of these rituals is precisely oriented toward manipulating the porous boundary between quotidian reality and the divine presence. For instance, the early Buddhist esoteric work, the *Mañjuśrīmūlakalpa* (MMK) devotes considerable attention to its own ritual for the practitioner to translate herself into the presence of buddhas. The supreme practice (*uttamasādhana*) set forth in this scripture accomplishes much the same goal as we saw in the *Samādhi of Face-to-Face Confrontation.*[45] In this case, the visualization (and translation) is aided by the use of a depiction of the deity (in this case, Śākyamuni himself) painted on a cloth scroll. During the rite, the practitioner sets this scroll up in front of himself and makes offerings of various substances before it. The scroll is then supposed to blaze with light, whereupon the practitioner circumambulates it thrice. Taking hold of the scroll, he is then able to soar up to the heavens, where he will meet and receive teachings from the Buddha Saṅkusumitarājendra and thousands of bodhisattvas, including Mañjuśrī.[46] It is worth noting that this procedure too may be used to account for the existence of teachings attributed to heavenly realms.

Likewise, the ritual of consecration (*pratiṣṭhā*) of divine images also (in principle) allows devotees to interact with the divine face-to-face and is predicated on the notion that buddhas are available for intervention in the ordinary world.[47] However, rather than bring the practitioner to the divine (as in the supreme practice of the MMK), consecration brings the divine to the practitioner by inviting a buddha or bodhisattva to inhabit her/his likeness in painted or sculptural medium.[48] It is most fascinating to observe that, among the scriptures that treat of consecration, there are some that explicitly address the mechanisms through which it is thought to be efficacious. In this connection, the question arises concerning the very need for consecration in a reality that is always already sacred.[49] That is, in line with the notion that buddhas are omnipresent in reality, why would one need to consecrate an image that is already a locus of divine power ipso facto its mere existence (as, indeed, are prosaic things such as rocks or old rags)? The *Concise Consecration Ritual Tantra* states, "all the buddhas are present (**pratiṣṭhita*) without any 'presencing' ritual (*pratiṣṭhā*: a.k.a. consecration); like space they are everywhere . . . primordially unborn—how could [they] be 'presenced?' [The rite] is only done so that beginners will understand."[50]

In sum, the constitutive imagination of the Mahāyāna communities was quite different from that reflected in the ideal-typical notion of a Buddhism dependent upon the ephemeral teachings of Śākyamuni. Rather, these groups conceived of the divine power of the buddhas as being omnipresent in space and time, and of the teachings of the dharma as being universally available to those spiritually so attuned. There were evidently many among the contemporaneous Buddhist communities who were not entirely comfortable with the direction things were moving. The rise of widely-accepted visionary revelations was recognized as a new innovation and troubled the more conservative elements.[51] However, the Mahāyāna communities in which esoteric Buddhism developed took this vision of the world and revelation for granted.

HISTORIOGRAPHY AND COSMOLOGY IN ESOTERIC BUDDHISM

Based upon the foregoing, one can abstract five models available to esoteric Buddhist groups (of which the Tantric movements were a part) by which to construct an account of the revelation of their innovative new scriptures. Following common precedent, esoteric Buddhists could (1) merely assert that they were taught by Śākyamuni, period; or, (2) claim that they were taught by Śākyamuni in some other world. Alternatively, following trends popular among the various prolific Mahāyāna "proclaimers of Dharma" (*dharmabhāṇaka*),[52] they could (3) maintain that the esoteric Mahāyāna method of mantra (*mantranaya*) represents the ancient and honorable teachings of all the buddhas, more venerable and profound than the transitory teachings of either the Śrāvaka Way or the exoteric Mahāyāna method of the transcendent virtues (*pāramitānaya*). To this general model they further could add the details that (4) the scriptures were retrieved from sacred caskets hidden in stūpas or caves for future, predestined revelation, or (5) that they represent teachings presented anew in direct encounters with buddhas other than Śākyamuni (or even from Śākyamuni himself).[53] The various historical conceptions put forth by the esoteric Buddhist communities took shape in relationship to these precedents. In many ways, as we shall see, the esoteric traditions did not innovate beyond the basic models of scriptural revelation accepted already by the exoteric Mahāyāna. Except in local detail (particular names, places, etc.) the esoteric narratives follow these five well-established patterns.

The *Gaṇapatihṛdaya*, for instance, takes a rather prosaic view of things, presenting the bare historical viewpoint (no. 1). This teaching presents a special recitation that purports to accomplish just about anything. It is explicitly stated to have been delivered by the Buddha to his faithful butler Ānanda in the conventional mainstream scriptural setting of Rājagṛha.[54] The *Amoghapāśa Mahākalparāja*, which represents a kind of transitional exo/esoteric scripture, also conforms in its basic narrative structure to the models accepted in Mahāyāna cultural circles. In this work, Śākyamuni clearly appears to be the teacher; however, the action is set on mythical Mount Potalaka, in the palace of the bodhisattva Avalokiteśvara, thus conforming to the motif of revelation in a heavenly realm (no. 2).[55]

At first glance, like the *Gaṇapatihṛdaya*, the *Mahāśītavatī Dhāraṇī* seems to depict itself in a conventional narrative framework, also being set in Rājagṛha, and addressed to the Buddha's son Rāhula. However, a closer look reveals that this work clearly adopts strategy no. 3, positioning itself as a transcendental teaching given by all the buddhas. This is stated explicitly at conclusion:

> Furthermore, this very Mahāśītavatī knowledge-spell was spoken [in the past], will be spoken [in the future], and is spoken [in the present] by Lord Buddhas equal to the number of grains of sand in ninety-one Ganges rivers.[56]

Likewise, the very influential *Chanting the Names of Mañjuśrī* (*Mañjuśrīnāmasaṃgīti*) seems to advance a bare historical model insofar as its authors claim that it was "spoken by the Lord, the transcendent lord Śākyamuni."[57] The location of the teaching is not specified, though it is requested by and given to the esoteric hero Vajrapāṇi, which might imply a transcendental location of some sort. Although an aggressively Tantric work in many ways, it articulates the general Mahāyāna model that these traditions are the overarching, core teaching of the buddhas of all times. This is clear at the outset of the work where the provenance of the teaching is clarified:

> The supreme *Chanting of Names*, good in the beginning, middle and end,
> Profound in meaning, of exalted meaning, great in meaning, unequalled, auspicious—
> That which was spoken by the buddhas of the past, and will be spoken by future buddhas
> Is also taught by the buddhas of the present again and again.[58]

This is not the exclusive teaching of Śākyamuni, but is an eternal revelation that is given not only by numerous buddhas in past and future, but by many in the present (grammatically, at least three, but presumably countless) all the time.[59]

Vajrapāṇi also appears in the *Vajravidāraṇī*, this time as the teacher of the scripture. However, in doing so, Vajrapāṇi acts as a surrogate for all buddhas and bodhisattvas in a manner accepted even in early communities.[60] In the opening sequence, the Lord (*bhagavān*) constitutes the world as made of adamant (*vajra*) and by means of his spiritual power (*anubhāva*) causes Vajrapāṇi to become absorbed in the adamantine samādhi. Then, by the power of the Buddha, Vajrapāṇi declares special mantras that derive from the blessing of all the buddhas and bodhisattvas.[61] As we shall see, this Vajrapāṇi becomes a favored character in esoteric Buddhist accounts of the revelation of their scriptures.

In addition to the shared model of the eternal teaching of the Mahāyāna, however, the esoteric traditions also advanced narratives of revelation cast in more prophetic or visionary terms (modes 4 and 5). The extremely influential *Mahāvairocana Tantra* (MVT), for instance, takes its narrative completely out of the ordinary world, presenting itself as the teaching of the cosmic buddha Mahāvairocana, not Śākyamuni. The setting is clearly divine and reflective of a notion that this revelation was not one that occurred in the conventional human world, but in a miraculous realm:

> Thus have I heard at one time the Lord was residing in the residence of all transcendent lords, the great and extensive adamant palace of the realm of reality, the assembly-hall of all vajradharas, the playful emanation of the zeal of the transcendent lords, without center or periphery, [with] a soaring dome, a storied palace made of and extremely beautifully adorned with [veritable] kings of gems, seated on a lion-throne composed of the bodies of bodhisattvas.

This is not to say, however, that this scripture does not place its teachings in the historical framework of the life of Śākyamuni. Rather, the MVT claims—as several other subsequent scriptures do—that it was precisely with this teaching that the Buddha became enlightened:

> The mantra methods are incomparable. By their means, the savior Śākyasiṃha overcame the irresistible host of Māra and [his] vast army.[62]

Nonetheless, this claim needs to be understood in context. Rather than stressing the ownership of Śākyamuni (here called Śākyasiṃha, the "Lion of the Śākyas"), this claim serves two functions: Most coarsely, it validates the new esoteric methods as central to the enlightenment of the prime (current, or local) exemplar of buddhahood; more subtly, it serves further to decenter and provincialize Śākyamuni, who is here cast as a disciple of other buddhas.[63]

This theme is given detailed elaboration in the *Sarvatathāgatatattva-saṃgraha* (STTS: "Compendium of the Reality of All Transcendent Lords"). This scripture foregrounds a narrative of the enlightenment of Śākyamuni presented at the outset of the work. In this tale, the man destined to become the historical Buddha is encountered before his enlightenment experience as the bodhisattva Sarvārthasiddha. He is seated at the foot of the bodhi tree, absorbed in the unshakable samādhi (*āsphānakasamādhi*), whereupon he is visited by a great community of transcendent lords appearing in their miraculous forms (*sambhogikakāya*), invisible to ordinary beings. They ask him, "How can you become a buddha without the knowledge of all the transcendent lords?" Sarvārthasiddha emerges from his samādhi and respectfully requests, "Make me understand, Lords! How shall I find out what reality is?" All the transcendent lords urge him, "Find out, O Noble One, by means of the meditative focus that attends to your own mind." They then teach him five mantras, initiating him as the esoteric bodhisattva Vajradhātu, in which form he then becomes enlightened. Upon his enlightenment, they escort him to the pinnacle of Mt. Sumeru to a storied palace with an adamant-, gem-, and jewel-encrusted dome, where they seat him on the lion throne of all transcendent lords.[64] That is, he is taken to a place very much like the setting for the revelation of the *Mahāvairocana Tantra*. In fact, the homology is straightforward: The four transcendent lords other than Vairocana seat themselves in the cardinal directions, forming a maṇḍala around Śākyamuni, who is subsequently referred to as the transcendent lord Vairocana.

In this acccount, the Buddha is not merely presented as a conduit for the ancient and eternal teaching of all the buddhas; rather, he becomes a disciple of all the buddhas who occasion his enlightenment through teaching and initiation. As a consequence of this reframing, Śākyamuni becomes a subordinate, albeit significant, character from a spiritual point of view: Luke Skywalker to the Jedi Council of the cosmic buddhas, as it were. The transcendent lords are the real teachers, who reveal themselves to the spiritually prepared in miraculous visions in their beatific forms (*sambhogikakāya*). There is an implicit homology: Sarvārthasiddha was initiated into the practice just as the contemporary disciple/practitioner is. Thus, just as the Buddha obtained a visionary teaching and initiation, the same is available to anyone who is prepared for the practice.

After the *Mahāvairocana Tantra*, most of the esoteric scriptures cast their narratives using elements from modes two, four, and five: Revelation in heaven, ancient teachings hidden away, or revealed in visionary encounters with buddhas in their beatific forms. Thus, for instance, the *Sarvadurgatipariśodhana Tantra* ("The Purification of All Bad Rebirths Tantra") is taught by "the Lord" (*bhagavān*) in the "grove of the highest delight of all the gods" (*sarvadevottamanandavana*). This venue is presumably in the heaven of Trayastriṃśa, because the entire audience is composed of deities and Indra inquires about the fate of a fellow god who passed (died) "from here, the abode of the gods of Trayastriṃśa."[65] The Lord in this case turns out to be Śākyamuni, but this is clearly another example of teachings delivered outside the conventional, mainstream Buddhist historico-cosmic framework.

The historical narrative of the *Catuṣpīṭha* ("Four Chapters") is most interesting as it reveals a three-fold typology of sites of revelation. According to this scripture:

> The great king of Tantras, the glorious *Four Chapters* [*Catuṣpīṭha*] in 180,000 [verses], was uttered by the Lord, Glorious Vajradhara, in the congregation of deities of the Śuddhāvāsa Heaven.[66] Then Vajrapāṇi, having condensed [this Ur-Tantra] into the King of Tantras in 12,000 [verses] in the glorious land of Oḍiyāṇa[67] [where it was comprehended?] by eight hundred million yogins and yoginīs. Then Glorious Nāgārjuna having gone there [to Oḍiyāna] and very secretly heard the Root Tantra of 1,200 [verses], he disseminated [it] in the world.[68]

Thus, the scripture is said to have been revealed in three stages from the divine to the human. It is initially revealed in a divine realm by the somewhat impersonal Lord Vajradhara (the leader of "all the transcendent lords"). It is then redacted by Vajrapāṇi (here considered distinct from Vajradhara) and taught in this form to yogins and yoginīs in the special land of Oḍḍīyāna.

As we shall see, this latter motif of revelation of Tantras in Oḍḍiyāna becomes a central element in much subsequent indigenous historiography. As one can infer from its location in the *Catuṣpīṭha* narrative, Oḍḍiyāna occupies a place intermediate between divine realms and the human realm. It is neither fully divine (as it is located on Earth), nor fully human (it is difficult of access and inhabited by semidivine beings). In Oḍḍiyāna, the Tantra is again redacted into a shorter version (suitable for lesser beings), in which form it is learned by a great saint, Nāgārjuna, who returned to teach it in the ordinary world. It may also be observed that this narrative appears to be organized as well around the concept of the three buddha bodies, such that Vajradhara≡dharmakāya, Vajrapāṇi≡sambhogikakāya, and Nāgārjuna≡nirmāṇakāya. This structure is also utilized in Chinese and Tibetan sources.

A similar account may be found in an esoteric Buddhist commentary from around the same time.[69] Jñānamitra's commentary on the *Prajñāpāramitānaya-pañcaśatikā* provides a remarkable tale of the revelation of Tantras such as the Guhyasamāja after the death of the Buddha. It is a remarkable document and rewards close attention.

> Earlier, during the eighty years when the Buddha lived in the human realm, there were none in the human realm of Jambudvīpa who were [suitable] to be disciplined by or to be vessels of the [spiritual] ways of the *Sarvabuddhasamāyoga*, the *Guhyasamāja*, or the like. Thus, the gods and fortunate bodhisattvas in the heavens of the Four Kings,[70] the Thirty-three (Trayastriṃśa), Tuṣita, and so on, being [suitable] vessels, at that time those scriptural collections resided there.[71]

The narrative thus makes quite clear that the esoteric scriptures were not revealed during the lifetime of Buddha Śākyamuni in the context of his ordinary teaching career, as the world was not ready for them. The text maintains, however, that they did exist at that time, being the provenance of the divinities of Trayastriṃśa and other heavens. It is not explicit whether they were taught there by Śākyamuni or predated him.

> Subsequently, after the Buddha passed into nirvāṇa [i.e. died], there was a king of Zahor[72] who, along with his retinue, had amazing faith in the Dharma. Having the good fortune to be disciplined by that [spiritual] way and being a [suitable vessel], the Eighteen Great [Scriptural] Collections, such as the *Sarvabuddhasamāyoga* and the like, came to the country of Zahor, by the blessing of Vajrapāṇi.[73]

Thus, the esoteric Buddhist scriptures miraculously appeared in the human world some time after the passing of the Buddha. They were brought there—evidently in the form of texts—by the power of Vajrapāṇi, who perceived that the time was ripe for their revelation, because there was a suitable disciple. However, the scriptures were incomprehensible to the king, so he needed to find someone who could explain them.

> The King of Zahor, Indrabhūti, inspecting those scriptures, [could] not decipher the writing. Then, having obtained clairvoyance by the force of prior karma, looking, [he saw] the Ācārya Kukkura in the Central Land (Magadha) in the region of Malapa.[74] During the day, [the Ācārya] would teach the Dharma to about a thousand dogs; at night, he enjoyed the sacraments with those dogs and acted as [Tantric] mentor to the dogs. [Seeing that the Ācārya] was a [suitable] vessel for that [spiritual] way and seemed also to have the fortune to discipline him, the King sent an ambassador to invite the Ācārya to come.[75]

Thus, the king made overtures to Kukkurāja, the "king of the dogs," evidently an antinomian yogin of the kind we will explore in chapters 5 and 6. There is a slight anachronism here, insofar as Kukkura is depicted as a kind of practitioner of nondual Tantric yoga, enjoying sacraments (*samaya*: presumably the consumption of revolting substances we will discuss in chapter 4, but also perhaps implying sexual yogas) with a pack of dogs (one of the most spiritually polluting of animals according to regnant brahminical mores). Yet, these practices—being the provenance of exactly the Tantras whose history is being narrated—had not yet appeared in the world. However that may be, the teacher (*ācārya*) sensed that he could be of service, but he wanted to check out the goods first.

> As the Ācārya, due to the force of prior karma, had the five clairvoyances, he investigated [therewith] whether or not the king had the fortune to be disciplined by him, and whether or not he himself was a [suitable] vessel for those scriptures, and concluded that the king did have the fortune to be disciplined by him and that he himself was a [suitable] vessel for the scriptures. [The Ācārya thought,] "I may [be able to] eliminate the king's doubts; however, since I've never seen those scriptures before, if at some point[76] I [am not able to] eliminate his doubts it would be extremely bad." So, he sent a missive back with the ambassador, [saying,] "As I would like to see those scriptures beforehand, please send them here." When the scriptures arrived and he inspected [them,] as he did not know which end [of the text] was the beginning and which the end,[77] he sank down right there, crying "I have no savior! No refuge!"

> Glorious Vajrasattva came in person and asked, "What do you desire?"
> [The Ācārya] begged, "I wish to understand these profound scriptures by merely looking at them."
> [Vajrasattva] having said, "I grant that it be so," thenceforth without even opening the texts of the *Sarvabuddhasamāyoga* and so on, the meaning of those became clear to the mental direct perception [of the Ācārya]. Then, the Ācārya went to Zahor and taught those Dharmas to the king and his retinue.[78]

Thus, in the end, Kukkurāja is blessed to understand the esoteric revelations by means of a miraculous vision of the esoteric buddha Vajrasattva. Based on this divine intervention and using the texts that miraculously appeared, Kukkurāja becomes—like Nāgārjuna in the *Catuṣpīṭha* narrative—the first transmitter of the Tantras in the ordinary human world. In sum, this narrative represents a hybrid of models 4 and 5: The texts appear physically (no. 5), yet require divine revelation for their proper interpretation.

The final centuries of Indian Buddhism witnessed the rise of a new esoteric revelation that had its own historical vision. The *Kālacakra* ("Wheel of Time") *Tantra* returns to a more realistic vision, insofar as it explicitly claims to have been taught by Śākyamuni Buddha. The *Vimalaprabhā* ("Stainless Radiance") *Commentary*, which forms an integral part of the basic text, gives the following tale of its origins, which places the chronology of its revelation quite precisely in a mainstream Buddhist framework:

> In this Land of the Nobles (India), the Lord Śākyamuni was enlightened at dawn on the full moon day of the month Vaiśākha. At the end of the fifteenth lunar day of the waxing moon, upon the waning moon commencing, [He] set the Wheel of Dharma in motion and created the Three Ways. In the twelfth month, on the full moon day of [the month] Caitra, at Śrīdhānyakaṭaka [He] displayed . . . the six-chapter Ādibuddha [Tantra].[79]

However, the realism of this tradition should not be overestimated. Even though this narrative thus strives to locate the revelation of the Kālacakra in the teaching career of Śākyamuni—one month after his enlightenment, in South India at the site of the Amarāvatī Stūpa—it is not clear that this revelation was the proximate source of the tradition in India. For the teaching is said to have been redacted and taken to Sambhala (or Śambhala)—a special realm much like Oḍḍiyāna, also imagined to reside in the northwest—where it was transmitted for centuries during which time the *Stainless Light Commentary* was composed by one of its kings. Only then was it, like the *Catuṣpīṭha*, redacted and taught in the human realm.[80]

However, in the Kālacakra traditions too the historicity of the revelation is further challenged (or, at least, augmented) by more visionary models. This same *Stainless Light Commentary* itself refers to the verse of the *Nāmasaṃgīti* we considered earlier, and explicitly invokes the same Mahāyāna notion we have seen throughout these histories—that the later revelations are the eternal, ancient, and constant teachings of all the buddhas, not just Śākyamuni:

> Just as the *Nāmasaṃgīti* was spoken, will be spoken, and is spoken by the transcendent lords of the past, future, and present, just so is the *Ādibuddha* [the Ur-*Kālacakra Tantra*]. The *ādi-* [in the word *ādibuddha*] means without beginning or end, that is "in beginningless time, it was taught, will be taught, and is taught [by] the primordial buddha." It is not taught only by Śākyamuni or the transcendent lord Dīpaṅkara. [Here the text cites *Nāmasaṃgīti*, vv. 12–13.] Hence . . . all the transcendent lords taught the Way of Mantras.[81]

A later commentator, Sādhuputrapaṇḍita Śrīdharānanda, suggests that there might in fact be simultaneous teachings taking place elsewhere. Citing a verse (presumably from the larger [divine, Ur-] *Kālacakra Tantra*):[82]

> At Vulture's Peak, Maitreya [will teach] the Prajñāpāramitā;
> [And] Buddha will teach the pure way of mantra at Glorious Dhānya.
>
> From this passage [we know] that the Lord's teaching of the way of mantras [took place] at Glorious Dhānya. However, elsewhere, as [or "when"] needed by those oriented toward that [way],[83] a great bodhisattva of the tenth stage [and/]or another revealer of scripture give the Tantra-teachings in detail.[84]

That is, Sādhuputra claims that although, yes, Śākyamuni did teach the *Kālacakra* at the Dhānyakaṭaka Stūpa in South India, its revelation is not limited thereto. For those who do not have access to that tradition, the Tantra is taught in various locations by various revealers whenever there is someone who can benefit from these teachings.

In addition to the Tantras themselves and the scholastic authors mentioned here, there survives one (and, apparently, only one) Sanskrit work on the history of esoteric Buddhism in a specifically narrative genre. The so-called "Shamsher Manuscript"[85] begins its history of the esoteric scripture(s) with Buddha delivering mainstream teachings to śrāvakas, but the scene then quickly moves to the South (*dakṣiṇāpathe*) where he is said to have emanated a divine world (*maṇḍala*) including a retinue of bodhisattvas.[86] Much of the text is devoted to lists of lineage members (*paramparā*). These strongly suggest the idea of visionary revelation insofar as the lists are very short (there only ever occur three or four names before names datable to the late first millennium) and the lineages do not begin with Śākyamuni, but rather with a divine buddha emanation (*buddhanirmāṇa*).

This document serves as a bridge linking the Indian literature we have explored so far and the many such narratives also found in the East and Central Asian sources. One encounters esoteric saints (*siddha*) traveling to Oḍḍiyāna to fetch Tantras to bring back to India. One sees miraculous visions of deities, instructions and prophecies in dreams, saints retiring to sacred mountains to do antinomian practice, and students following them there for instruction. One sees them performing rituals as well as pursuing education in Śrāvaka Buddhism, Mahāyāna, and the Tantras, and composing commentarial works thereupon. The stories related in this manuscript are thus very much of a piece both with its Indian precursors and with those we find in Tibetan works composed around the same time or shortly thereafter. As Sylvain Lévi noted, "the work of which we have a fragment here gives the history, naturally legendary, of this tradition, its transmission from masters to disciples, and its ritual. It is a curious specimen of the documents that must have served as the basis for . . . compilations in Tibetan."[87]

For their part, the Tibetans seem to have been well aware of all of the historical models by which Indian Buddhists conceptualized their tradition. For example, Tibetan authors could (and would) cite prior revelatory antecedents such as the Abhidharma in defense of the continuing openness to scriptural innovation found in the Indian and Tibetan practice of scriptural revelation.[88] A notable analysis of this issue is found in the *General Presentation of the Tantras* (*Rgyud sde spyi rnam*) of the Sa skya scholar Bsod nams rtse mo (1142–1182). This work abstracts four modes of esoteric revelation:

1. Those taught by Śākyamuni in his regular form
2. Those taught by Śākyamuni and revealed at a later time (after his death)

3. Those revealed at a later time that were not taught by Śākyamuni
4. Those taught by him while emanated in another form[89]

The first category includes Tantras taught to ordinary disciples of the Buddha's life in ordinary places such as Vaiśālī and so forth. We have seen examples of these here, such as the *Mahāśītavatī*, taught to Rāhula at Rājagṛha. The second includes Tantras such as the STTS that specify that they only descended to the human realm later; hence, these were specifically taught by him (it narrates his particular enlightenment story, after all) in a heavenly realm and only revealed in the human realm some time later. The third, those revealed at a later time that were not taught by Śākyamuni, include the *Cakrasamvara Tantra*. To explain this, Bsod nams rtse mo invokes an Indian authority[90] to the effect that such teachings are always available:

> As the *Commentary on the Saṃvara Tantra* explains, this teaching has existed since beginningless time; it was around before Śākyamuni. Since the *Transcendent Virtue of Wisdom* and so forth disappear during the fiery and other apocalypses at the end of each age, [although it had been taught before,] the Lord Śākyamuni had to teach it again. This is not so for the glorious *Saṃvara*. It never declines since it resides with and is practiced by heroes and heroines and so forth throughout inexpressibly many buddha fields.[91]

Hence, this type of scripture does not require intervention by the historical Buddha. It is always available in countless alternate universes. The final category—those taught by Śākyamuni through an emanation other than his ordinary one—is said to include most of the Tantras such as the *Guhyasamāja* and so forth.

It is interesting to note that at the end of his discussion Bsod nams rtse mo relates a story of the revelation of the *Guhyasamāja* that becomes extremely influential in Tibetan historical thought. In this account, Śakyamuni Buddha himself reveals the GST to a King Indrabhūti of Oḍḍiyāna, who asked for a method of liberation that did not require him to leave worldly life and its pleasures, whereupon the Buddha creates the *Guhyasamāja* to order.[92] In fuller retellings than the one given in Bsod nams rtse mo, the Tantra (written on gold sheets with melted beryl ink) ends up concealed in a magical Heruka chapel (*he ru ka'i gtsug lag khang*) under a lake which dries up at a later time, exposing the chapel, and allowing the revelation of the Tantra. Hence, it does not actually fit neatly in any of Bsod nams rtse mo's categories, as this complex narrative presents the GST as taught by Śākyamuni himself, emanated as Guhyasamāja, in the special land of Oḍḍiyāna and not revealed in the ordinary human world until quite some time afterward, when the miraculous temple appears.

Bsod nams rtse mo's comments on the provenance of this narrative are particularly interesting. Before discussing this narrative, he first rejects another conception of the circumstances of the revelation of the GST, saying that it is "not taught in any tantra, ritual manual, or śāstra—not even in oral tradition—[and] hence should be known to be a fabrication by innovators."[93] Immediately thereafter, he gives this Indrabhūti story—which he ultimately accepts as accurate—prefacing it with the comment that others claim this narrative *is* part of the oral tradition.[94] If this is true, it would account for the fact that—however popular it may be in Tibet—this narrative does not seem to appear in extant Indian sources.

It is also interesting to note that Bsod nams rtse mo goes out of his way to reject a narrative in which the Tantras fall on the roof of the palace of a King Ja, who does not understand them, enlists the aid of a monk named Kukkurī ("Bitch"), who himself gains knowledge through Vajrasattva's intervention. This should look familiar, as it is basically the narrative given in Jñānamitra's commentary. Bsod nams rtse mo points out issues that he thinks make it implausible to his view and also dismisses it as "a fabrication by innovators."[95] Although this may seem rather a serious blunder in light of the fact that a very similar narrative occurs in Jñānamitra's work, in his defense Bsod nams rtse mo is not entirely off base in this assessment. The version of this narrative featuring King Ja rather than Indrabhūti seems not to derive directly from an Indian source, but rather is a hybrid narrative mediated through a late first-millennium[96] Tibetan apocryphon called the *Scripture Collecting the Intention* (*Mdo dgongs 'dus*).[97] It is perhaps worth noting that this latter esoteric scripture describes itself in such terms that it would fall within our and Bsod nams rtse mo's third categories insofar as it claims to be taught eternally in the "mind stream of the Victors" (*rgyal ba'i dgongs brgyud*) in *dharmakāya* and *sambhogikakāya* forms.[98]

Tibetan literature is filled with marvelous narratives of many sorts concerning the revelation of various Tantras: Narrative historiography of this sort seems to have been particularly appealing to Tibetans and—in contrast to the Indian situation—many of these have been preserved. Although this is a fascinating area of study, because we are concerned herein with Indian Buddhism, we will restrict ourselves to commenting on those narratives that have clear continuities with Indian traditions. However, there is one further narrative type that bears mentioning in this regard, insofar as it occurs in two, seemingly independent extra-Indian sources.

In Tibet, this narrative is found in the work of the celebrated polymath Bu ston Rin chen grub. In several of his works on the esoteric traditions, this scholar addresses the history of these revelations. He summarizes his knowledge of the Indian sources, referring to three paradigms, all of which conform to the "taught in heaven" model (no. 2). Ānandagarbha, for instance, maintains that the Tantras were taught in Paranirmitavaśavartin heaven for the sake of the gods—much like the Trayastriṃśas model and consonant with the statements of Jñānamitra's narrative that the Tantras existed only among the gods during Buddha's lifetime. Alaṃkakalāśa taught that the revelation of the Tantras was a miraculous display, conducted while the Buddha was still residing prenatally in Tuṣita, by an emanated form (*nirmāṇa*) produced from the elements of his own body. Others, he notes, assert that *all* the Tantras were taught in Tuṣita.[99]

Like Bsod nams rtse mo, Bu ston too privileges the Indrabhūti taught by the Buddha himself in Oḍḍiyāna narrative. However, he goes on to elaborate a second narrative of a King Visukalpa, born in the era when the Heruka chapel is said to have first appeared.[100] This monarch, from various scriptural indications, infers that there must be a special super-Mahāyāna that uses the passions as means. In a dream, he is told by esoteric angels (*ḍākini*-s) to go north to Oḍḍiyāna. There, he is told, he will find the Heruka chapel containing the scriptures of the *Guhyasamāja* that emerged after the desiccation of the lake that had formed over it. Having found the sacred chapel, the king proceeds to prostrate at all four doors,[101] returns to the first (eastern) door and prays. A girl emerges and asks, "Are you Visukalpa?" Replying in the affirmative, he is brought inside and granted entry into the actual[102] Guhyasamāja maṇḍala, given initiation, instruction, and so forth. The text of the Tantra too is entrusted to him.

This narrative bears striking similarities to the more popular of the two Sino-Japanese traditions concerning the revelation of the esoteric scriptures: that they were recovered from a miraculous library stūpa.[103] The Chinese esoteric patriarch Amoghavajra "goes into considerable ritual and textual detail concerning the opening of the 'iron stūpa' in India from which the teachings of the STTS were purportedly recovered, but identifies the adept in question only as a 'great worthy' (*dade*, Sanskrit *bhadanta*)."[104] Amoghavajra begins by declaring that the "great worthy" received the esoteric *Mahāvairocana Sūtra* in a direct vision (mode no. 5) of Vairocana, "who manifested his body and a multitude of bodily forms. In mid-air, [Vairocana] expounded this teaching together with its textual passages and lines. He had [the great worthy] write them down."[105] Later, seeking a great esoteric scripture "enclosed in an iron stūpa in south India" (mode no. 4), he circumambulated the stūpa for seven days. Gaining entry, "he obtained the instruction of all the buddhas and bodhisattvas and these [he] remembered and held and did not forget."[106] The similarity of the stūpa and the Heruka chapel should be plain, especially because this particular stūpa had the special characteristic of being secured by "iron gates and locks" and space behind the door containing "incense and candles" as well as "exquisite flowers and jeweled canopies hung in sumptuous array."[107] This is certainly an unusual stūpa and sounds rather like a chapel, albeit many stūpas, like maṇḍalas, consist of four gateways (*toraṇa*) leading to a central, domed structure.[108]

Another, similar tale is related of the fifth-century apocryphal Chinese *Consecration Sūtra* (*Kuan-ting ching*, Taishō 1331).[109] This work "is quite explicit about its claimed origins as a treasure,[110] describing at length its initial preaching by the historical Buddha, its subsequent concealment, and its eventual discovery from a grotto, where it had been hidden in a jeweled casket, written in letters of purple and gold upon sandalwood tablets."[111] It does not take a great leap of the imagination to grasp the homologies between this tale and that of the *Guhyasamāja*, taught by the Buddha to Indrabhūti, written in melted beryl on gold plates, concealed in a miraculous chapel, and rediscovered. There is a further similarity in the two narratives insofar as both claim that their scriptures existed for a period during and after the Buddha's lifetime until, due to their extreme efficacy, they had liberated everyone in their proximity and went "underground."[112]

The Chinese traditions (like the Indian and Tibetan) also reflect the short lineage that is the unavoidable consequence of scriptures revealed recently. Zhao Qian, a disciple of Amoghavajra, "recount[s] the transmission of the STTS from an 'iron stūpa' in a lineage encompassing Mahāvairocana, Vajrasattva, Nāgārjuna, Nāgabodhi, and Vajrabodhi."[113] The last in this list is the teacher of the author's teacher. He accordingly comments that "from the origin flows a single tradition perhaps comprised of only some ten persons and that is it!"[114] Likewise, a late eighth-century (781) stele inscription proclaims that "from Vairocana to the monk [Amoghavajra] are a total of six 'petals.'"[115] It may also be noted that Zhao Qian "makes plain . . . that . . . this doctrine was not preached by Śākyamuni."[116]

The Japanese esoteric Shingon tradition similarly advances the notion that the MVT was/is taught by Dharmakāya Buddha, not the *nirmāṇa* Śākyamuni. Kōbō Daishi distinguishes the exoteric teachings as the revelation of *nirmāṇakāya* and *sambhogakāya* buddhas, while the esoteric is the *dharmakāya* teaching.[117] This is essentially the position advanced by the younger brother and heir of Bsod nams rtse mo, Grags pa rgyal mtshan (1147–1216). The latter wrote a brief work on the "Origins of Heruka," in which he foregrounds the Mahāyāna theory of the three bodies with a hermeneutical spin, asserting that in definitive meaning (*nītārtha*) the Buddha attained enlightenment in Tuṣita, while in interpretable meaning (*neyārtha*) he "turned many wheels of dharma in many places having emanated many teachers."[118] On this model, then, the Tantras are the teaching of one or another *nirmāṇakāya*, and/or of the *saṃbhogakāya*. There are numerous such Tibetan accounts that are marked for their tendency to stress the quasi-Docetic[119] Mahāyāna cosmology of the three bodies, allowing for a consequently more flexible notion of Buddhic authorship, insofar as buddhas such as Śākyamuni are regarded as merely one of myriads of buddha-emanations that appear from the same source (*dharmakāya*) throughout multiple universes.[120]

Although all this historiography may seem rather bizarre to modern sensibilities—the mystical rationalizations of innovating Buddhist communities or charlatans—the Buddhist esoteric traditions were not alone in India in advancing such claims. Much the same was taking place in other, contemporaneous Indian religions that were participating in the efflorescence of Tantric movements in late first-millennium India. For instance, the means to reveal in the world the *Śiva Sūtra*—an important scripture for the Śaiva Tantric Trika traditions—is said to have been given to the sage Vasugupta in a dream vision.[121] The work, he was told, is written on stone, the text concealed by being placed face downwards. The sage was instructed to travel there to extract the text from its place of concealment (mode no. 4). In an alternate tradition, Vasugupta is said to have received the scripture directly from Śiva in the dream (mode no. 5).[122] Here we see utilized for one and the same scripture, both of the means of revelation described in the Buddhist *Face-to-Face Confrontation Scripture*—dream revelation and physical concealment.

Indeed, just as the Buddhists were encouraged to do in that scripture, the Tantric Śaivas also adopted the practice of actively seeking visionary revelations. As Alexis Sanderson has noted, the Krama literature attests to "the practice of seeking revelation by propitiating the goddess during a period of ascetic retreat at a remote Pīṭha [sacred site]."[123] The *Kālikākramapañcāśīkā*, for instance, claims to be the result of such a vision quest, "transmitted by Niṣkriyānanda through a [disembodied] voice to the cremation-ground dwelling Siddha Vidyānanda when he was propitiating the goddess in a cave in the mountains of the Pīṭha Śrīśaila."[124] Numerous similar examples of visionary revelation may be found in the Śaiva Tantras. The third chapter of the *Rauravasūtrasaṃgraha* relates the origins of the *Rauravāgama*, the "decent of the Tantra [into the human world]" (*tantrāvatāra*), in which the "supreme guru of the world" Ananteśa reveals the scripture in the form of a smokeless blaze of light to Śrīkaṇṭha [Śiva], who transmits it to the goddess Devī, and so to Nandīśa, Brahmā, and ultimately to various sages and ordinary human disciples.[125]

The conception that esoteric scriptures were to be found in—and could be retrieved from—the wonderful country of Oḍḍiyāna is also widespread in Śaiva religious culture. Jñānanetranātha, for instance, to whom all Krama authors trace their lineage, is said to have "received the Krama revelation in Uḍḍiyāna directly from its Yoginīs, known as Pīṭheśvarīs, or from their leader (cakranāyikā) Maṅgalā."[126] These Pīṭheśvarīs of Oḍḍiyāna play important roles in many of the origin narratives of the Śaivas. Such narratives are used to account for revelation of such esoteric scriptures as the *Vātūlanāthasūtra*[127] and others.

Thus, the historiography of the Śaiva Tantric traditions mirrors much of what was being articulated by the Buddhists at the same time. Although, because their chief object of devotion was unequivocally immortal, the historiography of Śaiva Tantra was correspondingly simplified. One need not bother oneself with bare history in the case of an eternal deity. Thus, in some sense, what required significant historiographical restructuring by the Mahāyāna—conceiving of divinity as active in all pasts, presents, and futures—was a fait accompli for the Śaivas. However, they still needed to account for their history, to place the tradition in a narrative trajectory. In the account of the *Rauravasūtrasaṃgraha*, one can clearly see the mode of eternal divinity (no. 3) articulated in concert with that of revelation in heaven (no. 2): The eternal (*ananta*) lord (*īśa*) Ananteśa transmits the teaching to the deity Śrīkaṇṭha [Śiva], he to his divine wife, she to her son, and he to Brahmā, before the latter revealed it in the human world. Likewise, the *Śiva Sūtra* concealed on a hidden stone tablet (no. 4) or in a dream vision (no. 5) give ample evidence that there was considerable historiographical consonance among the various esoteric traditions of the Tantric Age.

OBSERVATIONS ON STRUCTURE, FUNCTION, AND HISTORIOGRAPHY

Thus, much as we saw of modern historiography in chapters 1 and 2, in the case of the indigenous historiography of esoteric Buddhism one can likewise discern clear patterns in the articulation of historical narratives. Just as modern historiographers drew on the resources of their own cultures for conceptual models and stock narrative forms with which to make sense of esoteric Buddhism for their own readers, so too did the authors of the Tantric traditions turn to earlier Śrāvaka and Mahāyāna precedents in seeking to craft through historiography a corporate understanding that would make sense to their contemporaries. Both groups of historiographers employ well-established narrative prototypes; they merely have different prototypes, deriving from differing discursive traditions. They both sought to make the objects of their narratives comprehensible, by situating them in culturally familiar frameworks that provide a ready-made interpretative context.

In the preceding, we have abstracted five basic narrative modes used throughout Indian esoteric Buddhist historiography and its reflections in the esoteric literatures of Tibet, China, and Japan. As I have indicated elsewhere,[128] there is a remarkable structural continuity in the form of these narratives insofar as they all in some fashion account for scriptural revelation subsequent to the lifetime of Śākyamuni Buddha. Bare historical assertions may suffice for less significant works (such as the *Gaṇapatihṛdaya*) that merely articulate spells of protection or prosperity. These could easily be conflated with the quite large and well-accepted corpus of mainstream Buddhist protection texts (*rakṣā*, *paritta*). As Skilling has observed, "the chanting of certain auspicious verses or texts for protection against disease and malignant spirits and for the promotion of welfare was no doubt a 'pan-*nikāya*' practice."[129] Such a strategy was, however, impracticable for more significant expressions of the Tantric genius, such as the MVT, STTS, and GST—capacious works that present complex ritual programs quite distinct from prior Buddhist practices. Thus, special narratives were found necessary in these cases; and, faced with this challenge, the esoteric traditions were able to resort to well-established precedents that had seen service when the task had been to gloss over the canonization of the huge and novel literature of the Abhidharma and Mahāyāna.

With the exception of the bare historical model (no. 1)—which in the case of the Mahāyāna traditions is not "bare" at all insofar as it had been radically transfigured in concert with a new buddhalogy into mode no. 3—the other four all involve revelations that did not come through the usual channels. They were either taught to the gods, from which they later descended to the human world (no. 2), and/or they were the eternal teachings of cosmic buddhas (or Śākyamuni in cosmic form) that could be accessed at any time (no. 3), and/or they had been revealed before and hidden for later re-revelation (no. 4), and/or they were taught anew in miraculous visions (no. 5). These conceptions allowed the Buddhist traditions to account for scriptural anachronism by providing a conceptual structure within which even newly revealed teachings may be considered as possibly authentic.

Motivating this accommodation was a central intellectual value at the core of Indian culture of the time. As Granoff has noted, Tantric religion "required . . . a definition of scripture that would admit the validity of new religious visions and of individual beliefs and practices" insofar as Tantric practices were "explicitly acknowledged to be new rituals."[130] Yet, these new visions and individual innovations sought acceptance in a cultural context in which the true is generally understood to be found in the old. In the thought of the time—much like in the classical cultures of Europe—truths had to have always been true. New truths were not to be made. When expressed in a Buddhist idiom, this axiom requires that if a religious technique or philosophical concept were true, it had to have been taught by the Buddha or, at least, a buddha.

That this culture of truth was pan-Indian is clear when one notes the consonance of Buddhist thought with Śaiva. Although the cultural imaginations of the various Śaiva traditions differ in certain significant respects from those of the Buddhists, we have seen that they structured the histories of their revelations in remarkably similar fashion. Like the esoteric Buddhists, the new literature and novel practices of the Śaivas emerged in dialog with already existing ideas and the people and institutions that perpetuated them. These narratives were thus crafted in a context of cultural contestation—and contested they were. As in the case of the Buddhists,[131] the claims of the esoteric Śaivas were not met with unanimous acceptance. Those who were not of a mind to accept the new approaches "expressly declared their human origin and consequent unauthoritativeness."[132] For those more positively inclined to the new formulations, however, the narratives we have explored provided an imaginative framework in which these religious practices could appear plausible to Buddhist and Hindu communities alike.

To comprehend properly the function of the historical discourses of Mahā/Vajrayāna Buddhists in context, it is perhaps helpful to think about the Buddha less as a concrete human being, and instead to understand the manner in which "Buddha" served an ongoing epistemic function in Buddhist cultures. For the esoteric Buddhist traditions, clearly, Buddha was not a historical Buddha (and certainly not "the" historical Buddha of some modern scholars and Buddhists), but an epistemic Buddha. Throughout the Buddhist world, the word of the Buddha is considered equivalent to truth and vice versa.[133] Hence, the famous statement that "whatever is well said [i.e., true] was said by the Buddha."[134] On the one hand, this allowed the co-option of ideas from other groups in the culture. Phyllis Granoff has, for instance, drawn attention to passages in the *Mañjuśrīmūlakalpa* that forthrightly claim that esoteric teachings of the Vaiṣṇava and Śaiva traditions "were actually proclaimed by Mañjuśrī disguised as one of the Hindu deities."[135] On the other hand, however, it also required that whatever claimed to be the word of the Buddha have been sufficiently vetted for consensual acceptance by the community. Such historiography is thus best understood as one feature of an ongoing process of epistemological negotiation in Indian cultured circles.

In this process of consensus building, new ideas could be tested in actual practice, and perhaps articulated in part through commentaries or works attributed to named persons, providing for some discussion and debate. The process of getting something accepted as scripture and thus (at least theoretically) binding on larger communities, however, required more substantial vetting through consensual critique. In this sense, it is worth bearing in mind that not all new scriptures were accepted by all or even a majority of communities, as can be inferred from the prophylactic passages in Mahāyāna scriptures (exo- and esoteric) referring to those who would reject them as "not the word of the Buddha."[136] In such cases, "hard-edged realism" was the order of the day. As Matthew Kapstein has observed concerning similar negotiations in Tibet, there were in all Buddhist communities

> two opposing tendencies: the tendency to anathematize and the tendency to canonize. The former was supported by elements of a realistic historical

> orientation. . . . The latter, by contrast, drew its strength from the belief that the canon could be held closed only on pain of self-contradiction, and from a fundamentally idealist vision of the Buddhist world.[137]

That is, Buddhists were well aware of the possibility of works being misrepresented as scripture and were concerned not to be led astray from the correct teaching. Thus, no doubt, many contenders for community approval were anathematized as not the word of the Buddha. Others, however, were found suitable and—based on the precedents we have reviewed here, including the idealist notion that enlightened speech was available anywhere, anytime—certain well-elaborated literary statements were accepted as valid articulations of the perspective of the community. By this process was gradually created a respected body of knowledge.

It is essential to understand that this process is by no means limited to mystical religious traditions such as Tantric Buddhism and Śaivism, but was a fundamental feature of Indian cultural discourse in virtually all fields. During the same first-millennium period that witnessed the revelation of the Mahāyāna and Mantrayāna scriptures, similarly consensual understandings deriving from years of social experience across the cultural spectrum were crystallized into major statements of theoretical and practical knowledge. Yet, due to the aforementioned axiom that all that is good and true must have been known of old by divine or semidivine beings, these knowledge systems too were attributed to miraculous revelations. As Sheldon Pollock has noted, in India

> *śāstra* [knowledge] must exist primordially. Extant *śāstras*, consequently, come to view themselves as either the end-point of a slow process of abridgement from earlier, more complete, and divinely inspired prototypes; or as exact reproductions of the divine prototypes obtained through uncontaminated, unexpurgated descent from the original, whether through faithful intermediaries or by sudden revelation.[138]

Both of these forms of understanding will be quite familiar from the aforementioned esoteric Buddhist narratives. The former (the slow process of abridgement) is precisely the narrative we saw in the case of the *Catuṣpīṭha Tantra*, which decreased by stages from a 180,000-verse divine edition, through a 12,000-verse Oḍḍiyāna redaction, to 1,200-verse text that is known in the human world. The same is related of the work on social duties and etiquette (*dharmaśāstra*) the *Nāradasmṛti*, which is said to have been composed in 100,000 verses by the divine sage Manu, abridged by Nārada to 12,000, eventually to emerge in the human world as the extant 2,700-verse redaction.[139] We have also observed that the latter process (direct revelation) is also very common in Tantric historiography. In exactly the same cultural register, key works on dramatics, astrology, cuisine, and archery—the *Bharatanāṭyaśāstra*, *Sūryasiddhānta*, *Pākadarpaṇa*, and *Bṛhatśārṅgadharapaddhati*—are attributed to direct revelation to humans by the Brahmanical gods Brahmā, Sūrya, Yama, and Śiva, respectively.[140]

Consequently, what is perhaps most remarkable about the indigenous historiography of esoteric Buddhism is that it is not remarkable at all. During the first millennium in India, every branch of human knowledge and practice (*śāstra*) was given identical treatment. Whether the subject was religious history (*purāṇa*), erotics (*kāma-śāstra*), poetics (*alaṃkāra-*), architecture (*śilpa-*), astronomy (*jyotiṣa-*), dramatics (*nāṭya-*), cookery (*pāka-śāstra*), or medicine (*āyurveda*), all tell similar stories of the derivation of their key literary statements from divine revelation. Although we have traced the Buddhist antecedents to this practice to illustrate the particular resources on which our authors drew, ultimately what we have described is a pan-Indian phenomenon common to all the knowledge systems of the time, whether religious or secular. In all of these areas, these corpora were negotiated, with some being anathematized and others being canonized. The commentarial process allowed subgroups to negotiate sometimes conflicting canons and to create their own synthetic traditions drawing on the materials provided in the authorized scriptures.[141] This conception of systematic presentations of community knowledge as deriving from divine revelation was culturally sanctioned across the board in literate Indian cultures, providing a space in which people could understand, authenticate, and share innovative new approaches without challenging the privilege of the ancient.

Of course, Indians (and Tibetans) often were skeptical of such claims. The use of this device was subject to critical reception; limits did exist outside of which these exceptions were not granted within an otherwise quotidian perspective. The attitude toward the miraculous in Indian culture is not entirely dissimilar from that taken in the classical Greek traditions where, as Veyne has noted:

> Among the learned, critical credulity, as it were, alternated with a global skepticism and rubbed shoulders with the unreflecting credulity of the

> less educated. These three attitudes tolerated one another, and popular credulity was not culturally devalued.[142]

Veyne provides the instructive example of Galen, the physician. Although skeptical of the existence of centaurs in general (because no one had ever seen one), "when the same Galen no longer seeks to impose his ideas but to win new disciples, he seems to pass to the side of the believers."[143] That is, when narrating the history of Greek medicine, he will readily describe its original teaching by Apollo to Chiron, the centaur.

We moderns, of course, cannot live in that world (we may not even want to); but the work of cultural criticism demands that we at least be able to understand the language used to articulate it. On that basis, we can discern more subtle dynamics of their historiography. Failure to do so will inevitably result in misconstrual of the object of our studies. On the one hand, to construe the indigenous historiography of esoteric Buddhism as engaging in the same cultural practice we do—to assume that traditional authors mean the same thing we do when they attribute works to the Buddha—is to import distorting assumptions into our representations. This problem is pervasive in studies of esoteric Buddhism, and we have seen the results in these chapters.

On the other hand, neither should we delude ourselves into thinking that what we do and what they do are so terribly different. Frequently, modern historians do not differ very significantly in their methods from the ancient Greek mythographers. Giuseppe Tucci, for instance, in discussing the narrative of the revelation of the Kālacakra, asserts that "it is evidently a pious tale, without the least historical foundation, . . . but everything leads us to think that there is much truth in the rest of the narrative."[144] In so doing, his method is not at all distinct from that of Roman historians such as Livy who "limited themselves to removing details that seemed false or, rather, unlikely or unreal . . . [and] presumed that their predecessors were telling the truth" or the Greek mythographer Pausanias who sought to separate the kernels of truth from the "puerilities—nymphs and river fathers—that can easily be corrected."[145] Indeed, recent speculation that the nonhuman spirits described as inhabiting remote meditation spots "reveals the social reality that Buddhists began to encounter tribal and semi-nomadic peoples extensively in the early medieval period"[146] reveals exactly the type of thinking that created euhemerism and other forms of Greek rationalization of myth. Much the same intellectual move can be seen in classical Indian writers, as well.

"Vedottama," for instance, "in his *Pāñcarātra-prāmāṇya* has gone so far as to declare that the original tantra works of the Śaivas that are believed to have been revealed by Maheśvara were compiled by an ordinary human being named Maheśvara and some credulous people were mistaken to identify him with the god Maheśvara only on the flimsy ground of the similarity of names."[147]

Thus, the contemporary interpreter finds herself betwixt and between—neither able to assume seamless continuity between herself and the culture that is her object, nor yet able to radically distinguish her own intellectual projects from those of the indigenous traditions. As Veyne answered his own question in *Did the Greeks Believe in Their Myths?*:

> Anyone with the slightest historical background would immediately have answered, "But of course they believed in their myths!" We have simply wanted also to make it clear that what is true of "them" is also true of ourselves and to bring out the implications of this primary truth.[148]

In some very important respects, the formal aspects of histories are always oriented more toward crafting the historical subject, than revealing the historical object. The discursively constructed position of the narrator and the "ideal reader" suggest to the actual reader an orientation, an endorsed subjectivity, an interpretative perspective with regard to the phenomenon whose history is being narrated. The stock of narratives hegemonic in a community encapsulate stylized orientations of the group and tend—as we have seen in modern and indigenous historiography—to be used again and again to interpret unfamiliar events and traditions, to make the unknown known.

Scholars will do well, then, to eschew well-worn paths of origins and historical narrative until close, scholarly work allows a much better sense of the meaningful discourses and practices—the semiology—of these traditions. Much more spadework needs to be done before responsible historical synthesis can be undertaken. If we do not fully understand who these communities were and what they thought they were doing—if we fail to understand the constitutive imagination of esoteric Buddhists—how can we essay larger synthetic projects? We will just end up recapitulating well-worn rhetorics to fill in the gaps in our own ignorance.[149]

As Veyne has also suggested, after Foucault we can no longer naively tell stories of eternal figures like esoteric Buddhism, Śaivism, and so forth. Rather, we need to focus on relations (structures), for it is relations that constitute what these things really are in history.[150] As Pollock has likewise suggested, such a mode of analysis "would include listening to the questions the texts themselves raise . . . rather than, like inquisitors, placing the texts in the dock and demanding that they answer the questions we bring to them; in other words, focusing on their critical processes rather than on our critical positions."[151] The type of discursive analysis exemplified in the foregoing—and to be continued in subsequent chapters when we advance our interpretation of Tantric Buddhist discourses—can facilitate this process insofar as it can bring to the fore stylized rhetorical patterns in both the scholarly subject and its objects.

If, as some have suggested, the real vocation of a historian is the analysis of evidence,[152] we may then logically pass from the domain of historiography to the interpretative challenges that confront the interpreter of the literary remains of Indian Tantric Buddhism. As I suggested in the introduction, it is here that a semiologically-inflected philology sensitive to the structures that pattern its rhetoric can provide some assistance. This is now where our path of investigation must lead—to a close and critical reading of the Buddhist Tantras. As I will endeavor to demonstrate, the critical lenses of semiological analysis allow us to approach the data with fresh eyes—to attend to patterns discernible within the discourses and to interpret their significance without recourse to an imagined social context or historical frame, operating on the presumption that the discourses are coherent and, if a large enough sample is taken, will demonstrate reliable things about the aggregate. The second part of this book will focus on the analysis of primary sources for the study of Tantric Buddhism. In particular, we will bring these tools to bear on that aspect of the esoteric Buddhist traditions that has most frequently been associated with the idea of Tantra—that with which we began this book—the transgressive discourses and rites found in the Mahāyoga and Yoginī Tantras.

II

INTERPRETATION

[4] THE SEMIOLOGY OF TRANSGRESSION

tattvaṃ na paśyati hi so 'kṣaramātradarśī candraṃ didṛkṣur iva cāṅgulim īkṣamāṇaḥ |

The one who sees only the literal, does not see reality—like one who wants to see the moon, gazing at the finger [pointing at it].

—Candrakīrti, *Pradīpoddyotana*

THE TIME has now come to return to the question posed at the beginning of this work: How to make sense of the fact that the seemingly antisocial, antinomian behaviors advocated in much of the later Tantric literature—that seem at first glance to be the ravings of madmen—are in fact "reckoned to be the sacred scripture of millions of intelligent human beings."[1] What is one to make of a tradition whose most revered scriptures seem to counsel its devotees to violate not only its own most basic moral precepts, but to violate all the most essential contemporaneous standards of human decency? What might all these outré statements (and, presumably, behaviors) mean?

Here too a close attention to rhetoric allows a more nuanced assessment of the place of transgression in the social and symbolical economy of esoteric Buddhist communities. We have seen in the foregoing how, in the case of historiography at least, human communication is rarely if ever a straightforward process. What may seem at first glance to be first-order statements about the origins or history of esoteric Buddhism—whether modern or indigenous—appear upon analysis as highly complex and ramified modes of expression whose ultimate referents encompass a range that includes expressing intercultural judgments, reinforcing and celebrating shared systems of valuation, and negotiating intracultural discussions over epistemic authority.

The antinomian discourses and practices of Tantric Buddhism are no less complex than those used to communicate its modern and traditional historiography. In the face of such complexity, in order to understand how (and what) they signify in their proper cultural settings, one must again move beyond the particular expressions (*paroles*) and endeavor to grasp the larger semiotical system (*langue*) of which they are but a part. Otherwise, as Pierre Bourdieu (among others) has warned,

> Those who take the short cut which leads directly from each signifier to the corresponding signified, who dispense with the long detour through the complete system of signifiers within which the relational value of each item is defined (which has nothing to do with an intuitively grasped "meaning"), are inevitably limited to an approximate discourse which, at best, only stumbles on to the most apparent significations.[2]

This chapter will begin the work of discerning this total system: to see how Tantric Buddhists can make sense with (and, we, of) the odd and often repulsive statements that appear in the scriptures of the Mahāyoga and Yoginī Tantras. The primary focus of analysis will be the so-called five meats (*māṃsa*) and five ambrosias (*amṛta*) as they appear in the most renowned and influential of the Buddhist Mahāyoga Tantras, the *Guhyasamāja (Esoteric Community) Tantra*.[3] These two sets of five substances—beef, dog, elephant, horse, and human flesh, and feces, urine, blood, semen, and marrow[4]—feature prominently in the literature of the later Tantras, and are a conspicuous element of their ritual performance.

With this focus in mind, before turning to my own philological and semiological analysis, it may be helpful to review the positions modern scholars have taken concerning the interpretation of these disturbing elements of Tantric ritual and scripture: That is, on the question of whether or not this transgressive discourse is to be taken literally. I will subsequently suggest that, to truly appreciate the semiology proper to the antinomian aspects of Tantric Buddhism, one must look beyond the level of plainly denotative (what I will also call natural) language. Those who argue that these injunctions should be taken literally and those who argue for a figurative interpretation both fail, I argue, precisely on account of a narrow focus solely on denotation. To the contrary, one may clearly discern in these traditions a coherent system of what Roland Barthes has called mythic speech or, more precisely, connotative semiotics. On the basis of the data of ritual prescription and analysis of Tantric scriptural narratives, I will endeavor to demonstrate that, by recognizing that these antinomian signs derive their significance from such a connotative semiotical system, scholars may better be enabled to address the fundamental question of their meaning(s) and, on this basis, reconstruct (in chapter 6) the social contexts that created and sustained them.

THE LITERAL AND THE FIGURATIVE IN TANTRIC HERMENEUTICS

In general, in addressing the question of Tantric interpretation, modern scholars have reduced the problem of interpretation to one of determining direct reference. This is, in seeking to resolve Mitra's quandary, the question is construed as: Did they do these outrageous things or not? Underpinning this approach is the assumption that words are found in the texts, that they denote various meanings, and that consequently the question of interpretation is simply one of deciding precisely what it is that they denote. Conforming to this general orientation, one may discern two major tendencies. Many assert that the Tantras—being the secretive, esoteric scriptures they claim—express themselves via a kind of special code (twilight language or intentional language), which must be broken in order to understand what the real meaning is behind what seem, taken literally, to be antinomian statements or references to exotic meats or revolting bodily fluids. Others (currently among the most vocal) claim that the Tantras say exactly what they mean and this question of interpretation is ultimately an artificial one born of naïvely giving credence to the later, "bowdlerizing," "sanitizing," and/or "semanticizing" tendencies found in the commentarial literature. This latter, it is averred, seeks to explain away the literal meaning intended by the original (lay) authors in order to render them more palatable for a very different (monastic) audience.[5] That is to say, scholars have tended either toward literalism or figurativism.

Scholars of the literalist tendency claim that the Tantras were intended as straightforward, literal statements, and that this literal meaning must be taken as the primary basis for cultural interpretation. They assert that the authors of the Tantras meant exactly and only what they said on the ostensive level of discourse. This is essentially the attitude one finds in the earliest modern writings on the Tantric traditions. It was clearly with a literal reading in mind that Eugène Burnouf (writing in 1844) made his now-famous statement (later repeatedly attributed to T. W. Rhys Davids) that "the pen refuses to transcribe doctrines as wretched in form, as they are odious and degraded in their foundations."[6] Rajendralal Mitra also—following what he considered to be the literal meaning of the *Guhyasamāja* concerning the meats and ambrosias—maintains that "the most appropriate food for devotees while engaged in [Tantric] worship is said to be the flesh of elephants, horses and dogs" and that "not satisfied with the order . . . to make offerings of excrementitious matter on the homa fire, the author [of the Tantra] goes to the length of recommending such substances as human food."[7]

In general, it may be said that these scholars assume that the Tantric movement in Buddhism originated in a desire to loosen the moral discipline enjoined by the tradition, to allow for what they consider a more natural enjoyment of life's pleasures. Many, most even, of these interpreters assume some model of the lustful monks etiology and/or the degeneration narrative as a guide to their readings. As Monier Monier-Williams expressed it: "The eternal instincts of humanity . . . insisted on making themselves felt notwithstanding the unnatural restraint to which the Buddha had subjected them."[8] Mitra's son, Benoytosh Bhattacharyya—whom we have seen was a strong advocate of a "natural" life—goes so far as to praise the *Guhyasamāja* for having "done Buddhism the service" of eliminating all its disciplinary measures. Although all sorts of luxuries were prohibited in the early days, he tells us

> in the Guhyasamāja everything is permitted. Not only flesh of the most harmless kind but all kinds of flesh-meat are permitted such as the flesh of elephants, horses, dogs, cows, nay, even of human beings.[9]

Nor is this approach limited to these early Orientalists. Such notable recent scholars of the Tantras as David Snellgrove and Ronald Davidson have made similar claims and have argued quite stridently against those who take such terms to mean anything other than what they literally denote. Snellgrove, for example, laments "a tendency nowadays, much promoted by Tibetan lamas who teach in the Western world, to treat references to . . . worship carried out with 'impure substances' (referred to usually as the 'five nectars') as symbolic."[10] Contrary to "whatever later refined interpretation was placed upon such prescriptions," he assures his readers, "there need be little doubt that such 'sacraments' were used in the circles of tantric yogins, where these texts had their actual origin."[11] Davidson similarly dismisses those who disagree with the literalist approach as apologists, and devotes considerable attention to refuting the notion that the language of the Tantras could bear significance beyond the literal. Like early Victorian scholarship on Buddhism—Davidson maintains that the Tantric scriptures were composed out of the desire of Buddhist monks to have scriptural warrant for their lusts for "drinking wine and making love to nubile women."[12] Like Bhattacharyya, Davidson sees in the history of Tantric Buddhism the final act in "a narrative about the extended testing of preceptorial boundaries by the morally challenged."[13]

Not all scholars of Tantric Buddhism, however, have been satisfied with this approach. Others have drawn attention to the important testimony of the surviving Tantric commentarial literature (many examples of which seem to suggest readings other than the literal) as well as to noteworthy indications native to the Tantric "primary scriptures" (*mūla-tantra*) themselves, which seem to indicate that these works were not intended to be understood entirely or exclusively literally. These scholars—evidently the target of Snellgrove's methodological ire—tend to describe the language of the Tantras as metaphorical or symbolical. A. K. Warder, for example, in his 1970 work *Indian Buddhism*, noted that "putting aside conjectures . . . the commentators are solidly in favor of the text[s] being metaphorical."[14] This line of thinking may draw some support from the fact that the commentaries on the Tantras often do not accept the literal meaning as the intended sense. In many treatises of this sort, what might seem to be antinomian terms or injunctions are interpreted as references to inner yogic processes. For instance, in several passages of Candrakīrti's *Pradīpoddyotana* (an influential commentary on the *Guhyasamāja*), expressions such as eating of feces and urine are glossed as "pacifying" the sense objects and the sense organs.[15]

Responding directly to Snellgrove's dismissal of the commentators' readings as representing a later trend than the root scriptures,[16] Warder contends that "since the [*Hevajra*] Tantra itself stresses the metaphorical meaning of its statements we cannot accept his opinion."[17] This point has been made again more recently by Anthony Tribe, who noted that this so-called symbolic interpretation cannot be attributed solely to later commentators as the *Hevajra Tantra* includes its own nonliteral exegesis within itself.[18] After a classical Tantric statement that "you should kill living beings, speak lying words, take what is not given, consort with the women of others" (i.e., break four of the five basic Buddhist moral rules), the Tantra itself interprets this passage to mean that one "kills living beings" by "developing one-pointed cognition by destroying the life-breath of discursive thought;" that one lies by vowing to save all sentient beings; and so on.[19] Such a move is by no means novel in the history of Buddhist exegesis for, as Tribe comments, "the whole device—of saying something that appears to be shocking and then explaining what is really meant—is reminiscent of passages from the [exoteric Buddhist] Perfection of Wisdom sūtras."[20]

On the basis of such observations, Michael Broido articulated a general methodological critique of modern Tantric studies, writing:

> One of the reasons for the weakness of current western work on the Tantras is the almost complete neglect of the methods of interpretation which were used by the commentators and teachers who interpreted them. We may not have access to the methods used in oral instruction, but there is no good reason for this neglect of the methods used in the traditional commentaries.[21]

Thus, in recent decades, more attention has been paid to these traditional methods of interpretation, with scholars such as Broido himself and Robert Thurman exploring the complex, polysemous modes of Tantric interpretation found in the commentarial and hermeneutical literature, such as the aforementioned *Pradīpoddyotana*, which sets forth a system of interpretation that allows for multiple, simultaneous readings of individual passages—including, but not limited to, the literal meaning. As this hermeneutical system was considered authoritative in a wide range of later Indian and Tibetan Tantric circles, research into Candrakīrti's work has shed much valuable light on these historically-influential principles of Tantric exegesis.[22]

Although the work of the figurativists has thus done much to advance discussion in the area of Tantric hermeneutics, it is not in fact the only or even the best way to approach the issue. Each of these two approaches to interpretation has contributed to efforts to understand Buddhist Tantrism; yet, each also has rather serious limitations. For instance, although Broido and others are exactly correct to stress the necessity of documenting and analyzing the historical actuality of particular instances of Tantric exegesis as found in the surviving commentarial literature, we cannot assume that the surviving texts constitute a comprehensive catalogue of all such interpretations. Indeed, it might be argued, a literal interpretation of the text does not need a commentary to defend it; so the fact that the only surviving commentaries interpret the text in nonliteral ways appears neither surprising, nor significant.[23]

However this may be, somewhat more to the point, I think, is the fact that many of the surviving commentaries do advocate literal readings of the texts. Indeed, literal sense (*yathāruta*) is one of the six exegetical alternatives outlined by Candrakīrti's magnum opus on Tantric hermeneutics. The sex and death for which the Tantras are famous are by no means regularly and uniformly excised by the commentaries. Although Davidson locates Candrakīrti among those he considers "puritanical" commentators, the *Pradīpoddyotana* includes numerous passages in which he details sexual rites in explicit and literal language—more so, even, than the primary scripture itself.[24] Thus, there is certainly a place for literal interpretation, even according to the later commentators. To assert that the Tantras were written comprehensively in code and were not to be understood literally at all is clearly untenable.

Even a somewhat attenuated form of literalism, however, is equally problematical. Besides the difficulties mentioned here, the very notion of literal is not nearly so simple and straightforward as it might be made to sound. For instance, in chapter 8 of the *Guhyasamāja Tantra*, there is a half-verse which runs, roughly translated, "one should always smear feces, urine, water, and so on, in order to worship the Victors."[25] Here the literal meaning seems clear as day: It is typical Tantric disgustingness, obviously, claiming that one should offer worship to the buddhas by the slathering of such foul substances as raw sewage. However, although that might seem literal, it is in fact itself already interpretative. What is meant in this passage by "feces and urine" is, in fact, feces and urine. However, unlike many occurrences of these terms in the Tantra, in this context what is meant (as confirmed by the commentaries in a gloss that in no way seems forced)[26] is cow dung and cow urine. Such a smearing of feces, urine, water, and the like, is then (to an Indian eye) quite normal and not foul or disgusting in any way. In orthodox Indian ritual contexts one routinely smears cow dung, urine, and water to purify a ritual site: There is nothing revolting, transgressive, or Tantric about it. As Freud is reputed to have quipped, "Sometimes a cigar is just a cigar . . ."

How, then, to resolve this scholarly quandary? Is it merely the case, then, that determinations of literal- or figurativeness must be resolved on a case-by-case basis? Is it simply not possible to elaborate a global theory of reference? Although ultimately there is no comprehensive rule that can be applied across the board, I do believe that much of this debate can be resolved by thinking more broadly about the nature of signification in this literature. What is striking about these approaches is that they take a remarkably narrow view of the possibilities (actualities, even) of human discourse. In approaching the question of interpretation as a choice between literal and figurative (or even as a polysemous mixture of literal *and* figurative), earlier discussions all proceed from the assumption that these discourses are examples of directly denotative (natural) language. Starting from this premise, scholarly method is reduced to the realist (one might even say positivist) project of attempting to determine if the Tantras really meant what they said. That is, the fundamental—even exclusive—question becomes "What signified or signifieds correspond to the signifiers found in Tantric discourses?" When it says beef, for instance, does that mean (real) beef or something else? The questions that have guided research in this area have all been posed accordingly.

It is by no means clear, however, that the authors of the Tantras intended to use language in the straightforward, prosaic way that this framing of the question suggests. To take only one example, consider the following verse found in the *Dhammapada* (and its Sanskrit version, the *Udānavarga*), a work of impeccable pan-Buddhist authority: "Having killed mother and father as well as the king and two learned Brahmans, and having beaten the kingdom along with [its] attendants, a man is called pure."[27] As the tradition makes clear, this injunction was meant to be interpreted—a fact signaled by its hyperbolic (yet culturally precise) transgressiveness. "Mother, father" and so on, which one is to kill, refer to obstacles such as desire, which are to be overcome by the practitioner. Likewise, the *Mahāyānasaṃgraha* makes statements such as "the bodhisattva is the supreme slayer of living beings," meaning thereby (according to a hermeneutical etymology) that he "cuts beings off from the round of rebirths."[28] These usages bear witness to a Buddhist penchant to use language in ways other than merely denoting literal meanings in a direct, simple, and discursively naïve way. In this exoteric context, it may be noted, no one questions the use of such literary devices, but there has been great reluctance to admit that such may have been the case with the Tantras. There are, I believe, very good reasons to believe that the discourses we find in the Mahāyoga Tantras are similarly complex in their semiotics; and that one of the primary modes of signification employed is, in fact, not that of natural language, but rather the higher-order semiological system of connotative semiotics.

CONNOTATIVE SEMIOTICS AS EXEGETICAL METHOD

The notion of connotative semiotics was first advanced by the Danish linguist, Louis Hjelmslev, and later elaborated by the French semiologist, Roland Barthes. Connotative semiotics—what Barthes also called mythology or mythic speech—is a second-order system of signification. It presupposes the conventions of natural language, and uses them to indicate complex ideas, obliquely yet strongly. The basis of the model is the structure of the linguistic sign first set out in Ferdinand de Saussure's *Cours de Linguistique Générale.* According to this model, a linguistic sign can be analyzed into an arbitrary signifier (usually one or more phonemes or graphemes) and a signified (a sense being indicated). The union of these two is what is known as the sign—a complex, dual phenomenon comprising the plane of expression (the signifier) and the plane of content (the signified).

In ordinary, prosaic, directly referential language—the kind that, many assume, is used in Tantric scripture and ritual—this is all one has. Signification takes place directly and, generally, unambiguously: I speak of a "table," and you know exactly what I mean. However, this is by no means the only level on which human beings express themselves—particularly when they take to expressing more complex meanings of their common culture or to signifying ideological (or otherwise highly-motivated) propositions that for one reason or other do not lend themselves to straightforward denotation. Transcending these first-order systems of direct signification, or denotation, then, are two higher-order systems.

The first of these is that used to speak *about* language and the structure of signs—what has been called metalanguage. This type of second-order discourse is used by linguists such as de Saussure to describe the functioning of signs. (It is, in fact, the mode of discourse used in the passage you are now reading.) In this case, a complete sign from natural language

FIGURE 4.1 Structure of the linguistic sign according to F. de Saussure

1. Signifier	2. Signified
3. Sign	

FIGURE 4.2 Structure of metalanguage

Language:		1. Signifier	2. Signified
		3. Sign	
META-LANGUAGE:	I. SIGNIFIER	II. SIGNIFIED	
	III. SIGN		

becomes a signified in the metalanguage, with terms such as sign, signifier, and signified serving as the signifiers. This mode of discourse may be schematized in figure 4.2.

The other second-order system, connotative semiotics, is (arguably) a rather more subtle and (certainly) a more pervasive mode of human communication. Unlike metalanguage, which—although accessible to the untutored—is largely the province of professional linguists, connotative semiotics (while no doubt also susceptible to professionalization) is well-attested as frequently used by ordinary speakers. In this mode, a complete sign from the natural language serves, not as a signified, but as a signifier in the higher-order system.

Barthes famously gives two examples of this mode of signification in *Mythologies*—that of a phrase serving as a grammatical example in a textbook and that of a picture of a saluting French soldier on the cover of

FIGURE 4.3 Structure of connotative semiotics

Language:	1. Signifier	2. Signified	
	3. Sign		
CONN. SEM:	I. SIGNIFIER		II. SIGNIFIED
	III. SIGN		

Source: Adapted from Barthes (1972), 115.

FIGURE 4.4 Barthes' first example

Language:	1. *quia ego nominor leo*	2. "because my name is lion"	
	3. Sign [the meaningful phrase]		
CONN. SEM.:	I. SIGNIFIER		II. PREDICATE AGREEMENT
	III. "I AM A GRAMMATICAL EXAMPLE."		

Paris Match. Each example highlights an important aspect of connotative semiotics, so we should examine each in turn.

The first example Barthes gives is of the phrase *quia ego nominor leo*, occurring in a Latin textbook as an example of the grammatical rule of subject-predicate agreement.[29] Here, it is important that the signifier be a real sign produced out of natural language—a meaningful statement rich with its own significance—and not merely an arbitrary signifier within the natural language. This first level of signification has already been expressed in the denotative enunciation of the rule that subject and predicate should agree. What is wanted in this case is a concrete example, which (to be effective) can only be such a sign. Here, what is being signified is not the meaning of the phrase ("because my name is lion"), but the grammatical rule it instantiates. Surely, this is a very different use of language than the merely literal, yet one which we encounter in a variety of forms nearly every day, with nary an eyebrow raised. This usage may be schematized as shown in figure 4.4.

Barthes' second example derives from his experience seeing a picture on the cover of *Paris Match* of a French soldier of African heritage saluting the tricolor. Here, the basic signifier is a photograph, which depicts the soldier just described. However, this literal analysis does not capture the signification taking place on the cover of that magazine. It is not just a picture of a soldier meant to communicate his appearance innocently to those readers with a special interest in soldiers and their appearance. As Barthes indicates, the presence of that particular kind of soldier displaying just that kind of patriotism itself (as a signifier) expresses a higher-order content—a content that, in

FIGURE 4.5 Barthes' second example

Language:	1. Photograph	2. Saluting Soldier	
	3. Saluting Soldier		
CONN. SEM.:	I. SALUTING SOLDIER (QUA PATRIOTIC COLONIAL)		II. FRENCH IMPERIALITY
	III. "THE FRENCH EMPIRE? IT'S JUST A FACT!"		

fact, may be said to be the (if not schematically or temporally, hermeneutically) primary signification of the image. The signified expressed by this image—the patriotic colonial—is, as Barthes insightfully indicates, "French imperiality." The sign thus constituted serves ideologically to naturalize the French colonial presence in West Africa: The viewer is semiotically seduced into a world of meaning wherein the French empire is "just a fact."

Based on these two examples, Barthes says of connotative semiotics that it "is a type of speech defined by its intention (*I am a grammatical example*) much more than its literal sense (*my name is lion*)." But he adds that "in spite of this, its intention is somehow frozen, purified, eternalized, made absent by this literal sense (*The French Empire? It's just a fact: look at this good Negro who salutes like one of our own boys*). This constituent ambiguity of mythical speech," he says, "has two consequences for the signification, which henceforth appears both like a notification and like a statement of fact."[30]

This constituent ambiguity of connotative semiotics—that its signification is defined primarily by its intention, yet this intention is obscured or mystified in the process of signification by the manifest content of the natural language sign—is of central importance to how I understand this mode of signification to be operative in Tantric Buddhist ritual and scripture. It is precisely this ambiguity which, I argue, makes connotative semiotics a powerful tool in ritual performances of the kind undertaken by its practitioners.

CONNOTATIVE SEMIOTICS IN TANTRIC RITUAL

The quotidian rituals of the esoteric Buddhist traditions that advocate consumption of the five meats and ambrosias consist essentially of variants on a basic rite called a *sādhana*, literally an accomplishing or effecting. As Yael Bentor very clearly demonstrates in her work on Indian and Tibetan rites of consecration,[31] the structure of the *sādhana* constitutes the ritual template for all Buddhist Mahāyoga and Yoginī Tantra rituals. Whether they be fire ceremonies (*homa*), offerings of ritual cakes (*bali*), rites of prosperity or curing (*pauṣṭika-* or *śāntika-karma*), consecrations of statues or the like (*pratiṣṭhā*), all are not only based upon but actually nested within the overarching and primary ritual pattern of the *sādhana*. The *sādhana* rite is also called the self-creation or, perhaps one might say, self-resurrection (*ātmotpatti*). We learn of its structure and nature from several sources, but in the various traditions of the Guhyasamāja, among the most authoritative are the self-creation rites attributed to Nāgārjuna and Candrakīrti.[32] It is these sources upon which I will base my presentation here.

The central aim of this self-creation yoga is for the practitioner to do away with the perception of herself as ordinary—as well as the pride that is believed to be associated with that perception—and to replace it with a perception of herself as a divine, enlightened being, with the sense of proud empowerment and universal efficacy that characterizes such a being. Such a profound transformation is not considered to be an undertaking that can be accomplished just so; rather, it is a highly ramified process that involves meditatively dying from the previous, unenlightened embodiment and ritually taking rebirth with a new, perfected identity. The ritual texts ascribed to Nāgārjuna and Candrakīrti describe the following main stages of the rite: Determining the site where the ritual should be performed; focusing on great compassion as the motivation; meditating on a protective perimeter; focusing on voidness as a way of eliminating ordinary perception and its pride; creating the cosmic foundation for the maṇḍala world; constructing the divine palace and its maṇḍala environs; entering into the maṇḍala of ultimate reality (i.e., death) and arising in the form of the Buddha Vajradhara; performing a series of yogic exercises to bless one's newborn enlightened body, speech, and mind; again entering into ultimate reality/death; arising in a new embodiment to benefit others; and performing various enlightened activities.[33] The various ritual activities besides self-creation (consecration, destruction, etc.) all are thought to gain their efficacy on account of being enacted, not by an ordinary person, but by an enlightened being. It is through self-resurrection as a deity in the *sādhana* as just described, that the practitioner assumes this omnipotent ritual identity.

The first three stages are quite straightforward, and fall within the general patterns of Indian and Buddhist ritual practice: Finding a suitable spot (lovely and somewhat off-the-beaten-track), setting the correct motivation of universal compassion as required of a Mahāyāna practitioner, and delimiting the site with a proper protective boundary (analogous to the rite of *sīmabandha* in the Buddhist ordination rite).[34] The practitioner then focuses on the fact that all things (including herself) are void of an intrinsically-real status—which serves in this context as the epistemological precondition for such a rite of radical reenactment of the cosmogony. She then imaginatively creates a divine environment for this recreated personality to inhabit: the *maṇḍala*, with its glorious palace suitable as the residence of a fully-enlightened divinity. The yoginī then "enters the maṇḍala of ultimate reality" (i.e., dies, leaving her ordinary personality), and arises in a thoroughly-accomplished, perfected form whose mind is suffused with the great compassion and wisdom of voidness cultivated previously. A variety of yogas involving the arraying and recitation of mantras and/or manipulation of vital airs are then prescribed to reinforce and consecrate this identity; whereupon she enjoys the type of beatific body known as the *sambhogakāya*, a special lucid embodiment in which she interacts with other enlightened beings. She then dissolves this rarified form again into the clarity of death, thereby reentering the so-called *dharmakāya*, an enlightened form in which the practitioner-qua-deity pantheistically identifies with the entire universe. Having heard the pleas of enlightened angels to take birth once again in order to benefit others, she subsequently arises in a concrete bodily form visible to all (called a *nirmāṇakāya*) and performs enlightened activities.

According to the instructions found in the rite ascribed to Nāgārjuna, it is in this final state of realization and compassionate diremption that "one performs the activities of eating [things] such as the five ambrosias and so on."[35] It is here, then—situated in the context of the culmination of the Tantric ritual of self-creation—that I suggest one look to try to understand the meaning of the five meats and the five ambrosias for the Mahāyoga traditions.

In order to grasp the semiosis implicit in the consumption of the meats and ambrosias at the climactic moment of the Tantric *sādhana*, it is essential to understand what these substances signify in the overarching discourse of contemporaneous, mainstream Indian culture. Bhattacharyya's suggestion that these meats were delicious luxuries much desired by a repressed Buddhist ecclesia could not be further from the mark. I do not believe we are justified in maintaining that they appear in the Tantras merely because they are tasty and the monks were seeking scriptural legitimation for an exotic barbeque.[36] They appear, rather, because they signify (or, better, instantiate) the violation of ritual purity. All five of these meats are distinctive within first-millennium Indian culture as, for lack of a better word, taboo meats. In the compendia of the *dharmaśāstra*-s, which (among other things) discuss in detail the rules governing the preservation of ritual purity in Indian society, these foods are among those generally classified as *svabhāva-duṣṭa*, "polluted (and, thus, polluting) by their very nature."[37]

That these restrictions were not merely academic notions, limited to the textbooks on dharma, but functioning social strictures,[38] is confirmed by the testimony of the Chinese Buddhist monk Xuanzang, who, in his seventh-century account of his visit to India, observes that "the meat of such animals as *oxen*, donkeys, *elephants*, *horses*, pigs, *dogs*, foxes, wolves, lions, monkeys, and apes is not to be eaten as a rule. Those who eat the meat of such animals become despicable and detestable to the public and are expelled to the outskirts of the city."[39] Although he does not specifically mention human flesh here, we may safely take it for granted (given what else we know of first-millennium Indian society) that this was also considered ritually impure.[40]

Much the same can be said of the five ambrosias. All five are bodily fluids, and thus polluting according to orthodox Brahmanical standards operative at the time. It is on account of their daily contact with such substances that physicians in ancient India were considered impure and excluded from the orthodox rites.[41] Such bodily excretions may also be said to fall into the polluting category of the *sahṛllekha*, that which is impure because it is "disgusting to the mind."[42]

In short, contact with the five meats and the five ambrosias so absolutely violates the most central purity strictures in Indian society that reference to them in Tantric Buddhist ritual and scripture could only have constituted a deliberate semiosis. They signify that which is disgusting and polluting. In fact, an explicit awareness of this is revealed in the text of the *Guhyasamāja Tantra* itself: In chapter 14, the Tantra specifically refers to feces and urine as "foul-smelling and disgusting."[43] Similar examples from Tantric Buddhist literature in Sanskrit could be multiplied almost indefinitely. The theme of the revolting (*jugupsa*) is a consistent trope in these traditions. It is clear that the authors considered these substances disgusting.[44]

Thus, perhaps somewhat ironically, it seems to have been the much-maligned early Orientalist scholars who—though reading the Tantras through the lenses of their own cultural presuppositions, and not those of first-millennium India—were able to "read" (if not understand) the Tantras correctly. To the early Indologists, the Tantras were full of the filthy and degrading, the foul and offensive. As I think should be very clear, a reader in first-millennium India would have thought much the same.[45] Nor, it is important to add, was this accidental—the disgusting nature of these substances was explicitly noted. The Tantric literature does not, therefore, as some would have it, reflect the naïve importation of marginal tribal magical techniques that just happened to be repulsive to the cultural mainstream. Rather, the authors of the Tantras were speaking precisely the mainstream cultural language of Indian society and pushing its buttons in such a systematic fashion that it could only have been deliberate. In short, in disparagingly referring to the Tantric *Subhāṣitasaṃgraha* as "a caricature of both the teachings of earlier Buddhism and legitimate Yoga,"[46] Cecil Bendall missed the most salient point: That is precisely what it was *meant* to be.

Further evidence for this may be derived from observing the two verbs that are consistently used in scriptural contexts related to the five meats and ambrosias—eating and offering. On my reading, every instance in which the five meats and ambrosias are mentioned in the *Guhyasamāja* places them in one of these two contexts. Of the twenty-nine references to meats and ambrosias in this scripture, twenty-one of them occur explicitly as the objects of acts of eating or offering or some variant thereof. Fourteen of these instances involve actions of eating or consumption;[47] while two further examples can be inferred to be so.[48] Seven occur in relation to acts of offering;[49] and one more is plausibly associated with this act in the commentary.[50] Of the five remaining, three do not refer to the five meats and nectars under discussion,[51] leaving only two out of the twenty-nine that are not explicitly associated in the primary text with eating or offering. A strong case, based on context and commentary, can be made to consider these two as also associated with consumption.[52] Hence, of the twenty-nine instances, all twenty-six relevant references to the meats and ambrosias in the *Guhyasamāja Tantra* associate them with actions of oral consumption and/or offering to divinities.

FIGURE 4.6 Suggested semiology of antinomian discourse in the Mahāyoga Tantras

Mainstream Indian culture:	1. Beef	2. Pollution	
	3. Polluting beef		
MAHĀYOGA TANTRA:	I. (EATING) POLLUTING BEEF		II. NONDUAL GNOSIS
	III. "I HAVE ATTAINED COMMUNION (YUGANADDHA)." ("IT'S JUST A FACT!")		

What, then, does this entail with regard to our understanding of their semiology within the Tantric traditions they represent? I think it is safe to say that these two activities—eating and worshipping/offering—are the quintessential moments of importance to orthodox, Dharmic purity strictures: They are prime occasions of danger, wherein one runs the risk of ritual pollution. In intercourse with the divine, much emphasis is placed on the notion that proper protocols be observed, lest one's status decrease—given the gods' transcendent purity, the postulant must be appropriately fastidious. Similarly, in the act of eating, wherein one accepts foreign bodies into one's own—and, thus, one's bodily constitution is potentially compromised—a concern for purity strictures is paramount in the Indian religious context. Thus, by interpolating these sets of polluting substances into the two archetypal liminal acts of the purity calculus, this literature seeks to hammer home the fact that what is at issue in these contexts is ritual purity. Fundamentally, this is a discourse about purity and pollution (notably, an overtly pervasive theme in the later Buddhist Tantras)—not the special, intrinsic qualities of particular meats and bodily fluids.

What does it mean, then, for a practitioner of the Mahāyoga Tantras, having gone through the process of self-creation as an enlightened Buddhist divinity, to eat from a skull a foul soup of polluting meats and bodily fluids? In this semiosis (as can be seen schematized in figure 4.6), the complete sign from the natural language of mainstream Indian culture—the signifier beef, and so on in semiological union with its signified "ritual pollution"—acts as a signifier in the process of ritual consumption considered as a discourse. The signified in this semiosis is the attainment of the enlightened state of nondual gnosis (*advayajñāna*), called in some sources[53] communion (*yuganaddha*)—the ultimate goal of the practitioner in which the deluded perception of things as having an intrinsic nature (pure or polluting, good or evil) is transcended.

This state of communion is described thus in the final chapter of Nāgārjuna's influential work on the practice of the Guhyasamāja, the *Five Stages* (*Pañcakrama*):

Defilement and purification—
Knowing them from the perspective of ultimate reality
The one who knows [them as] one thing
Knows [the] communion [stage].[54]

In particular, for our purposes, Nāgārjuna goes on to mention the following dualistic concepts which are likewise transcended by the accomplished practitioner.

As oneself, so an enemy . . .
As one's mother, so a whore, . . .
As urine, so wine.
As food, so shit.
As sweet-smelling camphor, so the stench from the ritually-impure
As words of praise, so revolting words . . .
As pleasure, so pain.[55]

Thus, by dramatically (and I use this term advisedly) demonstrating their transcendence of conventional dualistic categories of purity and pollution in the concluding portion of the rite of self-creation, the practitioners of these traditions signify ritually that their attainment of the enlightened state—which, it is worth remembering, is the starting point and the ending point of Buddhist Tantric practice—is, in fact, a fait accompli. In this way, the consumption of the five meats and ambrosias in these rituals constitutes an example of connotative semiotics.

What implications does this have for our understanding of text and ritual? If we return now momentarily to the examples given by Barthes, we will recall that there were two important points that he stressed with regard to the effect of connotative semiotics. For one, he said, it is speech that is guided primarily by its intention. That is, the phrase serving as a grammatical example means less its sense in natural language than it signifies its intention to serve as an example of a grammatical rule. This is the first point. Second, this intention, which is the key element of its signification, is occluded in the process of signification. "Its intention is somehow frozen, purified, eternalized, *made absent* by this literal sense.[56]

One can see how this is a very effective technique in the kinds of manipulative discourses of advertising and ideology that Barthes took as his primary objects of study. Viewers of the 1950s issue of *Paris Match* on which our Afro-French soldier stood saluting, who may well have been experiencing a crisis of confidence regarding the French empire in Africa, were meant to come away reassured—it is this intention that is primary in the signification. Yet, that intention is in no way explicit; it is occluded. As Barthes reads the image: "The French Empire? It's just a fact: look at this good Negro who salutes like one of our own boys."[57] The viewer is reassured of the strength of French imperiality via a profound, and seemingly ideologically innocent *coup d'œil*, in a way impossible to achieve through the rhetorical persuasion of, say, an op-ed piece on the viability of the situation in French West Africa. Yet this higher level of signification is shrouded by the primary act of signification, ensuring deniability: It's just a nice picture of a soldier, after all . . .

This type of signification is also present in advertising. Here the intention is obvious and clearly primary—to sell product. And it is this intention that it is also vital to keep occluded insofar as possible. If the rational mind is alerted to the signification, it loses much of its power—it is demystified. Connotative semiotics are thus rampant in the world of commercials: Products do not signify themselves, they signify ideas or pleasurable states. The SUV one sees climbing effortlessly into the garage of the Himalayan monastery does not signify itself: It signifies freedom, peace, and power. The boy who begs his mother for the one Christmas present he really must have—a Cross Your Heart bra—has clearly been reading the images he sees on television. Clever boy that he is—skilled at reading commercial discourse through hours spent before the tube—he is unconcerned with the direct denotative signification of the brassiere with which he is confronted, but is completely taken up with its connotative significance of total comfort and security.

Similarly, in the ritual context of the *sādhana*—calling as it does for the practitioner to renounce her rational, discursive knowledge of her own ordinary and limited personality—connotative semiotics are used as a more direct, mystifying mode of signification than ordinary rhetorical suasion. This latter had, in fact, been tried before in Buddhist pedagogical history. There is an extensive corpus of exoteric scriptures and philosophical literature devoted to advancing the notion that all beings are intrinsically enlightened by nature, that all are possessed of the *tathāgatagarbha*. This is by no means the most effective way of convincing someone of that fact, however.[58] There is simply too much evidence to the contrary available to the rational mind; just as, if one were to try to rationally convince a young boy of his need for a brassiere, one would be sorely pressed. However, in the ritual context of the self-creation rite, in which the practitioner blissfully eats conventionally-defiling substances with impunity, having adopted the attitude of the overlord of the maṇḍala (*maṇḍalādhipati*), there is no need for further convincing. The suggestion is accomplished in a *coup d'œil*—as (Vajra-) Barthes might say "The enlightened stage of communion? It's just a fact: Look as I savor this soup of beef, dog, semen, and feces!"

Elsewhere in his writings, in discussing an exhibition of shock photos, Barthes gives further indications of the important signifying function of connotative semiotics. Speaking of photos that deal with "the shocking," he notes that "it is not enough for the photographer to *signify* the horrible, for us to experience it."[59] What I believe he is getting at here, is the fact that there is a *distancing* effect to the structure of natural language. Recall the admonishment of a thousand writing teachers, to show, not say: It is not enough for one to inform another that something is horrible for that person to have a truly visceral, empathetic experience of its horror. If the intention is to share a taste of the horror and not merely to convince another that A or B falls into a certain abstract category of experience called horror, one cannot use merely denotative discourse. Connotation is essential: It allows communication to be guided by an ulterior intention (to shock), and yet for that intention to be occluded (so as not to make the experience overly contrived). Otherwise, if the signifiers chosen are drawn solely from natural, denotative discourse, says Barthes, they "have no effect on us; the interest we take in them does not exceed the interval of an instantaneous reading: It does not resound, does not disturb, our reception closes too soon over a pure sign."[60]

It is this understanding of the contrast between the prosaical discourse of denotation and the poetical discourse of connotative semiotics that I believe has been leveraged in this aspect of Tantric ritual. Thus, although such direct signification is found elsewhere in the rite of self-creation—the practitioner recites the mantra *oṃ śūnyatā-jñāna-vajra-svabhāvātmako 'ham* ("Oṃ I am the very adamantine nature of the gnosis of voidness"). Yet, in order to ensure the maximal experiential impact of the performance of self-resurrection, the autosuggestion of inhabiting a divine identity, transcending purity and pollution, the authors of the rite have also chosen to employ the more visceral, more instantaneous mode of connotative semiosis. It is here, in this semiotic process, I believe, that some of the "mystery" of the Tantras may be found.[61]

Seen in light of this dynamic, then, the original question of the meaning of the five meats and five ambrosias in Mahāyoga Tantra scripture and ritual would seem to call for some reconsideration. The question of whether these words—cow meat, dog meat, elephant meat, horse meat, human flesh, feces, urine, blood, semen, marrow—signify real beef, urine, and so on, I would suggest, is close to irrelevant. In the context of the self-creation rite we have analyzed earlier, what is important is their semiotical function, their ability to instantiate ritual pollution as a lived fact. What is essential to the signification of the rite are the five meats and five ambrosias as signs, insofar as they function as signifiers in the higher order system. In the natural language out of which that sign is borrowed, the actual signifier is, as de Saussure insists, arbitrary.[62] Thus, I would argue, the question that has troubled modern scholarship—is it "shit" or not?—is beside the point.In fact, much the same seems to have been indicated by authors of the *Guhyasamāja Tantra* itself—even in its earliest stratum (chapters 1 to 12). In chapter 12, after enumerating a set of five yogic accomplishments that correspond to eating each of the five meats, the text blithely notes that "if all these kinds of meat cannot be obtained, while meditating, one should conceive [of them] as really existent."[63] The concrete reality of flesh as a denoted signified is extraneous; what matters is its significance within the community of speakers of the Tantric yogin/ī.

CONNOTATIVE SEMIOTICS IN TANTRIC SCRIPTURE

To frame the question of the interpretation of antinomian elements in Tantric ritual in terms of what its signifiers denote in natural language is—in this case, at least—fundamentally to misconstrue the semiosis involved in the ritual act of consuming defiling substances. The two classical positions on Tantric hermeneutics, the literalist and figurativist, ultimately fail to account for the signification observable in these traditions. Both in the signs used in ritual performance and in the composition of scripture, the antinomian Tantras betray a clear semiotical structure. For reasons we will explore in chapter 6, the leading lights of the later esoteric movements sought to elevate a gnosis of nonduality as the central Buddhist goal, challenging (rhetorically, at least) concepts of purity and pollution (caste, astrological auspiciousness, etc.) widespread in the ritual and social mores of the earlier esoteric dispensations (e.g., the *Mañjuśrīmūlakalpa*[64]). The ritual consumption of the five meats and five ambrosias explored herein clearly reflect this central concern.

Given the sophistication of the Buddhist literary context out of which the Mahāyoga Tantras evidently arose,[65] I think we can only conclude that the notion that the literal meaning must be presumed to be original and primary can only be based on an unspoken assumption that Tantrism is primitive—an assumption with a long history in Orientalist scholarship (some of which we have traced in preceding chapters), yet one that would seem to be based on a failure to read the sources fully critically.[66] On the other hand, to suggest instead that the discourses of taboo meats and foul fluids constitute merely a code, hiding a secret transmission of esoteric yogic techniques, is to miss the historical resonance of these discourses in the contexts of both ritual performance and contemporaneous culture. In approaching the question of Tantric interpretation in such a way, scholars of the figurativist tendency have paid little attention to aspects of Tantric discourse besides the denotative. Even if the signifiers "feces" and "urine" refer to the sense organs and their objects (as Candrakīrti claims), this signification is still well within the parameters of natural language. That is, the code model merely replaces the signified in the sign relation with a variant element, such that one forms nothing more than a simple sign composed, for example, of the signifier "beef" and the signified "the form aggregate" (*rūpa-skandha*). This does not, I argue, capture the essence of the mode of communication used in the Tantric discourses, although I admit it is one suggested by some trends in the commentarial literature.

I suspect that much of the reason for the neglect of connotative modes of signification on the part of scholars of Tantrism has to do with the fact that these higher-order systems are seen to operate most clearly in ritual—a notoriously neglected area for much of modern religious (and, perhaps in particular, Buddhist) studies. Little attempt has been made to situate the discourses of the Tantric scriptures within their proper ritual contexts, although there survives a wealth of Indian Buddhist literature on precisely this subject. This is all the more paradoxical because—for most of the history of the modern study of the Tantras—it has been a scholarly mantra that the Tantras are primarily ritual (i.e., practical, not theoretical) texts.

On the other hand, I believe this semiosis can also be clearly and unmistakably discerned in the narratives of Tantric scripture. There are a number of important episodes internal to the *Guhyasamāja Tantra* itself, which I feel very strongly corroborate the view that these discourses are not meant to be taken as a direct, simple acts of denotative signification, but that—in scripture as well as in ritual—it is the experience of nondual gnosis that is the primary object signified. For instance, in a key passage that appears in GST chapter 5—a passage that has attracted a great deal of attention from modern scholars in that it is one of the most consistently and blatantly Tantric (i.e., transgressive) in the entire text—the Lord Buddha Vajradhara teaches the assembled buddhas and bodhisattvas that "even those who commit great sins such as the inexpiable sins (*ānantarya*) will be successful in this buddha vehicle, the great ocean of the Universal Vehicle (*mahāyāna*)."[67] Further, he teaches that those who violate the most basic Buddhist precepts—who take life, lie, steal, and are sex-maniacs—and even, notably, those who eat feces and drink urine, are considered by him to be "fit for the *sādhana*" (*bhavyās te khalu sādhane*). In a final flourish, he informs the assembly that those who commit incest with mother, sister, or daughter, will "attain vast success," while the one who makes love to the Buddha's own mother will attain buddhahood. At the conclusion of this pithy teaching, the bodhisattvas in attendance are said to have been "amazed and astonished." Why, they ask, is this bad speech (*durbhāṣita*) being spoken in the midst of the enlightened assembly? To this query, the buddhas in attendance reply that they should not speak so: That this is the pure teaching of all the buddhas. Upon hearing this reply, the bodhisattvas are so overwhelmed that they actually pass out, whereupon the Lord has to rouse them by the light rays of the meditative samādhi called (notably) the space-like nondual vajra (*ākāśasamatādvayavajra*).

This narrative is noteworthy in several ways; and a full unpacking of its implications has much to contribute to our understanding of the literary techniques of the Buddhist Tantras. First and foremost, it very clearly expresses a self-consciousness of the fact that the teaching given by Vajradhara in this very passage in the *Guhyasamāja Tantra* is blatantly heretical. However, it is far too simple to consider this merely a device for giving scriptural sanction to deviant practices[68] or as evidence of contemporaneous social opposition.[69] For this episode and similar passages elsewhere in the literature do not merely suggest the sanction of one or the other unorthodox religious praxis. Rather, in this sermon, the Buddha Vajradhara systematically hits virtually every subversive note in the Buddhist scale of religious values. Like the meats and ambrosias, this is in no way a semiotically innocent list: The practices advocated by Vajradhara represent the precise inversion of mainstream Buddhist ethical norms. The bodhisattvas, not surprisingly, are shocked and scandalized by this teaching, calling it bad speech (*durbhāṣita*). This term, too, is significant, as it alludes to the Buddhist hermeneutical rule of thumb that all that is well-spoken or good speech (*subhāṣita*) is the revealed Word of the Buddha.[70] Equally resonant here, however, is the fact that this term refers not merely to that which is poorly spoken in some abstract sense, but rather constitutes a distinct category of transgression of the Buddhist Monastic Discipline (*vinaya*).[71] Thus, the bodhisattvas' assessment of the teaching is that it is not Buddha speech (*subhāṣita*) but rather heresy (*durbhāṣita*); and when their enlightened classmates insist that this is, in fact, the "pure teaching of the buddhas," their imaginations are beggared—they simply cannot process the fact that the pure teaching of the buddhas and the defiled teachings of the heretics are nondual seen from the perspective of an enlightened being who has attained communion—and they black out. In the end, the reader is told, the bodhisattvas are enabled to come around—to digest the cognitive dissonance of this teaching, to tolerate the signification enunciated by the Buddha Vajradhara, enough so as to regain consciousness—only when they are touched by the "light" of the gnosis of nonduality.[72] On my reading, once again, in scripture as in ritual, the transgressive elements of the Tantras reveal themselves to be motivated discourses, whose primary semiotical interest is to stress the Tantric message of the nonduality of pure and impure, sacred and profane, immanent and transcendent.

It is worth stressing that this is not an isolated instance. Exactly the same semiotical structure informs a similar narrative that is the subject of chapter 9 of the *Guhyasamāja*. Both of these chapters, notably, are from the earliest stratum of the scripture (chapters 1 to 12) and thus may be considered reflective of the core values of the antinomian traditions. This chapter, too, consists of an initial sermon by Lord Vajradhara, astonishment of the bodhisattvas, and a rebuke and elucidation from the transcendent lords. It differs only insofar as the bodhisattvas do not in this case require spiritual light rays—a detailed explanation by the transcendent lords suffices.

The teaching given by Vajradhara in GST chapter 9 consists of five sections. Each gives instruction in a visualization in which a maṇḍala is transformed into one of the Five Transcendent Lords (Akṣobhya, Vairocana, Amitābha, Amogha, and Ratnaketu), whereupon the meditator is to envision performing a heinous act toward buddhas. In the first visualization, the buddhas of the three times emanated by Akṣobhya are pulverized by a blazing vajra and all beings, too, are similarly annihilated by the secret vajra. Ending on a more pleasant note, these all thereby become bodhisattvas ("sons of the Victors") in the vajra[-family] buddhafield [of Akṣobhya]. In the second visualization, Vairocana transforms into buddhas appearing as jewels that are then seized (i.e., stolen); these, too, become bodhisattvas, eminent among sages. The third involves visualizing Amitābha transforming into a space filled with buddhas who take on the form of women, whereupon they are enjoyed sexually. In the fourth, Amogha becomes all buddhas, who are then lied to and betrayed. Finally, the fifth visualization consists of Ratnaketu who radiates all buddhas, who are then verbally abused.

Naturally, just as in GST chapter 5, the bodhisattvas in the audience are "amazed and astonished" and inquire why the Lord would say such an astonishing thing. The transcendent lords reply that they should not consider it base (*hīna*) or revolting (*jugupsita*—note the recurrence of this term). They explain that this teaching is based upon the perception by buddhas of the voidness (and, thus, nonduality and purity) of all things, using well-established Buddhist philosophical similes.[73] The chapter then concludes with the "amazed and astonished bodhisattvas, their eyes wide with wonder," reciting:

> The conventional rings forth in the pure, the non-conceptual,
> In the most wondrous things that appear like space![74]

Once again, we see a narrative in which the Tantric teaching involves violating basic Buddhist precepts (against killing, stealing, sexual misconduct, lying, and verbal abuse); the bodhisattvas are befuddled; and the issue is clarified through reference to the nondual voidness of reality. In case there should be any doubt about what is intended, the chapter ends with a verse of praise that specifically refers to nonconceptuality and purity: the same complex of ideas that informs the entire antinomian orientation found in these Tantras.[75] Lest the reader worry that nonduality is not referenced, immediately following this verse is the chapter title[76] that reads "the ninth recital, the chapter on the pledge of the meaning of the nondual reality, the ultimate truth" (*paramārthādvayatattvārthasamayapaṭalo navamo 'dhyāyaḥ*).

◈ ◈ ◈

One can thus clearly see the utility of the model of connotative semiotics in the interpretation of the antinomian aspects of the Tantric Buddhist traditions. Indeed, this approach shows great promise in the interpretation more generally of those cultural formations we are in the habit of calling "religious." Barthes' analytical method allows a more critical approach to the uses of discourse in human society, which are rarely confined to literal denotation. This is true, evidently, not merely of the contemporary advertising and pop culture with which Barthes was concerned, but for classical traditions as well. It is one very powerful tool in discerning the structuring principles that inform discourses and practices—including modern historiography—that seem on the surface to be about something else, their manifest content.[77]

It has been noted in another context that a certain scholarly approach to the study of myths mistook them for explanations of natural phenomena, leading to the conclusion that they reflect a magical or pre-logical form of thought. Against this approach, it has been argued that "myths may think *with* natural objects or categories; they are almost never *about* natural objects or categories . . . the seasons may serve as a medium for thinking about periodicity, regularity, order, distinction, transformation and place."[78] Likewise, I would suggest that the currently prevalent, literalist approach to the interpretation of the rhetoric of the Buddhist Tantric literature errs in assuming that these discourses are *about* meats, fluids, and despised castes, thus failing to see beyond the ostensive content. Rather, I would argue, late-first-millennium Tantric Buddhist scripture and ritual use these signifiers to think with—as a medium for thinking about (and acting with reference to) ritual purity, freedom, and gnosis.

Though it may seem a trivial observation to scholars of Hindu Tantrism that ritual praxis should involve a calculus of purity and pollution, this is unfortunately not the case with much scholarship on Buddhist Tantrism. Much of this scholarship has been unfortunately limited to the corpus of Mahāyoga and Yoginī Tantras taken in isolation from their earlier esoteric forebears, and, among these, have focused almost exclusively on the soteriological, rather than ritual, aspects. Accordingly, they have not been attentive to the extent to which these traditions situate themselves against the purity concerns of the dualistic Buddhist Tantras and of broader currents in Indian society—an aspect of these traditions that is counterintuitive to those who approach them as "Buddhist." One is sometimes confronted, for instance, by stark claims such as "in the Buddhist Tantra of these periods [ca. A.D. 750–1200], caste purity and pollution are not fundamental issues, in contrast to Hindu Tantra."[79] One wonders how one could come anywhere close to such a view, having read even a handful of Buddhist Tantras. Although we have heretofore restricted our analysis to examples of meats and ambrosias, in chapter 5 we will see that caste discourses figure very prominently in antinomian Buddhist Tantras as well.

It is by grasping the essential semiological connection of the antinomian discourses to the broader discursive context of Indian and Buddhist concepts of purity and pollution—Bourdieu's "complete system of signifiers"—that one can avoid another misleading notion—that Tantric antinomianism is concerned with "transgression *as such*." As I think should be clear, the simple notion of a "transgressive sacrality"—"the ritual inversion of social taboos, as a way of laying claim to psychological and physical powers repressed by social convention"[80]—is inadequate to interpret the materials analyzed here. One does not see in these antinomian traditions a method to "overcome the fears that kept uncharted parts of the psyche repressed, with the aim of releasing those repressed forces and harnessing them for power and knowledge to be used in accomplishing specific ends."[81] This is merely to read the semiology of contemporary "spirituality" into late-first-millennium Indian religion, making sense of it through psychologization. The transgressions of this tradition are pointed and specific: They take their meanings from the cultural context within which they were deployed and are manifestly aimed at occasioning an experience (even if contrived) of nondual gnosis.

Lest my meaning and my opposition to literalism be misconstrued, however, it is important to note that, in stressing the semiotical nature of the rite of consuming the meats and nectars, I do not necessarily mean that these substances were not actually consumed. In fact, I would argue that—although I suspect that actual consumption was very rare in practice by any but virtuosi[82]—the *possibility* of such consumption must be available (at least as a limit case) for the system of semiosis to function. Although the real world may be irrelevant in many cases of human signification, in general it functions as the necessary horizon of possible experiences and signification. Consuming impure substances ritually would seem to be of this latter kind: The notion that one could (and might) actually do it is important for the full impact of the semiosis of (non-)revulsion to occur.

Consequently, whatever the commentators might say—and this is an area that calls for considerable further research—a strongly figurative reading of these rites is as flawed as a strongly literal approach. These two interpretative camps both fail to grasp the fact that human praxis takes place in a reality that is socially constructed and thus always already imbued with meaning. To put it in Lacanian terms, from the moment a child enters the symbolic order, her actions are inescapably significant; and yet the signification of each person (generated from their personal "imaginary order") is constrained by a concrete context (The Real). If one fails to account for either of these two aspects, one fails to account for a human phenomenon. What connotative semiotics offers is a way out of this dilemma.

To take one final example, consider the traditions concerning the Tantric saint Virūpa, of whom stories are told of his excessive imbibing of alcohol. Taking a literalist tack, Ronald Davidson rejects the "religious" interpretation advanced by the exegete Munidatta—which Davidson considers an example of later domestication for monastic consumption—preferring to construe the song as "a humorous acknowledgement that [Virūpa] preferred to spend time in a bar rather than in religious environments."[83] However, the approaches of Davidson and Munidatta both occlude the most essential aspect of the semiosis. On the one hand, Davidson's strongly literalist reading fails to account for references in the song to "sixty-four jugs," the "tenth door," and other tendentious allusions that belie a semiotical regime alien to ordinary drinking songs. On the other hand, Davidson is exactly correct to note that, in eliding the tippling altogether, Munidatta overshoots the interpretative mark. As he rightly observes "within India in particular, drinking is a low-status form of recreation."[84] In the context of Indian cultural norms, then, the sign of a saint drinking alcohol speaks much the same language of purity and pollution as that of a yogin consuming beef and semen—it signifies a transcendent attainment of nondual gnosis. The drinking is as essential to the semiosis as is the religious interpretation: Were the drinking omitted, nothing would remain but a standard exoteric saint; were there only the drinking, Virūpa would be nothing but a libertine. Different contexts might reveal differences of emphasis, but the integrated sign of a drinking saint is an essential and irreducible part of the discourse.[85]

[5] THE PRACTICE OF INDIAN TANTRIC BUDDHISM

As NOTED in chapter four, although the antinomian practices of the higher Buddhist Tantras feature an axial semiosis essential to their proper understanding,[1] this does not entail that these practices are not in fact to be performed. I suggested that at least the possibility of such performance is essential to the semiosis: If considered just a symbol, the full impact would not be possible and the semiosis of connotation would be reduced to mere flat denotation. In this chapter, we will advance our discussion of the transgressive aspects of the Buddhist Tantras by applying methods of structural discourse analysis to the antinomian (or, nondualist) esoteric scriptures that describe the practices followers of these traditions are to engage in. That is, we will inventory references to "practice" across a large corpus of primary sources. Such analysis will reveal that the transgressive acts advocated in this literature involve much more than mere consumption of revolting, polluting meats and ambrosias, comprehending as well sexuality, intoxication, and a broad range of other behaviors considered immoral. Moreover, it would seem as if the entirety of the prior Buddhist traditions is to be cast aside: These scriptures proscribe basic Buddhist devotional acts, scriptural recitation, ascetic disciplines, and a whole range of nonantinomian esoteric rites, such as fire-offerings, maṇḍala rituals, and mantra recitation.

As we shall soon discover, the interpretative challenges facing scholars of Tantric transgression are by no means limited to those involved in the semiotics of ritual and scripture. There are further issues of interpretative method that are crucial to grasp in order properly to understand the literary evidence available and, on that basis, to come to conclusions about how Tantric practice was envisioned among the communities that produced these fundamental sources. In this chapter, we will explore one such challenge in which once again we are confronted with signification that involves more than mere denotation. Throughout the scriptural corpus of the transgressive Tantras, the interpreter confronts an equally subtle challenge to interpretation—that posed by the pervasive employment of so-called terms of art. A term of art is "a word or phrase having a special meaning in a particular field, different from or more precise than its customary meaning."[2] Although they are similar in some respects, terms of art are to be distinguished from what are called technical terms. These latter bear specialized meanings, but their use is generally restricted to the one field. Terms of art, on the other hand, are often common words in the general vocabulary. For instance, byte is a technical term in computer science referring typically to eight units of digital information. Bit, however, is a term of art, referring to one such unit in the context of computing, yet its primary meaning is more general—simply, a small amount or piece.

In interpreting Tantric Buddhist scriptures, it would seem that several major terms of art have been almost entirely overlooked by modern scholars. This is perhaps understandable, given the polysemic nature of these words. Unlike technical terms such as *koṭava* (the name of a vital air in the subtle body[3]), which are unique to their particular contexts, or the use of code words such as camphor for semen, terms of art can seem like they are being used in their ordinary sense. Recognition of these terms as terms of art is, however, essential, insofar as failure in this regard creates and sustains broad and systemic misinterpretation of Tantric literature and of the traditions that produced (and were, in turn, produced by) these works.[4] One term in particular, of crucial importance to the question of the nature of Tantric practice, is the term practice (*caryā*) itself.

In this chapter, I will argue that modern scholarship has consistently and markedly misconstrued the nature of practice in the antinomian traditions, insofar as references to *caryā* employed as a term of art have been understood instead as referring in the generic to Tantric practice. For instance, the twenty-first chapter of the *Saṃvarodaya Tantra* (the chapter describing practice, or *caryānirdeśapaṭala*) has been described as presenting the religious practices of tantric teachers and their disciples.[5] More recently, the quite specific practice (*caryā*) I shall explain has been represented in quite general terms as "the post-initiatory practice which an initiate of tantric Buddhism is permitted to perform."[6] As will be clear from the evidence analyzed in what follows, the practice referred to in these passages (and many others) is by no means *the* practice of initiated Tantric Buddhists, but merely one, very rarified, practice. That is to say, it is perhaps better construed as a proper noun—not practice, but "The Practice."

This crucial term of art appears across virtually the entire corpus of Buddhist Mahāyoga and Yoginī Tantras (and some śāstras) as well as in a number of Śaiva Tantras. It frequently occurs with the term *vrata* ([religious] observance) in the same contexts. Both terms are, of course, of extremely common usage throughout Indian and Buddhist religious parlance. *Caryā*, for instance, is by far the most common generic term for the spiritual undertakings of buddhas and bodhisattvas. The *Mahāvastu*, for instance, frames its treatment of the career of the Buddha Śākyamuni by referring to four types of bodhisattva practices (*bodhisattvacaryā*) undertaken by the future buddha.[7] The famous work of Śāntideva on engaging in the practices of enlightenment is called the *Bodhicaryāvatāra*, while chapter 16 of his *Śikṣāsamuccaya* (Compendium of Learning) is devoted to the good conduct (*bhadracaryā*) of high resolve, dedication to the welfare of beings, and so on. The culminating chapter of Asaṅga's *Mahāyānasūtrālaṃkāra*, the stability in practice chapter (*caryāpratiṣṭhādhikāra*), treats inter alia of four practices leading to enlightenment: The practice of the [six or ten] transcendent virtues (*pāramitācaryā*), the practice of the [thirty-seven] accessories of enlightenment (*bodhipakṣacaryā*), the practice of the superknowledges (*abhijñācaryā*), and the practice of developing beings (*sattvaparipākacaryā*).[8] These same four practices are treated in the practice chapter (*caryāpaṭala*) of the *Bodhisattvabhūmi*.[9] Similarly, *vrata* appears regularly in Indian Buddhist literature, in even less marked a sense. For instance, in the *Bodhisattvabhūmi*, the renunciant bodhisattva is said to be superior to the householder bodhisattva on account of his maintenance of *vrata-niyama* (i.e., celibacy and restraint).[10]

Thus, encountering the term *caryā* in Tantric literature, certainly the most obvious and natural understanding would be that this term and related passages describe Tantric practice per se or in general, just as one would interpret the same word in works of exoteric Mahāyāna literature. Attentive reading employing structural analysis, however, reveals quite clearly that this term of art recurs throughout antinomian Tantric literature with a referent that is quite specific and markedly consistent across a variety of sources, Buddhist and non-Buddhist.[11]

In this usage, *caryā* and *vrata* appear to be largely synonymous and often occur in compound one with the other, with either of the two taking the dominant syntactical position. That is, one sees the terms *caryāvrata* and *vratacaryā*, with identical meanings.[12] In addition to these forms (which are the most common), the two also frequently occur in compound with qualifiers related to ideas of secrecy or madness, for example, *guhyavrata* (esoteric observance), *guhyacaryā* (esoteric practice), *prachannavrata* (concealed observance), *unmattavrata* (mad/insane observance), and so on. There also exists a cluster of interrelated terms that appear in the same contexts, and which seem to be largely synonymous, that appear to be variant species of the same genus. These may be seen in table 5.1, together with the works wherein they occur.[13] Of these, one in particular, *vidyāvrata* (knowledge observance, spell observance, and/or consort observance)—which is treated as essentially equivalent to *caryāvrata/vratacaryā* in Buddhist and Śaiva sources—is worth noting at this point as its signal significance will become more evident as our analysis proceeds. All of these expressions refer to the same class of ritual behaviors. This usage is consistent across a wide spectrum of texts, from which I conclude that this term of art is central to the ideology of the nondualist Tantras wherein they occur.

The injunctions of the rite include certain very specific things that are proscribed, things prescribed, sites wherein they are to be performed, specifications for the optimal time and duration of their performance, and specific accoutrements that are needed for or beneficial to the ritual acts. In what follows, we will examine each of these aspects of the *caryāvrata* so as to discern the essential parameters of the concept in the Tantric traditions. I will demonstrate that *caryāvrata/vratacaryā* is (1) a highly specific term of art in the literature of the Buddhist Mahāyoga and Yoginī Tantras, signifying a very precise undertaking, (2) that close attention to the semiology of the rite reveals a very clear ritual intent that is evident throughout the Buddhist literature, and (3) that the sources explicitly (if at times somewhat obliquely) stress that this rite is appropriate only in quite specific and elite ritual contexts with very specific prerequisites. I will also show (4) that this term of art is also common to the contemporaneous nondual Śaiva Tantras of the Vidyāpīṭha, and that the patterns of usage across the two traditions suggest an alternative way of understanding the interaction of these communities. Specifically, I argue that close attention to the available literature suggests that the semiology of the early Śaiva observance differs significantly from that of the early Buddhists as outlined in (2), and that the nature of the Buddhist and Śaiva variants further suggests that (5) this distinctively Buddhist semiology

TABLE 5.1 Central and related terms

CENTRAL TERMS AND SCRIPTURES WHEREIN ATTESTED
caryā ("practice"): GST, CPAMA, BK, ST, HT, SU, YS, CMT, VĀ, GS, CMP, YRM, KMT
vrata ("[ascetical] observance"): AVP40, (MVT), CPAMA, BK, KMT
caryā-vrata ("practice observance"): ST, LS/HA, CMP
vrata-caryā ("observance practice"): CPAMA, ST, HT, YS, YRM, KMT
guhya-vrata ("esoteric observance"): ST, GS
guhya-caryā ("esoteric practice"): GS
tattva-caryā ("reality practice"): ST
vīra-caryāvrata ("heroic practice observance"): LS/HA
trividhā caryā ("three-fold practice"): CMP, YRM
prachanna-vrata ("concealed observance"): GS
RELATED TERMS (PROBABLY SYNONYMOUS, OR CLOSELY SO)
vidyā-vrata ("consort observance"): (MVT), GST, KMT
unmatta-vrata ("mad/intoxicated observance"): ST, SU, GS, TD
bhusuku-vrata ("observance of eating, sleeping, and defecating"): CMP
yoga-caryā ("yoga practice"): ST, SU
samantabhadra-caryā ("universally good practice"): SU
*avadhūti-caryā (kun 'dar gyi spyod pa) ("central channel practice"): ST
*dig-vijaya-caryā (phyogs las rgyal ba'i spyod pa) ("practice victorious in all directions"): ST
*āliṅgana-caryā ('khyud pa'i spyod pa) ("embracing practice"): ST
paricaryā ("entertainment"?): MK

came ultimately to exert a profound influence on the later Śaiva understanding of the rite (and, indeed, their understanding of Tantric practice in general) after the ninth century. This conclusion further suggests that, contra the theories of a "substratum" or a total Buddhist dependence on Śaivism, (6) the features of religious observance (*vrata*) shared by these two groups are the product of a zeitgeist of antinomian practice wherein (as is in evidence throughout Indian religious history), groups utilized a common vocabulary of terms and rites to which they gave their own distinctive inflections, and in which the borrowing was mutual.

What, then, is the *caryāvrata*? In short, in the nondualist Tantric literature of the Buddhist Mahāyoga and Yoginī Tantras, this term and its equivalents come to encapsulate virtually all those features that have come most strongly to be associated with Tantrism (or so-called "Siddha Tantrism") in the modern mind: Sex, to be sure, but also eerie places (cemeteries, lonely fearsome forests, etc.), eccentric dress, and ecstatic behavior, including the wholesale rejection of the mainstream practices of exoteric Indian religion. This term is very prominent in the later Tantric literature—so much so that frequently an entire chapter is seen to be dedicated to this observance. This is the case for the *Guhyasamāja Tantra*, as well as the *Mahākāla*, *Buddhakapāla*, *Saṃpuṭodbhava*, *Hevajra*, *Caṇḍamahāroṣaṇa*, *Laghusaṃvara/Herukābhidhāna*, *Saṃvarodaya*, *Yoginīsaṃcāra*, and *Vajrāralli Tantras*. The ninth chapter of the *Buddhakapāla Yoginī Tantra*, for example, is devoted to the topic of *caryā*. It describes a rite that a yogin undertakes with an "absolutely excellent woman" (*atyantavarāṅganā*) presumably for the purpose of engaging in sexual yogas. Taking a skull bowl (*kapāla*) in hand, the yogin wanders naked, with hair unbound, begging from house to house and eating whatever is put in the bowl, regarding all things with equanimous delight. The yogin is here called, as elsewhere, a *vratin*—a practitioner who has taken on a specific religious observance (*vrata*).[14]

Considering the data set in aggregate (especially tables 5.2 to 5.6), it can easily be seen that the treatments as a whole in these Tantras foreground: (a) liminal, isolated spaces, and (b) funereal and horrific items of dress. They further consistently (c) advocate certain behaviors (sex, wandering, commensality, song and dance, and consumption of meats, alcohols, and bodily fluids) and (d) proscribe others (recitation, meditation, worship, burnt offerings, textuality, image devotion, and attention to astrological auspiciousness). A structural analysis of the range of these sites, accoutrements, prescriptions, and proscriptions is revealing.

Consulting the chart on sites (table 5.2), one can see that the most common are the mountain top, charnel ground, and either a generic uninhabited space (*vijana*) or varieties of liminal zones (the "suburban" *prānta*, crossroads, confluences of rivers, beaches, etc.). The *Saṃvarodaya Tantra* has quite an extensive list: charnel ground, a place with a lone liṅga or tree (*ekaliṅga*, *ekavṛkṣa*), forest, mountaintop, riverbank, ocean shore, garden, broken well, empty house, crossroads, city gate, palace gate, house of

TABLE 5.2 Sites of practice

	CROSS-ROAD	MOUNTAIN OR MOUN-TAIN PEAK	CHARNEL GROUND (ŚMAŚĀNA)	PLACE WITH ONE TREE (EKAVṚKṢA)	ONE LIṄGAM (EKALIṄGA)	ISOLATED PLACE (VIJANA)	LIMINAL ZONE / SUBURB (PRĀNTA)	WANDERING / HOMELESS	CONFLUENCE OF RIVERS	CAVE	VILLAGE/ TOWN (EMPTY?)	FOREST OR GARDEN	OCEAN BEACH	HOUSE (OF LOW-CASTE, EMPTY)
AVP40		X							X	X			Near water	
GST		X		X	X	X			X					
CPAMA			X			X	X	X						
MK							X				X	X		
ST	X	X	X	X		X	X		X	X		X	X	
HT		X	X			X	X			X	X			
LS/HA								X						
SU		X	X	X	X	X					X		X	X
GS		X	X			X		X			X	jīrṇodyāna		X
CMP		X				X			X			X		X
KMT	X	X	X	X	X			X	X		X	X	X	X
Total	2	7 or 8	6	4	3	7	4	4	4 or 5	3	5	4 or 5	3 or 4	4

mātaṅgī or cowherd's wife, house of female artisan, or concealed places (*gopita*).[15] Looked at systematically, this represents a list of isolated sites (mountaintop, empty house, concealed place), ritually-polluting places (houses of female artisans, cowherds, and outcaste mātaṅgī-s), and liminal spaces (crossroads, city gate, palace gate, etc.).

Similarly, the dress prescribed for the practice observance demonstrates markedly regular features across the literature (table 5.3). Occurring most commonly are a set of bone ornaments, funereal shrouds or other funereal items, skulls (*kapāla*, especially as begging bowls) and skull staves (*khaṭvāṅga*), animal skins (most commonly the tiger), drums, and the like. The *Hevajra Tantra*, for instance, specifies the following accoutrements for the practitioner of the practices (*caryā*), here also called the adamantine skull practice (*vajrakapālacaryā*): tiger skin (*vyāghracarma*), circlet (*cakrī*), earrings (*kuṇḍala*), necklace (*kaṇṭhamālā*), bracelets (*rucaka*), hip-belt (*mekhalā*),[16] garland of bones (*asthimālikā*), a headdress with the skulls of the Five Buddhas (*pañcabuddhakapālāni*), ashes (*bhasma*), a sacred thread of hair (*keśapavitra*), hand drum (*ḍamaru*), and skull staff (*khaṭvāṅga*).[17] Other sources suggest that the practitioner be naked (BT and LS/HA), have bound-up (or, alternatively, loose) hair (HT, BK), and/or bear shrouds or other funeral items (ST, SU, GS).

Among prescribed behaviors (see table 5.4), sex is the one most commonly advocated, followed closely by wandering. We have seen that the *Buddhakapāla Tantra* foregrounds practice with a female consort as characteristic of the *caryā*. One reads further in the *caryāvrata* chapter of the *Herukābhidhāna/Laghusaṃvara*: "The practitioner will obtain *siddhi* from [sexual] intercourse."[18] The *Hevajra* is also quite clear: "Taking a girl of the vajra [clan]—with a pretty face, wide eyes, with the glow of youth, with a body dark like a blue lotus, self-initiated, and compassionate—employ her in the performance of the practices (*caryā*)."[19] Also high on the list are commensality (i.e., eating with those of other, lower-status social groups), eating indiscriminately, or eating things our discrimination would typically cause us to avoid (sometimes strenuously), and (also quite prominently) singing and dancing.

In addition to those prescribed in the literature, there are also a variety of specifically *pro*scribed behaviors (table 5.5). Most prominent of these is—in line with the corresponding prescriptions—discriminating with regard to edible/inedible or potable/impotable, and value judgments in general, as well as recitation (*japa*), meditation, fire rituals (*homa*), and so on. As the *Hevajra Tantra* counsels the *vratin*, "Don't conceive of desirable

TABLE 5.3 Dress/accoutrements for practice

	RAGGED MONKS' ROBES (3)	NAKED	LOOSE HAIR	HIDE/ SKIN (TIGER)	FIVE ORNAMENTS/ BONE ORNAMENTS	SHROUD OR FUNEREAL ITEMS	HAIR-THREAD/ SACRED THREAD	ASHES	CREMATION ASHES	KHATVAṄGA	ḌAMARU	SKULLS	FIVE-INCH SKULL PIECES IN COIF
AVP40										X or staff			
CPAMA	X				X	X				staff			
MK					X						X		
BK		X	X									X	
ST				X	X	X	X	X	X	X	X	X	X
HT				X	X	X	X		X		X		X
CMT					X								
LS/HA		X		X			X			X	X	X	
SU				X	X	X	X						
YS				X	X		X			X	X	X	
VĀ					X								
GS					X	X							
CMP													
KMT					X					X	X		
Total	1	2	1	5	10	5	5	1	2	5 or 6	6	4	2

TABLE 5.4 Behaviors prescribed in practice

	WANDERING	SEX/ PLEASURE	EAT CARU OR PAÑCĀMṚTA	EAT WHATEVER	BEGGING	COMMENSALITY	EAT FROM SKULL	SONGS/ MUSIC	DANCE	PLAY OR LIKE A CHILD	LION-LIKE	DRINK ALCOHOL	EAT MEAT, DRINK BLOOD	BREAK FIVE VOWS
MVT				X										
GST	X	X	X	X	X	X						X	semen	X
CPAMA	X	X		X	X	X		X						
MK		X						X	X			X	X	
BK	X	X		X	X		X							
ST				X				X	X	X	X		X	X
HT		X	X	X		X	X	X	X		X	X	X	
CMT		X												
LS/HA	X	X	X			X				X		X		X
SU	X			X	X						X			
YS	X	X				X					X			
VĀ		X						X	X					
GS	X	X	X			X		X	X		X		X	X
CMP	X	X	X	X	X	X		X	X		X			
TD	X										X			
KMT	X	X				X								
Total	10	12	5	8	5	8	2	7	6	2	7	4	4–5	4

TABLE 5.5 Behaviors proscribed in practice

	RECITATION (JAPA)	MĀLĀ/ AKṢAMĀLĀ	MEDITATION (DHYĀNA)	WORSHIP (PŪJĀ)	FIRE-OFFERING (HOMA)	ASTROLOGY	PENANCE/ AUSTERITY (DUṢKARA)	DISCRIMINATING W/ REGARD TO IN/EDIBLE	VALUE JUDGMENTS/ CONCEPTUALITY	MAṆḌALA RITES	MUDRĀ	TEXTS	BATHING	HOMAGE TO DEITIES OR STŪPAS
MVT									X					
GST	X						X		X					
CPAMA								X				X		
BK									X					
ST	X		X	X	X		X	X	X	X	X	X		X
HT	X		X		X			X	X				X	X
CMT									X					
LS/HA	X		X	X				X	X					
SU	X	X		X	X	X		X	X					
YS	X							X	X		X			
GS						X			X	X	X	X		X
CMP	X		X		X	X				X		X		X
Total	7	1	4	3	4	3	2	6	10	3	3	4	1	4

and undesirable, or edible/inedible, potable/impotable, appropriate or inappropriate."[20]

INTERPRETING THE PRACTICE OBSERVANCE I: IRONY AND INVERSION

Of course, the specification of these types of sites, accoutrements, and behaviors will not likely surprise anyone considering what we have come to believe we know of the Tantric traditions. What is most notable here is the use of the terms *caryā* and *vrata* to describe them. Such a usage, it seems quite plain, is provocative—presumably, intentionally so. As we have seen earlier, in Buddhist religious contexts *caryā* typically refers to practices such as the six perfections and other conventional, beneficent practices of bodhisattvas. In non-Buddhist contexts as well it signifies similarly mainstream practices of restraint, generosity/offering, and so on. *Vrata*, too—a commonplace in Indic religions—involves conventional disciplinary restraint:[21] Giving up some thing or things, usually for a delimited time period, and typically with the intent of acquiring something else (sons, rain, etc.).[22] The terms that consistently arise in the context of *vrata* are those of renunciation—derivations of the root √*tyaj*, and so forth. It should be noted that, in general, this is true of the usage of the term in esoteric, as well as exoteric literatures. Thus, for instance, the great commentary on the *Kālacakra Tantra*, the *Vimalaprabhā* describes a five-fold *vrata* of renouncing violence, untruth, adultery, wealth, and intoxicants.[23] This is tantamount, of course, to the five-vow *pañcaśīla* of mainstream Buddhism, wherein similar sets of vows (frequently involving chastity, such as the eight fasting day vows or *poṣadha*) are similarly described as *vrata*.[24] In another esoteric context, Ratnākaraśānti, in his *Guṇāvatī Commentary* on the *Mahāmāyā Tantra* defines *vrata* quite straightforwardly as "rules of restraint (*niyama*) such as [keeping] silence, bathing, [and regulation of] foods."[25] However, several scriptures (GST, ST, HA/LS, and GS) specify precisely the violation of the five central Buddhist precepts as an element of the practice of the *caryāvrata*. Elsewhere as well, conduct such as purificatory ritual bathing is prohibited to the practitioner of the *caryāvrata*.[26]

The usage we are considering here, then, is clearly and markedly ironic: What we see in the Tantric *caryāvrata* is in essence an anti-*vrata*. What, then, may be said about its proper interpretation? What could have driven the nondual esoteric Buddhist schools to advocate such a seemingly precise inversion of mainstream practice (both exoteric and esoteric)—much or most of whose fundamental ritual and ethical framework remains intact in the later nondualist traditions?[27] What is at stake in the prescriptions of a *caryāvrata* that takes the form of such an anti-*vrata*?

All the major features of *caryā*, I would argue, reflect the overarching semiosis of Mahāyoga and Yoginī Tantra ritual that I essayed to describe in chapter 4. That is, just as (and, in fact, including) the deliberate engagement with the disgusting (*jugupsa*) discussed previously, the *caryāvrata* signifies through instantiation the attainment of nondual gnosis (*advaya-jñāna*) by the Tantric practitioner. As in the case of the ritual consumption of the polluting and repulsive five meats and five ambrosias (*pañcamāṃsa*, *pañcāmṛta*), the locations, dress, and behaviors of the *caryāvrata* so deliberately invert the purity strictures of orthodox society (including those accepted within the contexts of the dualistic Tantras), and are so consistent in their discursive articulation, that they manifestly constitute a deliberate semiosis. Much as we have seen concerning the ritual consumption of those sacramental pledges (and, in fact, the practices are related), the undertaking of the *caryāvrata* is a way of viscerally instantiating and ritually attesting to the attainment of the aim of Buddhist Tantric yogins: a nondual gnosis that sees through (and acts without regard for) the delusive sense that the constructed categories of conceptual thought are real and objective.

This much is clear throughout the literature, which consistently hammers home the theme of nonduality and nonconceptuality. The *Guhyasamāja Tantra* (GST) appears to be one of the earliest Buddhist Tantras to advocate the Practice in a developed form. It does so in chapters 5 and 7, each of which features this term in its title (the *Samantacaryāgrapaṭala* and the *Mantracaryāpaṭala*). Significantly, in the first passage on the *caryā* in GST V.1—whose central narrative we unpacked in chapter 4—the very first descriptive word is *nirvikalpārtha-sambhūtam*: "born with the aim of non-conceptuality." The same passage ends as well on the same note, in perfect essay form: "That one of the non-conceptual mind accomplishes buddhahood."[28]

The *Saṃpuṭodbhava Tantra*, too, explicitly indicates that this rite (which it also calls the reality-practice, or *tattva-caryā*—indicating its epistemic/gnostic intent[29]) is intended to cultivate a nondual perception with regard to purity and pollution, and similar conceptual dualities.[30] It lays great stress repeatedly on nonconceptuality: concepts lead to hell, nonconceptuality leads to liberation. Indeed, a quick look at the charts of prescribed and proscribed behaviors in the *caryāvrata* (tables 5.4 and 5.5) reveals beyond any doubt that the operative concern across the literature is the judging, valuing conceptuality that diverges from the nondual, enlightened gnosis that perceives all things as pure (*śuddha*), as divine by nature or *buddhamaya*, made of buddhas.

The inversive nature of this rite—wherein the practitioner signifies their attainment of nondual gnosis by cultivated contact with the conventionally defiling—is entire. Consider the *Saṃpuṭodbhava Tantra*: "Whatever things are not eaten in the world, those are to be eaten by the best of Reality-Practitioners. Whatever is unsuitable is suitable; that not to be done is to be done by him—the mantrin should not conceive of suitable/unsuitable, edible/inedible, desirable/undesirable, [or] potable/impotable."[31] We have already encountered at the beginning of this volume this scripture's notable and quite hyperbolic reflections on the yogin's food:

> Indeed, all is to be regarded with the yoga [of recognizing] appearances [as] unoriginated: having drunk dog, donkey, camel, and elephant[32] blood, [one should] always[33] feed on [their] flesh. Human flesh smeared with the blood of all species [of animals] is beloved. Entirely vile meat full of millions of worms [is] divine. Meat [rendered] putrid by shit, seething with hundreds of maggots, mixed with dog and human vomit, with a coating of piss[34]—mixed with shit [it] should be eaten by the yogin with gusto.[35]

The interpretative key here is found in the framing clause that references the "yoga [of recognizing] appearances [as] unoriginated" (*anutpādākārayoga*) that the entire rite is predicated upon. This is Buddhist jargon for the view of voidness (*śūnyatā*)—the void reality of all things is frequently indicated by their nonarising or noncreation.[36]

Furthermore, just as we observed in chapter 4 regarding the meats and ambrosias, the prescriptions for the *caryāvrata* are not only aggressively and thoroughly, but precisely inversive. In particular, they can be seen to correspond quite closely to some of the circumstances in Smārta orthodoxy that lead to a state of *anadhyāya*—a condition wherein one may not recite the Vedas. The rules concerning the circumstances during which one may or may not recite those most sacred Brahmanical scriptures encode a number of central Hindu (or, perhaps, Indian) purity strictures.[37]

Thus, with regard to the places whose polluting nature makes Vedic recitation prohibited, we find the following that correspond to recommended places for the practice of the *caryāvrata*: charnel grounds, barren land, roads, crossroads, liminal spaces (i.e., *prānta*), cities, and villages. It would seem that the very sites in which the *caryāvrata* is to be practiced were chosen due to their association with ritual pollution. However, an attentive reader will note that these sites do not exhaust the list of the principal places for the rite. What is one to make of these others: forests, empty houses, lonely places, and so forth? The rationale behind the presence of these becomes clear when compared to lists of generic yogic sites found in mainstream Buddhist and Śaiva literature. For instance, the *Mahāsatipaṭṭhāna Sutta* specifies its practices should be conducted in a forest (*arañña*), the foot of a tree (*rukkhamūla*), or an empty house (*suññāgāra*).[38] A transitional list, from an early dualist Śaiva source, specifies the following sites: "A lonely place, or a grove, or in an agreeable mountain cave, or in an earthen hut that is thoroughly secluded, free of insects, draught and damp."[39] Once one excepts these generic yogic sites, the remaining places correspond much more closely with the *anadhyāya* list.[40]

Regarding the behaviors enacted in the *caryāvrata*, these too correspond with situations in which one is prohibited from Vedic recitation, due to the impurity involved. Here, the correspondence is practically entire. The following circumstances create a situation of *anadhyāya*: contact with vomit, meat, blood, sex, funerary contexts and materials, urine and feces (even, it might be noted, having the mere urge to pass them), fear, dogs, donkeys, camels, music, drums, singing and dancing, and contact or commensality with low-caste persons. A quick consultation of tables 5.2 to 5.5 will confirm that these are precisely the situations to be courted by the practitioner of the *caryāvrata*.

It is also worth noting that this observance overturns the standard virtues elevated in exoteric Buddhism and Śaivism. Violation of the five basic Buddhist vows is frequently associated with the practice observance (as in GST chs. V and IX), as is the violation of the purity strictures of the dualistic Buddhist Tantras (e.g., *Mañjuśrīmūlakalpa*). Similarly, the characteristics of the dualistic Śaivasiddhāntin *vrata* are challenged by this rite. Our rite can again be seen to be an anti-*vrata*, insofar as the *vrata* of mainstream esoteric Śaivas is quite conventional in its asceticism, proscribing women, meat, alcohol, singing, dancing, conversation, playing, flowers, commensality with despised castes, and so[41]—all behaviors associated with the nondualistic *caryāvrata* of the nondualist Buddhist and (some) Śaiva Tantric traditions. The inversion is entire and precise.

In fact, our independent analysis of the literature is confirmed by the views articulated by indigenous intellectuals. The short treatise "Dispelling the Two Extreme [Views] with Regard to the Adamantine Way" attributed in the Tibetan canonical collections to Jñānaśrī[42] discusses inter alia the practices (*caryā*). In this context, the author mentions the practice of consuming the meats and ambrosias which is a commonly prescribed element of the practice observance.

> The practice of taking [impure] substances is articulated thus:
> The five meats and the five ambrosias
> Rely on these as appropriate, in order to dispel conceptuality.
>
> Because concepts such as "this is pure, this is impure" are fetters, if one methodically consumes sin-free meat[43] of extremely base sorts such as human, horse, cow, dog, and elephant, and the death-cheating ambrosias such as semen, blood, feces, urine, and human flesh, considering them void [of intrinsic reality] by the appropriate method and repeatedly considering those very things as if they were divine ambrosia, if one enjoys them without passion, gradually concepts such as pure and impure will not arise. Then will arise the certain knowledge that different concepts that arise with regard to all things are false; and certain non-human beings will on that account be delighted with that [person] and will protect [him/her] in accordance with the Dharma and receive religious instruction from him/her.[44]
>
> Meat and ambrosia are only examples: whichever objects are considered impure [like] meat and so on, those should be consumed without passion. When one sees [with] equanimous perception, one no longer needs to consume those for his/her own sake.[45]

Clearly, this author concurs with my own assessment of the role of the meats and ambrosias in these rituals, adding the interesting observation that the tradition believed that a side effect of the attainment of nonconceptual thought was charismatic power over (invisible) spirits. Although the passage here is brief, this is likely a kind of familiar (albeit presumably not animal) that would serve the needs of this type of advanced practitioner.[46] Although it may seem at present to be an extraneous element, this point is worth bearing in mind, as it will prove significant when we engage the question of the genealogy of this rite.

INTERPRETING THE PRACTICE OBSERVANCE II: PREREQUISITES AND TEMPORAL FRAME

Having considered the nature, interpretation, and purpose of the rite, let us turn now, for a moment, to the consideration of its intended practitioner, its context(s), and its duration. That the practitioner is necessarily an advanced one is also made clear throughout this literature. It would appear that in Indian Tantric Buddhism this rite was intended for (if not restricted to) virtuosi. On this point, the Indian and the Tibetan presentations of the *caryā* diverge. That is, contra the more liberal interpretation found in many Tibetan sources that allows (even prescribes) the practices in the context of the (Tantrically) propaedeutic creation stage (*utpatti-krama*), the authors of their Indian proof texts ([deutero-] Āryadeva and Candrakīrti) on the contrary restrict the practices to the most advanced practitioners of the perfection stage (*niṣpanna-krama*).[47] Careful reading of the Indian literature reveals clearly that these authors consider the practices to be appropriate only for those who have attained the third of the five stages of the Noble Tradition perfection stage sequence, the self-consecration (*svādhiṣṭhāna*), which corresponds to the attainment of the eighth bodhisattva stage—rather a rarified sort of person.[48]

The predecessor of Āryadeva and Candrakīrti, Padmavajra, held the same view. The first chapter of his masterwork on the Guhyasamāja, the *Esoteric Accomplishment* (*Guhyasiddhi*) is most explicit on this score. In making this point, he employs yet another term of art: One must, he says, first create the superficial (*saṃvṛtim utpādya*)—that is, generate the mind-made body (*manomayadeha*) of the self-consecration stage (*svādhiṣṭhānakrama*)—*then* one should undertake the Practice (*paścāt caryāṃ prakurvīta*). Immediately thereafter, Padmavajra asserts, the *vrata* is to be done with a consort (*vidyā*).[49] Likewise, in *Esoteric Accomplishment* III, he writes "having obtained a stage like this, the supreme deity yoga, then one should perform the *caryā* in order to accomplish the state of buddhahood."[50] The prior context makes clear that "a stage like this" means having obtained a rainbow-like deity body (*indrāyudhanibhaṃ kāyaṃ*)—precisely the distinctive characteristic of the self-consecration stage.

Although this specific qualification is characteristic only of the traditions of the Guhyasamāja, throughout the corpus of Mahāyoga and Yoginī Tantras, such a concern for prior qualifications (*adhikāra-bheda*) is pervasive. The literature surveyed here consistently stresses a variety of qualifications or prerequisites necessary for the practice of the *caryāvrata*. Most common of these (as can be seen in table 5.6) are the attainment of heat (*ūṣman*) or power (*sāmārthya*), or some attainment of meditative absorption (*samāpatti*). *Ūṣman* is a Buddhist term of art for an advanced meditative experience of voidness (*śūnyatā*) that came to be associated with the first stage of the second of the five paths of the Mahāyāna, the path of application (*prayoga-mārga*). In describing the realization of this *ūṣman* in his *Abhidharmasamuccaya*, Asaṅga says that it is "a samādhi that has obtained illumination (*āloka*) with regard to the Truth[s of the Nobles] internally, conjoined with critical wisdom."[51] Vasubandhu's *Abhidharmakośabhāṣya* also specifies that the heat arises when the practitioner, having focused on the mindfulness of things, sees them as impermanent, suffering, void, and nonself; it is described as a root of virtue (*kuśala-mūla*) and an element of the certain penetration of the path of the nobles (*nirvedhabhāgīya*). It is produced by [meditative] cultivation (*bhāvanā*), not learning or reflection (*śruti-cintā*); and is so-called on account of its being an intimation of the imminent attainment of the fire of the path of the nobles that burns the fuel of the defilements.[52] Thus, in a Buddhist context, to specify that a rite is for those with *ūṣman*, is manifestly to restrict it to a meditative elite, who are on the verge of attaining the path of the nobles (*āryamārga*), which is the path of seeing (*darśanamārga*). This latter, significantly, is said to be *anāsrava*—a key Buddhist term that refers to the purity of enlightenment and is often used to describe buddhas and arhats.[53]

This type of specification of prerequisites occurs in almost all of the works in our corpus. Thus, the *Buddhakapāla Tantra* stresses that the practitioner already have attained all eight worldly powers (*siddhi*); the *Saṃpuṭa* and *Hevajra* that one have meditative heat and ability to sacrifice one's own body; the *Catuṣpīṭhākhyāta-mantrāṃśa*[54] stresses meditative absorption and freedom from passion; and so on. *Saṃvarodaya*, interestingly, is most stringent, requiring not only yogic heat, and ability to sacrifice one's own body, but great learning (*bahuśruta*) and abandonment of wealth, life, and wife. For its part, the *Caṇḍamahāroṣana* emphasizes that the *vrata* is to be undertaken after significant prior practice (and—further confirming our semiological analysis—refers to the rite as constitutively inversive): "Having exhausted all sin, one will [then] succeed by means of inversion (*viparīta*)."[55] Presumably aware of the Indian scriptural sources bearing on this rite, an influential early Tibetan narrative of the life of the Tantric yogin Kṛṣṇācārya revolves precisely around his quest for the power (*nus pa*, **sāmārthya*) prerequisite to his undertaking the practice observance.[56]

TABLE 5.6 Qualifications/prerequisites for practice

	A LITTLE HEAT (ŪṢMA) OR POWER (SĀMARTHYA)	AFTER GIVING BODY	SELF-CONSECRATION	(TANTRIC) LEARNING (BAHUŚRUTA)	ABANDON WEALTH, LIFE, WIFE	ENDOWED WITH THE EIGHT (WORLDLY) SIDDHIS	AFTER SIN HAS BEEN CONQUERED	PASSIONLESS BODY	MEDITATIVE ABSORPTION/ REALIZATION
CPAMA								X	X
BK						X			
ST	X	X							
HT	X	X							
CMT							X		
SU	X	X		X	X				
YS	X								X
VĀ									X
GS			X						X
CMP			X						
TD			X						

On this basis, I would suggest that—somewhat like the cultivation of the realization of the so-called emptiness of emptiness in the exoteric context, which is used to refine an advanced understanding and prevent reification of the ultimate void—the inverted cultivation of a *vrata* of impurity is unambiguously characterized in the Buddhist Mahāyoga and Yoginī Tantras as an advanced, post-purification refinement of what we must consider an ongoing baseline esoteric Buddhist fastidiousness-in-quest-of-power such as is evidenced in the earlier, dualistic Buddhist Tantras, and which constitutes the common denominator of Tantric practice as a whole.[57] It was meant for elite practitioners alone and was not (as nearly all have taken it to be) the post-initiatory practice of the Buddhist Tantric communities *tout court*.[58]

Of further note is the fact that nowhere is the *caryāvrata* characterized as daily (*nitya*) or quotidian Tantric practice. Rather, it is consistently represented as a time-delimited, segregated practice generally performed in seclusion or in the virtual seclusion of a wandering lifestyle.[59] That is, the *vrata* is set apart in time as well as in space. As can be seen in table 5.7, there is less stress laid in these works on the duration of this ritual in the Tantric Buddhist contexts than on other aspects of the rite, but those that do weigh in on this point are quite clear about the occasional and time-delimited nature of this observance. Most (e.g., *Mahāvairocana*, *Guhyasamāja*, *Caryāmelāpakapradīpa*, etc.) specify six months as the proper (or maximum) duration of the rite. This point would not have required much stress, given the fact that all Indic *vrata*-s are considered to be time-delimited and supererogatory effectively by definition.[60] I do not think it is too great a leap to assume that by calling this conduct (*caryā*) a *vrata*, the authors of these traditions were indicating by implication that it was to be a temporary undertaking, restricted to a definite length (typically, six months). In fact, from the earliest appearances of this rite in Buddhist literature (whether one takes that to be the *Guhyasamāja* or the *Mahāvairocana Tantra*), the question of duration was prominent.[61]

INTERPRETING THE PRACTICE OBSERVANCE III: ŚAIVA PARALLELS

In the foregoing, we have observed that a cluster of related terms, centered on *caryāvrata*, functions as an important term of art in nondualist Buddhist Tantric traditions. We have noted its chief characteristics and its intended practitioners, including their qualifications, and the duration of

TABLE 5.7 Duration of practice

	1 MONTH	2 MONTHS	3 MONTHS	4 MONTHS	5 MONTHS	6 MONTHS	1 YEAR	12 YEARS	LIFETIME
AVP40	X	X	X	X	X		X	X	X
MVT						X			
GST						X			
CPAMA						X			
CMP	X (or fortnight)					X (max)			
KMT	X or (12 days/ fortnight)					X	X (1–12 years)		

its undertaking. Now, let us turn to what we can trace of the history and development of this observance, particularly with reference to the manner in which its appearance in Buddhist sources tracks closely its usage in Śaiva and Śākta Tantric contexts. A look at the semiology of this rite in the two contexts over time reveals interesting aspects of its development and its role in various esoteric systems in the two confessions. The perspective granted by this approach will clarify the earlier history of the rite in Buddhism and Śaivism and suggest a model for understanding their interrelationship, which is at variance from that which has been popularized in recent years.

In his important work on the Kāpālika and Kālāmukha sects of Śaivism, David N. Lorenzen notes that there were significant correspondences among several of the antinomian rites of the Buddhists and the Śaivas. He restricts himself, however, to the claim that, "the Buddhist parallels [to Śaiva Kāpālika practices] indicate that they must have also had some connection with Buddhist Tantrism, but, in absence of additional evidence, it is useless to speculate about what this might have been."[62] More recently, among authors working on the Hindu Tantras in particular, there has been a marked tendency to return to the early Orientalist view that the Buddhist Tantras are merely Śaiva Tantrism in "Buddhist garb"[63]—that is to say, that practically every element of Buddhist Tantrism may be accounted for as having been borrowed from the Śaiva traditions with merely a slight overcoding of Buddhist thought. Until quite recently, this view seems to have been based on the mere overgeneralization of a specific argument made by Alexis Sanderson about a degree of intertextuality that he maintains demonstrates that one influential Buddhist Yoginī Tantra incorporated textual material from a Śaiva source.[64] Nonspecialists, ignorant of the fact that Sanderson was analyzing a rather late and distinctive stratum of esoteric Buddhist literature (exemplified by the Yoginī Tantra, the *Laghusaṃvara*), took this to mean that all Buddhist Tantrism was derived from Śaivism. More recently, however, Sanderson himself has published an extensive piece in which he extends this argument to make much the same expansive claim himself.[65]

Most relevant to our own concern here, Ryugen Tanemura, in line with Sanderson's views, makes the claim that "probably the model of the [Buddhist] *unmattavrata* is the Śaiva post-initiatory observance [i.e., *caryā*]."[66] This claim is made somewhat offhandedly and is not substantiated, merely referring to the existence of an *unmattavrata* in the Śaiva Vidyāpīṭha *Picumata/Brahmayāmala*. Such a reference, of course, merely indicates the parallelism with which we must deal, and does not in itself resolve the question.

Looking at the literature as a whole, Buddhist and Śaiva, it appears that there certainly has been interaction and exchange between the Buddhist and Śaiva Tantric traditions—no one could or would deny that.[67] However, it seems that in the case of the *caryāvrata* what one sees is a fairly clear example of a Tantric feature that has developed, not in a Śaiva vacuum, nor even necessarily from a Śaiva prototype, but that gestated in a shared ascetical zeitgeist in which a number of similar regimens (*vrata*) were in circulation, and in which forms and features of the Buddhist and Śaiva idioms, as well as from the overarching orthodox Smārta traditions, were mutually emulated.[68] In fact, although the adoption of a funerary and transgressive idiom by the Śaivas *may* predate its adoption by the Buddhists (although this is by no means established), it seems clear that—while the interpretation and stated purpose of such observances by the Buddhists remained remarkably consistent—its representation in Śaiva literature shifted significantly over time, progressively approximating that found in the Buddhist sources. Consequently, it would seem that the later Śaiva practice of this rite (ca. ninth century and after) reflects a remarkable degree of influence from the Buddhist traditions with whom they rubbed shoulders throughout the ascetical milieux of the Tantric Age.[69]

It is worth recalling that funerary and transgressive antinomian elements were never the exclusive province of the Śaiva traditions. In fact, the transgressive *mahāvrata* or *kapāla-vrata*—which comes to be characteristic of the Śaiva *kāpālika* practices—is not itself specifically Śaiva. The earliest reference appears in *Yājñavalkyasmṛti* (ca. 100–300 C.E.) iii.243 as a penance for one who has killed a Brahman.[70] This work on the understanding of pious duty (*dharma*) was composed right around the period in which esoteric Śaiva sects began to emerge, and thus was one religious praxis among many available to the nascent Pāśupata-s and Lākula-s of the Śaiva Atimārga. In the adoption of this observance as a feature of regular practice by these ascetical traditions, one can detect a clear semiological intent: The rite is the great observance (*mahāvrata*) for the expiation of the greatest sin imaginable (by Brahmans, of course)—killing a Brahman.[71] If it were considered capable of such potent purificatory power, it would certainly recommend itself to be adapted to other mythological and ritual contexts as a trope for supreme asceticism and yogic purification. In the case of Śaiva mythology, in order to reinforce the reputation of Śiva as the supreme ascetic (although specifically invoked to account for the aftermath of his slaying of Brahmā, the Ur-Brahman), Śaiva communities began to represent Maheśvara himself as undertaking this rite as a part of his virtuoso ascetical regimen. When Śaiva ascetics undertook the imitation of Śiva with the goal of eliminating the stain of considering oneself as separate from the Great God (*bheda-mala*), the rite further recommended itself as a means for Śaiva ascetics themselves to identify quite publicly with Śiva's arduous practice of challenging religious observances (*duṣkara-vrata*).

It is also important to recall that, as in Buddhist circles, so too in early Śaiva esoterism, the terms *caryā* and *vrata* referred to (relatively) mundane ascetical exercises before they were gradually transformed in the later, nondualist Tantric contexts. When the terms *vrata* or *caryā* appear in the works of the dualistic Śaiva Siddhānta, for example, rather mainstream, pro-nomian definitions are regularly given. The *Mataṅgapārameśvarāgama* defines *caryāpāda* as "the character of our own tradition, constancy in vows, conduct, and truth-telling."[72] Similarly, Bhaṭṭa Nārāyaṇakaṇṭha's commentary on the passage in the *Mṛgendra Tantra* that discusses the mouth-washing of the student on entering the maṇḍala, glosses *vrata* as "eating the five cow-products and [sacramental] porridge, and so on"[73]—an entirely pro-nomian, exoteric, dualistic purity rite. Similarly, the *caryāpāda* of the *Mṛgendra* itself prescribes taking food only from non-despised castes (eschewing commensality), and characterizes those who undertake observances (*vratin*) as "those who abandon meat, women, and mead."[74] They are to shun women, song, dance, conversation, and play, as well as garlands and ointments (i.19). One might usefully compare table 5.4 for an indication again of how closely this tracks the *pre*scribed behaviors of the *caryāvrata*. It is also noteworthy how closely this corresponds to the discipline of the Buddhist monk (not only fully ordained *bhikṣu*-s, but novice monks as well), and the regular (frequently semimonthly) ascetical behavior of lay Buddhists during the ancient practice of *poṣadha* (Pāli *uposatha*), perhaps the most popular supererogatory practice of Buddhists around the world.[75] Here, again, the ascetical regimes of the various Indian traditions were quite similar both in terminology and in practice.

Some have pointed to the famous Pāśupata *vrata* as one source for a shift in later Tantric communities toward a nondualist, antinomian observance.[76] The existence of Pāśupata communities is attested in the early-mid first millennium (fourth century), so its practices would certainly be prior to any fully formed Buddhist or Śaiva esoterism of which we are aware at present. Its *vrata* is known to us through such sources as *Atharvaveda Pariśiṣṭa 40* (ca. late first millennium) and the better-known *Pāśupatasūtra* (ca. fourth century). In one short phase of this *vrata* as it is explained by Kauṇḍinya's late-first millennium commentary on the *Pāśupatasūtra*, the practitioner courts scorn by means of acting crazily—as advocated in the later nondualist prescriptions for the *unmatta-vrata*. There are also some few correspondences with regard to site and dress: The *Pāśupatavrata* is to be kept at a confluence of rivers, mountain cave, or near water, one is to bathe in ash, is to make offering to the image (*liṅga*) with laughter, song, and music, is to have only one garment or go naked. Also, as with most observances (*vrata*), the Pāśupata vrata is to be kept for a delimited number of months or years (AVP 40 1.3).

However, the pious comportment of this ritual overall is so thoroughly contrary to the *caryāvrata* of the Mahā- and Yoginī Tantra Buddhists (and, as we shall see in a moment, the similarly later and nondualistic Vidyāpīṭha and Trika Hindu Tantrists), that the Pāśupata *vrata* is better considered a conditioning type rather than a true cause.[77] In the Pāśupata *vrata*, except for a handful of token contrarian accoutrements and actions (*khaṭvāṅga*, singing and dancing, etc.), the central behaviors are entirely dualistic and the practitioner must be a (pure) Brahman.[78] The sites that correspond are generic sites of religious practice (*yogasthāna*) or auspicious sites (e.g., mountain caves, confluence of rivers); and singing and dancing are elsewhere attested as exoteric offerings to images. Indeed, only the *khaṭvāṅga* seems to have any connection to the nondualist *vrata* (a consideration that may suggest caution in overinterpreting this element in this regard). Images are worshipped; fire sacrifices (*homa*) are performed; pure altar ashes (rather than funereal ash) are used for bathing; the *vratin* fasts, observes chastity, avoids women and *śūdra*-s; and astrologically auspicious days are to be chosen for the rites. It is worth noting that the goal of this *vrata* is not liberation through a gnostic transcendence of conceptuality, but either nearness to Rudra or union with [Śiva] Paśupati in the afterlife.[79]

A more probable link—one that also serves as a bridge between the dualistic Śaivas and their nondualistic brethren—is the practice of the later division of the Śaiva Atimārga, the Lākula ascetics also known as the Kālamukhas.[80] Consider the testimony of the *Niśvāsatattvasaṃhitā* on what is called therein the skull observance (*kapāla-vrata*), the world transcending observance (*lokātīta-vrata*), or great Pāśupata observance (*mahāpāśupata-vrata*):

> Touched by the five secret [Brahmamantra]s and initiated, he should wander, carrying a skull-staff (*khaṭvāṅga*) and skull bowl (*kapāla*), either shaven or with dreadlocks, [wearing] a sacred thread [made of] hair[81] and adorned with skull-pieces,[82] wearing [nothing but] a codpiece, smeared with ashes, ornamented with divine decorations; considering the world [to be] made of Rudra, [he is] a devotee of Rudra; firm in his vow, [he] takes all [food and drink] and does all, devoted to meditation on Rudra. Knowing that "there is no other to protect me than Rudra, the supreme divinity," the fearless one should perform the [ascension through] the eleven levels.[83]

Here we see more of the characteristics of the later nondualist *vrata*, although on the whole it is not a large advance beyond the Pāśupata *vrata*, which is described just previously in this section of the *Niśvāsa*.[84] As we have seen, the *khaṭvāṅga* appears in the dualist Pāśupata *vrata* (and is probably a stylized representation of the Smārta *mahāvratin*'s banner-topped skull[85]). The great Pāśupata *vrata* articulated here does add a skull bowl (*kapāla*) and funerary ornamentation (hair thread and skull ornaments), but largely this is identical to the earlier Pāśupata rite—the flamboyantly antinomian practice of the *caryāvrata* is not clearly in evidence in the Lākula rite.[86]

It is not until the next phase of the development of Śaiva Tantrism that a thoroughgoing antinomianism is found. Alexis Sanderson has described the skull observance of these higher Śaiva traditions as follows:

> Wearing earrings, armlets, anklets and girdle [of human bone] with a sacred thread (*upavīta*) made of twisted corpse hair, smeared with ashes from the cremation-pyres, carrying the skull-bowl, the skull-staff and rattle-drum (*ḍamaru*), intoxicated with alcohol, he alternated periods of night wandering (*niśāṭana*) with worship (*pūjā*) in which he invoked and gratified the deities of the *maṇḍala* into which he had been initiated. This gratification required the participation of a . . . consecrated consort with whom he was to copulate.[87]

Here, quite clearly, in the eighth-century[88] Vidyāpīṭha traditions, is the Śaiva correlate of the Buddhist *caryāvrata* we have explored earlier. It is not, however, referred to as *caryāvrata* in the influential *Picumata/Brahmayāmala*. Although the term *vratacaryā* does occur a number of times therein, it does not appear to function as a term of art. Rather, *Picumata* XXI, the *vrata* chapter (*vrata-paṭala*), treats of nine variant *vrata*-s available to practitioners of this tradition, including the *unmattaka*- and *kapāla-vrata*-s as numbers four and five.[89] These latter are, of course, part of the cluster of interrelated *vrata*-s under consideration here and in this scripture clearly advocate the deliberate cultivation of antinomian behaviors.

Interestingly, the term *vrata-caryā* does appear in the Trika Tantra (*yathālabdha*) *Siddhayogeśvarīmata*, whose tenth chapter is devoted to the *vidyāvrata* or *vratacaryā*. Here, however, the *vrata* presented corresponds to the more dualistic vision of the Lākula-s rather than the more transgressive idiom of the *Picumata*.[90] The practice involves the anticipated ash smearing but is a thoroughly pronomian rite described in four iterations, evidently corresponding to the four powers (*siddhi*: purification, prosperity, domination, and destruction). One wears either a white, yellow, red, or black garment, respectively, with ashes and a sacred thread of the same color and is generally restrained and disciplined. The observances are to be kept for five days (SYM X.16). The only elements corresponding to the nondualist *vrata* are wandering and laughing, but these too are found in the dualistic Pāśupata *vrata*.[91] On the whole, the (*yathālabdha*) *Siddhayogeśvarīmata*—although considered one of the major scriptures of nondual Śaiva/Saktism—does not display a marked antinomianism or nondualism.

The *vidyāvrata* also appears in the Trika *Tantrasadbhāva*, from whence it was later incorporated into the *Kubjikāmata Tantra* xxv.29–171. Here we see all the key elements that we know from the Buddhist materials—dreadlocked or bald, ash-smeared, bearing the five signs (*mudrā*), naked or wearing strips of bark, wearing ornaments, clean or dirty, wandering with a *khaṭvāṅga*.[92] The sites, too, are essentially the same (xxv.46–48)—charnel ground, grove, cave, empty capital, crossroads, mountain peak, seashore, confluence of rivers, and so forth.[93] Yet again, as in the *Siddhayogeśvarīmata*, the practitioner of the *Tantrasadbhāva/Kubjikāmata* observance is chaste and bathed (*brahmacarī tu snātakaḥ*, KMT xxv.30d) and is to engage in meditation, worship, recitation, and fire offerings (xxv.41–42)—all elements prohibited in the Buddhist nondualistic *vrata*. Like *vrata*-s in general, it is delimited by time—six months, a year, or any number of years up to twelve (KMT xxv.54–55). The connection to the prototype dharmaśāstric *mahāvrata* is also explicit: "If a mantrin should practice [the *vrata*] twelve years, even a Brahman-killer will succeed."[94] It is worth noting that the *Tantrasadbhāva/Kubjikāmata* and the *Siddhayogeśvarīmata* clearly take the terms *vidyāvrata* and *vratacaryā* to be synonymous.[95]

The *vidyāvrata* appears as well in the "left-current" *Viṇāśikha Tantra*, albeit incidentally. However, even its brief attestation therein does allow us some further confirmation of one other aspect of the *vrata* we have been considering here—its elite status. *Viṇāśikha* 180, in praising the effectiveness of a murderous rite it teaches, claims that "hence, [even] one who is renowned [as accomplished in] the *vidyāvrata* [and] adorned with fame and so on, is affected by this procedure and dies without further ado."[96] This kind of self-promoting hyperbole might profitably be compared to statements in the Buddhist Tantras that, for example, such-and-such a ritual will "kill even a buddha" (see, for example, *Guhyasamāja* XIII.66). In both instances, the rite in question is being praised as capable of even such remarkable power as killing a being of outstanding power—in the one case a buddha, in the other a practitioner of the *vidyāvrata.*

What, then, of its history in the Buddhist context? As I have already stated, this rite appears exclusively in the later, nondualist Tantras classified as Mahāyoga or Yoginī Tantras. The usage of the term *vrata* or *caryā* for the aggressively transgressive rite we have identified is not found in any of the early, dualistic Tantras such as the *Susiddhikara*, *Mañjuśrīmūlakalpa,* or the like, up to and including the so-called Yoga Tantra, the *Sarvatathāgatatattvasaṃgraha.*

Among its earliest appearances as a term of art, then, would seem to be the famed *Guhyasamāja Tantra* in its fifth and seventh chapters. These two, called the "foremost of total practices" (*samanta-caryāgra*) and "mantra practices" (*mantra-caryā*), are explicitly concerned with this issue and are, notably, among the most antinomian of the entire scripture. The *vidyā-vrata* (which, here too, is essentially synonymous) is itself explicitly treated in chapter 16.[97]

As noted earlier, the entire antinomian discourse in chapter 5—advocating violating the basic, fivefold Buddhist ethic (*pañcaśīla*), commensality with impure castes, incest, and other transgressions, and (most telling) contempt for the guru—is framed by the notion of transcendence of conceptuality (*vikalpa*). Likewise, chapter 7 is devoted to sexual yogas (which, we have seen, are a central element of the *caryāvrata*) that involve perceiving the world and its contents as divine transformations of buddhas. It climaxes near the following verse on the transcendence of dualities to be attained through meditation on mindfulness of nonorigination (*anutpādānusmṛtibhāvanā*):

All is brilliant by nature, signless, without syllables,
Not dual, not nondual, peaceful, like space, thoroughly stainless.[98]

Chapter 16 elaborates specifically a consort observance (*vidyāvrata*) in which sexuality features prominently (although the consort may be a dryad or similar nonhuman being), is to be carried out in a forest, involves begging, is associated with antinomianism of the sort advocated in chapter 5, and is to be performed for six months. Thus, in the GST one sees the development of an idea of *caryā* and [*vidyā*]*vrata* that is very similar to the form found in the Yoginī Tantras, albeit less explicitly involving funerary elements, kāpālika insignia, and so on.

There is, however, an important exception to the rule that these terms do not appear in the earlier Tantras and that is essential to a proper understanding of the connotation of *vidyāvrata* in the *Guhyasamāja* and subsequent Buddhist literature. This is the intriguing use of the term *vidyāvrata* found in the *Mahāvairocana Tantra*. The entire fifteenth chapter of this important early Buddhist Tantra is devoted to the *vidyāvrata* (*rig sngags brtul zhugs*). Its usage in this context contains many of the features associated with the later nondualist *vidyāvrata*, minus the sexual sense of *vidyā*-qua-consort (in the MVT *vidyā* seems to have its more general meaning of knowledge or spell). It is notable that it uses the terms *caryā* and *vrata* as interrelated concepts: Vajrapāṇi specifically requests instruction on the *vidyāvrata*, "for the sake of those who engage in the practices (*caryā*) of the bodhisattvas by means of mantra."[99] This special observance in the MVT also pointedly contains some prototypical features that are central to the later practice of the rite, such as a focus on nonconceptuality and nondiscrimination in eating. It involves nondual perception of good and bad ("gold and gravel becoming equal," *gser dang bong rdo mnyam gyur*) and involves special eating and breathing rites, including (at one point) eating food without selectivity (*ma blangs pa yi zas*). Here, too, as in the *Guhyasamāja* and elsewhere, the *vidyāvrata* is a special, six-month practice that is said to yield no less than buddhahood.[100]

I would suggest that this usage, functioning in the shared cultural and religious idiom, was a further component of the ironic resonance of its new usage in *Guhyasamāja* and subsequent Tantras. Given the evident dependence of the *Guhyasamāja* on the earlier dispensations such as the *Mahāvairocana*, it is virtually certain that the authors of the GST rite intended this to be a commentary of sorts on the rite appearing in the MVT. That is, in addition to the semiological changes being played on the baseline, traditional sense of *vrata*, there is a certain Tantric intertextuality evident here as well in which proto- or semi-nondualism is challenged to go to its logical conclusion. As we observed in chapter 4, the antinomian inversions of the Mahāyoga and later Tantras are in part directed at the dualistic purity/pollution obsession of many earlier esoteric traditions, and this would seem to be another notable case in point.

The continuity between the prototype MVT *vidyāvrata* and the later, fully nondualist *vrata/caryā* of the Mahāyoga and Yoginī Tantras is further confirmed by a purported side effect of these practices described in the MVT:

> Gods such as Śakra, Brahmā and the like, piśāca-s, and mahorāga-s,
> Paying homage from afar, will also protect all [associated with the mantrin].
> They will all pay heed and do what they are commanded.
> [Divine] physicians, men, gods, vidyādhara-s and mantradhara-s
> Will come before [him] and say "what shall we do?"
> Obstructers (*vighna*), evil gremlins (*vināyaka*),
> demons (*rākṣasa*) and demonesses (*mātṛkā*)—
> When they see the one who upholds the mantras, they pay homage from afar.[101]

This passage may profitably be compared with the results promised the practitioner of the *caryā* in the **Vajrayānāntadvayanirākaraṇa*, to wit: "Certain nonhuman beings will on that account be delighted with that [person] and will protect [him/her] in accordance with the Dharma and receive religious instruction from him/her."[102] Tanemura seems to have considered this merely a curiosity of Jñānaśrī's presentation. However, it seems clear that the idea of nonhuman protection following upon a properly nondualistic perception of reality has deep roots in esoteric Buddhist ideology (if not Buddhist ideology as a whole).[103]

Thus, one can see real continuity between the earliest Buddhist attestation of a *vidyāvrata*, the transgressive *caryā* of the *Guhyasamāja*, and the fully developed *caryāvrata/vratacaryā* of the Buddhist Yoginī Tantras. They all focus on the attainment of nondual gnosis, which is the key soteriological virtue in these Mahāyāna Buddhist traditions. The development we see corresponds to a) the adoption of sexual yogas in the case of the

GST, and b) a progressively more aggressive semiology of transcendence of purity/pollution dualities in the Yoginī Tantras. Although the latter (especially employment of the five polluting meats and ambrosias) is a major element of the GST, it does not appear directly in its treatment of the *vidyāvrata*, so interpretative caution would urge making this distinction, although in so doing we may be exaggerating the difference. Further, the funereal focus is clearly more marked in the Yoginī sources than in the Mahāyoga scriptures, although (again) charnel ground imagery and practice is by no means absent and appears throughout even early Buddhist ascetical literature.

What, then, is the relationship of this rite to the very similar practices of the Śaiva traditions? Albeit—as Lorenzen and others have noted—there is clearly a relationship, from what we have seen in the case of the *caryāvrata*, that relationship would seem to have been rather more complex than has been acknowledged by many recent interpreters. That is, the influence would seem clearly to have been mutual. There is a lot of evidence to support the notion that the various Tantric communities interacted frequently if not constantly, sharing ideas and practices, often in an environment of mutual (if, at times, begrudging) recognition.[104] The communities shared the same civic space, and were generally patronized by the same royal or aristocratic donors.[105] In these circumstances, in India of the Tantric period, there flourished what Phyllis Granoff has called a culture of "ritual eclecticism" in which "rituals [were] a form of religious practice that was essentially non-sectarian or trans-sectarian."[106] Furthermore, as Sanderson has indicated, the *Guhyasiddhi* of Padmavajra suggests that Buddhist communities practicing the Mahāyoga Tantras were likely familiar with (able, at least, to simulate) the Śaiva tradition of the *Niśvāsatattvasaṃhitā*.[107] Similarly, among some Śaiva communities, Buddhist Tantrism was considered a perfectly valid (if less elevated) Tantric revelation. The Kaula *Matasāra*, for instance, reckons Buddhist Tantra one of the five streams (*pañcasrotas*) of lower Tantric initiation, along with Śaiva Siddhānta, Vaiṣṇava, Saura and Gāruḍa.[108]

Thus, in these shared ascetical contexts—in which an eclectic ritual culture was widespread (if not universal[109])—deities, rituals, and observances were practiced and propagated across traditions. It is certainly possible (as some have suggested) that as part of this process, the Buddhist communities emulated funereally-oriented ascetical practices of Śaiva Tantrikas. It is not clear, however, that they needed to turn to specifically

Śaiva prototypes. This is not to say that they may have taken the practices from an "Indic substratum" as suggested by David Seyfort Ruegg. Davidson, Sanderson, and others have succinctly indicated the problems of this model, insofar as it seems to postulate an otherwise unattested tertium quid as the source of inter-tradition commonalities.[110] However, I think it is clear that the adoption of some version of the Dharmaśāstric *mahāvrata* skull rite as a virtuoso ascetical observance is not an exclusively or distinctively Śaiva phenomenon, but was available as an option for a variety of ascetical groups.[111]

Furthermore, as is also well-known, funereal practices in charnel grounds were nothing new to Buddhist communities. In the (ca. late-fourth/early-fifth century[112]) *Laṅkāvatāra Sūtra*, for instance, charnel ground ascetics (*śmaśānika*) are listed as one of many types of Buddhist yogins.[113] The yogin is therein said to live in "an empty house, a charnel ground, the foot of a tree, a cave, on straw, or in the open air"[114]—very similar *yogasthāna*-s to those one sees in the *caryāvrata*. Also, by the time of the *Laṅkāvatāra*, the Buddhist communities were already well along in developing a discourse of transcendence of purity and pollution:

> As all things are unreal, there is neither defilement nor purity.[115]

They also boasted a well-developed critique of the conceptual representation of reality (*vikalpa*) that the Buddhist *caryāvrata* was intended to overcome, to wit:

> There is no truly existent thing as conceptualized by the [epistemically] naive;
> Liberation [is] precisely [predicated] on unreality—why don't sophists accept this?[116]

Thus, on entering the Tantric Age, the Buddhist communities had long since developed the institutional base and the intellectual apparatus to adapt elements of the shared ascetical zeitgeist (the eclectic ritual culture) into the rite of nondual transcendence of conceptuality that found place in the *Mahāvairocana Tantra* and developed through the *Guhyasamāja* and into the Yoginī Tantras.

The Śaiva communities also shared the charnel ground ascetical milieu and they were inspired by the skull-bearing *mahāvrata* of the

Paurānic Śiva. In the early period, however—pre-tenth century—the Śaiva Tantric traditions did not have an epistemology or soteriology that would support the idea that deliberate transgression of conventional norms would generate a gnosis that would occasion liberation. Rather, the literature we have examined would seem to indicate that, as the *caryāvrata* took shape among Tantric communities, the later Śaiva traditions (or, rather, some of them) gradually adapted their observance to bring it more in line with this distinctively Buddhist gnostic orientation. For, in the earliest forms of Śaiva *vrata* up to and including the *Picumata*, the rationale for the adoption of the polluted status of the (anti-)*vratin* has virtually no epistemic or gnostic focus. It seems to represent merely an attempt to mimic the ascetical behavior of their god Śiva, reflecting a devotion to his worship, a desire for identification or union with him, and a trend toward publicly marking their sectarian allegiance with funereal accoutrements. Lorenzen has noted this in his work on the Kāpālikas:

> The ultimate aim of the Kāpālika observance was a mystical identification or communion with Śiva. Through their imitative repetition of Śiva's performance of the Mahāvrata, the ascetics became ritually "homologized" with the god and partook of, or were granted, some of his divine attributes, especially the eight magical powers (*siddhis*).[117]

The Pāśupata observance is predicated on much the same idea. Its ritual mimesis is articulated thus in *Atharvaveda Pariśiṣṭa* 40:

> I shall take a bath in ash, which destroys all evils, because Rudra,
> when bathed in a bath of ash, became purified by himself.[118]

The early Śaiva Tantric paradigm for the transgressive *vrata*, then, was one of *imitatio dei*—mimicking the activity of the god in the interest of eliding the (presumably mistaken) sense of a gulf between him and the devotee. In none of these rites is there mention of transcendence of conceptuality or attainment of any epistemic nonduality—the concern seems entirely to be one of nonduality in the sense of union with the god Śiva.[119]

Consider, too, the items carried by the Śaiva *vratin*-s. These are described in the *Tantrasadbhāva/Kubjikāmata* XXV.51–52 as *āyudha*—literally weapons, but in this context (as another term of art) more pointedly referring to the various trademark items carried by the gods—that is, the trident of Śiva, the discus of Viṣṇu, and so on. This usage reinforces the notion that these items are employed for their mimetic—rather than their gnostic—value.

Nor do the formative scriptures of the Āgamic Śaivas represent the transgressive *vrata* as involved in a gnostic, liberative transcendence of conceptuality. Even the internal, esoteric interpretation of the *vratacaryā* given in *Tantrasadbhāva* and the *Kubjikāmata*, for example, does not mention nonduality at all.[120] In the *Brahmayāmala*, the *vrata* "from village to village" is characterized merely as "appearing in the form/appearance of the divinity."[121] Likewise, the *Jayadrathayāmala*—in its Fourth Ṣatka where the similar *vīra-melāpa* ritual is detailed, the focus is merely on "personifying [the] Aghora [form of Śiva]" and so on.[122] Here, again, the rite is a dramatic enactment of the practitioner's ultimate unity or identity with Śiva, not of his attainment of a specifically liberative nondual gnosis. It is the former (or rather the excitement by the former of the potential planted during *dīkṣā* [initiation]) that yields liberation, not gnostic realization as in the case of the Buddhists.

It is only in the later Śaiva sources, those posterior to the (late) eighth century—and thus subsequent to the Buddhist *Guhyasamāja Tantra*—that transcendence of conceptuality or attainment of nondual gnosis figures in their discourses about the *caryāvrata*. It would seem evident that *vikalpa-s* are good in the Pāśupata and Lākula *vrata*-s (or even the SYM *vidyāvrata*), for the authoritative Śaiva map(s) of the universe, which are to be navigated until one reaches union with Śiva, are precisely conceptual formulations of reality (*vikalpa*). This is even true of the later Āgamic Śaivas, who simply elaborated a more complex and ramified vision of the universe, subsuming the earlier revelations within their new vision. It is only with the more developed Śaiva thought of the Krama and Trika traditions of Kashmir (quite obviously formed under the influence and challenge of Buddhist philosophical and ritual discourses[123]) that the Śaiva systems begin to move beyond an ontological nondualism to adopt an epistemological nondualism.[124] The earlier Śaiva sources cited by Abhinavagupta in discussing transgressive observance merely refer to overcoming a sense of difference from Śiva (*bhedamala*) or an aim of entering into the heart of Bhairava (*bhairavahṛdayānupraveśa*) as a result of antinomian observance.[125] It was only the Krama scriptures that began to speak of liberation through a nondual practice of gnostic insight; and, in doing so, they used characteristically Buddhist terminology, speaking of eliminating concepts (*vikalpa*) and conceptual elaboration (*prapañca*).[126] Eventually, the Kashmiri Śaiva thinkers of the tenth century and subsequently (i.e., Somānanda [ca. 900–950)], Utpaladeva [ca. 925–75], and Abhinavagupta [ca. 975–1025]) began to conceive of a system wherein "the only impurity . . . [was] a state of ignorant self-bondage through the illusion that purity and impurity, prohibitedness and enjoinedness were objective qualities residing in things, persons and actions."[127] If developing such a view within an otherwise epistemologically realist Śaiva context is not enough to earn one the label "crypto-Buddhist" (*prachanna-bauddha*—as Śaṅkara is said to have been called), it is hard to imagine what would be.

The discourse of the Buddhists, as we noted earlier, and as we have seen throughout this discussion, is suffused from the very outset with a discourse of epistemic nonduality and transcendence of conceptuality—even, as we have seen, in its earliest form in the *Mahāvairocana Tantra* (which well predates the Krama scriptures), as well as in the *Guhyasamāja* (which was probably roughly contemporary). Thus, the only reasonable conclusion would seem to be that the scholar-practitioners of the later Śaiva Tantric traditions—particularly the Krama and the scholastic authors of Trika of the tenth centuries and subsequently[128]—while maintaining an established practice of various antinomian *vrata*-s that were commonly practiced in the diverse ascetical communities of the Indian charnel grounds (and other major *yogasthāna*), gradually transformed their understanding of the place and purpose of the transgressive rites in line with the more epistemological, gnostic focus articulated in Buddhist circles (who, for their part, were not shy about adapting congenial aspects of the Śaiva and Vaiṣṇava Tantric ritual traditions and pantheons).[129]

In this chapter, we have observed the very specific sense in which the terms *caryā*, *vrata*, and so on function as terms of art in the discourses of Indian Tantric Buddhism. The palpable irony of this usage, the semiology of the inversions characteristic of this observance, and the prerequisites and proper contexts advocated throughout the Indian literature that treats of it have also been noted. We have also made some first tentative steps toward a more complete discussion of its history in Buddhist and Śaiva esoteric circles, noting the thoroughgoing focus on gnostic transcendence of conceptuality in the Buddhist context, an orientation that became normative for later Śaiva esoterism as well. The analysis here has, unfortunately, only scratched the surface of a widely ramified and critically important aspect of Indian esoteric religion in the late first millennium.

To make such a beginning, however flawed, is important to progress in making sense of Tantric Buddhism. As a term of art, *caryāvrata* (and the many terms largely synonymous with it, such as *tattvayoga*, *unmattavrata*, *vidyāvrata*, etc.) has been widely misconstrued—if not overlooked entirely. The reasons are readily comprehensible, insofar as the terms *caryā* and *vrata* have wide currency as generic terms in Śaiva and Buddhist Tantric contexts. However, the failure of modern scholars to notice that what seemed to be descriptions of quotidian Tantric practice were in fact references to a very special observance has resulted in widespread misunderstanding and misinterpretation of the tradition. This was not just generic practice, or a practice, but "The Practice" extraordinaire—an occasional, time-delimited practice to be undertaken by elite practitioners. Having identified this distinctive usage, and given the fact that it is pervasive in literature, the contours of scholarly interpretation of esoteric Buddhism (and esoteric Śaivism) will necessarily change rather dramatically.

This transformed understanding opens up new questions and provides a powerful new lens with which to understand aspects of the South Asian traditions that had not previously been known to relate to this specific observance. The early "proto-Bengali" Caryāpāda-s, for instance, are an important case in point. While it has been clear for some time that these sources are important documents for the study of Bengali Tantrism, they have been taken by a number of authors as reflective of Tantric thought and practice broadly construed. However, a moment's reflection may now suggest to those familiar with their rigorously antinomian contents that the famous literature of the *Caryā Songs* (*caryāgīti*) should not thus be construed as representations of a generic Tantrism, but should rather be carefully interpreted with particular and pointed reference to the valences of this distinctive observance. For instance—to revisit a prior point—the drinking song of Virūpa discussed at the end of chapter 4—taken by Davidson as evidence for widespread alcoholic libertinism in Tantric Buddhism—is found precisely in such a collection of Practice Songs (*caryāgīti*).[130]

If one accepts this interpretation of the Mahāyoga and Yoginī Tantra literature, what consequences does it entail for our understanding of the Indian Tantric traditions as a whole? If, in fact, these "characteristically Tantric" practices turn out to be "The Practice" reserved only for intensive retreats by elite practitioners or for similarly special ritual occasions, what does this suggest concerning the sociology of Buddhist Tantrism? It is to this issue that we will turn in chapter 6.

[6] TANTRIC BUDDHIST TRANSGRESSION IN CONTEXT

Make a maṇḍala with an eight-petaled multi-colored flower in the center; in the center of that, on top of a sun disk, a blue letter hūṃ transforms into a black Akṣobhya in earth-touching gesture. Then . . . reciting oṃ āḥ vajrapuṣpe hūṃ, *one should offer every greatly desired thing.*[1]

—Advayavajra

Not reciting mantras . . . not performing maṇḍala rites, and not creating maṇḍalas: that is reciting mantras, . . . that is performing maṇḍala rites, that is creating the maṇḍala.[2]

—Advayavajra

HAVING BEGUN to trace the outlines of the semiotical system that structures the discourses and ritual logic of the nondual Buddhist Tantras, there remains the question of how to synthesize the observations we have made so as to advance the larger project of making sense of Tantric Buddhism. We have observed how modern scholars have advanced theories of the origins of Tantric Buddhism or cast its history in narrative form, by which means they construct a social context within which to interpret and explain its transgressive discourses and practices. We have explored the indigenous historiography of the Tantric traditions and its continuities with currents in the broader sphere of contemporaneous Indian culture. We have analyzed the semiotical process by which consumption of polluting meats and ambrosias makes sense—enacts meanings—for practitioners of the Mahāyoga and Yoginī Tantras. We have also observed the systemic misunderstandings of the scope of Tantric antinomianism generated by a failure to appreciate *caryāvrata* and related terms as terms of art and thus misconstruing the distinctive, elite time-delimited Practice as the ordinary, quotidian ritual of all nondualist Tantric Buddhists. What, then, do we really know of Tantric Buddhism as it was actually practiced or, as it is now fashionable to ask, "on the ground?" How did these traditions fit into the broader social fabric of late first-millennium Indian Buddhism and among other Indian religions? Based on what we have been able to discern of the semiology and practice of Tantric antinomianism can we better reconstruct a social context within which to locate Tantric Buddhism? Were there in fact, as has recently been claimed,[3] two distinct factions of esoteric Buddhism: One in the monasteries, taught by ambitious monks to royal patrons, and another in the wild, taught by tribal shamans to lay Buddhists (only later to be coöpted by monks and semanticized, bowdlerized, etc.)? In this chapter, we will address these unresolved issues, exploring the evidence that attests to the sociology of Indian esoteric Buddhism.

THE SOCIAL LOCATION OF ESOTERIC BUDDHISM AS AN INTERPRETATIVE PROBLEM

In recent studies of Tantric Buddhism in Southern Asia, two subgroups are postulated, which are depicted as belonging to differing social spheres—what have been called institutional esoterism and siddha esoterism. The former, it is asserted, is "principally the domain of monks, who wrote and preached in a hermeneutical method that emphasized the development and integration of esoteric ideas and models into institutional requirements." The latter is sharply contradistinguished from this more socially acceptable Tantrism, being "the somewhat anarchical domain of the Perfected (*siddha*), those sometimes scruffy, long-haired denizens of the margins of the Indian social institutions."[4]

It must be admitted at the outset that the literatures associated with these two spheres of esoteric Buddhism do indeed focus on rather different concerns. Institutional esoterism—constructed largely on the basis of what come to be classified as lower Tantras by later exegetes—is devoted to elaborate rites for attaining both worldly powers and enlightenment. One finds therein detailed prescriptions for the production and worship of caityas, the manufacture and consecration of buddha images in various artistic media, rites for bathing them and worshipping them, for the recitation of holy scriptures, for the performance of fire offerings, and for conducting initiation rites in which disciples are led into visionary worlds of divine power (*maṇḍala*) and consecrated therein as regnant buddhas. Characterized by a general ritual fastidiousness, these scriptures emphasize methods for (and the crucial importance of) preserving ritual purity through baths, diet, and behavior. They advocate conducting ritual observances on astrologically auspicious occasions. These scriptures further stress conventional Buddhist ritual forms such as taking refuge, cultivating the spirit of enlightenment, maintaining conventional Buddhist morality such as the vows of liberation, and cultivating personal restraint and asceticism.

The "siddha" literature, on the other hand, seems to many to be quite different. It appears to reject conventional morality and recommends violating the five (and other) vows; doing as one pleases. It heaps scorn on such niggling, ritualistic details as keeping track of lunar days (*tithi*), the progress of the moon through asterisms (*nakṣatra*), or that of the sun through the zodiac (*rāśi*). The accomplished ones (*siddha*-s) seem to recommend renouncing mundane Buddhist concerns such as caitya worship, reciting scriptures, offering to images of deities, or honoring monks. Rather than bathe, worry about clean clothes, white robes, a vegetarian diet, sexual restraint, and so on, the siddha literature recommends growing dreadlocks, playing with skulls, eating meat and feces, wandering from village to village with young girls, wearing rags or nothing. Rather than shunning persons of impure caste, as the Mahāyāna and dualistic Tantric scriptures do,[5] they advocate feasting and having sex with them.

Based on these palpable divergences, one can certainly understand how one might conclude that these scriptures were composed and followed by very different groups of people—groups that would not get along on account of the tremendous difference in their ritual protocols. However, to do so is, I believe, unwarranted. The conclusion that the institutional Tantrikas and the transgressive siddha Tantrikas constituted separate communities is based entirely on this divergence of literary content. There is no corroborating evidence to suggest the radical sociological separation suggested by this model; and, to assume that a discursive disjuncture corresponds to a sociological one is rather an interpretative leap. It also contradicts the preponderance of evidence in this regard and results in a fundamentally distorted picture of the sociology of Indian esoteric Buddhism.

There are, in fact, very good reasons to believe that the transgressive (siddha) communities were from the start entirely integrated with the nontransgressive esoteric Buddhist (institutional) communities, growing from and remaining well within the same cultural sphere, addressing similar concerns in their clients with similar ritual arsenals. There are, for instance, numerous indications that when transgressive practitioners did retire to socially marginal locations this move was entirely contrived. That is, these were privileged, educated Buddhist professionals (monks or quasi-monks [dedicated, professional lay religious]) affecting social marginality (and the associated ritual impurity) as an expression of the logic of the preeminent ritual observance of the nondualist traditions, The Practice. Additionally, attention to the divergences in rhetoric between the nontransgressive and transgressive traditions reveals that the latter does not reflect an independent ritual and social milieu, but rather an intimate awareness and tacit acceptance of the traditions of the former. Finally, although rejection of the mores and strictures of mainstream Buddhism and dualistic esotericism may seem on the surface to indicate a radical challenge, cultural criticism has more than adequately established that such inversions as frequently play a conservative, as a radical, social function. Hence, the notion that these traditions were a challenge to monastic institutions, and consequently divorced from centers of Buddhist education and power, misses the degree to which, ironically, such practices serve to uphold a conventional religious order that they assume through negation.

CONTRIVING MARGINALITY

As we briefly discussed in chapter 1, modern scholars have long considered antinomian Buddhist Tantrism to have emerged from marginal communities outside of the hegemony of mainstream Indian religions. In particular, we have seen how there is a pervasive imagination of the Tantric traditions as representing tribal or folk traditions of the underclasses oppressed by Brahmanical (and śramaṇical) orthopraxy. We have also observed that the arguments for this point are methodologically unsound, based on systematic misinterpretation of the literature. The tribal references interpreted by Sharma and others (see chapter 1) are quite evidently instances of the use of connotative semiotics, with low caste persons signifying ritual impurity in much the same manner as meats and ambrosias. Likewise, the more recent arguments of Davidson, based upon allegedly abundant tribal references in the literature, are revealed upon inspection to be nothing but references to bucolic, rural sites for yogic practice. That these interpretations rest entirely on precritical assumptions is confirmed by simple misreadings, insofar as the *Mataṅgapārameśvara Tantra* has nothing to do with communities of outcaste Mataṅgas, and on an observable interpretative double standard, insofar as similar instances of attribution to tribals such as the famed commentary ascribed to Śabara are not likewise construed as marginal, tribal traditions. As I read the evidence, there are no cogent grounds to consider Tantric authors with similar names tribal other than the widespread scholarly assumption that Tantrism is primitive.

This assumption is not merely prior, but contrary to the preponderance of evidence. There are clear indications that the tribal or outcaste identities of major figures in Tantric Buddhism—and Śaivism—are entirely contrived. This is exactly what one would expect given our earlier arguments concerning the semiology of transgression in these traditions. For instance, the so-called "Shamsher Manuscript" (discussed in chapter 3) relates the story of a boy with the (remarkably Buddhist) name of Triśaraṇa, who becomes a Tantric accomplished one (*siddha*) under the tutelage of Nāgārjuna.[6] Subsequently, Triśaraṇa is said to have "checked out the sites for The Practice, Manobhaṅga and Cittaviśrāma." That is, *after* he had become an accomplished Tantric master (*siddha*) through Nāgārjuna's guidance, he investigated the conditions at various sacred places wherein he might undertake the *caryāvrata*. When he had settled on a site, the reader is told, Triśaraṇa then "adopted the guise of a śabara and resided there."[7] There is no ambiguity here: The boy was raised in mainstream society; he practices Tantric Buddhism, becomes a master in his own right, and he contrives the appearance of a low-status tribal as an element of his transgressive observance of cultivated impurity.

Later in the document, there is another, similar narrative. This latter tale concerns a boy named Dāmodara, who is sent to the same two *caryā* sites, Manobhaṅga and Cittaviśrāma.[8] There, he is to seek a Tantric master by the name of Śabareśvara—presumably the same Triśaraṇa we read about earlier in the text in the guise of the Lord of Śabaras. Meeting him, he becomes his student, is instructed to display "the illusory appearance of killing things and the like,"[9] and eventually becomes a Tantric master in his own right under the name Advayavajra ("Nondual Adamant"). We will discuss this narrative in more detail shortly; for now, what is of primary importance is that this Tantric master, who joins Śabareśvara in the charnel ground to engage in The Practice, is in matter of fact a pure Brahman through paternal and maternal descent.[10]

The idea of religious figures from mainstream communities pretending to be marginal, low caste, or tribal types in the course of virtuoso practice of inversive observances is likewise attested in Śaiva Tantric literature. There one may read, for instance, of a certain Aṭavīla: To all appearances a tribal, whose very name implies he hails from the forest wilderness (the so-called tribal regions). However, it is clear in the narrative that this Aṭavīla was, in fact, "a Siddha who had assumed the appearance of a member of a forest (*aṭavī*) tribe."[11] That is, here we have the exact Śaiva parallel to the Śabareśvara of the Buddhists. In both of these instances, one sees accomplished esoteric masters taking on an ascetical observance of appearing as of impure birth, outside or oppressed by the purity strictures of mainstream society. Such references occur frequently and are certainly more convincing than, for instance, the narrative that appears in *Abhayadatta's *Stories of the Eighty-four Siddhas.* In this latter work, heavily relied upon by scholars even though it is almost certainly a Tibetan apocryphon,[12] the siddha Śabara is presented as a tribal hunter (*śabara*) who is converted by Avalokiteśvara, who reveals to him the sufferings of hell so that he gives up his un-right livelihood and becomes a compassionate, vegetarian bodhisattva.[13] This narrative is scarcely credible: It is precisely the sort of story one would expect to be composed (as such stories quite frequently are) merely on the basis of a figure's name by authors who had no other information at hand (and needed to fill out a list of eighty-four).[14]

One does not look far (although one must be observant) to come across numerous other instances in which it is clear that Tantric adepts are artificially adopting a primitive, marginal guise. The Śaiva Krama master Vidyānanda is likewise said to have "taken on the appearance of a śabara" (*śabararūpadhṛk*). Such references are so prevalent in Śaivism that Alexis Sanderson—much as I am suggesting here—identifies this as a primitivist theme that pervades the nondualist Śaiva traditions.[15] The Buddhist *siddha* Lokeśvara similarly "assumed the appearance of a śabara (*śabararūpadhāriṇā*) while practicing the sādhana of Vidyādharī-Vajrayoginī."[16]

THE COMMON REPERTOIRE OF BUDDHIST PROFESSIONALS

Indeed, it is difficult to conceive of how the situation could have been otherwise; for the nondualist Buddhist Tantras evince throughout an intimate knowledge of and thoroughgoing commitment to the dualistic structures of the nontransgressive Tantras. There is, for instance, a self-creation ritual in the *Garland of Practices* (*Sādhanamālā*) attributed to the same Śabara mentioned earlier that conforms entirely to the conventions of nontransgressive Buddhist esoterism.[17] The practitioner takes a comfortable seat, visualizes buddhas and bodhisattvas, and performs the first five procedures of the standard Mahāyāna seven-fold practice—homage (*praṇāma*), worship (*pūjā*), confession of one's own sins (*deśanā*), rejoicing in others' virtues (*anumodana*), and dedicating merit (*pariṇamana*)—before going for refuge to the Three Jewels, generating the spirit of enlightenment, and contemplating the four pure states (*brahmavihāra*) of love, compassion, joy, and equanimity. Then, dissolving all into voidness with the mantra "Oṃ I am the very nature of the adamantine gnosis of voidness" (*oṃ śūnyatājñānavajrasvabhāvātmako 'ham*), the practitioner is subsequently to visualize herself as the goddess Kurukullā. On a lotus in the practitioner-qua-Kurukullā's heart is another, detailed Kurukullā, quite daunting, with hair on end, three eyes, baring her teeth, Amitābha on her crown, and with green snakes as Brahmanical thread. This signifier Kurukullā (*samayasattva*—the unsanctified image) is consecrated through the ingress of the "real," signified Kurukulla (*jñānasattva*), accompanied by the four remaining transcendent lords (other than Amitābha, of whom she is the reflex) and the four goddesses. The practitioner then recites a mantra that promises dominance of the world and another to attain the eight worldly masteries (*aṣṭasiddhi, aṣṭaiśvarya*). In short, this is an entirely standard issue, Mahāyānically-inflected practice no different from those associated with, for instance, the dualistic, nontransgressive esoteric *Mahāvairocana Tantra*.

Furthermore, just as we saw of the antinomian semiology in chapters 4 and 5, the transgressive rejection of the practices of the dualistic Tantras is a precise inversion, likewise indexed to the notion of nondual gnosis:

> [Auspicious] lunar days, asterisms, or fasts—none of these are enjoined.
> The one with the nondual gnosis will have the power of the blissful ones (*sugata*).[18]

Or:

> One need not perform caitya rituals; one need not recite the scriptures . . .
> Likewise, one need not venerate deities nor honor monks . . . .
> Nor need one make ritual gesticulations (*mudrā*) or recite mantras.[19]

Or the many injunctions to the effect that one should break the primary vows of mainstream Buddhism that we have observed in preceding chapters: These could only have been written by someone with a knowledge of nontransgressive Buddhist esoterism. Consider, too, that they are negative injunctions. As Jan Nattier and others have noted concerning the challenge of gleaning historical information from normative scriptural sources, "statements of the type 'One should not believe X' or 'One should not do Y' . . . far from revealing what people actually did not believe or do—can serve as evidence that at least some members of the community were involved in the offending practices."[20] That is, the only reason to make a special statement prohibiting something is if people are actually doing it. In the case of the antinomian injunctions, these were meaningful precisely because the entire community to which these injunctions were directed understood these practices to be proper ethical and ritual behavior. There would be no reason to reject recitation of scripture, respecting monks, caitya worship, mantra recitation, and so on, if that was not already the tacitly accepted order of the day. Indeed, for every one of these radical injunctions, one could cite chapter and verse of a dualistic Tantra that says exactly the opposite; and—one may be certain—so could the authors of the nondualist scriptures.

Given these observations, the most likely explanation is that the antinomian traditions of the later Buddhist Tantras grew out of and were initially practiced within Buddhist monastic or quasi-monastic enclaves. This literature reflects not the ethos of marginal teachers, cobbling together rites from a mishmash of tribal practices and folk magic, but rather that of learned urban(e) Buddhist professionals. Whichever groups began to experiment with antinomian observances, undertaking them as an elite supplement to deity yoga and eventually integrating the theme of transcendence of purity and pollution into the rituals and the scriptural narratives, these were practitioners who were steeped in Buddhist lore and the techniques of the dualistic Buddhist Tantras. Transgressive esoterism, that is to say, did not grow out of marginal, outcaste, or tribal communities, but was crafted, developed, and preserved largely in centers of Buddhist learning and ritual practice. Many of these centers were monasteries and many of the important players in early Tantric esoterism were monks.

That the dualistic Tantric traditions were largely the preserve of Buddhist monastics is not in dispute. The *Susiddhikara*, for instance, is careful to distinguish renunciant and nonrenunciant practitioners,[21] following the pattern of the exoteric Mahāyāna scriptures. Like these exoteric works, the *Susiddhikara* privileges the renunciant and accords fully-ordained monks (*bhikṣu*) higher status than others.[22] Likewise, the *Mahāpratisarā* (an early esoteric work on amulet making) describes its techniques as being used by monks and nuns as well as others.[23] In fact, the order in which these are listed suggests that monastics were the primary target audience.[24] Similarly—although it has been little remarked upon—an early version of the esoteric *Mahāmāyūrīvidyārājñī* appears in the Bhaiṣajyavastu of the *Mūlasarvāstivāda Vinaya*,[25] suggesting a very early monastic provenance of these esoteric teachings. Elsewhere in this influential and voluminous Vinaya, a story is told of a monk who reanimates a corpse through mantra.[26] Given that this fact is part of the background of a narrative whose purpose is to illustrate varieties of monastic downfall (*pārājika*), we may infer that the idea of monks engaging in mantric ritual was taken for granted at the time this collection was redacted (early-mid first millennium).[27]

There are further indications in the nondual Tantric literature itself that suggests that ordained monastics were a primary audience. Consider this verse from the transgressive *Hevajra Tantra*:

> The body is said to be the ordination lineage (*nikāya*); the womb is the monastery (*vihāra*).
> One comes to be in the uterus from lack of passion (*vītarāga*).
> The placenta is the immaculate monastic robe (*cīvara*).[28]

The metaphors used by authors can often reveal quite a bit about their assumptions and the circumstances of their lives. The author(s) of this passage are clearly comfortable with the terminology of the Buddhist monastery: The different ordination lineages (*nikāya*), the epithets for renunciants as free of passion (*vītarāga*), and the vestments (*cīvara*) of the Buddhist monastic Community. Clearly, these were terms that had resonance for the community of Hevajra practitioners—presumably, because they were themselves monastics (or ex-, or quasi-monastics).

An attention to clothing is also in evidence elsewhere in the Tantric literature. For instance, *Catupithakhyatamantrāmsa*, in describing the *vrata* (i.e., *caryāvrata*) speaks of the practitioner of The Practice abandoning the "three religious robes."[29] These three robes (*tricīvara*) are the distinctive apparel, not merely of monks, but of fully ordained bhikṣus.[30] Here, again, the practitioner assumed by the text is an ordained monk. Many of the inversions of the antinomian rites could in fact have only been directed at monks, not laypeople. Setting aside the prominence of sexuality, consider the significant role of song and dance in the transgressive rites. How does this fit in to the overall semiosis? It fits because song and dance are prohibited by the Buddhist monastic discipline.[31] It would not be a transgression for a layperson. Hence, once again, the Tantric literature implicitly presupposes a monastic practitioner readership.[32]

Likewise, when one comes across evidence of Tantric practice outside of the literature, monks also occupy positions of great prominence. For instance, the transitional dualist/nondualist scriptures such as the STTS—which feature the practice of sexual union as a means to attain power and enlightenment—were transmitted to East Asia by missionaries, all (or most) of whom were monks.[33] In Southeast Asia too in the Kawi literature of Bali, one may read of a king of Singasari, Kĕrtanagara (1268–1292), who received initiation and engaged in nondualist Tantric practices. The existence of this Vajrayānist king is confirmed by a surviving statue of him, the Jaka Dolog. This image bears an inscription on the pedestal that records that the king was initiated in a cremation ground, whereupon he erected this image of himself in the form of Akṣobhya Buddha.[34] In this monument, the king is depicted wearing a monk's robes. Hence, this king evidently considered that a representation of himself-qua-tantric-practitioner should appear as a monk—presumably because viewers would expect the same. Similarly, the *Nikāya-saṃgrahawa*, a fourteenth-century Singhalese chronicle, speaks of a Vajra Mountain School (*vajraparvata*) in ninth- to eleventh-century Sri Lanka; and Rahul Sankrityayan has cogently demonstrated that this group practiced a form of Vajrayāna Buddhism.[35] The first mention of the tradition in the chronicles states that "during the reign of the King Mat-vala-sena (846–866 A.D.) a *monk* of the Vajra-parvata school went to Ceylon, and lived in the monastery of Virankura."[36] Hence, like Chinese esoterism, this early Tantric tradition too was transmitted by fully ordained Buddhist monks (*bhikṣu*).[37]

One might also consider the evidence of the Shamsher manuscript's story of Dāmodara, discussed briefly earlier. This Dāmodara, we observed, was a Brahman who undertook The Practice with Śabareśvara in charnel grounds. His earlier career is quite interesting. According to this narrative, the boy became an ascetic at eleven years old, learned Pāṇinian Sanskrit grammar and all the traditional sciences in the course of seven years. He then studies with Nāropāda (Naḍapāda). Remarkably, he does not learn esoteric Buddhism from this famous Tantric guru, but rather the Buddhist epistemological traditions (*pramāṇa*), Centrist philosophy (*madhyamaka*), and the exoteric Mahāyāna wisdom traditions (*prajñāpāramitā*). Only thereafter does he spend five years learning the mantra way (*mantranaya*) with a certain Rāgavajra, which esoteric studies are consummated under the great master Ratnākaraśānti. Eventually, after all this esoteric study, at the age of forty-six, what does he decide to do? "He then went to Vikramapura and became a fully-ordained Buddhist monk (*bhikṣu*) in the Sammatīya order under the name Maitrīgupta."[38] Only then does he travel to the charnel grounds to undertake The Practice with Śabareśvara. Clearly, the traditional authors who penned this document did not consider the antinomian Tantras—even the radical Practice—to be the preserve solely of nonmonastics. Rather, Dāmodara's ordination comes at the peak of a distinguished career, undertaken just as he sets off for a "graveyard shift" dedicated to The Practice in a charnel ground.

Tibetan esoteric literature also preserves narratives that reveal similar unstated assumptions about Tantric practitioners. Bu ston Rin chen grub, for instance, relates a story about a Bengali Brahman named Rāhulabhadra.[39] He, too, studied Sanskrit grammar as a child before taking Buddhist ordination and becoming learned in the exoteric Buddhist teachings. So successful is he in this regard that he eventually becomes abbot of the royally-endowed Vikramaśīla Monastery. He hears of Visukalpa[40] from some esoteric angels (*ḍākinī*), travels to meet him, requests and is granted initiation into the Guhyasamāja. He gets some stability in the two stages of Tantric practice, but subsequently seeks to consummate his attainment. To this end, he "conceals his monk's status" and heads off to undertake The Practice (*caryā*).[41]

In the Tantric traditions of other Indian religions, one sees the same prominence of professional renunciants among the practitioners of the later Tantric traditions. The Jaina *Jvālamālinīkalpa*, for instance, was revealed to/by a Jaina monk.[42] In the Hindu esoteric traditions, one clearly sees that these movements were spearheaded by renunciants; only later did they begin to be practiced by laypersons. For instance, the antinomian practices of the Kula traditions (and their prototype, the Yoginī cults) were originally the province of professional ascetical groups and only in later years were the practices adapted to form the Kaula tradition (*kaula*: derived from *kula*) appropriate for householder tantrikas.[43] Alexis Sanderson has noted that the "exotic ascetic observances (*vidyāvratam*, *puraścaryā*, *caryāvratam*)" found in the higher, nondualist Śaiva Tantras "disappeared from the foreground" of Kashmiri scriptural exegesis due in part to a social shift—not from householder to celibate ascetic—but *precisely the reverse.*[44] That is to say, the antinomian practices of the nondual Tantras were largely (and, perhaps, originally) the province of professional renunciants, not of laypeople.

It is important to understand in this regard that the operative distinction (in the Buddhist context, at least) is not between lay and monastic, but between professional and amateur; and these two categories do not correspond neatly. There were almost certainly lay Buddhists involved in the early nondualist traditions. However, to consider these laypeople ipso facto amateurs, not steeped in the learning and culture of Buddhism taught in the monastic institutions, is an unwarranted assumption. It is not the case that Buddhists were divided between professional, learned monastics and their lay clients: the former living in cenobitic vihāras, learned scriptures, practiced meditation, and taught; the latter living a life of family and work, occasionally (or, regularly) popping in at the monastery to give food, robes, or other necessities, but not engaging in Buddhist practices more sophisticated than that of giving (*dāna*), the paradigmatic practice of the layperson in Buddhist normative literature. This vision of the sociology of Buddhist communities does not capture the complexity of the actual situation; it is an oversimplification that reflects merely an ideal of Buddhist social relations.

Careful reading of the Buddhist scriptures themselves reveals a situation that does not quite conform to this ideal model. In her work on the Mahāyāna scripture, the *Enquiry of Ugra* (*Ugraparipṛcchā*), for instance, Jan Nattier critiques the common understanding of the term *upāsaka*, which is generally rendered "layman." As Nattier indicates (and had previously been noted by Louis de La Vallée Poussin), "an *upāsaka* is not simply a 'nonmonastic Buddhist'; rather, the term refers to a specific category consisting of lay Buddhists (one might better use the terms 'lay brother' and 'lay sister') who are particularly diligent in their Buddhist practice."[45] These lay brothers and sisters took part in the curriculum of the monastery, learning everything from the intricacies of monastic discipline to meditative techniques.[46] They were set apart too, by special religious dress: The distinctive mark of a white robe, insofar as "the wearing of white clothing in India . . . signified . . . a degree of renunciation midway between that of the householder . . . and the *saṃnyāsin*. . . . White garments are also worn by those who are renunciants but are less than fully ordained."[47]

The professional religious among Indian Buddhists were thus not restricted to those ordained under the full regimen of the monastic discipline. "These dedicated lay-Buddhists," however, "did not constitute a free-standing community, but were rather members of particular monastic organizations."[48] Many of these professionalized lay brethren attained renown as teachers in their own right. For instance, the seventh-century Chinese pilgrim Xuanzang (A.D. 602/3–664), in the report of his travels in India in search of the Dharma, describes a lay teacher named Jayasena:

> There was . . . an *upāsaka* named Jayasena. . . . He preferred to live a plain and simple life in the mountains and forests, and although he stayed in the world of illusion, his mind dwelt in the state of reality. He was learned in the subtle meanings of both Buddhist and heretical texts, being eloquent in discussion and perspicuous in his thinking. Various Śramaṇas, Brahmans, heretical and heterodox scholars, kings, ministers, elders, and wealthy and powerful people approached him to seek his instructions with full conviction. His disciples were found in six families out of ten.[49]

Here we see a clear example of a kind of professional layperson, no less steeped in the doctrines and practices than any monk: So much so that he took students from every stratum of society, including professional renunciants. This Jayasena, however, did not operate completely independently of the monasteries. Rather, he would invite monks for important religious functions and services, such as the consecration of stūpas.[50] Xuanzang, himself a monk, was a student of Jayasena for two years.[51]

Further confirmation of the synergy between lay and monastic religious professionals in Indian Buddhism is the Tantric master Naḍapāda (Nāropā). Like Jayasena, we have a pilgrim's report of a visit with this famous Indian esoteric teacher and author—this time a Tibetan pilgrim, Nag tsho Lo tsā ba Tshul khrims rgyal ba (A.D. 1011–1064), as reported by the Sa skya hierarch Grags pa rgyal mtshan.[52] Naḍapāda was a layman (at least at this time), yet we read that he was living in a monastery (*gtsug lag khang*, **vihāra*), Phullahari. On the day Nag tsho arrived, an important visitor (a regional ruler, probably one of the local patrons of the monastic institution) was coming to pay his respects to this prominent lay teacher. Given the nature of the visit, one may conclude that Naḍapāda was the leading teacher of the monastery. Nag tsho considered it a lucky break that he got to see such a famous teacher, as this public event happened to be scheduled for the day he arrived. Although a layman himself, in Naḍapāda's audience were monks such as Nag tsho (and presumably many others, because the site was a monastery). The teacher appeared with all the pomp traditionally accorded a royal teacher, was carried on a palanquin, and his head ornamented with ritual sindhur.[53] The literary evidence for this renowned master of the antinomian traditions attests to his being an extremely erudite scholar.[54] As we saw in the case of Jayasena, learned and widely respected lay teachers of this sort had been around for centuries.

Approaching this division from the other direction, there is also evidence from a number of sources that not only were there professional religious who were not ordained, there were also many who were ordained yet lived rather like householders, even within cenobitic communities. Old Karoṣṭhī documents from around the third or fourth centuries of the Christian Era, for instance, attest to monastics taking wives and mention is made of monks' children.[55] Likewise, the Mahāyāna scripture *The Enquiry of Rāṣṭrapāla* contains a prophecy that in the future there will be monks who "like householders have wives, sons, and daughters,"[56] suggesting strongly that there were indeed such monks in the early first-millennium India context of the composition of this polemical scripture. Kalhaṇa's twelfth-century poetic history of Kashmir, the *Rājataraṅginī*, speaks of the foundation of a monastery in Kashmir prior to the seventh century, which was divided into two sections, half for those monks (*bhikṣu*) who followed the precepts and the other half for householders with "wives, children, cattle and property."[57]

Thus, it should be clear that, in India of the Tantric period, whether a person was ordained as a monk or not did not necessarily correlate with keeping of the monks' vows, such as chastity. It likewise does not correlate to being or not being learned in the Buddhist teachings. Ordination status does not determine whether or not one lives in or near a monastery, or how much intercourse one has with ordained monastics. It also is no sure indication of orientation toward elite Buddhist practices: The aforementioned lay teacher Jayasena, for instance, put tremendous effort into making little clay stūpas, a practice that has been (erroneously) considered a lower, lay undertaking.[58] Yet, he also practiced meditation. Consequently, it would seem that ordination status is no measure or strong cleavage point in Indian Buddhist communities. Rather, the relevant criterion is professionalization: There were professional Buddhist priests on both sides of the lay/monastic divide, as there were amateurs, dilettantes, and idlers as well.

The authors of the antinomian traditions were nothing if not Buddhist professionals. The scriptures they revealed are composed (with some few exceptions) in standard Sanskrit, a learned language.[59] Even the "barbaric" Apabhraṃśa that is the linguistic medium for many of the transgressive Tantras was nothing more or less than a "pan-Indic koine": Like Pali, both were "learned languages and at least as dependent on the textbook as Sanskrit itself." Even more intriguing perhaps, given what we have seen earlier concerning the contrived marginality of the Tantric ethos, authors would employ Apabhraṃśa precisely "to suggest rural simplicity and joyful vulgarity."[60] Further, as noted in great detail in chapters 4 and 5, the scriptures of these traditions clearly reveal a specialized knowledge of Buddhist categories of ethics, philosophy, and cosmology such as could only have come from a learned professional.[61] We have seen how dramatically this implicit knowledge is on display in one of the earliest transgressive scriptures, the *Guhyasamāja*, as well as across a wide spectrum of later, nondualist Tantras. To take one more example, consider the following verses, from another important, early transgressive scripture, the *Union of All Buddhas*:

> Yoga is not produced in consecrated images, and the like;
> Yogins [who cultivate] the great yoga of the spirit of enlightenment are divinities due to that.
> Oneself is verily all buddhas and the very sagacity of beings.
> Hence, one should master oneself by the yoga of one's own tutelary divinity.[62]

Clearly, this passage is not an expression of illiterate, tribal rituals. Rather, one sees a literate, cultivated Buddhist author using technical terms such as *svādhidaivatāyoga* ("the yoga of one's own tutelary divinity") and *bodhicitta* ("spirit of enlightenment"). The author is stressing that the ultimate practice of Tantric Buddhism is to become a buddha oneself by finding the enlightened being within, rather than seeking communion with buddhas through mediations such as consecrated statues and the like. It should be noted that although *bodhicitta* is, of course, a general Mahāyāna Buddhist term, *svādhidaivatāyoga* is prominent in the nontransgressive Tantras, which aim to cultivate a personal, divine identity.[63]

In fact, the cultural continuities between the nontransgressive esoteric and the transgressive Tantric systems are so profound and pervasive that—although some might be surprised to hear it—the ritual regime of the Tantras is rather prosaic on the whole. Its rites involve exactly the things that the inversive (and temporary) *caryāvrata* excludes. Initiates are introduced to maṇḍalas, elaborately constructed or painted, and consecrated with rites installing the deities therein as, for instance, in the *Hevajra Tantra*:

> First, the yogin-qua-divinity should purify the site [of the ritual] . . . then draw the maṇḍala.[64]

These transgressive scriptures also enjoin intricate fire offerings involving clarified butter and numerous substances, long mantra repetitions, and other ritual accoutrements. Exemplary in this regard is the fire offering (*homa*) chapter of the transgressive *Saṃvarodaya Tantra*.[65] It gives extremely specific details on the size of the various hearths that can be used, the measure of its rim, how it is to be decorated, and what colors should be used. It describes visualizing and creating the main deity, reciting its mantra, visualizing and inviting the fire god Agni, and making offerings to him (the standard offerings of mainstream Buddhist practice: water, perfume, incense, food, music). It gives instructions on prognosticating from the appearance of the fire and the various substances to be offered, such as four types of wood, sesame seed, whole grains, curds, cooked rice, and two types of sacred grasses typically offered in orthodox fire offerings.

The central rite of these traditions is—just like the nontransgressive Tantras—the sādhana of self-creation as a divinity. The same *Saṃvarodaya Tantra* describes the rite in its thirteenth chapter.[66] The practitioner is to emanate light rays to pay homage to his guru and the buddhas, make offerings to them (flowers, etc.), take refuge, generate the spirit of enlightenment, and meditate on the four pure states. Dissolving all into voidness with the standard mantras recalling the purity of all things and one's own innate gnosis,[67] a maṇḍala universe is created, in which the main deity takes up residence in all his glory.

The rites advocated in the transgressive Tantras involve numerous mantras, visualizations of expanding and contracting light rays, divinities being called in from their heavenly homes, offering divinities emitted from the self-visualized-as-deity's heart, and similar features. From the *Guhyasamāja Tantra*:

> In the middle of [your] heart visualize the adamant of the [buddhas] of gnosis-adamant: the meditation of the meaning of the adamant mantra, situated in the center of the adamant maṇḍala. . . . Install all buddhas in

> the vicinity of all maṇḍalas; sending out five[-colored] light rays, enlightenment will be attained.[68]

Its results include such standard, Pan-Indian yogic powers as clairvoyance (to see distant pure lands), clairaudience (by which to hear teachings remotely), ability to read minds, knowledge of past lives (such as attained by the Buddha under the Bodhi Tree), and the ability to emanate numerous created bodies (*nirmāṇa*) as buddhas had long been understood to do.[69]

Like virtually all other such socio-religious formations, the antinomian traditions promise benefit and succor to the people, such as protection, power, and benefit. This was certainly nothing new to the Buddhist traditions. As Peter Skilling has observed, "Certainly, protection through recitation and ritual was—and continues to be—one of the main functions or even duties of Buddhist monastics."[70] The esoteric traditions differed only in their techniques, although even in this regard there is considerable congruence with earlier Buddhist forms. The very early Buddhist *Vaiśālīpraveśa* Mahāsūtra, for instance, features Buddha sending Ānanda into Vaiśali—then in the grip of an epidemic—to recite "*mantrapadas* and *gāthās*" which brings an end to the depredation of the disease.[71] The Mahāyāna author Asaṅga too speaks of the use of meditative absorption (*samādhi*) combined with "mantra-words (*mantrapada*) to appease the distress [*īti*: e.g., plague, drought, vermin, etc.] of beings."[72] Mantras of protection of this sort were a significant preoccupation of the Mahāyāna in general, featuring prominently in such classic scriptures as the *Laṅkāvatāra*, *Suvarṇabhāsa*, *Śūraṃgamasamādhi*, *Lotus*, and many others. A large section of Śāntideva's *Śikṣāsamuccaya*, a survey of the exoteric Mahāyāna curriculum, is dedicated to mantras of protection, which are prescribed for such things as curing diseases.[73] Likewise, the master of the *Guhyasamāja Tantra*, utilizing his own meditations and mantras, could promise to deliver for the community such services as striking fear in foes, protecting crops from rain, curing poisoning, curing diseases afflicting whole towns and villages, as well as alleviating more personal afflictions as goiter, boils, and dermatological and other diseases.[74]

Thus, it would seem that the social role of the esoteric Buddhist professional—even those practicing the transgressive traditions—was much the same as that of exoteric Buddhists, whether Śrāvaka or Mahāyāna, as well as that of esoteric Buddhists in general. Such specialization in scripture, ritual, and meditational/magical care of the community (and the Community) was very much the métier of professional

Buddhists of all stripes, enabling them to attend to the needs of both other professionals and their clients, whether royal or less-than-royal. Very much the same may be observed in contemporaneous nondualist Śaiva communities that also retained the basic social role and ritual structures of the dualist traditions they considered lower. As Alexis Sanderson has observed, the more transgressive, nondual traditions of Śaivism did not operate independently of the ritual structure of the dualist Siddhānta,

> for they are essential to their survival. This is partly because [they] draw meaning from these wider contexts as gnostic disciplines that *transcend the Tantric systems from within*. But it is also because the systems defined as lower provide these Śākta . . . Tantric adepts of sudden enlightenment with the means of operating on other levels as occasion demands and patronage expects.[75]

I think it is clear that the same is true of the nondualist Tantric systems of Indian Buddhism. These, too, "transcend the [dualist] Tantric systems from within." They do not diverge from the basic ritual structures of dualist esoterism (*maṇḍala, mantra, mudrā, homa*); they assume it. They merely claim an elite, gnostic superiority to the dualistic traditions that they flout by means of antinomian imagery and (to a certain degree) practices.

In short, all the evidence we have points to the conclusion that Vajrayāna Buddhism emerged in monastic or quasi-monastic settings, among those of significant religious and cultural learning. As we have consistently seen, such transgressions make sense only in contexts in which the corresponding prohibitions apply. Such inversions only flourish within a framing structure in which the opposite is understood. As Steven Collins has noted, for instance, renunciation is not in general the province of those with nothing to renounce.[76] Renunciation is not meaningful (nor terribly attractive) to impoverished people with nothing to give up; rather, it is the wealthy who find the idea most sensible and appealing. Similarly, despised underclasses vowing to engage in polluting activities is a failed semiosis. India of the Tantric Age would have been unimpressed by an outcaste in a loincloth, filthy and muttering mantras while he ate roadkill dog, feces and all. Such a modality of transgression is merely pathetic or disgusting. Contrariwise, famous, wealthy, or otherwise privileged persons pushing the limits of propriety and transgressing the same boundaries are objects of awe and respect. An esteemed religious figure descending into poverty and crossing over to the side of society's rejects in order to express divine insight, compassion, and selflessness—that signifies. Inversion of social strictures only makes the right kind of sense if the person inverting them is already firmly established on the "correct" side of the duality. It is no coincidence that the practitioners for whom the Śaiva *pāśupatavrata* was prescribed were pure Brahmans.[77]

CARNIVALESQUE OR RITUALS OF REBELLION?

Here one might object: Even if we accept that the Tantric esoterists knew the literature and ritual regimen of nontransgressive esoterism, surely—advocating the transgressive program that they did—the siddha leaders and their communities must have located themselves elsewhere, outside the fold of "institutional" esoterism. How could two such diametrically opposed systems have occupied the same ritual and social space without conflict? There might be some merit in this objection were it not so obviously the case that these inversions served the purpose, not of overturning the standard mainstream and esoteric Buddhist programs, but of reinforcing them. Once again, I have to differ from Davidson's interpretation in this regard. Citing Bakhtin's discussion of the carnivalesque (wherein he claims that social inversions serve a leveling, equalizing function), Davidson maintains that the "social inversion [of the siddhas and others] replaces the rules of one social strata [*sic*] with those of another."[78] That is, he portrays the siddhas as a distinct social group with a "preference for brothels and bars," who sought the ascendency of their own libertine values at the expense of "Brahmanical religion, court-sponsored Śaivism, and Buddhist monastic decorum."

In interpreting the social inversions of antinomian esoterism in this manner, however, Davidson makes two crucial errors. The first is one of observation, one that we have critiqued in detail in the preceding: The transgressive literature does not reflect a struggle of the mores of one social stratum against those of another, hegemonic one. Rather, these mores are demonstrably (and at times explicitly) inversions (*viparīta*) of an assumed social order—that of dualistic Buddhist esoterism. The second is one of interpretation. This is the more crucial error: For these inversions are not "corrosive discourses" that "eat away at the claims and pretensions of discourses and speakers who try to arrogate authority for themselves."[79] Rather, they are themselves authoritative counter-discourses, merely replacing and inverting that which it presupposes through its rejection. The process of inversion—far from eroding—actually reinforces the established order insofar as it assumes and demonstrates the authority of the former through its rejection. As Bruce Lincoln has noted:

> For all that inversion can be an effective instrument of agitation . . . dominant orders are capable of employing their own symbolic inversions. . . . To be sure it is a powerful act to turn the world upside down, but a simple 180-degree rotation is not difficult to undo. An order twice inverted is an order restored, perhaps even strengthened as a result of the exercise.[80]

A similar case is made by Roland Barthes, when he describes a semiosis common in commercial advertising, wherein inversion serves as "a kind of homeopathy" whose purpose is not to reject, but to preserve and reinforce the values challenged.[81]

One does not need to look far in Buddhism for a similar discursive inversion resulting in reinforcement of preestablished values. As noted in chapter 4, the Transcendent Virtue of Wisdom literature (*prajñāpāramitā*) is saturated with it. Indeed, this would seem to be one very important function of the very voidness doctrine on which the nondualism of the antinomian Tantras is predicated.[82] Consider the narrative arc of the dialectic of Nāgārjuna: It too begins with the rejection of the ultimate reality of every conventional Buddhist notion assumed by its (intramural Buddhist) audience. These constitute the very foundation of the entire religious system, such as moral action (*karma*), its results (*phala*), and its conditioning imprints (*saṃskāra*), suffering (*duḥkha*), liberation (*mokṣa*), even the buddha himself (*tathāgata*), and the Four Truths of the Nobles (*caturāryasatya*) that inform the entire therapeutic structure of the Buddhist path.[83] In the end, the entire Buddhist religion is reduced to mere conventional, conceptual imposition from the perspective of the ultimate reality of voidness. However, just as in Barthes' homeopathic reinforcement,[84] at the conclusion of Nāgārjuna's analysis the established order rises like a phoenix from the ashes. In fact, one is assured—far from voidness undermining the religio-ethical foundations of Buddhism—the opposite is the case: Voidness, conventionality, is the very condition of possibility of an established order. The reality of voidness, then, is said to entail the validity of bondage, liberation, karma, buddhas, the Dharma, and—perhaps most importantly in this regard—the authoritative religious Community (*saṅgha*)—precisely the order overturned by the first stage of the dialectic.

Similarly, the shocking antinomianism of the nondualist Buddhist Tantras does not represent a first order critique corrosive of the authority of the Buddhist order. Rather, these function as instances of what Max Gluckman identified as "rituals of rebellion." Such rituals involve "an instituted protest demanded by sacred tradition, which is seemingly against the established order, yet which aims to bless that order."[85] Tensions within a social system can be mitigated—ritually incorporated and mollified—through stylized enactments of the breakdown of that order. That is, counterintuitively, "to act the conflicts, whether directly or by inversion or in other symbolical form, emphasizes the social cohesion within which the conflicts exist."[86]

But, what conflict do these rites resolve? What threat to social cohesion and the stability of the cultural system did they mitigate? In my reading, the antinomian rituals in Tantric Buddhism reflect—and constitute an arena for negotiating—the central epistemic/ontological paradox at the heart of elite Buddhism. That is, throughout documented history, the Buddhist traditions have attempted to navigate what seems to most to be fundamental contradictions in their system.[87] That is, there is said to be no real self, yet there is insistence on the reality of rebirth and the consequent necessity of a rigorous ethics. There is no reality to conventional, discursive thought; yet we can rely upon reasoning to discover reality. Nirvāṇa is unconditioned, yet the path to it is conditioned. Buddhist literature is filled with discursive attempts to resolve this intrinsic tension.

The esoteric ritual systems for their part were not immune to this difficulty—quite the opposite. We have seen this tension expressed in the dualistic *Mahāvairocana Tantra* and similarly in the *Concise Consecration Ritual Tantra*.[88] Both of these scriptures raise and attempt to resolve the fundamental tension between an undifferentiated ultimate reality and the conventional or superficial (*saṃvṛti*) details of perceived reality, particularly as expressed in ritual ceremonial. An important, early chapter of the *Mahāvairocana Tantra* raises this very issue.

> Vajrapāṇi bowed to the feet of the Lord and said this to the Lord, "buddhas are without [specific, finite] attributes, residing [as they do] in the body of reality (*dharmakāya*). They teach a Dharma unequalled, uncompounded and without [specific, finite] attributes. Why, then, O Great Hero, do you teach this rite that has such attributes [as] the mantra practice?"[89]

The same concerns are raised throughout the esoteric Buddhist literature on consecration rites. If everything is already enlightened by nature, if buddhas are everywhere, why are there such detailed rituals for inviting them and installing them into images? The same issue may be observed behind the various positions taken regarding the competing models of sudden versus gradual enlightenment in mid-to-late first-millennium Indian Buddhism.[90] In such scriptures as the *Laṅkāvatāra Sūtra*, and in scholastic treatises such as Kamalaśīla's *Bhāvanākramas* or Āryadeva's *Caryāmelāpakapradīpa*, Indian Buddhists tried to give a satisfactory account of how ultimately foundationless conventional behaviors and conceptually inflected practices could result in an unconditioned, nonconceptual experience of ultimate reality. Therein one can observe various intellectual and discursive approaches by which Buddhist communities sought to resolve this paradox.

The antinomian inversions of the Buddhist Tantras represent the same conceptual tension being resolved not by discursive, conceptual means, but through ritual performance. Observance of the ritual minutiae of esoteric maṇḍala rites, fire offerings, and so forth, meant that Tantric Buddhist professionals were confronted daily with the inherent problematic of attempting to reach an ultimate nondual goal by discursive, dualistic means. These rituals are predicated upon voidness, yet appear to be anything but to officiants and their clients, replete as they are in conventional details. Incorporating a visceral reminder of nonduality and transcendence of convention into their otherwise dualistic rituals provided a means to digest performatively the anomaly of such a highly ritualized mode of Buddhist practice, so as to allow the maintenance of such a complex ceremonial without obvious self-contradiction.

Thus, much as we observed in the case of the semiology of antinomian ritual, the rebellions against the order found throughout the transgressive Tantras are intramural. They reflect cultural negotiations within the community, and were not meant to set them apart from the mainstream of society. Professionals of the sort these Tantric practitioners seem to have been rely on patronage: Rituals take time and money (sometimes quite considerable amounts of both). Whatever religious literature might say, no one meditates in wilderness regions, undertakes serious asceticism, or executes elaborate liturgical observances without a substantial subtending support system. Behind every successful practitioner (*sādhaka*) there is a ritual assistant (*uttarasādhaka*) to deal with food, water, housekeeping, and so forth. The same might be said for the extensive literature through whose practically sole testimony we know of the antinomian claims of the transgressive Tantras. Such a corpus could not have been composed, transmitted, nor preserved without a considerable institutional apparatus.

It is thus by no means the case, as has been suggested, that antinomian Tantric rituals such as the host circle (*gaṇa-cakra*) require "a commitment to a permanent liminal status in which the individual will never be reintegrated into any village anywhere."[91] As we observed in chapter 5, even the more extensive and demanding antinomian *caryāvrata* only lasted a few months. The host circle—in some respects The Practice in miniature (transgressive, albeit with generally less emphasis on the revolting)—was a one-night affair. The liminal status is entirely constructed through the semiology of antinomian ritual; and, at the conclusion of the rite, the participants disperse and return to their usual occupations. The transgressive host circle too seems to have been an elite practice,[92] performed in isolated places, with restricted admission.

BUT . . . DID THEY REALLY DO IT?!

As I suggested earlier, however, it would seem that at least the possibility of enacting these rites (even if merely tacitly accepted by the community, not actual) would be necessary for the semiology to truly work. We are brought back, then, to the question of actual observance. However, it is not at all clear how one might determine where, how often, or by whom these rites were performed. There is no secure evidence of any transgressive ritual of this type being enacted in late first-millennium India, outside the insecure testimony of normative texts. Tantric literature provides a detailed look into the ideals of these traditions, but we can unfortunately make very few claims about what actually happened in the centuries during which Indian esoteric Buddhism flourished. As Alexis Sanderson has noted, the surviving sources for the Tantric traditions

> provide no data, and we are not likely to discover any from other sources, that would enable us to judge, for example, what percentage of the population of a given region and time was involved in the practice or support of the religion, or how its followers and supporters were distributed between castes, economic classes, age-groups, genders and levels or type of involvement. In other words the texts tell us what was possible for various groups but not the extent to which these possibilities were put into practice.[93]

It is interesting, however, to observe the manner in which the issue of the actuality of the practice of the antinomian host circle ritual has been treated by modern critics of a literalist tendency. When confronting the issue of whether or not such transgressive rites were actually performed—in the absence of any contemporaneous evidence—modern scholars have often turned to the example of contemporary communities or, rather, reports of contemporary communities. David Snellgrove, for instance, substantiates his claim that these rites took place literally in India of the Tantric Age entirely by reference to a discussion in George Briggs's 1938 work on Gorakhnāth.[94] Briggs, for his part, relies on three types of evidence: translations of normative sources, the testimony of William Ward (1817) and of Edwin Aitkinson (1882–86), as well as his own "more recent inquiries."[95] The limitations of normative works has been noted earlier; and, because Briggs does not report having seen such rites himself, his "recent inquiries" presumably consist of secondhand evidence. This leaves the reports of Ward and Aitkinson as Briggs's (and, thus, Snellgrove's) critical source of evidence.

Ward does indeed give a detailed account of a host circle.[96] Notably, given our discussion, he observes that at the beginning of the rite, "the teacher . . . informs his disciple, that from henceforward he is not to indulge shame, nor dislike to any thing, nor prefer one plan to another, nor regard ceremonial cleanliness or uncleanness, nor cast[e],"[97] conforming to the classical works and our own semiotical interpretation. As noted by Briggs, Ward claims that these rites "are performed in secret; but that these practices are becoming very frequent among the bramhŭns and others, is a fact known to all."[98] However, upon inspection, Ward's evidence is clearly secondhand or, rather, thirdhand. Concerning his sources, Ward writes: "Ramŭ-nat'hŭ, the second Sŭngskritŭ pŭndit in the college, informed a friend of mine, that he once watched one of these groups unobserved, when spirits were poured on the head of a naked woman, while another drank them as they ran from her body."[99] Concerning another source, he comments, "The brahmŭn who gave me this account had procured it from a brŭmhŭcharēē, by pretending that he wished to perform these rites."[100]

Briggs's other source is Edwin Aitkinson's *Himalayan Gazetteer*, an amateur compendium of information about this region.[101] This source gives detailed information on the alleged practice of the "orgies of the left-handed sect." However, all the details in Aitkinson's account are admittedly drawn from literary works such as the *Daskarma* and are described as being "prescribed" in the normative texts. Notably, Aitkinson draws a contrast between esoteric practice in Gárhwal and that in Kumaon. In Kumaon, one is told, these orgies are "observed in secret, and none but the initiated are admitted even to the public ceremonies." In Gárhwal, on the other hand, Aitkinson reports "the more frequent public exhibition of the ceremonies there."[102] One gets the impression (much like that of Ward) that these rites are being performed all the time for all to see. However, a quick glance at the preface to the *Gazetteer* reveals that Aitkinson only ever visited Kumaon and Dehra Dun—never Garhwal.[103] Presumably, then, the information on Garhwal was reported at second- or thirdhand.

In sum, the reports of widespread (even increasing) practice of antinomian host circles in contemporary Bengal—perhaps even their very existence—turns out to be an early-nineteenth-century urban legend.[104] "Everyone knows," because everyone knows someone who knows someone who has heard it happens. Snellgrove cites Briggs; Briggs cites Ward; and Ward has it from the best of sources: A friend of a friend assures him it is so.[105] Upon this impeccably secure foundation, Snellgrove and others then assert with great confidence that this proves that these rites were performed quite literally in late first-millennium India. Given that no one reports firsthand knowledge of these rites, one may quite reasonably doubt the veracity of these accounts.

On the other hand, there does seem to be one person who did have firsthand experience of these circles: Horace Hayman Wilson, the famed Sanskrit scholar of early nineteenth-century Calcutta. Wilson makes the following, revealing observations on the practice of antinomian Tantrism in his time:

> It is contrary . . . to all knowledge of the human character, to admit the possibility of these transactions in their fullest extent; and, although the worship of the SAKTI . . . may be sometimes performed, yet there can be little doubt of its being practised but seldom, and then in solitude and secrecy. In truth, few of the ceremonies, there is reason to believe, are ever observed; and, although the *Chakra* is said to be not uncommon, and by some of the zealous *Sáktas*, it is scarcely concealed, it is usually nothing more than a convivial party, consisting of the members of a single family, or at which men only are assembled, and the company are glad to eat flesh and drink spirits, under the pretense of a religious observance.[106]

Here, Wilson is very likely responding to the somewhat hysterical assessment of the Chukra by Ward. He makes a number of important points to which contemporary scholars might attend.

First of all, Wilson makes the very simple observation that truly antinomian rites—eating offal or human fluids, engaging in rituals involving socially reviled women—are not popular undertakings for most people. Of course, a scholar of religion has always to take into account the fact that people are indeed capable of remarkable things. Nonetheless, it seems unobjectionable to state (as, indeed, the Tantric texts themselves assume) that these practices involve things that normal people avoid; and most religious practitioners are fairly normal people in this regard (although one does find notable exceptions). Were they not so objectionable and unappealing, these rites would not be doing their job insofar as they mean to express transcendence of conventional purity strictures. Wilson allows that they may, indeed, sometimes be performed as prescribed but that this would be in secrecy and rarely—both also qualities supported by the textual injunctions, yet which would entail no reportage. Ultimately, however, he notes that—insofar as anyone has actually witnessed (and reported) on them—these wild rites turn out to be nothing but a kind of family barbeque in which the less objectionable esoteric sacraments (booze and meat) are consumed with, presumably, varying degrees of professional ritual.

Of course, it is very difficult to infer from nineteenth- and twentieth-century practices what actually took place in the late first millennium. The contemporary practices may have little or nothing to do with the traditions in the earlier period, sharing little but the name. This is certainly true of much of what passes for Tantrism in contemporary Bengal.[107] However, it does seem likely, as Wilson suggests, that these rites were performed rarely and in secret. In fact, as one can clearly observe in the cases of Ward and Aitkinson, there can thereby emerge a widespread perception that such transgressions are taking place without much or any actual engagement in these activities. Such a public reputation, of course, would be enough to sustain the semiosis of the community. One suspects very much that this was (and is) largely the case with the radical Buddhist Tantras—the reality more than likely did not conform to the hype.

An objection may be anticipated here. Some may not accept the reading I have here offered of antinomian esoteric Buddhism, regardless of how much evidence from varied sources might be adduced. In so doing, one may expect to hear another story familiar to readers of Tantric studies:

That one cannot trust the surviving evidence, for the materials that have come down to us have been worked over, deodorized, or semanticized. There is one significant weakness to this line of reasoning, however: There is no direct evidence for an earlier, more primitive form of Tantrism that was domesticated for monastic consumption. All the surviving evidence comes from one or another sectarian tradition: Buddhist, Śaiva, Vaiṣṇava, or Jain. As Alexis Sanderson observed:

> The problem with [the] concept of a "religious substratum" or "common cultic stock" is that they are by their very nature entities inferred but never perceived. Whatever we perceive is always Śaiva or Buddhist, or Vaiṣṇava, or something else specific. Derivation from this hidden source cannot therefore be the preferred explanation.[108]

In a certain sense, this argument that the Tantric traditions derive from some presemiotic, nonsectarian substratum—whether aboriginal or tribal—is similar to that advanced by some traditional apologists to the effect that, even though there is no evidence for it, Tantric Buddhism must be centuries older than we think, perhaps even taught by the Buddha himself. For the traditionalist, lack of evidence is not a problem, but a confirmation: There is none because the Tantras are said to have been taught in secret. For the primordialist/literalist, too, evidence is not a problem: All the evidence for the contrary view may be said to derive from later sectarian traditions and is thus ipso facto (and a priori) tainted. In both cases, then, a lack of evidence is oddly construed as evidence for; both, too, are based upon precritical assumptions that refuse to be dislodged. Taking such a tack, however, the scholar ends up like the prurient Buddhist monk depicted in the satirical *Mattavilāsaprahasana*—determined to find the hedonistic teaching he is sure exists and asking "where are the uncorrupted root texts?"[109]

One might very well entertain the hypothesis that there was such a primitive form of Tantrism, prior to an alleged assimilation by Buddhism, Śaivism, Vaiṣṇavism, and Jainism. To accept this, however, would require that one of two conditions hold: Either (1) these traditions all conspired and were devilishly clever (and remarkably successful) in eradicating all traces of it, or (2) that historical, cultural, economic, or other circumstances conspired to eradicate all traces of it. The former, of course, is both paranoid and absurd. The latter is more cogent, insofar as these postulated preassimilated forms of Tantrism were allegedly practiced by marginal, illiterate tribals, without the skills and finances necessary to leave lasting traces such as texts, statutes, and inscriptions. Militating against this, on the other hand, is the fact that there is not even any literary evidence for these supposed traditions and their communities. The best that can be marshaled are vague and ambiguous traces such as busty Harrappan terra-cottas, sanguinary rites of tribal groups, or speculations on non-Āryan elements in the secret Tantric codes (*chommā*).

Because there is no direct evidence, scholars are then reduced to circular reasoning to establish their conclusions. Given the manner in which its proponents argue their case, this hypothesis becomes unfalsifiable and, thus, not a scientific hypothesis. Any evidence to the contrary—such as the various arguments put forth in the second part of this book—are taken as evidence of their theory. That is, any evidence that suggests significant presence of Buddhist and monastic ideals is rejected as representing later transformations and, thus, evidence for such a transformation. There are, however, no independent grounds on which to justify such a tendentious reading. Rather, what one observes is a preestablished conclusion for which the evidence is interpreted such that it is inevitably arrived at. The real, original Tantrikas must have existed—Occam's razor be damned.[110] We return then to the impasse we mentioned at the end of chapter 1: Given the axiom that all Buddhist elements are ipso facto construed as not Tantric and vice versa, the study of Buddhist Tantrism becomes impossible, because it cannot possibly exist or, if it does, it is an aberration.

The model of monastic domestication is so widespread, that even otherwise careful scholars are led to errors. One author, for instance, having claimed that the *Cakrasaṃvara Tantra* was "evidently composed at the margins of Indian society" seeks to demonstrate accordingly that the "tradition was adopted, and adapted, by Buddhist monastic communities."[111] This is substantiated, on the grounds that the earliest extant commentary, by Jayabhadra, stresses sexual practices, whereas a later commentator, Bhavabhaṭṭa—said to be the fifth Tantric preceptor of the prominent Buddhist monastery of Vikramaśīla—stresses gnosis. One is hard pressed to understand how this commentarial divergence can be attributed to the need to conform to monastic mores when the first commentator, Jayabhadra, was himself an ordained monastic official in the very same institution![112] Furthermore, Buddhist Tantric traditions do not uniformly become more conservative in monastic contexts. There are many examples in addition to Jayabhadra of monastics who were perfectly comfortable with sexual yogic rites in their practice.[113] Furthermore, the opposite may also be observed—some monastic authors may be observed to move their traditions in a more accommodating direction.[114]

That this tale of monastic bowdlerization is another example of a story we moderns like to repeat to ourselves is clear when one compares narratives related of other, contemporaneous traditions. For it is remarkable that those narrated by some scholars of Hindu Tantric traditions are structurally identical to those one sees in the Buddhist context. That is, if one replaces "Buddhist monastics" with "Brahmanic circles," one finds exactly the same rhetoric repeated: There was an originally wild and crazy, primitive tradition that got tamed by the urban, literate schools:

> Elite brahmanic circles . . . sublimated the "hard core" of Kaula [*sic*] practice into a body of ritual and meditative techniques that did not threaten the purity regulations that have always been the basis for high-caste social constructions of the self.[115]

Here one sees the same story of stodgy elites taking all the fun out of the sport of freewheeling commoners. It is noteworthy that the materials White relies upon as sources for the original Kula practices date from a period significantly after that of the alleged semanticization carried out by figures such as Abhinavagupta, whereas the truly early Śaiva Tantras are those of the dualistic (and decidedly un-sexy) Siddhānta.[116] Once again, the evidence is made to fit the theory, not the theory the evidence.[117]

Scholars have in general erred in taking the antinomian Tantric literature too seriously on its own terms and neglecting to inquire beyond the ostensive content to discern the structure of the system that provides coherence to the lived, social, second worlds of these communities.[118] By focusing on theory rather than practice or taking the discourses hyperliterally, a distorted picture emerges. Eager to make general assessments, some err in privileging vague, programmatic statements such as "liberation through desire" and "do as you like" mistaking these for reality rather than expressions of informing theoretical perspectives. As we have seen in chapter 5, such statements refer to the ideal—the transcendent attained one (*siddha*) who undertakes The Practice—not to the everyday life of Tantric practitioners and their communities of professional ritualists. Likewise, some err in taking the literary portraits of the accomplished ones (*siddha*-s) as reflecting reality—as if these people could craft and sustain these sometimes hyper-literate traditions while roaming around doing nothing but acting weird, getting wasted, and doing rude things. Rather, critical analysis of the liturgical and scriptural remains of these traditions reveals the transgressive traditions to be woven of the same cloth as conventional dualistic esoterism.

CONCLUSION

NO TWO "WAYS" ABOUT IT

The whole is a riddle, an ænigma, an inexplicable mystery. Doubt, uncertainty, suspence of judgment appear the only result of our most accurate scrutiny, concerning this subject.

—David Hume, *The Natural History of Religion*

The storyteller makes no choice; soon you will not hear his voice. His job is to shed light, not to master . . .

—Robert Hunter, "Terrapin Station"

IN THE foregoing, I have suggested a number of ways in which the methods of semiological analysis provide critical tools for advancing the scholarly study of Tantric Buddhism in India. Subjectively, scholars can gain critical distance—a more acute awareness of their own participation in dialectics of representation—through greater attention to the stock of conceptual models and narrative forms that circulate throughout the discourses that structure their fields of study. Objectively, analysis of the rhetorical patterns evident across the corpus of Tantric Buddhist scripture and ritual reveals an informing semiotical structure to the transgressions characteristic of the later Tantras, suggesting in turn a revised appraisal of their cultural meaning(s) and social context(s).

Heretofore, etiological and narrative historiography—both recapitulating stock tropes of the modern historical imagination—have served as guides to interpretation of Tantric transgression by suggesting a social context within which to construe the meaning of such discourses and practices. The effect of this mode of cultural analysis has not been to open up new lines of inquiry, challenging scholarship to expand and refine its understandings. Rather it has been to foreclose the very necessity of further investigation. By defining an essential character of Tantric Buddhism and/or locating it in familiar narratives—situating it as something already known—these models have provided the illusion of an already successful interpretation. More critically, however, by identifying the origins of these cultural forms in physical impulses or primitive thought—thereby suggesting that they lack a fully formed semiological dimension—such historiography cum hermeneutics has inhibited students of religion from inquiring more deeply into the social meaning(s) of transgression. Viewed from such a perspective, the familiar forms taken by modern histories of Tantric Buddhism seem strange, and rightly so: They are precisely examples of modern scholarly myth—"ideology in narrative form."[1]

Setting aside these well-worn recitations, and looking with new eyes attentive to cultural relations, it quickly becomes clear that the discourses of Tantric Buddhism and their associated practices do in fact make sense and are, in fact, very much continuous with practices and doctrines across the contemporaneous Indian cultural landscape. Although culturally other, viewed semiologically, Tantric Buddhism does not seem so strange after all. In its rhetorical aspect, esoteric Buddhist historiography is not so radically different from modern historiography. It, too, makes sense of an unknown object by locating it as something known and constructs an ideal subjectivity and an associated valuation with regard to its object. So, too, for all its ostensive talk of divine beings and visionary revelations—seeming mystical nonsense—esoteric Buddhist historiography is part and parcel of a Pan-Indian intellectual practice aimed at synthesizing and consensually authorizing specialized systems of knowledge and practice (*śāstra*).

Likewise, ritual consumption of repulsive ambrosias begins to appear less like the ravings of madmen and even to evince a certain logical sense. This is not the half sense of primitive tribal rituals, or of a vague system of transgressive sacrality, but a robust, culturally nuanced, and elaborated network of signification that ritually crystallizes, communicates, and reinforces a core value of these communities. Tantric literature expresses this value consistently, through the medium of narrative and in the rituals they describe. Close attention to the discursive structures of Tantric literature similarly provides greater purchase on the actual structures of practice in these communities. This, in turn, allows one to begin to make sense of Mitra's quandary: Transgression was not, in fact, required of everyone involved in Tantric Buddhism any more than monastic ordination or meditative retreats were required of exoteric Buddhists. In both contexts, these elite options exist as informing ideals that reflect and reinforce the values of the community. They need only the horizon of possible enactment—occasionally by a virtuoso or even just rumors of the same—to sustain the community's sense of corporate identity.

Applying these methods to the available evidence, an entirely different picture emerges of the Tantric Buddhist communities. Unlike previous models, my interpretation suggests communities deeply integrated into the intellectual, institutional, and social structure of prior Buddhist traditions. Thus, although the nondualist literature is wont to contrast the Tantric Vajrayāna with the exoteric Mahāyāna as two distinct ways (*yāna*) to pursue enlightenment, the distinction is largely rhetorical, reflecting ideology not sociology. These constructs did not represent two separate factions, but rather a negotiation intramural to one encompassing tradition.

The fundamental re-visioning of Tantric Buddhism suggested here may seem to some counterintuitive, requiring too fundamental a realignment to seem plausible in light of nearly two centuries of prior scholarly consensus. It may be reassuring, therefore, to reflect that scholarship on the exoteric Mahāyāna traditions has itself undergone a very similar, fundamental restructuring in recent decades. For much of the history of modern scholarship, a similar story was told of the relationship of two other ways—the Mahāyāna and the Hīnayāna. Mahāyāna too distinguished itself against what it argued was a lesser tradition. The Mahāyāna, scholars asserted, emerged as a radical challenge: In its case, a rejection of the institutional monasticism of the various Buddhist schools (*nikāya*-s). It too was said to be sociologically distinct, developing in geographically separate locations (stūpa sites, rather than monasteries) with a distinct clientele (laypeople, not monks).[2] It also was periodically attributed to "foreign, especially Persian, influence,"[3] and featured culture heroes depicted as mavericks living on the fringes of society, in forest hermitages, and other marginal places.

So, as well, was this myth of two radically divergent ways "no more than an assertion propped up by repetition,"[4] and is likewise belied by the available evidence. As the work of numerous scholars has established, the evidence suggests that the Mahāyāna did not practically challenge the core ideology of the Śrāvaka traditions. Rather, it accepted it wholesale, merely claiming to go beyond it, transcending it from within. Likewise, there is substantial evidence that the same institutional foundations in India supported both Śrāvaka and Mahāyāna monks; and these "bodhisattvas" were indeed largely monks—as Jan Nattier has put it, "a few good men."[5] So, as well, were these communities that—although they revered the figure of the lone saint meditating in the wilderness—were not likely (or predominantly) products of the contexts they thus idealized.

Consequently, in researching the Tantric Buddhist traditions, I have often found myself confronting the same challenge faced (until very recently) by scholars of the exoteric Mahāyāna. That is, as Peter Skilling lamented, "I have dutifully consulted the secondary literature, but usually find it to be at variance with the texts."[6] The article in which Skilling makes this comment summarizes the newly revised consensus that has emerged from recent, more rhetorically sophisticated research into the history and literature of the early Mahāyāna. In so doing, Skilling identifies ten key points on which—much as I have claimed with regard to prior scholarship on Tantric Buddhism—one finds that "modern misconceptions . . . are projections of Western preconceptions and preoccupations, and have no foundation in Buddhist thought itself." Of Skilling's ten points, five are worth stressing as examples in which similar distortions have become entrenched as well in the modern interpretation of Tantric Buddhism:[7]

(1) Just as in the case of the Mahāyāna, Tantric Buddhism was not "a concession to lay needs . . . all [were] obliged to address the needs of both lay-people and monastics."

We have observed that the social function of Tantric siddhas was essentially identical to that of the priests of both Śrāvaka and Mahāyāna Buddhism. All engaged in some form of protective rite on behalf of their clients, promising relief from sickness, drought, and similar afflictions. These rites all involved some form of recitation of words considered powerful (*mantrapada*). All participated in cults of images, including consecration and worship of the same with the aim of deriving worldly and transcendental benefits therefrom. In all these contexts, professionals both lay and ordained participated in conducting rituals and other forms of community outreach in exchange for patronage. Buddhism of whatever stripe, it bears remembering, rarely—if ever—consisted solely of "strict ethico-religious practices." As La Vallée Poussin reminded us, "Indian Buddhists were willingly idolatrous, superstitious or metaphysicians."[8]

(2) Tantric Buddhism is likewise "not morally lax. . . . On the contrary, many of its [scriptures] advocate a rigorous morality, often a strict ascetic life in the forest."

The Tantric literature reflects a community of practitioners bound by a common ritual repertoire, calendar, cosmology, and soteriological ideal. These were professionals engaged in a complex cultural tradition; and that tradition was committed to a rigorous discipline. Tantric rituals of rebellion—far from undermining—precisely rearticulate and reinforce the tacit, communitywide acceptance of a common ethical commitment.

(3) Just as the Mahāyāna did not reject the texts or practices of the Śrāvaka Buddhist traditions, the Tantric movements too "cannot be understood without a thorough grounding" in the literature of the earlier dispensations.

As we have outlined in some detail here, the semiological inversions of the Tantras reveal a detailed knowledge of Śrāvaka and Mahāyāna Buddhism. The ritual forms, the benefits desired, and the informing ideologies derive from and are by no means in conflict with these earlier forms of Buddhist practice that they seek to "transcend from within."

(4) For, in fact, Tantric Buddhism was "not a religion, church, or sect. In India it had no independent institutional existence. It was dependent on the monasteries and nunneries of the eighteen schools."

Attentive reading of the historical record suggests that many if not most of the leading lights of the transgressive Tantric communities were fully ordained Buddhist monks. What laymen were involved likewise appear to be accomplished professionals, learned in the knowledge systems transmitted in Buddhist institutions and generally affiliated with monasteries for ritual and patronage purposes. The transgressive "revolution" of nondual Buddhist Tantrism was, like many before it, intramural.

In addition to these specific points, there is one final general point of similarity that is worth stressing: An injunction of crucial importance not only to research on Tantric Buddhism, but to the study of religion and culture as a whole. That is,

(5) "We should never lose sight of its diversity."

Tantric Buddhism existed throughout India over the course of five centuries and was no doubt practiced and/or patronized by a wide range of people: People of differing regional cultures and languages, different social strata, various degrees of wealth, a variety of locations relative to political power, and including a wide range of levels of education and personal quality. Tantric Buddhism, as all historical movements, has been ambi- or polyvalent: like the individuals involved, complex. In what I have presented here, I have been concerned to discern and articulate a common thread of signification evident across a wide range of documents considered most important by these communities. As a consequence, this volume has not addressed the complexity of the many local variant forms Tantric Buddhism has taken historically and geographically.

These reflections, therefore, are not meant to be definitive or exclusive. I do not claim that the synchronic interpretation I have advanced is adequate to describe each and every instance of transgression in Tantric Buddhism. Rather, these excurses are meant as a methodological corrective to what I consider a premature calcification of the rhetorics and methods used to make sense of these traditions and a constructive attempt to sketch out a new approach to their interpretation. The methods applied herein do not pretend to reveal what is—or should be—the only possible form of transgressive discourse, practice, and community in Indian esoteric Buddhism. Significant work remains to be done to refine and nuance scholarly understanding in this field. There is, and can be, no master narrative.

The interpretation I have advanced, however, does have the simple virtue of being based clearly and unambiguously upon evidence. It works from concrete documents, applies clear principles of method, and consequently comes to conclusions about the nature of the traditions that produced them and the communities that considered them authoritative. It may very well be that this approach fails to address certain marginal groups that did not leave traces behind in the historical record; However, as Veyne has observed, "one cannot write the history of events of which there remains no trace."[9] Whatever transgressive Tantric discourses or practices may have existed in late first- and early second-millennium India, we can only come to know (and can only responsibly speak about) those for which we have evidence: Scholarly speculation should be constrained, that is, by the surviving textual sources. I believe the account given here to represent a cogent interpretation of the semiology of these documents, the system of meanings shared among Tantric Buddhist communities in India. It has been said that the objects of historical research are "things that would be as banal as our lives if they were not different."[10] Herein, then, one may perhaps find the real history of the Tantric tradition: In a culture constitutively semanticized and even socially conservative; in a word, banal.

APPENDIX I: THE INDRABHŪTI STORY ACCORDING TO PAD MA DKAR PO (CA. 1575)[1]

WHEN THE Lord was staying in Varaṇāsi, in the land of Oḍḍiyāna five hundred *yojanas* to the west, there was a king named Indrabhūti. When he was ascending his palace made of seven precious jewels, he saw communities of śrāvakas in the sky, going west in the morning and returning east in the evening. He asked his minister Candrabhadra, who replied, "some say they are gods. I've never asked; I'll ask someone else." When the wise minister and others asked the townspeople, some said, "five hundred yojanas east of here there is a town called Varaṇāsi. There, the son of King Śuddhodhana, the crown prince Sarvārthasiddha, has become enlightened and resides, turning the wheel of Dharma. They are his retinue."

Then, having heard the name "Buddha," the King became [filled with] especial faith, thinking, "if even his retinue has that kind of miraculous power, He must certainly have miraculous power and great compassion." Placing one knee on the ground and facing east, he folded his hands [in supplication] holding a flower and prayed out loud, "Omniscient, Compassionate, Wielder of Miraculous Powers, come here tomorrow with your retinue [that I might offer you] your noontime meal."

The Lord came there the next day with his retinue. The king with his retinue proffered many offerings, asking "please teach us and those like us a method for liberation from the suffering of the life-cycle."

The Lord, knowing [his mind], said "go forth from home to homelessness and there is a way."

The king, again making offerings, replied, "since passionate beings like us cannot renounce the five objects of sense desire, please teach a method for liberation in which one doesn't renounce those."

The Lord there contracted his passionless appearance and in the form of a universal emperor emanated the thirty-two deity maṇḍala of Guhyasamāja Akṣobhya. He initiated the king and his retinue, taught them the Tantra, and entrusted it to them. The king, understanding its meaning, created a palace of seven precious jewels, in which they were arrayed thus: In the place of the chief [deity], the king himself; in the place of the four buddhas and the four mothers, his sons and queens; in the place of the heroes and heroines, the ministers; in the place of the wrathful ones, the servants. They performed the Great Practice with elaboration[2] that takes defilement as the path until they achieved [the result]. Shedding their impure bodies like a snake sheds its skin, they attained bodies marked with the colors of the rainbow, and they traveled from buddhafield to buddhafield in order to perfect the communion beyond learning.

Hence, the land of Oḍḍiyāna became emptied and in the south a lake grew. The land became filled with many nāgas. Then, Vajrapāṇi wrote the Tantras such as the *Guhyasamāja* in a book of gold with melted sapphire ink. Ripening the nāgas of the lake [through initiation], he explained the Tantra and entrusted the volume to them. Then, most of them became human and lived in a town on the shores of the lake. By practicing the points of Method Tantra [such as the Guhyasamāja], most attained the common and supreme powers. Their sons became yogins and their daughers ḍākinīs. Henceforth, and still today, [the land] is called Glorious Orgyan, Land of the Ḍākas.

The other nāgas, perceiving the smell of the humans, went to another lake. Then, at some point, the lake dried up and there emerged an exquisite, self-created chapel of Glorious Heruka. In its treasury were the volumes of the Tantra.

APPENDIX II: CHAPTER NINE OF THE *BUDDHAKAPĀLA TANTRA*, THE "PRACTICE" (*CARYĀPAṬALA*)

Now, henceforth I will explain
The "Practice Chapter," which is extremely rare.
The yogin always performs the practices
With an extremely good woman. 1.

One endowed with the eight powers (*siddhi*)
May then undertake the practices.
Whatever powers beings desire
Those [powers] it always grants. 2.

Taking a skull-bowl in hand
The performer of the observance (*vratin*)
Wanders, [performing the] practices (*caryā*),
Naked, hair loose, everywhere at all times.
Thus should the practices be performed. 3.

Free of all ornamentation,
Like space,
Without doubt, the wise one wanders
From house to house [begging] for food. 4.

All must be considered as pleasing to the mind.
[This is] without a doubt the very foundation of meditation.
Whenever the yogin requests alms,
He regards it with a delighted mind. 5.

[If the donor says] "no," [the yogin] gives the empty state.[1]
[If the donor says] "sure," [the yogin gives] meditation.
[If the donor says] "go," [the yogin gives] the unexcelled gnosis.
That is called the Great Seal. 6.

Merely hearing "quit," the yogin devoted to the Dharma
Should eat [whatever] substance [is] placed in[2] the skull-bowl.
Immediately upon eating the substance,
The wise one falls asleep. 7.

In the house, in the yard, on a heap of ashes, at the foot of a tree,
Wherever, whenever, there and then,
Whoever with a delighted mind,
Performs this sort of practice-yoga (*caryāyoga*)
Will certainly attain the Great Seal (*mahāmudrā*). 8

As is said in the Tantra:

However, wherever, and by whatever, [one] becomes a buddha.
Whatever objects[3] are experienced, all are pure by nature.

Of the *Buddha Skull Tantra*, the Unexcelled Secret of Secrets of the Yoginīs: Chapter the Ninth, on the Practice.

NOTES

INTRODUCTION

1. *Saṃpuṭodbhavasarvatantranidānamahākalparāja*, unpublished Sanskrit MS, Tokyo University Library, new catalog nr. 428 (old nr. 319), f. 38b[4–5].
2. Mitra, *Sanskrit Buddhist Literature,* 257–260.
3. Henri Bergson likewise asked, in more general terms, how "beliefs and practices which are anything but reasonable could have been, and still are, accepted by reasonable beings" (H. Bergson, *Two Sources of Morality and Religion*, 103; cited in Evans-Pritchard, *Theories of Primitive Religion*, 15).
4. See Austin, *How to Do Things with Words.* Even though limited in its scope, Austin's work is extremely useful for thinking through the semiotics of ritual and ritual systems, in particular his discussion of what he calls the "performative" aspects of verbal expression.
5. In a sense, this last point is just basic philology. Yet, however thorough and unremarkable this practice may be in the more limited and highly professionalized field of textual editing, I fear it is rather underutilized in the higher order practice of textual interpretation.
6. Said, *Orientalism*, 5.
7. See Said, *Orientalism*, 94. One need not necessarily agree with Said's assessment that all knowledge of India is "somehow tinged and impressed with, violated by, the gross political fact" of European colonialism (and later American Coca-Colonialism), to recognize that scholarly discourses tend to replicate themselves.
8. Bloch, *Historian's Craft*, 10.
9. "For History not to signify, discourse must be confined to a pure, unstructured series of notations"; Barthes, "The Discourse of History," 15.
10. Barthes, "The Discourse of History," 16.
11. Nietzsche, "On Truth and Lies in a Nonmoral Sense," 84.
12. R. Inden, *Imagining India*, 38–39.
13. See F. de Saussure, *Course in General Linguistics*, "Introduction, Chapter III, §3 Languages and their Place in Human Affairs."

14. Barthes, "Structural Analysis of Narratives," in *Image-Music-Text*, 80.
15. Barthes draws this distinction, of course, from F. de Saussure; see *Course in General Linguistics*, 13–14.
16. Collingwood, *The Idea of History*, 1.
17. This term was coined by Andrew Tuck in his *Comparative Philosophy and the Philosophy of Scholarship* (see esp. 8–10 and 16), referring to the "reading into" texts that is the unavoidable correlate of the "reading out" of exegesis.
18. One recent critique of modern discourses on Tantra, for instance, has suggested a solution

> not unlike what Michael Taussig has called "mimetic excess"—his own attempt to resolve the intense conflicts and contradictions raised by anthropology in a postcolonial context. Mimetic excess is the acute reflexive awareness of the mimesis that is at work in all cross-cultural representation—"an excess creating reflexive awareness as to the mimetic faculty."

The problem with this formulation is that it contains little substantive content and the subsequent unpacking of this vague proposal is similarly unilluminating: "This means both that we must be extremely self-critical, ever aware of the potentially destructive effects of our representations of others, and that we must be always open to the creation of new ways to represent both others and ourselves" (Urban, *Tantra*, 280). This approach strikes me as either essentially contentless or, at best, utopian. Self-criticism here is reduced to remaining aware that our representations have effects (sometimes negative) in the world. Surely, most scholars are aware of that, even value it, insofar as it implies that their work is not without consequence. So what, then, exactly is the method recommended? That the scholar remain open to new modes of representation? Yet, how exactly is one to cultivate such openness? Does one do so through a particular mode of textual analysis? Through psychotherapy? Empathy?

19. Indeed, a large part of modern philosophy has been devoted precisely to the pursuit of such an ideal epistemic position, with limited success.
20. *Oxford English Dictionary*, second edition, s.v. *esoteric*.
21. Michel Strickmann has identified some remarkable documents in Chinese that attest to an initiatory ritual structure as early as the fifth century of the Christian era. See *Mantras et Mandarins*.
22. H. White, *Metahistory*, 22.

1. ORIGINS, RELIGION, AND THE ORIGINS OF TANTRISM

1. Durkheim, *Elementary Forms*, 15.
2. "Le Tantrisme bouddhique, ses charactères, ses origines," section heading in *Bouddhisme: études et Materieaux*, 130.
3. Article entitled "Die Entstehung des Vajrayāna."

4. It should be observed there that I do not treat three other prominent theories of origination of esoteric Buddhist traditions: (1) the theory that they are derived from the Vedas (in particular the *Atharvaveda*), (2) the theory that they may be traced to a drive by Buddhist communities to address larger, less educated populations (the "popularization" thesis), and (3) the theory that esoteric Buddhism is, in essence, a reaction to the political context of "medieval samānta feudalism" of mid-first-millennium India. I set aside all of these models in what follows insofar as they are theories of the origins of the ritual forms of dualistic esoteric Buddhism, rather than of the transgressive forms of Tantric Buddhism that are the subject of this book.

   I nonetheless believe that there are fatal problems with each of these theories as well. The theory of the Vedic origins of the Tantras has rightly fallen into desuetude. If shared religious ideas are a criterion for a tradition having its origins in the Vedas, one would be hard pressed to find any Indian religious formation that does not. Even the contrarian Carvākas articulate their atheism in Brahmanical terms. Likewise, the view that the esoteric traditions represent an accommodation to the popular masses by introducing magic and worldly spells to Buddhism is (like the "degenerate monks" theory noted in this chapter) a creation of scholarly speculation and is based upon a number of problematical assumptions about the nature and sociology of religion: a classical expression of what has been identified as "Protestant presuppositions" in the study of Buddhism (Schopen, "Protestant Presuppositions"). Finally, while scholars such as Ronald Davidson (*Indian Esoteric Buddhism*) have indicated quite clearly the consonance between the language of Buddhist esoterism and that of contemporaneous Indian politics, this does not constitute an adequate account of its origins, but merely a description of its nomenclature. As Evans-Pritchard observed in 1965, "it is true, of course, that . . . the experience of social relations must furnish a model for [religious] conceptions," but he further cautions that that this may "account for the conceptual forms taken by religion, but not for its origin, its function, or its meaning" (*Theories of Primitive Religion*, 77).
5. Bhattacharyya, *Sādhanamālā*, xxviii.
6. Bhattacharyya, "Tāntrika Culture Among the Buddhists," 88.
7. Bhattacharyya, *Sādhanamālā*, xxix.
8. Bhattacharyya, *Introduction to Buddhist Esoterism*, 23.
9. Bhattacharyya, *Introduction to Buddhist Esoterism*, 32.
10. Bhattacharyya, *Introduction to Buddhist Esoterism*, 24.
11. Bhattacharyya, *Introduction to Buddhist Esoterism*, 15.
12. Bhattacharyya, *Introduction to Buddhist Esoterism*, 24–25. Chapters 4 and 5 will explore the ways something quite different is revealed to the less-than-casual reader.
13. Bhattacharyya, *Introduction to Buddhist Esoterism*, 24.
14. Kramrisch, "Pāla and Sena Sculpture," 112.
15. Thomas, *History of Buddhist Thought*, 245–246.
16. Meisezahl, "Amoghapāśahṛdayadhāraṇī," 266–267.

17. Bareau, "Le Tantrisme," 200: "Les origines du mouvement tantrique remontent assez loin dans le temps et semblent liées à de vielles croyances magiques et religieuses, demeurées vivantes dans l'Inde comme ailleurs."
18. Van Gulik, *Hayagrīva*, 4.
19. Chakravarti, "Antiquity of Tāntricism," 114.
20. Shaw, *Passionate Enlightenment*, 21.
21. Samuel, *Civilized Shamans*, 410.
22. See Davidson, *Indian Esoteric Buddhism*, 211–214.
23. The first to put forward this view was John Marshall, Director of the Archaeological Survey of India. As A. L. Basham (*Wonder That Was India*, 23) has noted, "the most striking deity of the Harappā culture is the horned god of the seals. He is depicted . . . seated . . . with the legs drawn up close to the body and the two heels touching. . . . The god's body is nude . . . he wears a peculiar head-dress, consisting of a pair of horns . . . with a plant-like growth between them. . . . [H]e is surrounded by four wild animals. . . . The animals, the plant-like growth from his head, and the fact that he is ithyphallic, indicate that he was a fertility god. . . . Marshall boldly called this god Proto-Śiva, and the name has been generally accepted; certainly the horned god has much in common with the Śiva of later Hinduism, who is, in his most important aspect, a fertility deity, is known as Paśupati, the Lord of Beasts." Doris Srinivasan ("Unhinging Śiva") has explored this question in detail and demonstrated definitively that there is no cogent evidence or argument to establish Śiva's origin in the Indus civilization.
24. E. Burnouf, *Introduction*, 549: "Ce sont donc des Buddhistes qui tout en gardent leurs croyances et leur philosophie, consentent à pratiquer certains rites çivaïtes qui leur promettent le bonheur en ce monde."
25. H. H. Wilson, "Notice of Three Tracts Received from Nepal," 451.
26. L. de La Vallée Poussin, "Tāntrism (Buddhist)," 193.
27. D. Snellgrove, *Indo-Tibetan Buddhism* I, 147–152.
28. A. Sanderson, "The Śaiva Age," 128.
29. Though (as Evans-Pritchard said of similar etiologies in the study of primitive religions), "I suppose, it could be claimed to be psychologically, or virtually, true in the sense that a myth may be said to be true in spite of being literally and historically unacceptable." See E. E. Evans-Pritchard, *Theories of Primitive Religions*, 42.
30. For an example, see R. Davidson, *Indian Esoteric Buddhism*, 242.
31. A. Wayman, *The Buddhist Tantras*, 6.
32. See R. Davidson, *Indian Esoteric Buddhism*, 242. This argument is predicated on the evidence of the farce play, the *Mattavilāsaprahasana*, wherein (as Davidson tells it) a Buddhist monk character laments "that the elders were hiding the real scriptures wherein the Buddha extolled the benefits of drinking wine and making love to nubile women." Davidson concludes, "if the seventh-century monk could not find the scriptures that he suspected his superiors had kept from him, by the eighth century siddhas had successfully located the holy texts through the act of composition."

33. A recent (2002) example, however, may be found in M. C. Joshi, "Historical and Iconographic Aspects of Śākta Tantrism."
34. "There is no archaeological evidence to support claims of special sexually oriented aspects of Harappan religion," Dales's "Sex and Stone," cited in D. Srinivasan, "Unhinging Śiva," 87.
35. See Chakravarty quote, 21–22.
36. C. von Fürer-Haimendorf, "Les Religions Archaïques," 279: "persisté dans une organisation économique et sociale qui, ailleurs, était tombée en désuétude dès la fin de l'ère néolithique." Von Fürer-Haimendorf here clearly commits the error, common among less recent anthropology, of projecting less technologically-advanced societies of the present into an imagined past. The methodological difficulties of such a move (suggested already quite early by Max Müller) are discussed in, for example, J. Fabian, *Time and the Other.*
37. G. Samuel, *Tantric Revisionings*, 86 and 90n14. A similar case is made by Poornima Paidipaty in her 2009 Columbia dissertation, "Tribal Nation: Politics and the Making of Modern Anthropology in India."
38. K. Suresh Singh, "Study in State-Formation," 319–320.
39. B. C. Law notes that, based on numismatic evidence, the Śibis "formed a gaṇarāṣṭra or some sort of a republican state" (*Tribes in Ancient India*, 83).
40. R. S. Sharma, "Material Milieu," 179.
41. K. Suresh Singh, "Study in State-Formation," 317–318.
42. V. Jha, "From Tribe to Untouchable," 69–70; the sources for these three observations are the *Aitareya Brāhmaṇa*, the *Śrautasūtras* of Āpastamba, Kātyāyana, and Varaha, and the *Mānava Śrautasūtra*, respectively.
43. Padmavajra, *Guhyasiddhi*, VIII.11–16; cited in A. Sanderson, "History Through Textual Criticism," 6n3.
44. A. Sanderson, "Śaiva Religion among the Khmers," 361.
45. In general, discourse on "tribes" in India (especially during the period before A.D. 1000) is incoherent and rife with speculation. Consider that B. C. Law's work on *Tribes of Ancient India* includes discussion of such groups as the Licchavis, Cōḷas, Keralas, Śākyas (!), Videhas, etc.—groups that were well-known to have a high degree of cultural, political, and economic development from as far back as we have concrete evidence; and thus do not conform to the accepted anthropological understanding of a "tribe": that is, "a whole society, with a high degree of self-sufficiency at a near subsistence level, based on a relatively simple technology without writing or literature, politically autonomous and with its own distinctive language, culture, and sense of identity, tribal religion being also coterminous with tribal society" (see A. Southall, "The Illusion of Tribe," 28). Furthermore, what little literary, epigraphic, and numismatic evidence we have for the allegedly "primitive" tribes all derives from the same handful of sources, which tend to lump them all together and tar them with the same brush in broad generalities, indicating that these terms—referring notably to groups of remarkably wide geographical dispersion—were merely derogatory epithets, much like the American expression "nigger." Consider the following "ethnographic" description of the Bhils by Sir

Michael O'Dwyer (cited in L. A. Krishna Iyer and L. K. Bala Ratnam, *Anthropology in India*, 53): "a black man but more hairy. When he meets you in his jungle, he shoots you in the back with an arrow and throws your body into the ditch. Thus you may know the Bhil." It seems clear that the authors of the literary sources from the late first-millennium had similarly sensitive and nuanced understandings of their "tribal" compatriots.

46. R.S. Sharma, "Material Milieu," 181.
47. R. S. Sharma, "Material Milieu," 183.
48. N. R. Bhatt, ed., *Mataṅgapārameśvarāgama*, xxiv: "C'est là l'explication du nom de ce traité qui a été '(emis) par Parameśvara (et transmis finalement à) Mataṅga."
49. N. R. Bhatt, ed., *Mataṅgapārameśvarāgama*, 6–8. Likewise, the figure Śabarī, who plays a very minor role in Valmīki's *Rāmāyana*, is therein described merely as "an ascetic named Śabarī" (*śramaṇī śabarī nāma*), as an accomplished one (*siddhā*), and as an ascetic established in a religious observance (*śramaṇīṃ saṃsthitavratāṃ*). See *Rāmāyaṇa* III.69.19c, and III.70.6a and 7b. Intriguingly, this character is considered to be a grand-disciple of a sage named Mataṅga. Lutgendorf ("Dining Out," 120–124) draws attention to the absence of tribal association with this character in Valmīki, but attributes its lack to omission based on a "Brahmanical agenda." However, it seems more likely instead that the much later, second-millennium versions *created* a notion of her "tribalism" based upon her name.
50. R. Shafer, *Ethnography of Ancient India*, 142.
51. Semiologically speaking, this would seem somewhat akin to the opinion some contemporary rural Americans have of New Yorkers: They are of suspicious character religiously and socially, due in part to the presumed miscegenation that takes place in such metropolitan areas.
52. *Kulārṇava Tantra*, VII.42, 215.
53. Many thanks to Richard Salomon, who first suggested this reading to me, and Yigal Bronner and Wendy Doniger, who helped me think through the various readings.
54. R. Davidson, *Indian Esoteric Buddhism*, 226.
55. These are GST XII.2, PU 107; and *Kṛṣṇayamāri Tantra* XI.9.
56. R. Davidson, *Indian Esoteric Buddhism*, 169.
57. Monier Williams, *Sanskrit-English Dictionary*, 11: "'place to roam in,' forest;" Apte, *Practical Sanskrit-English Dictionary*, 36: "a forest, wood." In Shafer's *Ethnography* (see 117), all the ethnonyms that contain *aṭavī* are compounds such as *aṭavī-śabara*, *-śikhara*, *-śivira*, etc.; i.e., "wilderness" is added on as a qualifier to other quasi-ethnonyms ("hunter/gatherer"). While derivatives of *aṭavī* do occur in Kauṭilya's *Arthaśāstra* in reference to polities on the periphery of the ruler's domains that are considered less civilized, there is no trace of this usage in these passages or elsewhere in the Tantric literature.
58. GST XII.2: mahāṭavī-pradeśeṣu phala-puṣpādy-alaṃkṛte | parvate vijane sādhyaṃ sarva-siddhi-samuccayam |.
59. Other instances could be attested wherein this term has no "tribal" referent. For instance, the term appears in *Guhyasiddhi* VIII.17 which (again) deals with sites at

which the special *caryā* is to be practiced (see chapter five). It reads, "[Practice] on mountains, at the seashore, in a country free of faults, in great forested regions, in a town, or in old caves" (parvateṣu samudrānte rāṣṭre doṣavivarjite | mahāṭavīpradeśeṣu nagare jīrṇaguhāsu ca ||). The following line corresponds to the *Pradīpoddyotana*, recommending those places that are "strewn with clear waters" (*svacchodakasamākīrṇa*) and "beautified by fruits [and] trees (or, 'fruit-bearing trees')" (*phalavṛkṣopaśobhita*). See S. Rinpoche and V. Dwivedi, eds., *Guhyādi-aṣṭasiddhi-saṅgraha*, 54.

60. A. Geden, "Tantras," 193. This article in the influential *Encyclopedia of Religion and Ethics* notes as well that Tantric rites "belong to a type of thought that is primitive and among primitive peoples varies little in the course of the centuries."
61. H.P. Shastri, "Introduction," 10: "Tantra came from outside India. Most likely it came with Magi priests of the Scythians."
62. See, for example, P. C. Bagchi, "On Foreign Element in the Tantra."
63. L. de La Vallée Poussin, *Bouddhisme: études et Materiaux* (1898), 6: "On regarde d'habitude le Tantrisme idolâtrique et superstitieux comme 'n'étant plus du Bouddhisme'; on oublie que le Bouddhisme n'est pas séparable des bouddhistes, et que les Hindous bouddhistes étaient volontiers idolâtres, superstitieux ou métaphysiciens."
64. See A. Sanderson, "The Śaiva Age."
65. Arguments to this effect may be found in chapter five.
66. See chapter five for evidence of Buddhist influence on Śaiva Tantrism and consideration of their mutual conditioning; cf. R. Davidson, *Indian Esoteric Buddhism*, 202–206, and D. Lorenzen, *Kāpālikas and Kālāmukhas*, 4.
67. H. Rodrigues, *Introducing Hinduism*, 257–258. These points, that "Tantra derives mostly from the non-Vedic religious traditions of the Indian subcontinent, and may date back to the period of the Indus Valley Civilization," and that the "Buddhist Tantras appear to have Hindu, especially Śaiva, origins," are subsequently repeated in a bullet list of "Key points in this chapter" (268).
68. E. J. Sharpe, *Comparative Religion*, 95.
69. I take this to be the import of Harrison's use of the French term *origines* here. Compare contemporary Anglophone usage of, e.g., *imaginaire* and *habitus*.
70. Cf. J. J. Bachofen, *Myth, Religion, and Mother Right*, 75: "It is the origins which determine the subsequent development, which define its character and direction. Without knowledge of its origins, the science of history can come to no conclusion."
71. P. Harrison, "Searching for the Origins of Mahāyāna," 49.
72. G. Vico, *New Science*, §147, 58.
73. M. Bloch, *Historian's Craft*, 29.
74. D. Dubuisson, *Western Construction*, 22.
75. This is perhaps understandable, given how common such thinking is in contemporary discourses about religion, nation, etc.; one might very well suspect,

however, that this reflects an unconscious adoption of religious attitudes toward origins within the contemporary academic study of religions. As Bloch observed (*Historian's Craft*, 31),

> this preoccupation with origins, justifiable in a certain type of religious analysis, has spread . . . into other fields of research where its legitimacy is far more debatable. . . . [I]n many cases the demon of origins has been, perhaps, only the incarnation of that other satanic enemy of true history: the mania for making judgments.

76. Compare P. Veyne (*Did the Greeks Believe?*, 77) on the origin myths of ancient cities: "Etiology simply spoke from a need for political identity. . . . Once the historian had narrated its foundation, the city was fixed in space and time; it had its identity card."
77. D. Dubuisson, *Western Construction*, 152 and 167.
78. H. White, *Metahistory*, 2.
79. E. E. Evans-Pritchard, *Theories of Primitive Religion*, 8.
80. B. Lincoln, *Theorizing Myth*, 70.

2. NARRATING TANTRIC BUDDHISM

1. H. White, "Value of Narrativity," 9.
2. H. White, *Metahistory*, x–xi.
3. This is less clearly the case when, as not infrequently happens, the data are themselves narratives.
4. Note that "fictive" here does not imply that such elements are necessarily false, but rather to emphasize that they are elements native to the *rhetoric* used to describe human activity, rather than such activity itself.
5. Aristotle, "Poetics," 1462: "a whole [narrative] is that which has beginning, middle, and end."
6. Mink, *Historical Understanding*, 188.
7. Aristotle, "Poetics," 1462: "A beginning is that which is not itself necessarily after anything else, and which has naturally something else after it; an end is that which is naturally after something else, either as its necessary or usual consequent, and with nothing else after it; and a middle, that which is by nature after one thing and has also another after it."
8. H. White, *Metahistory*, 9.
9. H. White, *Metahistory*, 8n6.
10. H. White, *Metahistory*, 22.
11. I make this point in more detail, and with reference to a specific corpus of Sanskrit Buddhist literature, in a work-in-progress presented to the American Oriental Society in 2010, "Thus Have *We* Heard: Rhetorics of Seduction and Solidarity in Mahāyāna Sūtra Literature."
12. Cf. H. White, *Metahistory*, 6–7.

13. This, notably, was the name of a nationalist newspaper run by Mohandas Gandhi from 1919 to 1932.
14. Croce, *History as the Story of Liberty*, 46.
15. Cf. Lincoln, "How to Read a Religious Text," 127 and 139.
16. In criticizing general works on Tantric Buddhism available in the 1970s, Wayman (*Yoga of the Guhyasamājatantra*, 52) maintained that, "[Such] an introduction should show what the Tantra is all about, the underlying suppositions, the leading instructions, to the extent of recreating the Tantra as a viable entity to be liked or disliked. The trouble with so much of the present writing on Tantra is that the reader is, or should be, left with a feeling of distancy or bewilderment; he is neither genuinely for nor against it, because he does not understand it."
17. Croce, *History as the Story of Liberty*, 48.
18. Kværne, "Sahaja," 102.
19. de Bary, *Buddhist Tradition*, 110.
20. See, for example, La Vallée Poussin, "Notes de Bibliographie Bouddhique" (1934–35), 399.
21. Vico, *The New Science*, 17–18.
22. Collingwood, *The Idea of History*, 67.
23. See Ibn Khaldûn, *Muqaddimah*, 141–42.
24. Rousseau, "On the Social Contract," 194. Note the metaphor of the body politic—a Greco-Roman construct, later Christianized.
25. H. White, *Metahistory*, 123.
26. Bendall, *Subhāṣita-Saṅgraha*, 2.
27. M. Williams, *Buddhism*, 148. When this book was written, its author had not yet been knighted, so I here use the older, less cumbersome form of his name, rather than the post-knighthood, Monier Monier-Williams.
28. M. Williams, 151. Note the similarity here to Bhattacharyya's use of the term "natural."
29. M. Williams, 159. [emphasis mine]
30. M. Williams, 152.
31. La Vallée Poussin, *Bouddhisme: Opinions,* 19 [emphasis mine]: "la critique peut admettre cette division tripartite: un Bouddhisme peu dévot et exclusivement monastique, ou Petit Véhicule, qui remonte sans doute jusqu'au fondateur; un Bouddhisme beaucoup plus composite, monastique et séculier, dévot, polythéiste, parfois monothéiste, très mêlé de philosophie pure et de gnose: c'est le Grand Véhicule, . . . ; enfin le Bouddhisme dégradé et dénaturé des Tantras, attesté depuis le VIIe siècle chrétien."
32. H. White, *Metahistory*, 8n6.
33. This was also interpreted in some accounts as a valid justification for the Roman invasion.
34. Fell, *Etruria and Rome*, 139.
35. And, in the typical style of the Abrahamic traditions of one-upping each others' narratives, this trope was later turned on the Catholic Church itself by the vigorously youthful Reformation schools.

36. Edward Thomas put this reductionistic portrayal in its most undisguised form when he reported that Tantric Buddhism "consists in giving a religious significance to the facts of sex." See Thomas, *The History of Buddhist Thought*, 246.
37. Cunningham, *The Bhilsa Topes*, 2–3.
38. Compare Waddell's account: "during the three or four succeeding centuries [seventh–tenth/eleventh centuries A.D.] Indian Buddhism became still more debased. Its mysticism became a silly mummery of unmeaning jargon and 'magic circles. . . . ' In these declining days . . . , when its spiritual and regenerating influences were almost dead, the Muhammadan invasion swept over India . . . and effectually stamped Buddhism out of the country" (*Buddhism of Tibet*, 15–16).
39. Auguste Barth gives a similar, implicitly anti-Catholic, anti-ecclesiastical account of the decline of Buddhism (priests, too rigid, scholastic, dry, etc., so it died); see his *Religions of India*, 136–139.
40. Rhys Davids, *Buddhist India*, 320 [emphasis mine].
41. Davidson, *Indian Esoteric Buddhism*, 4.
42. Davidson, *Indian Esoteric Buddhism*, 101 [italics mine]. Curiously, one finds the following claim in Weber: "The whole history of monasticism is in a certain sense the history of a continual struggle with the problem of the secularizing influence of wealth" (Weber, *Protestant Ethic*, 174).
43. H. White, *Metahistory*, 22.
44. Shaw, *Passionate Enlightenment*, 20.
45. Tucci, *Tibetan Painted Scrolls*, 209 [italics mine]. In advancing this theory, Tucci may very well have been influenced by the views of Heinrich Zimmer (or "Henry R. Zimmer").
46. Tucci, *Tibetan Painted Scrolls*, 219.
47. Elder, "Saṃpuṭa Tantra," 3–4. His citation for this assertion refers the reader to Chakravarti's *Tantras* and the sixth chapter of Eliade's *Yoga*.
48. This is very much the perspective of formative anthropological works such as Tylor's *Primitive Culture*. One also finds the same axiom in the work of J. J. Bachofen, 105–107.
49. See Fabian, *Time and the Other*.
50. Tucci, *Tibetan Painted Scrolls*, 216.
51. Dasgupta, *Obscure Religious Cults*, 26.
52. Dasgupta, *Obscure Religious Cults*, xxv–xxvi.
53. Basham in de Bary, *Buddhist Tradition*, 112 [emphasis mine]; cf. Basham "Notes on Origins," 153.
54. Conze, *Buddhism: Its Essence and Development*, 176.
55. Conze, *Buddhism: Its Essence and Development*, 178. It may be observed that, although Conze does not explicitly specify that this Dravidian stratum is a *sub*-stratum, strata are always vertical, so the implication of hierarchy is evident nonetheless.
56. Tsuda, "A Critical Tantrism," 172. Although this article is cited widely in the scholarly literature on Tantric Buddhism, it is perhaps better considered as a contribution to Buddhist theology.
57. Eliade, *Yoga*, 201–203 [emphasis mine].

58. Hardy, "The Esoteric Traditions and Antinomian Movements," 649 [emphasis mine]. It is worth noting that this volume is widely cited in works on Indian Tantrism.
59. Chutiwongs, *Iconography of Avalokiteśvara*, 76. Similar claims may be found in M.C. Joshi's 2002 article "Historical and Iconographic Aspects of Śākta Tantrism."
60. *Das Mutterrecht: eine Untersuchung über die Gynaikokratie der alten Welt nach ihrer religiosen und rechtlichen Natur*.
61. Bachofen, *Myth, Religion, and Mother Right*, 78.
62. Bachofen, *Myth, Religion, and Mother Right*, 69.
63. Bachofen, *Myth, Religion, and Mother Right*, 71 [emphasis mine].
64. This historical model was in fact "accepted pretty generally among sociologists until about the beginning of the twentieth century" (Boas, "Preface," xviii). Bachofen's narrative was by no means widely discredited until some decades into the twentieth century; and, even so, studies of Oriental religions are very often several decades behind the times in terms of the theorists upon which they rely. (This very study may be considered a case in point, but I leave that for the discerning reader to determine.)
65. Though, as Margaret Mitchell has suggested (personal communication), it does "partake of the 'civilized/barbarian' dualism of the Greeks and Romans."
66. Bachofen, *Myth, Religion, and Mother Right*, 76–77.
67. This case is briefly made in Urban, *Tantra*, 179–186.
68. Note that Robinson had less to do with the contents of this book than one might assume. Even the first edition was published posthumously. The remaining editions were all produced by others.
69. These thirteen references occur over nine pages: 99, 101, 103, 114, 116, 124, 127, 131, and 140.
70. M. Monier-Williams, *Hinduism*, 122–123.
71. Hoffmann, *Religions of Tibet*, 33.
72. Snellgrove, *Indo-Tibetan Buddhism* I, 130.
73. R. Williams, *Keywords*, s.v. "medieval."
74. The *Oxford English Dictionary* does not attest any usage before 1827; see s.v. "medieval." Note also Bullen's conclusion that "in the mid-nineteenth century the concept of the Renaissance was relatively new and unstable. It had come into being almost accidentally at the end of the eighteenth century;" see, Bullen, *Myth of the Renaissance in Nineteenth-Century Writing*, 1.
75. *Annual Bibliography of Indian Archæology for the Year 1933*, xi.
76. See, for instance, Banerjee, "Hindus in Mediæval India."
77. B. Stein, *History of India*, 113.
78. Silk, "Bibliography on Ancient Indian Slavery," 277.
79. Many medievalists have advocated abandoning this and related terms altogether. See, for instance, Davis, *Periodization and Sovereignty*.
80. F. C. Robinson, "Medieval, the Middle Ages," 750.
81. In his inaugural address on taking up a professorship at Victoria University of Wellington, Peter Munz observed that "the word medieval can be used

meaningfully only if it refers to a period which lies between two civilizations and is not civilized in its own right. The word can be used intelligently only in its original sense in which it implied contempt for all those things Gothic and barbarous that had intervened between Rome and the Renaissance;" *The Concept of the Middle Ages as a Sociological Category*, 6.

82. Leauchli, *The Language of Faith*, 16.
83. F. C. Robinson, "Medieval, the Middle Ages," 752.
84. F. C. Robinson, "Medieval, the Middle Ages," 749.
85. J.I., "Gothic Architecture," 134. Compare the comments of Peter Munz, see note 81.
86. Notably, Robinson ("Medieval, the Middle Ages," 755) observes that in French there is no negative association to *medieval* ; rather, the derogatory connotation is confined to *moyenâgeux*. This latter term is, unsurprisingly perhaps, the term most frequently encountered in older Francophone discussions of esoteric Buddhism (e.g., La Vallée Poussin), while more contemporary authors (e.g., Strickmann) prefer *médiéval* (which I suspect to be proximately a loan word from English). It is worth noting in this regard that *moyen* as a noun means a conduit or intermediary to something else—that is, it refers to something fundamentally secondary or derivative.
87. Anecdotally, the most common defense of this term that I have heard in many discussions with self-professed medievalists is that it functions as a conceptual shorthand for a date range that straddles the turn of the millennium. That is, in short, it is easier to say than "sixth to the fifteenth centuries." Contrariwise, I have found it no real encumbrance to refer to my research as concerning "esoteric Buddhism between the eighth and fourteenth centuries."
88. Davidson, *Indian Esoteric Buddhism*, 28; and Wink, *Al Hind*, 219-223.
89. For instance in Sharma's work on Indian feudalism, Wink sees "an obstinate attempt to find 'elements' which fit a preconceived picture of what should have happened in India because it happened in Europe" (*Al Hind*, 222). A similar criticism is made in Wedemeyer, "Review of R. Davidson, *Indian Esoteric Buddhism*," 375–376.
90. Wink, *Al Hind*, 220.
91. Davidson, *Indian Esoteric Buddhism*, 28.
92. This is part of what Davidson calls a "culture of military opportunism" characteristic of medieval India. In this respect, at least, the analogy with Europe clearly breaks down, insofar as Western feudalism "rather than being a destructive political force breeding particularism and anarchy, was a constructive and unifying system that made possible the political rehabilitation of western Europe . . . and provided the conditions necessary for the formation of the strong centralized states" (Lyon, *Middle Ages in Recent Historical Thought*, 24).
93. Davidson, *Indian Esoteric Buddhism*, 53 and 127.
94. Indologist Alexis Sanderson has in fact maintained that "historians . . . in recent decades have shown the invalidity of the widespread view that it was a time of decline, de-urbanization, fragmentation, and general impoverishment in the aftermath of a glorious classical age that culminated under the Gupta

kings and ended with their demise." He suggests that the view of the decline of Indian culture after the Guptas "owes more, one suspects, to the concept of the European Dark Ages after the collapse of the Roman empire than to unbiased analysis of India's epigraphical and archaeological record" (Sanderson, "Śaiva Age," 253).

95. *Oxford English Dictionary*, s.v. *medieval*. Fred Robinson has further expressed his annoyance at "the way ultramodern techniques for administering torture and waging war are frequently described as 'medieval.'" In common usage, he wrote, medieval seems "to mean simply evil" (Robinson, "Medieval, the Middle Ages," 753).
96. Consider the following comment in a review of Davidson's book: "Early scholars of Buddhism found Tantricism to be so offensive that they could not bring themselves to study it dispassionately—and, as Davidson emphasizes, it is offensive" (D. Gellner, "Himalayan Conundrum?," 411).
97. Orzech, "Great Teaching of Yoga," 69. Orzech coauthored an encyclopedia article on Tantra with Davidson, so presumably he had some purchase on the latter's views. See, Davidson and Orzech, "Tantra."
98. "Sāmanta" does not carry any real semantic weight here. It is merely echoing Davidson's discourse. In essence, in Davidson's usage, "sāmanta feudalism" acts as what Sanskrit grammarians call a *karmadhārayasamāsa*, or appositional compound, in which the words are equated or serve to gloss each other.
99. *Oxford English Dictionary*, 2nd edition, s.v. "spawn."
100. After King, *Orientalism and Religion*, 9.
101. Sanford, "Abominable Tachikawa Skull Ritual," 11 [emphasis mine].
102. See chapter 2, 62.
103. See note 81.
104. cf. Chattopadyaya's *The Making of Early Medieval India*.
105. Ferguson, *Tree and Serpent Worship*, 65.
106. Davidson, *Indian Esoteric Buddhism*, 12.
107. H. White, *Metahistory*, xii.
108. It may be objected that there have been those who have exalted the European Middle Ages. While this is undoubtedly true, a) like those who exalt primordial religion, they are a minority, and b) this position has never to my knowledge been attested when speaking of medieval periods in non-European cultures. It is worth observing in this regard that contemporary Tantric Buddhist groups never refer to their traditions as medieval. Rather, one can observe a remarkable consistency in the reference to their traditions as ancient, whether they be pre-Gupta Indian forms or even Tibetan practices as recent as the mid-second millennium. In so doing, these groups manifest a clear awareness of the relative valuation of each term in modern discourses. Writing in the early mid-nineteenth century, Eugène Burnouf used the term modern to denigrate later Buddhism. Burnouf was writing before the shift that valorized the modern and devalued the medieval. See Burnouf, *Intro*, 583–586.

3. GOING NATIVE: TRADITIONAL HISTORIOGRAPHY OF TANTRIC BUDDHISM

1. This is true of Snellgrove, *Indo-Tibetan Buddhism*; Conze, *Buddhism*; Robinson, *Buddhist Religion* (1970); Gomez, "Buddhism in India;" Wayman, "Esoteric Buddhism;" and Williams with Tribe, *Buddhist Thought*. Two notable exceptions are Warder (*Indian Buddhism*, 462), who briefly notes the Japanese tradition of the Iron Stupa and the Tibetan Tāranātha's comments on the gradual revelation of the Tantras, and Joshi (*Studies*, 236 and 240), who comments on the traditional claims of divine revelation of the Tantras.
2. Joshi (*Studies*, 240), for instance, privileging the claims found in the Kālacakra literature, makes the unqualified assertion that "the Buddhist Tantras . . . claim to have been revealed by Buddha; the origin of Esoteric or Tāntrika Buddhism is therefore traced to Buddha himself."
3. Given that this text has come to be widely known under this form of the title, I preserve this usage. However, both the original manuscript used for Sâstrî's edition and a new manuscript that has come to light in Nepal indicate that the correct form may very well be *Mañjuśriyamūlakalpa*.
4. Bhattacharyya, *Introduction to Buddhist Esoterism*, 19.
5. Bhattacharyya "Tāntrika Culture among the Buddhists," 89.
6. See, for example, the passage from the *Mañjuśrīnāmasaṃgīti*, 80.
7. J. Z. Smith, *Relating Religion*, 4: "Anthropological thought begins with thinking about language itself, for it is in the linguistic project that we see most clearly the creation of a distinctively human world, our 'second environment.' In crude terms, language 'creates' the world; it does not merely 'reflect' it."
8. Dreyfus, *Sound of Two Hands*, 179: "To be compelling, soteriological practices must be presented within a narrative embodying values central to the tradition. Such narratives in turn require larger cosmological frameworks in which they can unfold. . . . To construct such a universe of meaning and to strengthen the faith of participants in such a soteriological possibility are the main goals of the study of the [*Abhisamayālaṃkāra*] and other related texts in the Tibetan scholastic tradition."
9. I explore the rhetorics involved in the former (reinforcing communal identity) in the scriptures of the Buddhist Universal Way in "'Thus Have *We* Heard': Rhetorics of Seduction and Solidarity in Mahāyāna Sūtra Literature," a paper delivered at the 220th Meeting of the American Oriental Society, St. Louis, MO, March 12, 2010.
10. J. Z. Smith, *Imagining Religion*, xiii.
11. This term is used by Paul Veyne in, for example, *Did the Greeks Believe in Their Myths?*, wherein he describes it as an imaginative faculty that "is not an individual creative gift; it is a kind of objective spirit in which individuals are socialized." Different constitutive imaginations in different cultures define different programs of truth "for 'reality' is the child of the constitutive imagination of our tribe" (113). Veyne further notes that "all this eliminates any way of making a profound distinction between cultural works that are true and the pure products of the imagination" (108).

12. This situation has changed dramatically, however, in recent decades. The pioneering work of Paul Harrison (e.g., "Mediums and Messages" and *Samādhi of Direct Encounter*), Ronald Davidson ("Introduction to Standards"), Matthew Kapstein ("Purificatory Gem"), Robert Mayer ("Caskets of Treasures" and "Scriptural Revelation"), and Janet Gyatso (e.g., "Signs, Memory, History" and "Drawn from the Tibetan Treasury"), among others, has taken this discussion in a direction of admirable thoughtfulness and sophistication. I am deeply indebted to their work in what follows, especially in the first two sections on "Historiography and Cosmology."
13. Indeed, there would be precious little left of Buddhist literature to study if this criterion were utilized.
14. Lincoln, *Authority*, 104.
15. That is, those that fall under Burnouf's rubric "works bearing the names of authors" (*ouvrages portant des noms d'auteurs*); see Burnouf, *Introduction* (1844), 646.
16. This much was noted as early as 1949 by Giuseppe Tucci, who wrote (*Tibetan Painted Scrolls*, 210), "the Tantric schools follow in the footsteps of the Mahāyāna, which (as we shall often repeat in this book) had also shifted the place of revelation, from the earth to spheres beyond the earth." Note that I use the term buddhalogy here on analogy with Christology.
17. On the traditions concerning the decline of the Buddhist teaching, see, for example, Nattier, *Once Upon a Future Time*.
18. See *Jātaka*, vol. I, 48: vassa-sahassassa accayena pana sabbaññu-buddho loke upajjissati.
19. "Mahāparinibbānasutta" (*Dīghanikāya* II, 142, 143): tesaṃ taṃ bhavissati dīgharattaṃ hitāya sukhāya; sugatiṃ saggaṃ lokaṃ uppajjanti.
20. Indeed, Jonathan Walters ("Mahāyāna Theravāda") suggests that this was a minority view and that the mainstream of the early traditions was open to new revelations.
21. A remarkable movement of neo-historical naiveté has recently appeared as seen, for instance, in the work of Richard Gombrich and Alexander Wynne.
22. Note that, strictly speaking, the term *pāli* refers to the corpus of scriptures, not the language in which they are written: "The dialect . . . usually called 'Pāli' by European scholars is nowhere so called in the Theravādin canon. The word *pāli* . . . has the meaning 'canon,'" (Norman, *Pāli Literature*, 1).
23. See "Āṭānāṭiya Sutta" the thirty-second chapter of the *Dīgha Nikāya*. Note that this is not an exceptional text, except perhaps in its popularity and antiquity. As Peter Skilling has noted (*Mahāsūtras* II, 575 and 577), "its influence seems to have been enormous" and it "is one of the oldest surviving Buddhist cult texts."
24. Harrison, "Mediums and Messages," 126.
25. Lamotte, *History* (163): "To judge from the explanations supplied by all the Vinayas one after the other—*Mahāsamghika Vin.* (T 1425, ch. 13, 336*a* 21); *Mūlasarv. Vin.* (T 1442, ch. 26, 771*b* 22); Pāli *Vin.* (IV, 15), *Dharmagupta Vin.* (T 1428, ch. 11, 639*a* 16); *Sarvāstivādin Vin.* (T 1435, ch. 9, 71*b* 1)—the Dharma is what is uttered by the Buddha,

without a doubt and above all, but also by the auditors (*śrāvaka*), wise recluses (*ṛṣi*), gods (*deva*) and apparitional beings (*upapāduka*)." Note also that canonized within the *Khuddaka Nikāya* of the Pāli are works not claimed to be the word of the Buddha, such as the *Milindapañha* and *Thera-/Therī-gāthā*; thanks to an anonymous reviewer for Columbia University Press for drawing my attention to this.

26. There was at least one notable exception to this—the so-called Sautrāntika schools that distinguished themselves through their refusal to accept the authority of the Abhidharma. "The Sautrāntikas are so called because for them the norm consists of the sūtras to the exclusion of the Abhidharma treatises (*ye sūtraprāmāṇikā na tu śāstraprāmāṇikāḥ*)" (Lamotte, *History*, 181).
27. Skilling, "*Dharma, Dhāraṇī, Abhidharma, Avadāna*," 53–54.
28. Trayastriṃśa is the abode of Śakra, king of the gods. On the motif of revelation in Trayastriṃśa, see Skilling, "*Dharma, Dhāraṇī, Abhidharma, Avadāna*."
29. Skilling, "Mahāyāna and Bodhisattva," 152.
30. ye ca buddhā atītā ca ye ca buddhā anāgatā | paccuppannā ca ye buddhā ahaṃ vandāmi sabbadā |; cited in Skilling, "Mahāyāna and Bodhisattva," 152.
31. David Drewes argues that "there was probably simply not much to early Mahāyāna apart from these texts. What the evidence collected over the last century and a half suggests is that early Indian Mahāyāna was primarily a textual movement, focused on the revelation, preaching, and dissemination of Mahāyāna sūtras" ("Early Indian Mahāyāna II," 67).
32. See Skilling, "*Dharma, Dhāraṇī, Abhidharma, Avadāna*," 48. There is a significant homology here, insofar as the change merely replaces one wisdom literature (the Theravāda Abhidhamma) with another (the *prajñā* literature of the Mahāyāna).
33. As David Drewes notes, "Mahāyāna authors never denied the facticity of the early Buddhist world; rather, they expanded on it to the point where it became largely irrelevant, left with little more than a toehold in a vast new universe" ("Early Indian Mahāyāna II," 66).
34. Lamotte, trans., *Śūraṃgamasamādhisūtra*, 168.
35. This theme is touched upon in the *Vimalakīrtinirdeśasūtra*, in which it is said that "the transcendent lord Śākyamuni teaches the Dharma there in a buddha-field of five corruptions to beings of inferior aspiration; . . . in order to cultivate beings, the buddhas do not reveal the [divine] buddha perception to all" (*Vimalakīrtinirdeśa*, 92–93: tatra śākyamunir nāma tathāgato dharmaṃ deśayati hīnādhimuktikānāṃ satvānāṃ pañcakaṣāye buddhakṣetre . . . satvaparipākāya tu buddhā bhagavanto na sarvaṃ buddhaviṣayaṃ saṃdarśayanti). Compare Thurman, trans., *Holy Teaching of Vimalakīrti*, 80.
36. For example, the stories of the prior buddhas Candrasūryapradīpa (in chapter 1, the "Nidānaparivarta") or Mahābhijñājñānābhibhū (in chapter 7, the "Pūrvayogaparivarta"), both of whom taught the *Saddharmapuṇḍarīka* "in a past time, incalculable æons, yet more incalculably long, immeasurably, inconceivably, infinitely, inestimably long, long ago" (atīte 'dhvani asaṃkhyeyaiḥ kalpair asamkhyeyatarair vipulair aprameyair acintyair aparimitair apramāṇais tataḥ pareṇa parataraṃ [or, paratareṇa] yadâsīt; Vaidya, ed., 11 and 104).

37. See Harrison, *Samādhi of Direct Encounter*.
38. "No Buddha has appeared in the past, and no future one exists anywhere who has not expounded and will not expound this peaceful, holy *samādhi*" (Harrison, *Samādhi of Direct Encounter*, 77).
39. The scripture was translated into Chinese in A.D. 179; Harrison (*Pratyutpanna*, 1–2) claims that "sometime in the first century C.E. may not be too wide of the mark."
40. Harrison, *Samādhi of Direct Encounter*, xx.
41. Harrison, *Samādhi of Direct Encounter*, 32.
42. Harrison, *Samādhi of Direct Encounter*, 33.
43. See Harrison, *Samādhi of Direct Encounter*, 103; cf. Harrison, *Pratyutpanna*, 52.
44. Cited in the *Śikṣāsamuccaya* of Śāntideva: āśaya-saṃpannasya punar bhagavan yadi buddhā na bhavanti gagana-talād dharma-śabdo niścarati kuḍma-vṛkṣebhyaś ca | āśaya-śuddhasya bodhisattvasya svamanojalpād eva sarvāvavādānuśāsanyo niścaranti | (Vaidya, ed., 150). Consider also the modes of revelation mentioned in the *Sarvapuṇyasamuccayasamādhisūtra* (extant in Chinese: T. 381 and 382), cited in Harrison, "Mediums and Messages," 125. The scripture is referred to as the *Nārāyaṇaparipṛcchā* in the *Śikṣāsamuccaya*:

> Vimalatejas, the Buddhas and Lords resident in other world-systems show their faces to reverent and respectful bodhisattvas and mahāsattvas wanting the dharma, and they cause them to hear the dharma. Vimalatejas, treasures of dharma are deposited in the interiors of mountains, caves and trees for bodhisattvas and mahāsattvas wanting the dharma, and endless dharma-teachings in book form come into their hands. Vimalatejas, deities who have seen former Buddhas provide bodhisattvas and mahāsattvas wanting the dharma with the inspired eloquence of Buddhas.

45. For an excellent treatment of this rite and its place in the MMK, see Wallis, *Mediating the Power of Buddhas*; cf. Kapstein, "Weaving the World."
46. For a translation of the relevant section of the MMK, see Wallis, *Mediating the Power*, 26–27. Note I am using the masculine pronoun, contrary to my typical usage, given the patriarchal assumptions of the text I am discussing.
47. For an excellent treatment of consecration rites and the theoretical and scriptural literature associated with it, see Bentor, *Consecration*.
48. The *Concise Consecration Ritual Tantra* (f. 146b[2]) specifies "worked, painted, cast, and so forth" (brdungs pa dang | bris pa dang | 'bur du byas pa la sogs pa).
49. This idea occurs at least as far back as the *Mahāvairocana Tantra*, as attested by the question Vajrapāṇi poses in chapter 2: "Then, Vajrapāṇi bowed to the feet of the Lord and said this to the Lord, 'buddhas are without [specific, finite] attributes, residing [as they do] in the body of reality (*dharmakāya*). They teach a Dharma unequalled, uncompounded and without [specific, finite] attributes. Why, then, O Great Hero, do you teach this rite that has such attributes [as] the mantra practice?'" (| de nas phyag na rdo rjes bcom ldan 'das kyi zhabs la gtugs ste | bcom ldan das la 'di skad ces gsol to | | sangs rgyas mtshan ma mi mnga' ste | | chos kyi

sku la rnam par bzhugs | | mtshan med 'dus ma byas pa yi | | mtshungs pa med pa'i chos ston na | | dpa' bo chen po ci slad du | | mtshan mar bcad pa'i cho go 'di | | gsang sngags spyad pa bstan par mdzad |; sDe, bKa', vol. tha, f. 99b$^{3-4}$).

50. *Rab tu gnas pa mdor bsdus pa'i cho ga'i rgyud* (**Saṃkṣipta-pratiṣṭhā-vidhi-tantra*), Tōh. 486, f. 147a$^{1-3}$: sangs rgyas kun ni rab tu bzhugs | | rab tu gnas pa gang na'ang med | | kun du mkha' ltar gnas pa la | . . . | gzod ma nas ni skye med pa | | ci 'dra ji ltar rab tu gnas | | dang po'i las can sems can rnams | | rtogs pa'i rgyu ru mdzad par zad |. Note that the Sanskrit title given at the outset of the work, *Supratiṣṭhatantrasaṃgraha*, is obviously an erroneous back-formation from the Tibetan title added by later compilers. My reconstruction is based on the title given in the colophon.
51. One may infer as much from an apologetic passage of the *Samādhi of Face-to-Face Confrontation* in which the Buddha warns that, when such visionary texts are produced, the close-minded will object, arguing that "*Sūtras* like this are fabrications, they are poetic inventions; they were not spoken by the Buddha, nor were they authorized by the Buddha."(Harrison, *Samādhi of Direct Encounter*, 56.) Here, the objector assumes two consensually-accepted modes of revelation: direct address and authorization. The latter was the mode by which many of the early communities accepted the validity of the Abhidharma.
52. On these figures, see esp. Drewes, "Early Indian Mahāyāna II," 69–70; cf. Harrison, *Samādhi of Direct Encounter*, xx–xxi. See also, Nance, "Indian Buddhist Preachers."
53. We will also see that some claimed the Buddha taught the Tantras *after his death*.
54. evaṃ mayā śrutam ekasmin samaye bhagavān rājagṛhe viharati sma | . . . tena khalu samayena bhagavānn āyuṣmantam ānandam āmantrayate sma |; Iwamoto, ed., *Kleinere Dhāraṇī Texte*, 10.
55. Mt. Potalaka is not strictly speaking a heaven, as it is usually considered to be located on an island to the south of Jambudvīpa (India); but it is clearly outside the purview of the ordinary world of the Indian Buddhist; cf. *Amoghapāśakalparāja* I (14): evaṃ mayā śrutam ekasmin samaye bhagavān potalake parvate viharati sma |.
56. iyaṃ khalu punar mahāśītavatī vidyā ekanavatyāṃ gaṅgānadīvālukāsamair buddhair bhagavadbhir bhāṣitā bhāṣiṣyate bhāṣyate ca; Iwamoto, ed., *Kleinere Dhāraṇī Texte*, 5–6.
57. bhagavat-tathāgata-śākyamuni-bhāṣitā; Davidson, ed., 69.
58. MNS 11: gambhīrārthām udārārthāṃ mahārthām asamāṃ śivāṃ | ādimadhyānta-kalyāṇīṃ nāma-saṃgītim uttamāṃ || yâtītair bhāṣitā buddhair bhāṣiṣyante hy anāgatāḥ | pratyutpannāś ca saṃbuddhā yāṃ bhāṣante punaḥ punaḥ ||.
59. The plural number in Sanskrit signifies three or more agents. The expression *punaḥ punaḥ* (lit. "again and again") implies that the action is at least frequent, if not constant.
60. See note 25.
61. evaṃ mayā śrutam ekasmin samaye bhagavān vajreṣu viharati sma | sarvaśarīraṃ vajramayam adhiṣṭhāya vajrapāṇiś ca buddhānubhāvena vajrasamādhiṃ samāpannam | tato vajrapānir buddhānubhāvena sarvabuddhādhiṣṭhānāc ca sarvabodhisattvādhiṣṭhānāc ca mahakrodhasaṃbhūtaṃ vajrasārapadaṃ bhāṣate sma |; Iwamoto, *Kleinere Dhāraṇī Texte*, 7.

62. MVT, ch. 2, sDe bKa', vol. tha, ff. $160b^7$–$161a^1$: | gsang sngags sbyor ba mnyam med de | | shākya seng ge skyob pa yis | | bdud sde shin tu mi bzad pa | | dpung chen dag kyang de yis bcom |.
63. Although the future Śākyamuni Buddha does learn from other buddhas in narratives cast in his previous lives, I am not aware of any Śrāvaka or Mahāyāna source that depicts him as such in his final life as a bodhisattva (*carama-bhāvika*).
64. This narrative may be found in *Sarvatathāgatatattvasaṃgraha*, [41–44].
65. bhagavan itas trayastriṃśaddevanikāyād (Skorupski, ed., 122 and 124).
66. Or, "in the dwelling of [the deities of] the Śuddhāvāsa."
67. According to the most recent work on Oḍiyāna by Alexis Sanderson, "Uḍḍiyāna, also written U/Oḍiyāna, U/Oḍyāna, and U/Oḍḍayana, was the petty kingdom known to the Chinese as Wuzhangna (Jap. Ujōna) and to the Tibetans as U rgyan or O rgyan, located west-north-west of Kashmir to the north of Peshawar in what is now Pakistan. Its capital on the river Swāt beyond the Indus was only about 150 miles from the capital of Kashmir as the crow flies" ("Śaiva Exegesis," 265).
68. yad aṣṭadaśa-lakṣaṃ śri-catuṣpīṭha-mahātantrarājaṃ bhagavatā śrīvajradhareṇa śuddhāvā[sakāyikā]nikāye bhāṣitam || tasmāc chrī-vajrapāṇinā saṃhṛtya dvādaśasāhasrikaṃ tantrarājaṃ śrimad-oḍiyāne 'śītikoṭi-yoga-yoginībhiḥ | prabodhya ta++++taṃ tasmād api śrī-nāgārjuna-bhaṭṭārakena tatra gatvā mahāguptena śrutvā dvādaśa-śatika-mūlatantraṃ loke pracāritam ||; text from Szántó, "Antiquarian Enquiries," 9; translation adapted from that of Szántó; text in brackets my emendation.
69. Davidson dates this as early as 810 CE.
70. Davidson (*Indian Esoteric Buddhism*, 242) translates the final sentence as follows: "Therefore, the four Great Kings caused the scriptures to reside in the realm of the Thirty-three, Tuṣita, etc., or wherever there were gods and bodhisattvas of the good aeon who were fit vessels for the teaching." In so doing, he follows the sDe dge edition which mistakenly reads an instrumental here (*pas*) instead of a conjunction (*dang*). Both the Ganden MS and the sNar thang xylographic Tangyurs read *dang*; Bu ston also reads *dang* in his citation of this passage in *Yo ga gru gzings*, f. $60a^3$. The reading *dang* is to be preferred as a) the verb *bzhugs* does not take an instrumental agent, and b) the Four Kings do not exhibit the authority to distribute Tantric texts anywhere else in the literature. Eastman ("The Eighteen Tantras," 21) renders this "the four kingly mountains." Note that these are the same Four Kings who revealed the mainstream *Āṭanāṭiya Sutta*, mentioned earlier.
71. Jñānamitra, *Prajñāpāramitānayaśatapañcāśatkaṭīkā* (edited text; cf. sDe dge ff. $272b^7$–$273b^2$): gsung rab 'di'i lo rgyus bshad na | | sngon sangs rgyas mi yul na lo brgyad cu bzhugs pa'i tshe na | sarva buddha sa mā yo ga dang | guhya sa mañca la sogs pas 'dul zhing theg pa de dag gi snod du gyur pa 'dzam bu'i gling gi mi yul na med pas rgyal chen ris bzhi dang | sum cu rtsa gsum dang | dga' ldan la sogs pa'i gnas na lha rnams dang bskal pa bzang po'i byang chub sems dpa' la sogs pa snod du gyur nas de'i tshe mdo sde de ni bzhugs so |.
72. Matthew Kapstein (personal communication) has argued that the toponym "Zahor" refers to Sauvīra.

73. | slad kyis sangs rgyas mya ngan las 'das pa'i 'og tu za hor gyi rgyal po 'khor dang bcas pa ngo mtshar du chos la dad pa dag cig 'dug pa theg pa de'i 'dul skal du gyur cing snod du gyur nas | sarva buddha sa mā yo ga la sogs pa sde chen po bco brgyad phyag na rdo rje'i byin gyi rlabs kyis za hor gyi yul du gshegs pa dang |.
74. So read the bsTan 'gyur redactions; Bu ston (*Yo ga gru gzings*, 119) reads *ma la va.*
75 za hor gyi rgyal po indra bhū tis mdo sde dag bltas na brda ma phrad nas sngon gyi las kyi dbang gis na mngon par shes pa thob pas bltas na yul gyi dbus yul ma la pa na ā cārya ku ku ra nyin zhing ni khyi stong tsam la chos 'chad | mtshan zhing ni khyi de dag la dam tshig longs spyod mdzad pa khyi'i slob dpon mdzad pa zhig bzhugs pa de theg pa'i snod du gyur la | bdag gi 'dul skal du gyur pa yang 'dra nas rgyal pos pho nya btang ste slob dpon gshegs su gsol pa dang |.
76. *brgya la*; this somewhat obscure form is attested as an equivalent of Skt. *kadācit* ("sometime"). Davidson's reading "in a hundred ways" (243) is too literal. Eastman ("Eighteen Tantras," 22) also reads this as "hundred doubts."
77. *mgo 'jug gar lta ba'i cha ma mchis*; Davidson reads "he became turned upside down, uncertain on where to look. Throwing himself down in front of the books." Eastman reads "from beginning of unparalleled content, his body collapsed on them, helpless."
78. slob dpon de yang sngon gyi las kyi dbang gis na mngon par shes pa lnga dang ldan nas | rgyal po de bdag gi 'dul skal du 'bab bam mi 'bab mdo sde de dag gi snod du bdag gyur ram ma gyur brtags na | bdag gi 'dul skal du yang 'bab | bdag kyang mdo sde'i snod du yang gyur | rgyal po'i the tshom yang sel bar 'gyur mod kyi | 'on kyang mdo sde dag sngar ma bltas na brgya la rgyal po'i the tshom dag ma sol bar gyur na shin du ma legs pas pho nya la slar spring ba | mdo sde dag kho bos sngar blta 'tshal gyis tshur bskur cig ces spring ba dang | de nas mdo sde dag pas gshegs te bltas na mgo mjug gar lta ba'i cha ma mchis na de nyid du lus brdabs te mgon med do | | skyab med do zhes bos pa dang dpal rdo rje sems dpa' mngon par gshegs te khyod ci 'dod ces dris pa dang | bdag mdo sde zab mo 'di bltas pa tsam gyis shes par 'dod ces gsol ba dang | de bzhin gnang ngo zhes gsungs nas de nas sarva buddha sa mā yo ga la sogs pa'i glegs bam rnams ma phye bar de dag gi don yid la mngon sum du gsal bar gyur to | | de nas slob dpon de za hor gyi yul du gshegs nas rgyal po 'khor dang bcas pa rnams la dharma de dag bshad de |.
79. *Vimalaprabhā* III.1.5: ihâryaviṣaye śākyamunir bhagavān vaiśākha-pūrṇimāyām aruṇodaye 'bhisaṃbuddhaḥ | śukla-pratipadādi-pañcadaśakalāvasāne kṛṣṇa-pratipat-praveśe tato dharmacakraṃ pravartayitvā yāna-traya-deśanāṃ kṛtvā dvādaśame māse caitra-pūrṇimāyāṃ śrī-dhānyakaṭake. . .ṣaḍ-vibhāgikam ādibuddhaṃ. . .visphāritavān |. Essentially the same narrative may be found in Raviśrījñāna's *Amṛtakaṇikā*, 1.
80. See Newman, "A Brief History," 54–76.
81. *Vimalaprabhā* (18–19): yathā nāmasaṅgītir atītānāgatapratyutpannais tathāgatair bhāṣitā bhāṣiṣyate bhāṣyate tathâdibuddham api | ādiśabdo 'nādinidhanārthaḥ | anādikāle anādibuddha-deśitaṃ deśayiṣyate deśyata iti | naîka śākyamuninā dīpaṅkara-tathāgatenâpîti | . . . | ato. . .sarvatathāgatair mantrayānaṃ deśitam iti |.

82. This verse is similar to one cited in Raviśrījñāna's *Amṛtakaṇikā* (1) as from the Great Ādibuddha (*bṛhadādibuddha*) and Nāḍapāda (Nāropā)'s *Sekoddeśaṭīkā* (66) who cites it as from the "Root Tantra" (*mūlatantra*).
83. *tatrādhimukto*; perhaps emend to "oriented toward the Tantras" (*tantrādhimukto*).
84. *Sekoddeśaṭippaṇī* (Shāstri, *Descriptive Catalogue*, 152): gṛdhrakūṭe 'pi maitreyaḥ prajñāpāramitānayam | buddho mantranayaṃ śuddhaṃ śrīdhānye deśayiṣyati || iti vacanād bhagavataḥ śrīdhānya eva mantranaya-deśanā | anyadeśe punar yat tatrādhimukto janas tad abhiprāyena daśabhūmīśvara-mahābodhisattvaḥ [*sic*] saṃgītikāro 'nyo vā tat taṃtra-deśanāṃ vistareṇa karoti |. Newman ("Outer Wheel," 73) reads this *punar* as "later," but I believe it is meant to be contrastive—the Buddha taught it at Śrīdhānya, but others teach it elsewhere as needed.
85. This manuscript is quite rare and remarkable in that it contains esoteric Buddhist narratives in Sanskrit. It was first brought to scholarly attention in independent articles by Giuseppe Tucci ("Animadversiones Indicae") and Sylvain Levi ("Un nouveau Document"). The moniker "Sham Sher Manuscript"—based upon the name of the Nepalese minister who controlled the texts (Kaiser Shamsher Jang Bahadur Rana, 1892–1964)—seems to have been coined by Mark Tatz in a pair of articles on these narratives in 1987 and 1988 ("Life of Siddha-Philosopher Maitrīgupta" [696] and "Maitrīpa and Atiśa" [481, where he uses the spelling "Sham Shere"]). Ronald Davidson follows this usage in his 2003 *Indian Esoteric Buddhism* (306). The name is not particularly apt, as there are thousands of manuscripts in the Kaiser Manuscript Collection, but I here follow the usage of Tatz and Davidson for consistency and familiarity.
86. tatrâdau dharmacakre 'smin śrāvakaiḥ parivāritaḥ | upatasthe sa bhagavān diśan pāramitādikam || tatas taṃ samparityajya gatavān dakṣinapāthe | nirmāya dharmadhātvākhyam maṇḍalaṃ sumanoramam ||; Lévi, "Un Nouveau Document," 421.
87. S. Lévi, "Un Nouveau Document," 417: "L'ouvrage dont nous avons ici un fragment donnait l'historique, naturellement légendaire, de ce culte, la transmission de maîtres à disciples, et le rituel. C'est un spécimen curieux des documents qui ont dû servir de base ou lama Tāranātha pour ses précieuses compilations en tibétain." Lévi mentions the rather late Tibetan historian Tāranātha because he was well-known to Western audiences. The point he makes, however, is applicable to much earlier (indeed, contemporaneous) Tibetan documents.
88. For instance, the *History* of Mkhas pa Lde'u notes, "if one objects that the Seven Abhidharmas are not [revealed] Word, since they were spoken later by the seven saints, it is certainly not the same. The Teacher [Śākyamuni] first declared the meaning in parts; later, the saints synthesized it and it was included in the Word of the Individual Vehicle and the Treatises of the Universal Vehicle" ('o na mngon pa sde bdun dgra bcom pa bdun gyis phyi nas gsungs pas bkar cang 'gro 'am zhe na | gcig tu ma nges te | ston pas don dang por sil bur gsungs pa la | phyi nas dgra bcom pas bsdus pas theg chung gi bka' la theg chen gyi bstan chos su 'gro skad do | (Mkhas pa Lde'u, *Chos 'byung*, 88–89).

89. Bsod nams rtse mo, *Rgyud sde spyi rnam*, f. 52a$^{1-2}$: spyir gsang sngags mtha' dag sngar bshad pa'i tshul gyis shā kya thub pa'i snga rol du sprul pa'i sku mchog gis gsungs la | phyis shā kya thub pas bzlas te gsungs pa'ang yod | phyis bzlas te ma gsungs pa'ang yod | de nyid kyi rnam 'phrul gzhan gyis gsungs gsungs pa'ang yod do |.
90. Bsod nams rtse mo here cites Bhavyakīrti's *Śrīcakrasaṃvarapañjikā śūramanojñā*; David Gray (*Cakrasamvara Tantra*, 30) has translated the relevant passage from its Tibetan translation: "I, Bhavyakīrti, hold that since the primal buddhas know no cessation, this teaching formulation has a beginningless continuum, existing even before Śākyamuni, as has been well stated by tens of millions of buddhas and heroes. This means that when the *Prajñāpāramitā*, and so forth, wane due to the power of time, the burning eon, and so forth, the Lord Śākyamuni teaches them again. The *Śrī Cakrasamvara* is not like that, for it exists without interruption in inexpressible buddhalands, and it is experienced through meditative states, and so forth, by the heroes and heroines such as Īśvarī."
91. Bsod nams rtse mo, *Rgyud sde spyi rnam*, f. 52b$^{1-3}$: | dpal bde mchog rtsa rgyud kyi 'grel pa las | chos kyi rnam grangs 'di ni thog ma med pa'i rgyud can yin te | bcom ldan shākya thub pa las snga ba nyid du gnas so | | dus kyi dbang gis sreg pa'i bskal pa la sogs pas shes rab kyi pha rol tu phyin pa la sogs pa nub pa na | bcom ldan 'das shākya thub pas slar yang gsungs pa yin no | | dpal bde mchog ni de lta ma yin te | sangs rgyas kyi zhing brjod du med pa na dpa' bo dpa' mo la sogs pas nyams su blangs te gnas pa'i phyir ma nub bo | | zhes bshad pa lta bu'o |. This is a *very* close paraphrase of the cited text.
92. This narrative, which appears in a number of tellings throughout Tibetan scholastic literature, has been translated in Wedemeyer, *Āryadeva's Lamp*, 26–28, from the work of 'Jam mgon A myes zhabs. The elaborate version found in the history of Pad ma dkar po may be found in Appendix I.
93. Bsod nams rtse mo, *Rgyud sde spyi rnam*, f. 53a$^{1-2}$: rgyud dang rtog pa dang bstan bcos las kyang ma bshad la gtam du yongs su grags pa'ang ma yin pas | rang bzo mkhan rnams kyis rang bzor byas pa yin par rig par bya'o |. The view in question is that "in the vaginas of the vajra ladies," which is the site of revelation of the GST, refers to when the bodhisattva was in his mother's womb.
94. *gtam tu yongs su grags pa*; literally, "well-known in stories."
95. *Rgyud sde spyi rnam*, f. 56a^{1}.
96. Jacob Dalton ("Uses," 3) dates the work to the "second half of the ninth century," however Matthew Kapstein (e-mail communication, June 2, 2011) maintains that it is "not possibly 9th c[entury]. Perhaps late 10th."
97. On this work, see Dalton, "Uses of the *Dgongs pa 'dus pa'i mdo*." Dalton makes the important inference that the moniker "Ja" (Tib. *dza* or *tsa*) is an abbreviation of Kuñjara, which full form occurs elsewhere in the text. On the Tibetan provenance of King Ja, see Karmay, "King Dza/Tsa," 207.
98. See Dalton, "Uses of the *Dgongs pa 'dus pa'i mdo*," 58.
99. For these three theories, see Bu ston, *Gsang 'dus bshad thabs*, ff. 27a^{5}–27b^{1}.
100. The Visukalpa narrative is found in *Gsang 'dus bshad thabs*, ff. 28a^{3}–28b^{4}.

101. Evidently, the Heruka chapel is designed like a maṇḍala, with a gateway in each cardinal direction.
102. That is, not a pictorial or ritual representation, but the real maṇḍala itself, manifesting there.
103. The second is that it was accidentally found by monkeys and a woodcutter.
104. Orzech, "Great Teaching of Yoga," 51. I would speculate that this is probably meant to be Nāgārjuna, insofar as he is frequently referred to in Sanskrit sources with the honorific *bhaṭṭāraka*. Japanese tradition indeed considers this to have been Nāgārjuna.
105. Orzech, "Legend of the Iron Stūpa," 316.
106. Orzech, "Legend of the Iron Stūpa," 316–317.
107. Orzech, "Legend of the Iron Stūpa," 316.
108. It might also be noted that above the maṇḍala of the Esoteric Community (Guhyasamāja) there is said to be an "adamant canopy, resembling a caitya" (*vajrapañjaraṃ caityam iva*); Candrakīrti, *Vajrasattvasādhana*, 8, line 7.
109. On this work, see especially Strickmann, *Mantras et Mandarins* and "Consecration Sūtra."
110. That is, a sacred text revealed and subsequently concealed for later re-revelation. Strickmann ("Consecration Sūtra," 81) claims that it is "apparently the first Buddhist scripture to represent itself as a hidden 'treasure-text.'" However, I do not think this view can be sustained. Already at the time Strickmann was writing, Paul Harrison's work on the *Pratyutpanna Sūtra* was demonstrating a much earlier example.
111. Mayer, "Caskets of Treasures," 143.
112. "By the second hundred years [after the Buddha's passing], however, most of the Buddha's disciples would already have obtained deliverance and so there would be less recourse to the scripture. During the third hundred years, the scripture . . . were to vanish into the earth, for there would be no further need of them at that time" (Strickmann, "Consecration Sūtra, 86).
113. Orzech, "Great Teaching of Yoga," 53, translating Taishō 2056, 50.292b20-25.
114. Orzech stresses the influence of Ch'an discourses on this presentation. Nonetheless, the basic idea of a "short lineage" is clearly of Indian heritage.
115. Orzech, "Great Teaching," 53.
116. Orzech, "Great Teaching," 56.
117. See Tajima, 241. Wayman strangely characterizes Tajima as claiming that the Tantras "goes back to the Buddha" ("Appendix Essay" to his translation, 351.)
118. gnas du mar ston pa du mar sprul nas chos kyi 'khor lo du ma bskor ba; Grags pa rgyal mtshan, *Dpal he ru ka'i byung tshul*, 253a^6 (298-4-6).
119. Like Christian Docetism, the Mahāyāna theory of three bodies lays emphasis on the idea that the concrete, embodiments of the Buddha are derivative of prior—and more fundamental—transcendental, spiritual, and immortal, forms.
120. For a very clear expression of this idea in Tibetan literature, see Lessing and Wayman, *Introduction*, 21, 23, 25.

121. Chatterjee, *Kashmir Shaivaism*, 26.
122. Chatterjee, *Kashmir Shaivaism*, 29.
123. Sanderson, "Śaiva Exegesis," 268.
124. Sanderson, "Śaiva Exegesis," 269.
125. *Rauravasūtrasaṃgraha* III vv. 6–10 (tantrāvatāra); *Rauravāgama*, 7.
126. Sanderson, "Śaiva Exegesis," 263. The *Ahirbudhnyasaṃhitā*, a Vaiṣṇava Tantra, is said to have been abridged, like the Buddhist *Catuṣpīṭha*; see Schrader, "Introduction," 116.
127. Sanderson, "Śaiva Exegesis," 345–346.
128. Wedemeyer, *Āryadeva's Lamp*, 29–35.
129. Skilling, "The Rakṣā Literature of the Śrāvakayāna," 168.
130. Granoff, "Tolerance in the Tantras," 300.
131. Cf. *Mahāvairocana Tantra*, chapter III: "Regarding that, Lord of the Secret Ones, in the future, beings with weak minds and no faith will not trust this teaching, will be of two minds and full of doubts. . . . They will say 'this belongs to the non-Buddhists; it is was not spoken by the Buddha.'" (Sde, Bka', vol. tha, f. 177a[1–2]: de la gsang ba'i bdag po ma 'ongs pa'i dus na sems can blo zhan pa ma dad pa gang dag bstan pa 'di la dad par mi 'gyur zhing yid gnyis dang som nyi mang ba | . . . dag 'byung bar 'gyur te | . . . | 'di skad du 'di ni phyi rol pa rnams la yod de | sangs rgyas kyis gsungs pa ni ma yin no zhes smra bar 'gyur).
132. See Chakravarti, *Tantras*, 27.
133. In the famous opening verse of Dignāga's *Pramāṇasamuccaya*, the Buddha is called *pramāṇabhūta*, the very embodiment of a criterion for truth. See Jackson, "Buddha as Pramāṇabhūta."
134. *Adhyāśayasaṃcodanasūtra*: "Whatever, Maitreya, is well-spoken (*su-bhāṣita*), all that is spoken by the Buddha (*buddha-bhāṣita*)" (*yat kiñcin maitreya subhāṣitaṃ sarvaṃ tad buddhabhāṣitam*); cited in Śāntideva, *Śikṣāsamuccaya*, see P. L. Vaidya, ed., 12. Compare *Aṅguttara Nikāya*, vol. IV, 164: *yaṃ kiñci subhāsitaṃ sabban taṃ tassa bhagavato vacanaṃ arahato sammasambuddhassa.*
135. Granoff, "Other People's Rituals," 409; in this regard, Granoff cites a verse from the MMK (II.39) that she translates, "All of the *laukika* (Hindu) mantras that are proclaimed in this ritual text are proclaimed by me [Mañjuśrī] taking this or that form for the sake of teaching living beings" (yāvanto laukikā mantrāḥ te smi kalpa udāhṛtāḥ | vaineyārthaṃ hi sattvānāṃ vicarāmi tathā tathā ||).
136. See, for example, *Pratyutpannasaṃmukhāvasthita Sūtra* (Harrison, ed., 52): mdo sde 'di lta bu dag ni rang gis byas pa | rang bzo byas pa ste | 'di ni sangs rgyas kyis gsungs pa ma yin | sangs rgyas kyis gnang ba ma yin no | zhes de skad kyang rjod cing smod par byed de |; and *Mahāvairocana Tantra* (f. 177a[1–2]): ma 'ongs pa'i dus na blo zhan pa ma dad pa gang dag bstan pa 'di la dad par mi 'gyur zhing yid gnyis dang som nyi mang ba | . . . | 'di skad du 'di ni phyi rol pa rnams la yod de | sangs rgyas kyis gsungs pa ni ma yin no zhes smra bar 'gyur.
137. Kapstein, *Tibetan Assimilation*, 135.
138. Pollock, "Theory of Practice," 512.
139. Pollock, "Theory of Practice," 512–513.

140. Pollock, "Theory of Practice," 514–515.
141. Local canons of authority could be created, as for instance by Madhva, who wrote that "the Four Vedas, the *Mahābhārata*, the Pāñcarātra corpus, the *Valmīki Rāmāyana*, and texts consistent with these, constitute *śāstra* [(true) teaching]. All other texts are not *śāstra* by rather the evil way." Madhva, *SarvaDaSaṃ*, 157, cited in Pollock, "Theory of Practice," 503.
142. Veyne, *Did the Greeks Believe?*, 54.
143. Veyne, *Did the Greeks Believe?*, 55.
144. Tucci, *Tibetan Painted Scrolls*, 212.
145. Veyne, *Did the Greeks Believe?*, 7 and 101.
146. Davidson, "Reframing *Sahaja*," 58.
147. Chakravarti, *Tantras*, 27.
148. Veyne, *Did the Greeks Believe?*, 128–129.
149. Veyne, *Did the Greeks Believe?*, 103: "Historians are merely prophets in reverse, and they flesh out and animate their *post eventum* predictions with imaginative flourishes. This is called 'historical retrodiction' or 'synthesis,' and this imaginative faculty furnishes three-fourths of any page of history."
150. Veyne, "Foucault révolutionne l'histoire," 236, cited in Chartier, *On the Edge*, 70. Compare the epigram by Evans-Pritchard at the beginning of chapter 1 of this book.
151. Pollock, *Literary Cultures in History*, 13.
152. Momigliano, "Rhetoric of History," 265. It may seem strange for someone whose work is so heavily influenced by Hayden White to be citing Momigliano. I believe that both are careful historians with a principled concern for evidence and method. Momigliano, I believe, misreads White in this regard and accordingly underestimates the value of White's insights for the practical work of historiography.

4. THE SEMIOLOGY OF TRANSGRESSION

1. Mitra, *Sanskrit Buddhist Literature*, 257–260. This passage is cited approvingly by Benoytosh Bhattacharyya, "Origin and Development of Vajrayāna," 741.
2. Bourdieu, *The Logic of Practice*, 4.
3. This scripture is cited by name in a number of other Tantric scriptures as of particular sanctity and authority, such as the *Herukābhidhāna* and the *Saṃpuṭodbhava* (for translations of these passages, see, e.g., Gray, *Cakrasamvara*, 177, and Elder, *Saṃpuṭa*, 162).
4. There seem to be divergent traditions concerning the fifth ambrosia. It is named in none of the relevant passages in the GST: All either have merely "the five ambrosias" or some partial listing up to four (feces, urine, semen, blood), never mentioning the fifth. Most Tibetan traditions consider it to be marrow (*rkang mar*). Elizabeth English considers the fifth ambrosia to be flesh, citing the *Cakrasaṃvara Tantra*; English, *Vajrayoginī*, 210 and 491–492n493). However, the Śaiva *Kaulajñānanirṇaya* XI.11 (36) concurs in holding it to be marrow (*majjan*). The *Bod rgya tshig mdzod chen*

mo [*Great Tibetan-Chinese Dictionary*] gives the cryptic "adamantine dew" (*rdo rje'i zil pa*) as the fifth; Zhang, *Bod rgya*, 1362.

5. This very presupposition—that the authors of the Tantric movement were laypeople—may be said to be inextricably linked to the literalist viewpoint. Were this axiom set aside (and in chapter 6 we will address exactly this question), the implicit narrative undergirding the entire literalist project is significantly—if not fatally—weakened.
6. Burnouf, *Introduction*, 558: «La plume se refuse à transcrire des doctrines aussi misérables quant à la forme, qu'odieuses et dégradantes pour le fond.»
7. Mitra, *Sanskrit Buddhist Literature*, 258–260.
8. Monier-Williams, *Buddhism*, 151.
9. Bhattacharyya, *Two Vajrayāna Works*, xii.
10. Snellgrove, *Indo-Tibetan Buddhism* I, 160.
11. Snellgrove, "Categories," 1379. It is worth noting that the context of the passage he cites to substantiate this claim is that of the *caryāvrata* described in chapter 5.
12. Davidson, *Indian Esoteric Buddhism*, 242.
13. Davidson, *Indian Esoteric Buddhism*, 101.
14. Warder, *Indian Buddhism*, 475.
15. Chakravarti, ed., *Pradīpoddyotana*, 47–48, 108, and 164.
16. And this is indeed a cogent concern with regard to commentaries such as the *Pradīpoddyotana*. If, as I argue, the author of this commentary likely flourished in the late tenth or early eleventh centuries, this would place his floruit long after the composition of the *Guhyasamāja Tantra* itself; see Wedemeyer, *Āryadeva's Lamp*, 25n53.
17. Warder, *Indian Buddhism*, 499.
18. This is all the more notable, perhaps, insofar as the *Hevajra Tantra* is generally considered to belong to the class of Yoginī Tantra-s. That is, it belongs to a stratum of Indian Buddhist literature somewhat later than the *Guhyasamāja* that is considered by many scholars to represent a more radical, antinomian platform than that found in the Mahāyoga scriptures.
19. It is worth noting that this explanation is strikingly similar to the exegesis of the *Guhyasamāja* found in its explanatory tantra, the *Explanation of the Intention* (*Sandhyavyakarana*), on which see, for example, Wedemeyer, "Antinomianism and Gradualism," 184–187.
20. P. Williams and A. Tribe, *Buddhist Thought*, 237. Indeed, this motif appears much earlier, as can be seen in the *Dhammapada*, 225–226 (cf. *Udānavarga*).
21. Broido, "Killing, Lying, Stealing and Adultery," 72–73.
22. See, for example, Steinkellner, "Remarks on Tantristic Hermeneutics," Broido, "Killing, Lying, Stealing and Adultery," and Thurman, "Vajra Hermeneutics." Davidson, *Indian Esoteric Buddhism*, makes some use of Candrakīrti's work, but largely dismisses it out of hand.
23. On the other hand, Davidson's suggestion (*Indian Esoteric Buddhism*, 247) that the diversity of commentarial interpretations implies the literalness of the original signification is equally problematical. The fact of commentarial divergence does

cast doubt on the notion of a preexistent, secret interpretation hidden via a code. However, it is rather a logical leap then to assert that the original meaning must have been literal. Although little has been established concerning the sociology of scholastic commentary in Buddhist India, some degree of diversity is certainly to be expected, given the diversity of ideological (social, institutional, cultural) commitments of their authors.

24. See, for example, Chakravarti, ed., *Pradīpoddyotana*, 225. Clearly, the simplistic construct of later commentators bowdlerizing or domesticating the Tantras for monastic consumption is inadequate to the data at our disposal. For another example in which modern scholars have clung to this kind of construct concerning a monastic Tantric commentator, although it were manifestly contradicted by his available writings, see Wedemeyer, "Sex, Death, and Reform."
25. GST VIII.8: *viṇ-mūtra-toyādi-vilepanaṃ vā kurvīta śaśvaj jina-pūja-hetoḥ* |; here I am following the (notably more antinomian) reading found in the *Pradīpoddyotana Commentary*, rather than the edited text which reads "pure water(s), and the like" (*viśuddha-toyādi-*).
26. Chakravarti, ed., *Pradīpoddyotana*, 75.
27. mātaraṃ pitaraṃ hatvā rājānaṃ dvau ca śrotriyau | rāṣṭraṃ sānucaraṃ hatvā naro viśuddha ucyate || (*Abhidharmasamuccaya*, cited in Ruegg, "Allusiveness," 304). *Udānavarga* xxix.24 and xxxiii.61 read identically: mātaraṃ pitaraṃ hatvā rājānaṃ dvau ca śrotriyau | rāṣṭraṃ sānucāraṃ hatvā anigho yāti brāhmaṇaḥ ||; and *Udānavarga* xxxiii.62 reads: mātaraṃ pitaraṃ hatvā rājānaṃ dvau ca śrotriyau | vyāghraṃ ca pañcamaṃ hatvā śuddha ity ucyate naraḥ ||. *Dhammapada* has: mātaraṃ pitaraṃ hantvā rājāno dve ca khattiye | raṭṭhaṃ sānucaraṃ hantvā anīgho yāti brāhmaṇo || mātaraṃ pitaraṃ hantvā rājāno dve ca sotthiye | veyyagghapañcamaṃ hantvā anīgho yāti brāhmaṇo || (DP, 294–295).
28. Cited in Lamotte, "Assessment of Textual Interpretation," 18.
29. Pierre Bourdieu attributes this same example to Valérie, not Barthes, so I am not certain whether it may properly and originally be attributable to the latter, rather than the former; Bourdieu, *The Logic of Practice*, 32.
30. Barthes, *Mythologies*, 124.
31. Bentor, *Consecration of Images and Stupas*.
32. These are the **Sūtra-melāpaka* of Nāgārjuna and the *Vajrasattva-sādhana* of Candrakīrti. In the apparent absence of a surviving Sanskrit witness, I have consulted the former solely through a Tibetan translation by Dharmaśrībhadra and Rin-chen bZang-po: *rNal 'byor chen po'i rgyud dpal gsang ba 'dus pa'i bskyed pa'i rim pa bsgom pa'i thabs mdo dang bsras pa zhes bya ba (*Śrī-guhyasamāja-mahāyogatantrotpattikrama-sādhana-sūtramelāpaka-nāma)*, sDe dge bsTan 'gyur, rGyud 'grel, vol. ngi, ff. 11a^{2}–15b^{1} (Tōh. 1797). The latter I have consulted in a Tibetan translation by Tathāgatarakṣita and kLog-skya gZhon-nu-dpal, as edited by Dipaṃkārarakṣita and Bari Lotsāwa (*rDo rje sems dpa'i sgrub thabs zhes bya ba*: Peking bsTan-'gyur, rGyud-'grel, vol. gi, ff. 168b^{3}–178a^{3}) as well as in an unpublished Sanskrit manuscript found in the Rāhula Sāṅkṛtyāyana collection of the Bihar Research Society (Bandurski no. Xc 14/30, ff.

13b–19a). More recently, this has been edited by Luo Hong and Toru Tomabechi. On the vexed issue of the identity and dating of these two authors, see Wedemeyer, *Āryadeva's Lamp*, 7–43.

33. These stages are most explicitly systematized in: Nāgārjuna, *Sūtramelāpaka*, Pek. bsTan 'gyur, rGyud 'grel, vol. gi, f. 17a[1-6]. The structure of the rite as presented by Candrakīrti, although it varies in some minor details, is essentially identical.
34. Actually, it might be said to be more than merely analogous—the identical term (*sīmābandha*) is used, for example in Candrakīrti's *sādhana* rite, as part of the larger rite of the protection circle (*rakṣācakra*). In the Sanskrit manuscript this may be found at f. 14b[5]. The Tibetan translation may be found at: f. 170a[7].
35. bdud rtsi lnga la sogs pa'i zas kyi bya ba dag kyang bya'o |: Nāgārjuna, *Sūtramelapaka*, Pek. Bstan 'gyur, Rgyud 'grel, vol. gi, f. 16b[6]. It ought to be noted, for full disclosure, that Candrakīrti's rite does not mention the five meats or ambrosias.
36. Indeed, the presence of feces and semen on the menu might have already suggested to the attentive reader that this is no ordinary weenie roast!
37. Kane, *History of Dharmaśāstra*, vol. II, part 2, 771–786.
38. This is an important point; for contemporary scholarship on the *dharmaśāstra*-s does not believe these works to have functioned as first-order law codes to be applied in society, but rather more as second-order works intended to inculcate students in the proper modes of speaking about such social strictures. Thus, they cannot in themselves be taken as evidence of social practice without corroborating evidence.
39. Li Rongxi, trans., *Great Tang Dynasty Records*, 64. Note that the use of "ox" here may be taken to mean "cow." The character in question is *niu*, which can mean either cow or ox. Earlier in Beal's translation (70), he renders *niu* as "cow." Thanks to Tyson Yost for assistance with the Chinese of this passage. See also, Beal, *Buddhist Records*, 89 [italics mine].

    Similarly, in the early eleventh century, Alberuni reports that it is forbidden in India to kill (and, thus, eat) cows, horses, and elephants; Sachau, *Alberuni's India*, vol. II, 151. He does not mention either dogs or humans, but these are cases so well-known in Indian culture and so clearly proscribed in Islamic dietary laws, as perhaps not to require substantiation. On dogs and horses in Hinduism, one may now consult W. Doniger, *The Hindus*.
40. Kane, *History of Dharamaśāstra*, 781, mentions that Devala forbids all five of the meats (in a much longer list). Also, because human flesh is well-known to have been taboo in contemporaneous Chinese culture, Xuanzang's failure to mention it is not noteworthy.
41. Zysk, *Asceticism and Healing*, 21–27.
42. Kane, *History of Dharmaśāstra*, 771.
43. *pūtigandha-jugupsitam*: GST XIV.51.
44. Consider the testimony of the *Caryāmelāpakapradīpa* of Āryadeva (Wedemeyer, *Āryadeva's Lamp*), who refers to the meats and ambrosias as "pledge [substances] to be consumed, [which are] forbidden [to be eaten] in the world" (*lokagarhitaṃ*

bhakṣaṇīya-samayaṃ). The term that I here render "forbidden in the world," *loka-garhita*, could also be rendered "reviled by folk;" notably this term is also used by Candrakīrti when speaking of charnel grounds (*śmaśāna*—also a preëminent site of ritual pollution—see Chakravarti, *Pradīpoddyotana*, 104). In this regard, one might also consider the usage of *jugupsa* ("revolting") in *Advayasiddhi* (verse 21 about revulsion for low castes; see Shendge, *Advayasiddhi*, 19), *Jñānasiddhi* I.16 (on acts revolting to others; see Bhattacharyya, *Two Vajrayāna Works*, 32), and *Pradīpoddyotana* (on avoiding revulsion in ritual cunnilingus; see *Pradīpoddyotana*, 213).

Much the same awareness may be seen in a parallel instance in Śaiva esoterism. Jayaratha, in commenting on Abhinavagupta's *Tantrāloka* XXIX.10, cites the following verse that clearly indicates how these substances were perceived: "This Krama is to be worshipped with substances that are odious to folk and contrary to the aim of [exoteric] teaching, worthy of both revulsion and reproach" (dravyaiś ca loka-vidviṣṭaiḥ śāstrārthāc ca bahiṣkṛtaiḥ | vijugupsyaiś ca nindyaiś ca pūjanīyas tv ayaṃ kramaḥ ||; *Tantrāloka*, vol. XI, pt. 2, 8).

45. Shiníchi Tsuda ("Original Formation," 110–111) has also made this point, albeit in a somewhat different context: "it was in fact the expectation of the 'author' of [the *Guhyasamāja*] that this Tantric attitude of assuming intentionally the appearance of extreme obscenity by removing the worldly distinctions of good and evil or purity and defilement would be looked upon with astonishment or abhorrence by the people of the world or the people of commonsense."
46. Bendall, *Subhāṣitasaṃgraha*, 29n1.
47. Ten occur as objects of the verb √*bhakṣ* ("to eat": VI.23, VIII.26, XV.17–18, XV.36–48, XVI.37, XVII.9, XVII.10, XVII.11, XVII.47, XVII.60), three with *āhāra*+√*kṛ* ("to take [as] food": V.5, VI.21, VI.22), and one with *mukhe pra*+√*kṣip* ("to put in [one's] mouth": XII.5).
48. These references (XII.41–44 and XII.47) refer to the meats and ambrosias as *samaya*, "pledge [substances]"—a term closely associated with ritual consumption throughout this literature.
49. Two occur as objects of the verb √*pūj* ("to worship": VIII.24 and XVI.13), one as the object of *ni*+√*vid* ("to offer, give": IV.21), three with √*dā* or *baliṃ* √*dā* ("to give" or "to give an oblation": XVI.7, XVI.24–25, and XVII.32), and one in the instrumental with *āhutiṃ prati*+√*pad* ("to render an oblation": XVI.33–35).
50. XV.75–79: Verse 77 reads "It [the image of an enemy] should be made of beef, horse meat, dog meat [and] various [things] in a three-cornered maṇḍala; [then] even adamant will certainly be destroyed" (*gomāṃsahayamāṃsena śvānamāṃsena citriṇā | trikoṇamaṇḍale kāryaṃ dhruvaṃ vajro 'pi naśyati ||*). The *Pradīpoddyotana Commentary* reads "'Beef' and so on [means]: having drawn a three-cornered, i.e., fire, maṇḍala out of funereal ashes in a charnel ground, kindling a fire with *kaṭuka* kindling, having made an image of the enemy out of beef and so on, preceded by the invocation and reciting as before, cutting and cutting, one should sacrifice [it] in the fire" (*gomāṃsetyādi | citibhasmanā trikoṇam āgneyamaṇḍalaṃ smaśāne*

saṃlikhya tasmin kaṭukendhanenâgniṃ samādhāya gomāṃsādinā śatroḥ pratikṛtiṃ kṛtvā āvāhanapūrvakaṃ pūrvavat japan chitvā chitvâgnau juhūyāt |; PU, 173). The context of the passage as a whole, as well as the act being done in a "three-cornered maṇḍala" (the stereotypical form of the fire maṇḍala, as the commentary indicates), leads me to believe that this comment accurately indicates the meaning of the verse from the root scripture. Thus, we may safely take this to be another occurrence of the meats in conjunction with a verb of offering (in this case √*hu*, "to sacrifice").

51. Two of these (VIII.8 and XV.3) are examples of the smearing of cow dung mentioned earlier (again, the commentary and the context converge in indicating this reading); the other is a reference to *pañcāmṛta*, which the commentary glosses as the "five transcendent lords" (*pañca-tathāgata*)—in this context, reading *amṛta* as "immortal" (i.e., a divinity), rather than "ambrosia." Again, here I believe we can safely follow the commentarial gloss, as the action to which it is connected in this passage (*pātana*, "descending") is commonly found throughout this literature in reference to the five tathāgatas (as visualized in a yogic process); it occurs nowhere else in reference to the five ambrosias.
52. The examples are effectively adjacent (GST XVI.39 and XVI.42), so could even be considered one example; though, so as to err on the side of conservatism, I have counted them as two. In the former, the expression "fæces, urine [and] meat" (*viṇmūtramāṃsa-*) occurs with a derivative of the verb "to do" (√*kṛ*) ifc.; the commentary notes "the usage of [the word] 'action' (*kṛtya*) comprehends [the sense] 'eating and drinking the in[edible and] un[potable]'"; Chakravarti, *Pradīpoddyotana*, 194 (*kṛtyagrahaṇenâbhakṣyapeyādigrahaṇam* |). The latter instance merely states that one should place the five meats and ambrosias in equal portions in a vessel. The commentary specifies that they should be made into portions or pills and eaten daily. The verb used, again, is √*bhakṣ* ("to eat").
53. Notably the works of the Noble Tradition of the Guhyasamāja, including—but not limited to—Nāgārjuna's *Pañcakrama*, Āryadeva's *Caryāmelāpakapradīpa*, and Candrakīrti's *Pradīpoddyotana*. See Mimaki and Tomabechi, *Pañcakrama*; Wedemeyer, *Āryadeva's Lamp*; and Chakravarti, *Pradīpoddyotana*.
54. *Pañcakrama* V.3: saṃkleśaṃ vyavadānaṃ ca jñātvā tu paramārthataḥ | ekībhāvaṃ tu yo vetti sa vetti yuganaddhakam ||.
55. *Pañcakrama* V: 30–34a; yathātmani tathā śatrau . . . | yathā mātā tathā veśya . . . || . . . yathā mūtraṃ tathā madyaṃ yathā bhaktaṃ yathā śakṛt || yathā sugandhi karpūram tathā gandham amedhyajam | yathā stutikaraṃ vākyaṃ tathā vākyaṃ jugupsitam || . . . | . . . || yathā saukyaṃ tathā duḥkhaṃ.
56. Barthes, *Mythologies*, 124.
57. Ibid.
58. Compare Freud's comment on rational argument vs. jests (*Jokes*, 163): "Where argument tries to draw the hearer's criticism over on to its side, the joke endeavors to push the criticism out of sight. There is no doubt that the joke has chosen the method which is psychologically the more effective."
59. Barthes, *The Eiffel Tower*, 71.
60. Barthes, *The Eiffel Tower*, 72.

61. It may be noted that a similar feature has been observed of the performative aspect of ritual or ritual-like activities wherein, as Catherine Bell has noted, "one is not being told or shown something so much as one is led to experience something;" Bell, *Ritual*, 160.
62. Similarly, in connotative semiotics, although the choice is delimited in some measure by the range of available signs in any given cultural moment, the specific choice of signifier among this spectrum of suitable possibilities is arbitrary.
63. GST XII.44: alābhe sarvamāṃsānāṃ dhyātvā sattvaṃ vikalpayet. Elsewhere also, in chapter 6, the text recommends that one "imagine" eating human flesh.
64. The frequently-repeated injunctions in Mahāyoga Tantra materials against taking account of astrological phenomena such as lunar mansions (*nakṣatra*), lunar days (*tithī*), amd so on, in ritual practice would seem to be a response to earlier esoteric scriptures that enjoin practitioners, on the contrary, to schedule their ritual activities in accordance with such considerations. For passages in the older strata that enjoin attentiveness to astrology, see, for example, *Mahāvairocanottaratantra* I. 14, II.5, III.2, IV. 2 (English translation may be found in S. Hodge, *The Mahā-vairocana-abhisaṃbodhi Tantra*) or *Mañjuśrīmūlakalpa*, of which chapters 18–21, 24, and 32 deal at some length with issues of astrological auspiciousness, planets (*graha*), lunar mansions (*nakṣatra*), and so on, with regard to ritual practice (see T. G. Sâstrî, *Āryamañjuśrīmūlakalpa*; cf. Wallis, *Mediating the Power of the Buddhas*, esp. 99, 114, and 175–177). Examples of later esoteric Buddhist responses may be found in, for example, *Cittaviśuddhiprakaraṇa* vv. 71–6 (see Patel, *Cittaviśuddhiprakaraṇa*, 5–6; cf. Wedemeyer, *Vajrayāna and its Doubles*, 371), *Advayasiddhi* v. 1 (see Shendge, *Advayasiddhi*, 15). Matthew Kapstein has likewise noted of the *Mañjuśrīmūlakalpa* that purity "is clearly one of its predominant concerns;" Kapstein, *Reason's Traces*, 279 n. 13.
65. Notably, according to Bhāmaha's *Kāvyālaṃkāra*, the Tantras of this sort also flout the conventions of good poetic literature, by using cryptic expressions (*gūḍha-śabda*) and offensive words; Sastry, *Kāvyālaṃkāra of Bhāmaha*, 16–19. Bhāmaha actually uses "fæces" (*viṭ*) as an example of terms that are "offensive to the ear" (*śruti-duṣṭa*; note the apparent consonance of this term with the Dharmaśāstric term applied to the five meats, *svabhāva-duṣṭa*, "polluting by its very nature"). Thus, the Tantric semiosis may perhaps also have served to place its scriptures in implicit (agonistic) dialogue as well with contemporaneous conventions of fine literature. Cf. also Ruegg, "Allusiveness and Obliqueness in Buddhist Texts," 317–322.
66. It must be noted, however—lest clever critics accuse me of suggesting that the authors of these Tantras were adumbrating Barthes—that it is not crucial to my argument that the use of connotative semiotics have been self-consciously employed. As is clear from the work of Barthes and others, this type of signification is nearly ubiquitous in human communication, and—like other grammars of signification—is learned and used without the need for theoretical elaboration.
67. ānantarya-prabhṛtayo mahāpāpakṛto 'pi ca | sidhyante buddhayāne 'smin mahāyāna-mahodadhau ||; *Guhyasamāja Tantra*, 15. The "inexpiable sins" or "sins of immediate retribution" (*ānantarya*) are those that result in inescapable rebirth in hell immediately after death. The *Pradīpoddyotana* enumerates them

as follows: killing one's mother, father, or a monk/saint (the Sanskrit text reads *bhikṣu*, while the Tibetan translation reads the more common *dgra bcom pa*, i.e., *arhat*), damaging a buddha's body, and abandoning the Holy Dharma (*Pradīpodyotana*, 57: ānantaryetyādi | mātṛpitṛbhikṣuvadha-buddhapratimābheda-saddharmapratikṣepakākhyāni pañca karmāni maraṇānantaraṃ narakapātanād ānantaryāni/ [Chakravarti reads *narakayātanād*]); also, Peking Bstan-'gyur, vol. 60 (Rgyud 'grel, sa): sems can mtshams med ces bya ba la sogs pa la | pha dang ma dang dgra bcom pa gsod pa dang | sangs rgyas kyi sku 'jig pa dang | dam pa'i chos spong ba zhes bya ba'i las lngas ni | 'chi ba'i dus byas ma thag tu dmyal bar ltung bar 'gyur bas na mtshams med pa ste |.

68. Davidson (*Indian Esoteric Buddhism*, 253) characterizes a similar narrative found in chapter 1 of the *Guhyasamāja* as "a strategy to introduce new practices"—suggesting that encapsulating an idea in a scriptural genre and indicating its novelty by means of astonishment episodes were enough to validate such radical departures from mainstream doctrine. This seems to me rather to oversimplify the complex cultural negotiations to which these documents bear witness. A prototype of this position may be found in Waddell, who maintained (*Buddhism of Tibet*, 57) that the aim of Tibetan esoteric apocrypha was "to legitimize many of their unorthodox practices . . . and to admit of further laxity."
69. Bhattacharyya, "Tāntrika Culture Among the Buddhists," 95–96: "if this book is examined carefully, it will be seen that the teachings were opposed even when the work was first revealed. . . . [relates narrative of fifth chapter]. . . . This shows that there was considerable opposition to the teachings of the book, which people were not prepared to accept in their entirety."
70. *Adhyāśayasaṃcodanasūtra*: "Whatever, Maitreya, is well-spoken (*su-bhāṣita*), all that is spoken by the Buddha (*buddha-bhāṣita*)" (*yat kiñcin maitreya subhāṣitaṃ sarvaṃ tad buddhabhāṣitam*); cited in *Śikṣāsamuccaya*, 12. Compare *Aṅguttara Nikāya*, vol. IV, 164: *yaṃ kiñci subhāsitaṃ sabban taṃ tassa bhagavato vacanaṃ arahato sammasambuddhassa*.
71. Prebish, *Buddhist Monastic Discipline*, 24.
72. Winternitz, ("Notes on the Guhyasamāja," 3) gives the following, rather inadequate account of this narrative: "Lord Sarvatathāgatakāyavāk [*sic*] touched them with the rays issuing from his body *after a certain meditation*, and they were soon revived, and praised the Lord who had given them *a miracle instead of an explanation*" [emphasis mine].
73. The term "voidness" (*śūnyatā*) does not explicitly appear in this passage, but it is transparent that this is what is being referred to when it speaks of all things being like space and fire residing neither in the wood or the manual labor that rubs them together. Matsunaga, ed., GST, 28. Candrakīrti's commentary specifies that this is a discussion of *śūnyatā* (PU, 87–88).
74. GST IX.21: mahādbhuteṣu dharmeṣu ākāśa-sadṛśeṣu ca | nirvikalpeṣu śuddheṣu saṃvṛtis tu pragīyate ||.
75. Compare the analysis given in the next chapter of the antinomian chapters of the GST, especially 5, 7, and 16.

76. Chapter titles appear at the end of chapters, rather than the beginning, in Sanskrit works.
77. Adapting from Barthes, Bullen schematizes the semiotical structure of historical discourse as:

<table>
<tr><td>1. Signifier</td><td>2. Signified</td><td></td></tr>
<tr><td colspan="2">3. Sign
I. SIGNIFIER [form]
Documentary sources</td><td>II. SIGNIFIED
Ideology</td></tr>
<tr><td colspan="3">III. SIGN [SIGNIFICATION]
The historical text</td></tr>
</table>

Seen in this way, the historian's work may be seen to constitute a composite of documentary sources (historical evidence, composed of already-meaningful signs) arranged so as to serve itself as a signifier indicating as its signified the (implicit) ideology of the historian. "In this way, the historian's spoken or unspoken intentions, his conscious or unconscious pre-critical imperatives, his cultural values, or his religious and political prejudices, seem to be organically and innocently linked to the form of the myth to create an objective historical discourse."(Bullen, *Myth of the Renaissance*, 6.)
78. J. Z. Smith, *Drudgery Divine*, 128–129.
79. R. Ray, "Reading the Vajrayāna in Context," 182.
80. "Robinson and Johnson" [actually Wawrytko & DeGraff] *The Buddhist Religion*, 4th ed., 127.
81. *Buddhist Religion*, 4th ed, 129.
82. The traditions developed various ways of allowing this to happen. The *Vimalaprabhā* Commentary on the *Kālacakra Tantra*, for instance, speaks of eating each day a sesame-seed-sized pill composed of the five meats and ambrosias (Newman, *Outer Wheel*, 266). This "homeopathic" approach would allow for the consumption and semiosis to occur without significant revulsion. This would have been important for the tradition, if we credit the ritual instructions, for a reaction of revulsion is said to work in the opposite direction, "breaking the [semiotical] spell" and eroding rather than constructing the sense of divine identity. See *Caṇḍamahāroṣaṇa Tantra* IV: "One should drink urine . . . [and] eat feces as one likes. One may not be even slightly disgusted (*ghṛṇa*), otherwise there will be a decline in success (*siddhi*)" (yāvadicchaṃ pibet mūtrāṃ . . . | . . . viṣṭhāṃ yāvadicchaṃ prabhakṣayet | na kartavyā ghṛṇālpâpi siddhibhraṃśo 'nyathā bhavet |; see George, ed., 64).
83. Davidson, *Indian Esoteric Buddhism*, 258.
84. Davidson, *Indian Esoteric Buddhism*, 259.

85. One might recall in this context the comments of Barth concerning opposing views on the historicity of the Buddha's biography, the mythological and the euhemerist: "[To take either approach] is to mutilate Buddhism . . . and render it, as a religion, inexplicable. In Kern's book, the story lacks the man; in that of Oldenberg, the god" (c'est mutiler le bouddhisme . . . et le rendre, comme religion, inexplicable. Dans le livre de M. Kern, c'est l'homme qui manque à cette histoire; dans celui de M. Oldenberg, c'est le dieu; cited in Lamotte, "Le Légende du Bouddha", 42).

5. THE PRACTICE OF INDIAN TANTRIC BUDDHISM

1. As anthropologist Evans-Pritchard stressed (*Theories of Primitive Religions*, 7), "very fundamental semantic problems" confront the scholar of foreign religions insofar as there are "conceptions, images, words, which require for understanding a thorough knowledge of a people's language and also an awareness of the entire system of ideas of which any particular belief is part, for it may be meaningless when divorced from the set of beliefs and practices to which it belongs."
2. Clapp, *Random House Webster's Dictionary of the Law*, 427. Compare: Garner, ed., *Black's Law Dictionary*, 1511: "A word or phrase having a specific, precise meaning in a given specialty, apart from its general meaning in ordinary contexts"; and Wild, ed., *Webster's New World Law Dictionary*, 254–255: "A word specific to a discipline and having a special meaning within that discipline other than what it is understood to mean in common usage."
3. See *Caryāmelāpakapradīpa*, 181 and 374.
4. That something of the same is true across the Buddhist traditions is suggested by Peter Masefield (*Divine Revelation in Pali Buddhism*, xv), who comments "the sad fact is that much of the basic terminology and symbolism of the Nikāyas is still in need of detailed investigation. Indeed the fact that a good many terms were used with a distinctly technical sense [i.e., were terms of art] has often escaped most scholars."
5. Tsuda, *Saṃvarodaya-Tantra*, 46.
6. Tanemura, "Superiority of Vajrayāna," 488.
7. *Mahāvastu*, vol. I, 1: catvārīmāni bodhisattvānāṃ bodhisattvacaryāṇi | katamāni catvāri | prakṛticaryā praṇidhānacaryā anulomacaryā anivartanacaryā |.
8. *Mahāyāna-sūtrālaṅkāra of Asaṅga*, 175; see also, Jamspal, et al., trans., *The Universal Vehicle Discourse Literature*, 333–334.
9. *Bodhisattvabhūmi*, 256.
10. punaḥ pravrajito bodhisattvaḥ pareṣāṃ vrata-niyame sthitatvād ādeyavacano bhavati | na tu tathā gṛhī bodhisattvaḥ; *Bodhisattvabhūmi*, 213.
11. *Caryā* as a term of art seems to have been almost completely overlooked by contemporary interpreters. There seem to be no more than two or three mere references in modern scholarship to the notion that *caryā* refers in some contexts to a specific religious undertaking. These, too, refer to it only insofar as it was abstracted and discussed by commentators, not as it occurs in the revealed literature of the Tantras themselves; and there has been no systematic scholarly

treatment of the topic as a whole. I believe the first published piece to address this issue specifically was my own "Antinomianism and Gradualism." Ronald Davidson makes passing references to the related *vidyāvrata* in his *Indian Esoteric Buddhism*, published in the same year (see 199 and 326–327). To this may be added my own study of Āryadeva's *Caryāmelāpakapradīpa*; yet that presentation too is inadequate insofar as it is limited to the somewhat idiosyncratic presentation given in that particular śāstra and in no way represents a thorough, critical analysis of the phenomenon in the Tantric traditions as a whole. More recently (since these arguments were first presented at the June 2008 Congress of the International Association of Buddhist Studies), Ryugen Tanemura has published two contributions in this area: "Justification for and Classification of the Post-initiatory Caryā in Later Indian Tantric Buddhism," and "Superiority of Vajrayāna Part II." These, like my own 2002 essay, are rather brief, but within a limited scope attempt to lay out some of the key features of the rite.

12. In fact, Tathāgatarakṣita's *Yoginīsaṃcāratantranibandha* (133) glosses *vratacaryā* in the root text (XV.2) with *caryāvrata*, indicating that he took them to be synonymous. One might further infer from this that the form *caryāvrata* is more common and readily recognizable as the term of art we are interested in here. This is, I believe, supported by the pattern of occurrence of these expressions across the Buddhist literature. The inverse may be true, however, of the Śaiva literature wherein, for example, the *Picumata/Brahmayāmala* uniformly reads *vratacaryā*, although those usages do not appear to be terms of art. Thanks to Shaman Hatley for his assistance in providing scans of the manuscript of the PM-BY as well as drawing my attention to occurrences of *vratacaryā* therein.
13. Note that Tanemura, based largely on his reading of the (rather later) works of Abhayākaragupta, takes *samaya* to be a synonym for *caryā* ("Justification," 53); and it seems as if Alexis Sanderson shares this view (he translates *samaya* as "post-initiatory disciplines" in "Commentary," 116). Such a conflation, however, is unwarranted. In fact, Abhayākaragupta himself, in one of the works cited by Tanemura, glosses *caryā* as "relying thus on all those things such as *samaya* and so on" (*Āmnāyamañjarī*, f. 296a[6]: de ltar dam tshig la sogs pa thams cad la brten pa la sogs pa ni spyod pa ste). It is clear from this and many other instances that *samaya* refers to the polluting substances consumed in the rite of *caryāvrata*, not the rite itself. While *samaya* may occasionally be used in a synecdochic sense, it certainly does not in general directly denote the *caryāvrata*.
14. See appendix 2 for a complete translation of this chapter from the Tibetan and a folio preserved in the Cambridge University Library. This important work of Indian Tantric Buddhism and Abhayākaragupta's *Abhayapaddhati* commentary is currently being cooperatively edited by scholars from the China Tibetology Research Centre and the Department of Indian and Tibetan Studies at the University of Hamburg, based on manuscripts from Tibet. Information on this project may be found at: http://www.tantric-studies.org/projects/buddhakapalatantra-abhayapaddhati. I am grateful to Harunaga Isaacson for providing me with a scan of this important folio. The *Abhayapaddhati* itself has recently (2009) been edited by Chog Dorje.

15. *Saṃvarodaya Tantra*, chapter XXI "Teaching of the Practice" (*caryānirdeśapaṭala*), vv. 14cd–16cd (135): śmaśāne ekaliṅge vā ekavṛkṣe 'the kānane || parvatāgre nadītīre mahodadhitaṭe 'pi vā | udyāne bhagnakūpe vā prāsāde śūnyaveśmasu || catuṣpathe puradvāre rājadvāre maṭhe 'pi vā | mātaṅgī-ābhirīsthāne śilpikāgṛha gopite ||.
16. These last five are said to symbolize the Five Buddhas (see HT I.vi.11–12).
17. HT I.vi, 2–17.
18. *Herukābhidhāna/Laghusaṃvara* XXVII.3ab: sādhakaḥ siddhim āpnoti samparkāt. Here the word I render intercourse is *samparka*: Pace my friend David Gray's rendering of this term in his recent translation of this scripture as "association," I would suggest a stronger reading is apposite here. Bhavabhaṭṭa's commentary glosses this as *dūtīdarśanādi*, "observing the messenger-girl [i.e., consort] and the like." See Gray, *Cakrasamvara Tantra*, 271. For commentary, see Pandey, ed., vol. II, 488.
19. HT I.vi.8: cāruvaktrāṃ viśālākṣīṃ rūpayauvanamaṇḍitam | nīlotpala-śyāmāṅgīṃ ca svābhiṣiktāṃ kṛpāvatīṃ | vajrakanyāṃ imāṃ gṛhya caryāṃ kartuṃ vibudhyate ||. Both the *Yogimanoharā* and the *Muktāvalī* gloss *vibudhyate* as *yujyate*.
20. *Hevajra Tantra* I.vi.21: bhakṣyābhakṣya-vicāran tu peyāpeyaṃ tathaiva ca | gamyāgamyan tathā mantrī vikalpan naiva kārayet ||. These latter terms—*gamya* and *agamya*—presumably (that is, in my interpretation) refer here to the suitability of a sexual partner, a major focus of the *caryāvrata*. That is, though Farrow and Menon render this "what should and should not be done" (67), it more likely refers (in a manner of speaking) to "*whom* should and should not be done." Snellgrove renders this "nor should he ever wonder whether a thing is suitable or unsuitable" (*Hevajra Tantra*, vol. I, 65); cf. chapter 11 of Indrabhūti's *Jñānasiddhi*, which treats this topic (Rinpoche, ed., 127).
21. Cf. 6, where *vrata* occurs in compound paired with *niyama* (restraint) as qualities of ascetical renunciants.
22. Compare, for example, the Newar Buddhist *ahorātra-vrata* that entails the worship of a caitya for a day and a night, for which various results obtained may be kingship, health, good appearance, human birth, and so on. See Handurukande, ed., *Three Sanskrit Texts*, 9–22 and 104–107.
23. In commenting on pāda a of *Kālacakra Tantra* III.93, "abandon violence, untruth, adultery, wealth of self and others, and drinking mead likewise" (*hiṃsāsatyaṃ parastrīṃ tyaja svaparadhanaṃ madyapānaṃ tathaiva*), *Vimalaprabhā* comments "this refers to the restraint [that is] the five observances" (*iti pañcavratāni niyama ity arthaḥ*). See *Vimalaprabhāṭīkā*, vol. II, 88. Note that I am reading *madhu* here rather literally; presumably, this refers to fermented beverages in general. See likewise the *Mṛgendra* passage in note lxxiii, following.
24. *Lalitavistara*, for example, describes the ascetical chastity practice of Queen Mahāmāyā before the conception of the Buddha thus: "She remains stationed in her observance, like an ascetic, attending to [her] observance [yet also remaining the King's true, albeit chaste,] soul-mate" (vratasthā sā tiṣṭhati tāpasīva vratānucārī sahadharmacāriṇī | (*Lalitavistara* iii.14ab; 20). Virtually all sources (*Jātaka*, *Mahāvastu*, *Lalitavistara*) describe her in more specifically Buddhist terms

as either *poṣadhikā* or *poṣadhagṛhītā*, that is, as taking the eight fasting day vows. On *poṣadha* and its similarity to Śaiva Siddhāntin *vrata*, see also as follows, 36–37.

25. vrataṃ mauna-snāna-bhakṣyādi-niyamaḥ; Ratnākaraśānti *Guṇavatīṭīkā* on *Mahāmāyātantra* II.4 (27).
26. HT II.iii.41c: snānaṃ śaucaṃ na kurvīta.
27. This is true of both the Buddhist traditions, for which the maṇḍala rites of the Mantranaya continue to form the ritual core of the later Vajrayāna, and of the Śaiva traditions, for which the basic structures of Siddhāntin ritual continued to provide the basic ritual context for the higher systems. Alexis Sanderson has written: "Both the Saiddhāntika and the non-Saiddhāntika scriptures . . . taught a single ritual system, both in the ordering of their ceremonies and in the construction of each." See Sanderson "Śaiva Exegesis," 237–238. We will return to this point in chapter 6.
28. GST V.1–7: nirvikalpārthasambhūtāṃ rāgadveṣamahākulām | . . . sidhyate tasya buddhatvaṃ nirvikalpasya dhīmataḥ |.
29. This term, which highlights the gnostic intent of the rite, is also found in Anaṅgavajrapāda's *Prajñopāyaviniścayasiddhi* V.1, which describes it as *saṅkalpāri-niṣūdinī*, "exterminatrix of the enemy conceptions." Note the similarity of this verse with the one cited here in note 30.

    Later in the same chapter, Anaṅgavajrapāda equates the *tattva-yoga* with a rite of polluted sexual ritual (another instance in which the inversive injunctions occur in the context of The Practice): "The practitioner will quickly succeed by means of the reality yoga *(tattvayoga)*, loving a consort born in a clan (*kula*) such as the brahmin or one born as an outcast, another's wanton wife, likewise one deformed or crippled, [one's] mother, mother-in-law, one's own daughter, or sister." *Prajñopayaviniścayasiddhi* V.22-25 (93): brāhmaṇādikulotpannāṃ mudrāṃ vai antyajodbhavām | duḥśīlāṃ parabhāryāṃ ca vikṛtāṃ vikalāṃ tathā || janayitrīṃ svasāraṃ ca svaputrīṃ bhāgineyikāṃ | kāmayan tattvayogena laghu sidhyeta sādhakaḥ ||.
30. vikalpāri-nisūdanī sarva-dharma-samudbhūtā tattva-caryā niruttarā; *Saṃpuṭodbhava Tantra*, Tokyo MS 428, f. 37a[6]: "destroyer of the enemy conceptuality, born from all things—the reality-practice is unexcelled."
31. ye 'nye loke 'bhakṣyās te bhakṣyās tattvasādhakedrasya | ye 'gamyās te gamyās | ye 'kāryās tasya te kāryāḥ | gamyāgamya-vikalpaṃ bhakṣābhakṣam aniṣṭam iṣṭaṃ ca peyāpeyaṃ mantrī na kuryāt |; Tokyo Univ. Library MS 428 (old 319), ff. 38b[6]–39a[1]; Tokyo Univ. Library MS 427 (old 324), ff. 48b[6]–49a[1].
32. *gaja*; Tib. reads "ox" *glang po*; this could also be interpreted as "elephant," although *glang chen* would be preferable in this sense.
33. *nityaṃ*; or, perhaps "daily."
34. *vajrāmbu-marjikā-yuktam*; Commenting on the irony of this passage, Gary Tubb (e-mail communication, March 1, 2009) notes "*Marjikā* is an interesting word. It refers to the dessert now called shrikhand (at least in Maharashtra). As you no doubt know, this is a wonderful confection that is in the direction of cake frosting, both in texture and taste. So 'a coating' is not a bad translation; a word like 'glaze' or 'icing' would probably be more precise but might be confusing in this setting.

Its use here is quite amusing." Thanks are due to Prof. Tubb for discussing this and other oddities of this passage with me.

35. draṣṭvyāḥ khalu sarve tv anutpādākāra-yogena śvā-kharoṣṭra-gajādy-asṛk pītvā māṃsena bhojanaṃ nityaṃ || iṣṭaṃ sarva-viśeṣa-rakta-vilipta-mahāmāṃsaṃ samasta-kutsita-māṃsaṃ prāṇaka-śata-lakṣa-saṃyuktaṃ divyaṃ | vairocanenâtipūṭaṃ kīṭa-śataiḥ simisimāyamānaṃ śvāna-nara-cchardita-miśram māṃśaṃ vajrāmbu-marjikā-yuktam | vairocana-saṃmiśraṃ bhoktavyaṃ yoginotsāhaiḥ |; *Saṃpuṭodbhavasarvatantranidānamahākalparāja*, unpublished Sanskrit manuscript held by the Tokyo University Library, new catalog nr. 428 (old nr. 319) f. $38b^{4-5}$.

    Cf. Tibetan translation (Tōh. 381): sDe dge bKa' 'gyur, rgyud ga, f. $107b^{1-3}$: | khyi dang bong bu rnga mo dang | | glang po la sogs khrag 'thungs nas | | sha yang rtag tu bza' ba nyid | | sha chen khrag gis bsgos pa ni | | thams cad khyad par du ni blta | | dman pa'i sha ni thams cad dang | | srog chags 'bum phrag brgya ldan bza | | rnam snang shin tu rul ba yi | | srin bu brgya phrag zi zir ldan | | khyi dang mi skyugs bsres nas ni | | sha ni rdo rje'i chus gos ldan | | rnal 'byor pas ni spro ba yis | | rnam snang bsres nas bza' bar bya |.

36. The locus classicus of this are the dedicatory verses of Nāgārjuna's *Mūlamadhyamakakārikā*, of which the second word is *anutpāda*. It is worth noting that this verse celebrates the Buddha's teaching of dependent co-origination (*pratītyasamutpāda*), which is said to both stop conceptual construction (*prapañcopaśama*) and to be (in a quite non-Śaiva sense!) auspicious (*śiva*).
37. On *anadhyāya*, see Olivelle, "When Texts Conceal."
38. *Dīgha Nikāya*, vol. II, 291. See also *Śrāvakabhūmi* (I)-A-II-4-b-(10) on *prāvivekya* and (I)-C-III-13-a-(10) on the *dhutaguṇa*.
39. ekalinge nikuñje vā saumye vā giri-gahvare | bhūgṛhe suvibhakte vā kīṭavātodakojjhite ||; *Parākhya Tantra* XIV:2; see Dominic Goodall, ed., *Parākhyatantra*, 109 and 347. Tanemura ("Superiority," 502) translates *bhugṛha* as cellar, though it seems clear that it should be earthen hut" (as Goodall renders it here) or cottage (as I have rendered it in the passage from the CMP that Tanemura retranslates).
40. The Śaiva/Śākta *Siddhayogeśvarīmata* (VI.3) has sites very much like those specified for the *caryāvrata*, but in a seemingly dualistic ritual context. That is, the context is preliminary initiation (*samayadīkṣā*) and the rite involves bathing, fasting, and purity: ekaliṅge śmaśāne vā nadyor vā saṃgame śubhe | jaladher vā taṭe ramye parvatāgre 'tha vā punaḥ || sugupte śaraṇe vātha ekavṛkṣe manorame | mātṛgṛhe 'tha udyāne yatra vā rocate manaḥ ||. See Törzsök, "Doctrine of Magic Female Spirits," 14 and 121.
41. For citation of relevant Siddhāntin scriptural sources, 156.
42. *Rdo rje theg pa'i mtha' gnyis sel ba* (**Vajrayānāntadvayanirākaraṇa*): Sde dge bstan 'gyur, Rgyud 'grel, vol. tsu, ff. $15a^{7}$–$20a^{2}$ (Tōh. 3714). I am not at present entirely convinced that this is not a Tibetan pseudepigraphon. The Tibetan diction is a little clearer than one might expect in a true translation. However, even if it turns out to be a "grey text" or something similar, the work nonetheless stands as an unambiguous indigenous expression of this interpretation. In the interests of

consistency with prior scholarship, I am adopting here the reconstruction of the name used by Tanemura (and attributed to Alexis Sanderson); there are numerous possibilities, such as for example, *-nirghāta[na]*.

43. *sdig pa med pa'i sha*: that is, not killed by or for oneself: "roadkill," etc.
44. or, perhaps, "will uphold his/her religious precepts" (*de'i gdams ngag 'dzin par 'gyur ba*).
45. *Rdo rje theg pa'i mtha' gnyis sel ba* (**Vajrayānāntadvayanirākaraṇa*), f. 19a[4]–19b[1]: dngos po 'dzin pa'i spyod pa ni | | sha lnga dang ni bdud rtsi lnga | | rnam rtog spang phyir ci rigs bsten | | zhes brjod pa ste | | 'di ni gtsang ba'o | |'di ni mi gtsang ba'o zhes rtog pa nyid 'ching ba yin pa'i phyir | sdig pa med pa'i sha shin tu smad pa mi dang rta dang | ba lang dang | khyi dang | glang po che dag dang | thabs kyis zin par spyod pa dag gis 'chi ba zlog pa'i bdud rtsi khu ba dang | khrag dang | bshang ba dang | gci ba dang | mi'i sha dag ci rigs pa'i tshul gyis stong par bsam zhing | yang de dag nyid lha'i bdud rtsi ltar bsams nas | chags pa med par spyad na rim gyis mi gtsang ba dang | gtsang ba'i rnam par rtog pa mi 'byung la | de'i tshe chos thams cad la tha dad pa'i rtog pa 'byung ba brdzun yin par nges pa'i shes pa 'byung ba dang | mi ma yin pa kha cig de nyid kyis de la yongs su dga' ba 'byung zhing chos bzhin du skyob pa dang de'i gdams ngag 'dzin par 'gyur ba yod do | | sha lnga dang bdud rtsi lnga ni mtshon pa ste | yul gang na sha la sogs pa mi gtsang bar 'dzin pa de dang de nyid la ma chags par spyod do | | mnyam pa'i shes pa mthong ba na bdag gi don du de dag spyad par bya mi dgos so |.
46. Compare *Oxford English Dictionary*, 2nd edition, s.v. *familiar*: "3. A familiar spirit, a demon or evil spirit supposed to attend at a call." The usage "familiar angel" is also attested.
47. This assertion may seem counterintuitive to many, given the reputation Tibetan authors such as, for example, Tsongkhapa, have as monastic authors interested to restrict sexuality. Nonetheless, my own researches indicate that this is, in fact, clearly the case. See Wedemeyer, "Antinomianism and Gradualism."
48. Tanemura ("Superiority," 488) takes issue with my interpretation ("Antinomianism," 192ff.) of the "initiation" requisite for practice of *caryā* as the *sarvabuddhābhiṣeka* described in the CMP as taking place after the third of the five stages of the Noble Tradition system. He claims that "the sub-commentary [to the *Pradīpoddyotana* (PU)] . . . seems to understand the relevant part differently." In support of this claim, he merely cites the Tibetan text of the subcommentary, without explanation. The relevant portion, however, reads as follows: *dbang bskur ba thob pas kyang zhes pa ni le'u bzhi pa nas gsungs pa'i rim pas so*; that is, "[the phrase in the PU] 'by obtaining the initiation,' [means] by the process described in the Fourth Chapter." Now, Tanemura has evidently not consulted the Fourth Chapter of the PU, or he would have noted that it is concerned precisely with an initiation process into a sand maṇḍala (*rajomaṇḍalābhiṣeka*) for "students who are distinguished in their mastery of meditation on the subtle yoga" (*sūkṣmayogabhāvanāsādhitaviśeṣāṇāṃ śiṣyāṇāṃ*; Chakravarti, ed., 41). In *Caryāmelāpakapradīpa* III (f. A:16a), subtle yoga is used as a synonym for the yogas of the perfection stage; so, a student who had already mastered that/those would at least have attained the second (mind-isolation,

cittaviveka) stage, if not necessarily the third (self-consecration, *svādhiṣṭhāna*) stage. Pace Tanemura, this is hardly "understand[ing] the relevant part differently."

49. GS I.24cd: tad-anantaraṃ tu vai kāryaṃ vrataṃ vidyā-samanvitam.
50. GS III.83: īdṛśam tu kramaṃ prāpya devatā-yogam uttamam | tataś caryāṃ prakurvīta buddhatva-pada-siddhaye |.
51. ūṣma-gataṃ katamat | pratyātmaṃ satye 'py āloka-labdhaḥ samādhiḥ prajñā-saṃyogaś ca |; Asaṅga, *Abhidharmasamuccaya*, 65.
52. See *Abhidharmakośabhāṣya*, vi.17 (343): kleśendhanadahanasyāryamārgāgneḥ pūrvarūpatvāt |.
53. *Abhidharmakośa*, vi.1 (327): darśanākhyas tv anāsravaḥ ||.
54. Péter-Dániel Szánto seems to suggest in a recent, short article that this alleged explanatory tantra of the *Catuṣpīṭha* is actually a supplemented version of what was originally the fourth chapter of a *Catuṣpīṭhamaṇḍalopāyikā* written by Āryadeva. See his "Antiquarian Enquiries," 8–10.
55. sarva-pāpa-kṣayaṃ kṛtvā viparītenaîva sidhyati |, *Caṇḍamahāroṣaṇa Tantra*, unpublished MS, Tokyo University Library, New Catalog nr. 63 (Old nr. 186), f. 49a[4] (50 of 94); cf. Tokyo University Library MS nr. 64 (New; Old nr. 196, f. 51a[4]). Tibetan translation in Sde dge bstan 'gyur, vol. nga, f. 325b[4] (Tōh. 431): sdig pa thams cad zad byas nas | phyin ci log gyis 'di nyid 'grub |. The Sanskrit verse is unmetrical, but that just seems to be how it is; cf., the comments of Dominic Goodall (*Parākhya Tantra*, 143, fn. 18) concerning the *Parākhya Tantra*, to wit, "this particular type of hypermetry, in which the first two syllables are probably intended to be read rapidly together and must count for one, appears to be not uncommon in this sort of writing."
56. See Sa chen Kun dga' snying po, the "Narrative of the Lineage of Mentors of the Śaṃvara Kṛṣṇapā Tradition" (*bDe mchog nag po pa'i lugs kyi bla ma brgyud pa'i lo rgyus*). It is worth noting that the character of Kṛṣṇācārya is so closely associated with the *caryā*/*caryāvrata* that the Tibetan traditions came to translate his name not with the expected Nag po slob dpon, but as Nag po spyod pa: i.e., as if the name were actually Kṛṣṇa-caryā! In this work, Kṛṣṇapāda is also referred to as *Vratacaryāpāda (*brtul zhugs spyod pa ba*).
57. See earlier note 27.
58. This understanding carries forward into the later commentators. For instance Abhayākaragupta, in his eponymous commentary on the *Buddhakapāla*, notes that the mention of the eight powers in this context means that "the practices (*caryā*) are permitted . . . for the one who has thereby obtained potency" (anena labdha-sāmarthyasya . . . caryānujñātā |; *Abhayapaddhati*, 65; see also Sde Bstan, vol. ra, ff. 211b[5–6]). Saraha's *Gnostic* [*Jñānavatī*] *Commentary* on the *Buddhakapāla* is also explicit that the achievement of the eight powers (*siddhi*) is a prerequisite for practice of the *caryā*, commenting, "to unpack the half-line 'endowed with the eight powers,' [it means] 'when a yogin is endowed with the eight superhuman powers [*aṣṭaguṇaiśvarya*—a synonym for the eight *siddhi*-s] then he should commence the practices (*caryā*)" (| dngos grub brgyad dang yang dag ldan | | zhes pa ni gang gi tshe rnal 'byor pa yon tan gyi dbang phyug brgyad dang ldan pa de'i tshe | spyod pa yang dag par brtsam par bya zhes pa'i tha tshig go |; Sde Bstan, vol. ra, ff. 138b[7]–139a[1]).

59. We have seen earlier that isolated places (*vijana*) and other lonely spots are preferred for its practice. Padmavajra's *Guhyasiddhi* describes it as the concealed observance (*prachanna-vrata*) and the sites prescribed for its practice are secret regions (*guhya-deśa*).
60. There are some cases in which the duration of the adoption of a *vrata* may be for life, but this is an exceptional case and, given the subtending notion of continuous rebirth, may also be taken to imply a limited duration.
61. In the opening passage of the "Vidyāvrata Chapter" of the *Mahāvairocana Tantra*, several questions about this observance are asked of the Lord Vairocana by Vajrapāṇi: how does one do it, where, and so forth. Not neglected is the question of duration; Vajrapāṇi asked "on the passage of how much time will the observance be complete?" (dus ni ci srid lon gyur na | brtul zhugs yongs su rdzogs par 'gyur |; MVT XV.2ab; Sde dge Bka' 'gyur, Rgyud, vol. tha, f. 215b[4]).
62. Lorenzen, *Kāpālikas and Kālāmukhas*, 4.
63. La Vallée Poussin, "Tāntrism (Buddhist)," 193: "Buddhist Tantrism is practically Buddhist Hinduism, Hinduism or Śaivism in Buddhist garb."
64. Sanderson points to parallelism between the Buddhist *Laghusaṃvara* and the Śaiva *Yoginīsaṃcāra*. The textual correspondences are certainly noteworthy. The issue of the direction (or source) of the borrowing has created some ongoing (and arguably unresolved) controversy, however. While Sanderson has consistently maintained the position that the Śaiva sources are primary, his arguments for this view have shifted over time. At first, he was inclined to credit a thirteenth-century Śaiva myth that claims that Buddhist Tantrism was invented by the gods in order to make heretics of competing demons, thereby decreasing their Śiva-mojo, so that they might be defeated (see "Vajrayāna," 93). Presumably perceiving the limitations of this argument (the myth is, after all, transparently a latter-day calque on the "Buddha is an avatar of Viṣṇu" motif, and hardly credible historically), he later shifted the basis for his claim to philological interpretation ("History through Textual Criticism"). More recently, Sanderson has revised his assertion somewhat, maintaining that the source for both the extant Buddhist and Śaiva materials is likely some no-longer-extant third source, which Sanderson nonetheless continues to maintain was Śaiva ("The Śaiva Age," 191). Other perspectives have been articulated in recent years by David S. Ruegg ("Sur les Rapports," "A Note on the Relationship," and esp. *Symbiosis*), Ronald M. Davidson (*Indian Esoteric Buddhism*), and David B. Gray (*Cakrasaṃvara*). Both Sanderson and his student, Péter-Dániel Szánto, have very recently published replies to the arguments of these critics.
65. See "The Śaiva Age," 124–243. In doing so, he resurrects his argument based on the thirteenth-century myth mentioned here in note lxiv.
66. Tanemura, "Justification," 56 and 67, note 26. Tanemura does not advance any real argument for this claim. Presumably, he is following Sanderson who has maintained that antinomian consumption of meat, alcohol, and so forth, and sexual intercourse with polluting women "originated as part of the magical technology of certain extremist orders of Śaiva ascetics" ("Śaivism and the Tantric Traditions," 661).

67. Even Sanderson is forced to acknowledge that the Śaiva traditions adopted elements from the Buddhist traditions. However, in line with his marked tendency to use strongly derogatory terms with regard to Buddhism and Buddhists (language strikingly absent elsewhere in his writings), Sanderson refers to this as a "reflux" from Buddhism ("The Śaiva Age," 240).
68. As I will indicate further, this position is not to be confused with Ruegg's substratum theory that implies some tertium quid. Rather, I believe that the continuities between the traditions may be accounted for on the basis of their shared civic space/time in the midst of an eclectic ritual culture." Phyllis Granoff ("Other People's Rituals") likewise speaks of an "eclectic ritual culture" in late-first-millennium India in which sectarian boundaries were remarkably porous. Similarly, Francesco Sferra ("Some Considerations," 61) speaks of a "common *Weltanschauung*, which has necessarily resulted in the development of a massive literary output and conceptual re-elaboration, as can be seen in other areas of Indian (and not only Indian) culture." Thus, I believe a consensus is forming around a developing model of a shared culture/Weltanschauung/zeitgeist which is more subtle than either the "substratum" or "borrowing" hypotheses.
69. Sanderson has suggested this late-first-millennium period of Indian religions be referred to as the "Śaiva Age." However, I believe that Benoytosh Bhattacharyya's "Tantric Age" better describes the character of the period.
70. Lorenzen, *Kāpālikas and Kālāmukhas*, 13. It also appears in other *dharmaśāstra*-s; the commentary of Aparārka cites Gautama, Manu, Saṃvarta, and Vasiṣṭha on this topic; see *Yājñavalkyasmṛti*, 1053f.
71. The killing of a Brahman serves in some Dharma literature as a metonym for the worst class of crimes, for example, *Yājñavalkyasmṛti* ii.206–233. On this issue in general, see Kane, *History of Dharmaśāstra*, vol. IV, 10–12, 17–20, and 87–96.
72. samayācāra-sadvāda-sthitiḥ svāmnāya-lakṣaṇaḥ / caryāpādaḥ; N. R. Bhatt, ed., *Mataṅgapārameśvarāgama (Vidyāpāda)*, 30.
73. Bhatt, ed., *Mṛgendrāgama*, 114: *pañcagavya-caru-prāśanādi*. It may be noted in this regard that this term *caruprāśana* is another example of one that is carried over from dualist to nondualist Tantrism. In the later works of the Krama, *caruprāśana* is the key element of their (abbreviated) initiatory ceremony; however, the *caru* comes to mean the sexual fluids of the Krama ritual. See Sanderson "The Śaiva Exegesis," 260; and Sanderson 2005, 110–114n63.
74. *māṃsa-yoṣin-madhu-tyāga*; *Mṛgendra* caryāpāda i.18 (213). On *madhu*, see note xxiii here.
75. This practice, keyed to the lunar month, entails observance of eight vows of the ten required of a novice monk or nun: The five vows (including strict chastity) as well as eschewing artistic performances, wearing of perfume or jewelry, and sleeping on a high or fancy bed. In addition, the *poṣadha* involved observance of fasting after noon (as the clergy are enjoined to do). On the practice of *poṣadha* in Burma, see Spiro, *Buddhism and Society*, 46 and 214–219.
76. This is suggested by Ronald M. Davidson, *Indian Esoteric Buddhism*, 177–186 and 326.
77. The same might be said of the *vidyāvrata* of the Buddhist *Mahāvairocana Tantra*.

78. On this latter point, see Bisschop and Griffiths, "Pāśupata Observance," 325n49.
79. *Pāśupatasūtra* 19 mentions nearness to Rudra (*anena vidhinā rudrasamīpaṃ gatvā*); *Pāśupatasūtra* 33 and *Atharvaveda Pariśiṣṭa* 40 vi.14 both specify union with Paśupati (*paśupati-sāyujya)* as the result/goal.
80. Or, Kālāmukhas; on this group and their relationship to other Śaiva groups, see Sanderson, "The Lākulas."
81. *vālayajñopavīta*; Sanderson ("Lākulas," 164) reads this as "hair [of the dead]," though elsewhere ("Śaivism and the Tantric Traditions," 665) he rendered it "made from snake skins."
82. The text reads *śiromuṇḍaiś ca maṇḍitaḥ*, lit. "adorned with bald skulls." Sanderson interprets this as either "a chaplet fashioned from human skullbones" ("Lākulas," 165) or "a necklace of human bone" ("Śaivism and the Tantric Traditions," 665).
83. ālabdhaḥ pañcabhir guhyair ddīkṣitaś caiva so bhramet | khaṭvāṅgī ca kapālī ca sa jaṭī muṇḍa-m eva vā || vālayajñopavītī ca śiromuṇḍaiś ca maṇḍitaḥ | kaupīnavāso bhasmāṅgī divyābharaṇabhūṣitaḥ || jagad rudramayam matvā rudrabhakto dṛḍhavrataḥ | sarvādas sarvaceṣṭaś ca rudradhyānaparāyaṇaḥ || rudraṃ muktvā na cānyo'sti trātā me devataṃ param | viditvaikadaśādhvānaṃ nirviśaṅkaḥ samācaret ||; *Niśvāsamukha* f. 17b2–5 edited in Sanderson "Lākulas," 163–164. My translation differs significantly from the two (divergent) translations provided by Sanderson ("Śaivism and the Tantric Traditions," 665–666; and "Lākulas," 164–165). The last line could also be rendered, "knowing the eleven levels, the fearless one should practice."
84. *Niśvāsamukha* verses 4:69cd–4:87 describe the mainstream Pāśupata observance involving courting social censure in order to transfer demerit to the critic and rob them of their merit.
85. Cf. *Yājñavalkyasmṛti* iii.243: śiraḥkapālī dhvajavān. Aparārka's commentary on this verse indicates that this verse means that the Brahman-murderer should carry precisely a *khaṭvāṅga* ("a skull placed on the peak of a banner[-pole], *dhvajāgrāropitakapāla*) and gives a hermeneutical etymology for the term: Because it is torn (*khadvā*, perhaps for *khaḍvā*?) from a corpse [it is *khaṭvā-*], its body (*-aṅga*) is indicated by the word "banner" (*khadvā cātra śavanirharaṇārthā, tadaṅgam eva dhvajaḍabdena vivakṣitam* |). He also cites the *Saṃvartasmṛti*, which indicates that the keeper of this penance should beg from all four castes (a gesture toward commensality), carrying a khaṭvāṅga, and then retire back to the forest (*cāturvarṇyaṃ cared bhaikṣaṃ khaṭvāṅgī niyataḥ pumān | bhikṣās tv evaṃ samādāya vanaṃ gacchet tataḥ punaḥ* |). See *Yājñavalkyasmṛti*, vol. II, 1053.
86. There may be some dispute over this point, so a few further remarks are in order. Sanderson seems to infer such a thoroughgoing antinomianism from the half verse *sarvādas sarvaceṣṭaś ca rudradhyānaparāyaṇaḥ* (*Niśvāsamukha* 4:90cd), which he translates as "He may eat and drink anything. No action is forbidden him. He should remain immersed in contemplation of Rudra, thinking. . . ." However, the clause about thinking (4:91ab) is grammatically linked with the subject *nirviśaṅkaḥ* (the fearless one) in the following verse in which they are both found; and the content of this thought is related to this fearless attitude. The immersion (*parāyaṇa*), on the

other hand, belongs to a series of appositional terms in the preceding three verses (4:88–90) that describe the practitioner of the *vrata*. The final characteristic of the practitioner is that he is or should be (as I translate it) "devoted to meditation on Rudra" (or "visualization of Rudra," *rudra-dhyāna-parāyaṇaḥ*). Just previously, the text laconically specifies that the practitioner "takes all [food and drink] and does all" (*sarvādas sarvaceṣṭaś ca*), presumably (i.e., as I take it) meaning that this *vrata* does not (as most do) include restrictions (*niyama*) on food, drink, or other activities (song, dance, etc.).

Sanderson attempts to buttress his antinomian reading by translating *nirviśaṅkaḥ* as "without inhibition," but this interpretation cannot be sustained. Although *śaṅka* does occur in (later) Kaula sources with the meaning of inhibition with regard to engaging in prohibited behaviors, the straightforward meaning is one who is fearless or dauntless and there is no reason to take it otherwise in this context. The Śaiva yogin is here being told that, understanding the eleven levels of reality (*ekādaśādhvānaṃ*), he may practice free of timidity, secure in the knowledge that Śiva is his supreme protector. In short, any notion of transcending gnostic inhibitions with regard to purity and pollution strictures is not in evidence in this passage, although both the worldly (*laukika*) and transcendent (*lokottara*) Pāśupata observances described do involve some transgressive behaviors and attitudes.

Hence, I conclude, one does not see the dramatically deliberate antinomian elements of the *caryāvrata* in the Lākula observance. What one sees therein is still a (perhaps somewhat more edgy, but nonetheless) dualistic rite centered on one-pointed, constant devotion to a savior god. It may advance or enhance the funerary features of the earlier Pāśupata observance, but it does not move significantly beyond the basic framework of the ascetical and funerary elements of the (nonsectarian) *mahāvrata* of the Dharmaśāstra-s. The Lākula *mahāpāśupatavrata* described in the *Niśvāsamukha* is not yet the transgressive, antinomian rite of the later Buddhist and Śaiva *caryāvrata*.

It seems that Sanderson's interpretation of this passage has evolved somewhat, such that his most recent views appear to be closer to my own. According to his most recent contribution, this section of the *Niśvāsa* shows that the Lākula ascetics "stood apart from the Pāñcārthikas by taking on, like the Kāpālikas, the *visible attributes* of the brahmin-slayer" (emphasis mine); he concludes that they constitute a transitional point between these two other groups, evincing "a more radical disregard for conventional notions of ritual purity and intensifying the power of their inauspiciousness, but without, it seems, transcending the convention of celibacy" ("The Lākulas," 165–166).

87. Sanderson, "Śaivism and the Tantric Traditions," 670–671. Sanderson does not give sources here for this précis, but it would seem to reflect the *kapālavrata* as described in *Picumata* XXI and elsewhere.
88. On the dating of these materials (always a vexed task), see the discussion in Hatley, "The *Brahmayāmalatantra*," 211–228. P. C. Bagchi ("Detailed Notices on Manuscripts," 102) also considered it "probably . . . a compilation of the 8th century."
89. PM/BY XXI.1–3, ff. 98r[4–5].

90. It is, in fact, called the *pāśupatavrata* in SYM X.15.
91. Edition and (tentative) translation of the *Siddhayogeśvarīmata* found in Törzsök, "The Doctrine of Magic Female Spirits," 28–29 and 143–145.
92. The *khaṭvāṅga* is here interpreted (via classical hermeneutical etymology [*nirukti*]) as a levitation device (KMT xxv.124b: khaṭvāṅgaṃ kathayiṣyāmi khagatīkaraṇaṃ param |).
93. Interestingly, these are all given an esoteric, internal interpretation in KMT xxv.65–95.
94. dvādaśābdaṃ caren mantrī brahmaghno 'pi sa sidhyati |; KMT xxv.55d.
95. KMT xxv.23 Kubjikā asks Bhairava to teach her the *vidyāvrata*; when explaining their internal, esoteric meaning in xxv.123, Bhairava refers to it as *vratacaryā*. In SYM x.2 Devī asks Bhairava to teach her the *vratacaryā*; in x.3 Bhairava refers to it as the *vidyāvrata*.
96. tato vidyāvrataślāghī kīrtyādibhir alaṃkṛtaḥ | sādhyate 'nena prayogeṇa mriyate cāvikalpataḥ ||; Goudriaan (*Vīṇāśikhatantra*, 116) renders this "even a person who is proficient in the observance of wisdom and is adorned with fame and glory is victimized by such a practice and dies without delay;" he comments (142, note 55) that "the *vidyāvrata* ('observance of wisdom') is a practice or way of life described in some Tantras in which a yogin is constantly aware of the symbolic meaning of his attributes or aspects of his behaviour. It is only meant for those who have transcended the ritual level." Given what we see of the *vidyāvrata* in both Bauddha and Śaiva sources in this paper, one suspects that Goudriaan is here relying overmuch on the presentation in the *Kubjikāmata Tantra*, which he also collaborated in editing. Sanderson ("History," 13n11) also describes a very different rite when he speaks of *vidyāvrata* as an "initial period of ascetic japaḥ, etc. to be undertaken after one has received a Mantra," i.e., he takes it to be a kind of *pūrvaseva* or *puraścaryā*.
97. See esp. GST XVI.91–103.
98. GST VII.35: prakṛtiprabhāsvaraṃ sarvaṃ nirnimittaṃ nirakṣaram | na dvayaṃ nâdvayaṃ śāntaṃ khasadṛśaṃ sunirmalam ||.
99. MVT XV: phyag na rdo rjes gsang sngags kyi sgo nas byang chub sems dpa'i spyad pa spyod pa rnams kyi don du tshigs su bcad pa'i dbyangs kyis rigs sngags kyi brtul zhugs zhus so |; Sde Bka' Rgyud tha, f. $215b^2$.
100. This might also be considered noteworthy, given the common, mistaken notion that the early Buddhist Tantras were not soteriologically oriented. This view was most recently articulated by Tribe, "Mantranaya/Vajrayāna," 208.
101. MVT, Sde Bka' Rgyud, vol. tha, ff. $216a^7$–$216b^2$: brgya byin tshangs la sogs pa'i lha | | sha za lto 'phye srin po rnams | | rgyang ring nas ni phyag 'tshal zhing | | thams cad srung ba'ang byed par 'gyur | | de dag thams cad bka' nyan cing| | de yi bka' bzhin byed par 'gyur | | sman dang mi dang lha rnams dang | | rig sngags rnams dang gsang sngags kun | | ci dag bgyi zhes tshig smra zhing | | de yi drung na 'khod par 'gyur | | bgegs dang log 'dren ma rungs dang | | srin po dang ni ma mo rnams | | gsang sngags 'dzin pa mthong ba'i tshe | | rgyang ring nas ni phyag 'tshal 'gyur |.
102. See note xlv here.

103. Consider, for example, *Milindapañhā* VI wherein observance of the *dhutaṅga*-s (including living in a charnel ground) both provides protection (*ārakkhā*—presumably from non-human beings—is listed as one of twenty-eight qualities of keeping these vows) and is considered essential to the attainment of sainthood (*arahatta*) in one life (*na mahārāja dhutaguṇesu pubbāsevanaṃ vinā ekissā yeva jātiyā arahattaṃ sacchikiriyā hoti*). See *Milindapañha*, 351 and 353.
104. Davidson makes a cogent and detailed case for the sustained interaction and mutual influence of the various Tantric traditions in *Indian Esoteric Buddhism*, for example 171–235.
105. See Sanderson, "Śaiva Age," 70–123.
106. Granoff, "Other People's Rituals," 400–401.
107. See Sanderson, "History Through Textual Criticism," 6 (note 3) and 23.
108. Cited in Hatley, "Brahmayāmalatantra," 217n72.
109. Granoff also notes instances in which ritual eclecticism was rejected or proscribed. See "Other People's Rituals" (409) and "My Rituals and My Gods."
110. See Ruegg, "Sur les Rapports" and *Symbiosis*; for critical responses, see Sanderson, "Vajrayāna," 92–93, and Davidson, *Indian Esoteric Buddhism*, 171–173. Though I also disagree with Ruegg on the usefulness of the concept of a substratum, his *Symbiosis* makes a useful contribution insofar as it highlights how essential it is to have a strong grasp of pre-Tantric Buddhist literature in order to successfully interpret the Buddhist Tantras.
111. Sanderson himself suggests as much, noting that the notion of "taking on, like the Kāpālikas, the visible attributes of the brahmin-slayer," was available to the Pāñcārthikas as well from "the Dharmasūtras and other orthodox sources" ("Lākulas," 165). That is, both Śaiva groups were drawing on Smārta sources, not Śaiva.
112. See Takasaki, "Sources," 545–546.
113. See *Laṅkāvatāra Sūtra*, 103.
114. *Saddharmalaṅkāvatāra Sūtra* X.335: śūnyāgāre śmaśāne vā vṛkṣamūle guhāsu vā | palāle 'bhyavakāśe ca yogī vāsaṃ prakalpayet ||.
115. *Laṅkāvatāra Sūtra* III.37ab: abhāvāt sarvadharmāṇāṃ saṃkleśo nāsti śuddhiś ca |.
116. *Laṅkāvatāra Sūtra* III.16: na bhāvo vidyate satyaṃ yathā bālair vikalpyate | abhāvena tu vai mokṣaṃ kathaṃ necchanti tārkikāḥ ||. These sophists (*tārkika*), incidentally, are precisely the bête noire of the Tantrika communities (a usage also found in the *Saṃdhinirmocana Sūtra*, for example).
117. Lorenzen, *Kāpālikas*, 80.
118. *Atharvaveda-pariśiṣṭa 40* 4.1: bhasmasnānaṃ [tāvad] grahīṣyāmi sarvapāpapraṇāśanam | bhasmasnānena rudro hi snāto 'bhūt pūta ātmanā ||; text and translation from Bisschop and Griffiths, 335.
119. Note the duality (*dvandva*) overcome by the *rudra-vrata* in Śaiva works such as the *Mataṅgapārameśvara* (caryāpāda) is not a species of (mental) conceptual duality, but rather comprises contrasts (such as cold/hot) experienced by the *body*. Describing the result of that *vrata*, that scripture states that "after a year, one may conquer all dualities that vex the body (saṃvatsarāj jayet sarvān dvandvān deha-prabādhakān: see 410). Compare *Niśvāsamukha*, 4:76

120. KMT xxv.123–155. Interestingly, though, the evidence of the *Tantrasadbhāva*'s esoteric, internal interpretation of the *vratacaryā* and the varieties of consorts described (mother, sister, etc.; KMT xxv.123–167) demonstrates that, just as in the case of the *Guhyasamāja*'s transgressive idiom, in the Śaiva context as well, the allegedly later, bowdlerized interpretation is in fact integral to the earliest stratum of this type of literature.
121. BY/PM LXXXV.10ab: grāme grāme vrataṃ tasya devatā-rūpa-lakṣaṇam; note that the following pāda mentions the *unmatta-vrata* as one option here.
122. *Jayadrathayāmala*, ṣatka 4, ff. 206b[3]–207b[5]; cited in Sanderson, "Śaiva Exegesis," 287. Note that such *melāpa*-s are precisely where the transgressive rituals are also to be found in the Buddhist Vajrayāna.
123. See Rastogi, *Krama Tantricism of Kashmir*, 58–63. Sanderson ("Śaiva Exegesis," 369) has likewise noted that "the Krama authors . . . may well have been the first to adopt and adapt [the concept of the inseparability of cognition and its objects] from Buddhist circles"—precisely the epistemological orientation that would underlie a transgessive, gnostic rite.
124. Lorenzen (*Kāpālikas*, 77) suggests that the Kāpālikas were guided by a quasi-epistemological model of coincidence of opposites, such that "they were at the same time the holiest of all ascetics and the lowest of all criminals"—but the passages he refers to (loc. cit., and on 70) deal with Buddhist materials.
125. See, for example, Sanderson, "Commentary," 111.
126. See, for example, *Kālīkulapañcaśataka* ii.65–66 (M. Dyczkowski, ed.).
127. Sanderson, "Purity and Power," 198.
128. It may be worth noting that these authors were likely younger contemporaries of the Noble [i.e., Tantric] Āryadeva, whose *Caryāmelāpakapradīpa* is already at this time organizing a broad range of Mahāyoga and proto-Yoginī Tanta materials into a new, systematic treatment of the *caryāvrata* as a phenomenon. See Wedemeyer, *Āryadeva's Lamp*, esp. 112–120 and 277–328.
129. The word "adapting" is worth stressing here. While Sanderson goes to great length to demonstrate the common heritage of Śaiva and Bauddha communities—stressing those elements that seem to him to have Śaiva provenance—he rather downplays the fact that all of these accoutrements (deity clusters, observances, etc.) are in the service of radically divergent soteriological models in the different traditions. In such a circumstance, it makes little sense to speak of "overcoding"of one tradition on another. Rather, whatever exchanges took place, they involved considerable re-coding into distinctive (and, occasionally irreconcilable) models of the path to liberation.
130. Likewise, I think it is clear that a more critical understanding of the *caryāvrata* is essential to any successful interpretation of the so-called caryā dances (*caryānṛtya*) of Nepal's Newar Buddhist communities. There are very good reasons to believe that caryā dance is a contemporary, attenuated enactment of the Tantric rite of *caryāvrata*. To date, however, there has been a woeful lack of modern research on this phenomenon—and what little exists is largely derived from its twentieth-century artistic transmutation at Kalamandapa/Hotel Vajra (see, e.g., Kalamandapa's

Buddhist Ritual Dance and Ahmed, "Caryā Nṛtya of Nepal"). The nature of this "practice dance" can also illuminate our own concerns. The fact that *caryānṛtya* is performed "as a part of [Vajrayāna] ritual especially on the occasion of tantric initiations, great festivals and important pujas" (Kalamandapa, *Buddhist Ritual Dance*, 6) is an important one. In addition to the special, temporary *vrata*, the antinomian features of The Practice occur in only two other contexts in the literature: initiation (*abhiṣeka*) and host circle worship (*gaṇacakrapūjā* or [*yoginī*]*melā*[*pa*]). Outside of these three, I believe, with the partial exception of the consumption of meats and ambrosias that constitutes an element of the daily ritual (*sādhana*), the cluster of distinctive antinomian elements we have observed are not elsewhere evident in the literature or practices of the Buddhist Tantras. Establishing this is a larger project than possible here; however, the ritual logic is consistent. As we have seen, The Practice is an elite undertaking insofar as it semiotically indicates and instantiates the divine identity of the esoteric practitioner in concrete, lived, social space. It is precisely in initiation (when this identity is first simulated) and in the occasional feasts (when this identity is simulated corporately) that this semiology is most essential. Thus, it is not surprising that it is precisely in these contexts that the Tantras describe the antinomian practices.

6. TANTRIC BUDDHIST TRANSGRESSION IN CONTEXT

1. maṇḍalakaṃ kṛtvā tanmadhye viśvavarṇāṣṭadalakamalavaraṭake sūrya-maṇḍalopari nīla-hūṃkāra-pariniṣpannaṃ bhūmisparśamudrādharaṃ kṛṣṇavarṇam akṣobhyam tadanu . . . oṃ āḥ vajrapuṣpe hūṃ ity anena abhimantrya sarvam iṣṭataraṃ ḍhaukayet | (*Advayavajrasaṃgraha*, 5).
2. na mantrajāpo na tapo na homo na māṇḍaleyaṃ na ca maṇḍalaṃ ca | sa mantrajāpo sa tapaḥ sa homaḥ tan māṇḍaleyaṃ tan maṇḍalaṃ ca || (*Advayavajrasaṃgraha*, 35; citing HT I.x.43).
3. See, especially, Davidson, *Indian Esoteric Buddhism*.
4. Davidson, *Indian Esoteric Buddhism*, 114.
5. *Susiddhikara* I, ch. 7 (see Giebel, *Two Esoteric Sutras*, 146).
6. "Having obtained the [ritual] permission of Nāgārjuna, he then became a siddha" (āryanāgārjunājñāṃ prāpya siddhas tadâbhavat); Lévi, "Un Nouveau Document," 422.
7. manobhaṅga-cittaviśrāmau caryā-sthānāṃ vivecitam ākṛtiṃ savarasyâsau dadhan nivasati sma saḥ (Lévi, "Un Nouveau Document," 422). Lévi reads *vivecitam* as "he removed himself to" («il se retira . . . au»).
8. The Dāmodara narratives are also explored by Tatz ("Life of the Siddha-Philosopher Maitrīgupta") in light of Tibetan accounts of Maitrīpa.
9. prāṇātipātādimāyāṃ darśaya (Lévi, "Un Nouveau Document," 424); this is quite likely a reference to *caryā*, which we have seen, is associated with violating Buddhist morality. Not killing living beings is the first of the five Buddhist vows, hence this with the suffix -ādi ("and so on") implies the rest of the list of five.

10. tasmin sthāne bhāhmaṇajātir nānukā nāma brāhmaṇī ca sādhvīti nāma prativasati sma | tadā ca kālāntareṇa dāmodaro nāma tatputro babhūva | (Lévi, "Un Nouveau Document," 423).
11. Sanderson, "Śaiva Exegesis," 339.
12. See, for example, Martin, *Tibetan Histories*, 26–27.
13. This story is found on ff. 6a⁷–7b² of volume śrī (14) of the redaction in the *Sgrub thabs kun btus*.
14. Mark Tatz ("Life of Maitrīgupta," 702) describes the *Lives of the Eighty-four Siddhas* as "a flagrantly fictional siddha history." Note, however, the observations of Matthew Kapstein regarding Abhayadatta and a "tendency to historicization" that informs Western interpretations of this literature in "King Kunji's Banquet," 52–56.
15. Sanderson, "Śaiva Exegesis," 340n359.
16. Sanderson, "Śaiva Exegesis," 339n359.
17. On "institutional esoterism," see Sanderson, 360. This rite may be found in *Sādhanamālā* II, pp. 385–87.
18. *Advayasiddhi*, v. 24: na tithir na ca nakṣatraṃ nôpavāsao vidhīyate | advayajñānayuktasya siddhir bhavati saugatī ||.
19. Aryadeva, *Svādhiṣṭhānaprabheda*, vv. 48abc, 49ab, 50bc; these rites, it is said, may be effected by merely the yogic process of self-consecration (*svādhiṣṭhānakrama*) or may instead be performed "like a reflected image" (*pratibimba*): caitya-karma na kurvīta na ca pustaka-vācanam | karotu vācayec câpi svādhiṣṭhānakrameṇa tu || devān na vandayed evaṃ bhikṣuṃś câpi na vandayet | athavā vandayet sarvān svādhiṣṭhānakrameṇa tu || mantra-nyāsaṃ na kurvīta mudrābandhaṃ tathaîva ca | mantrajāpaṃ na kuryād vā kuryāc ca pratibimbavat ||.
20. Nattier, *A Few Good Men*, 67.
21. Giebel, *Two Esoteric Sutras*, 149.
22. Giebel, *Two Esoteric Sutras*, 150.
23. Hidas, "Remarks on the Use," 198n51.
24. "monks and nuns, male and female lay followers, kings, princes, royal ministers, or anybody else" (*bhikṣur vā bhikṣuṇī vā upāsako vā upāsikā vā rājā vā rājaputro vā rājāmātyo vā . . . tadanyo vā*): see Hidas, "Remarks on the Use," 198n51.
25. Pathak, "A Dharani-Mantra in the Vinayavastu;" see also Davidson, *Indian Esoteric Buddhism*, 368n10.
26. See Skilling, "Zombies."
27. Jan Nattier articulates this as the interpretative "principle of irrelevance": That is, "we may draw with some confidence on data found within a normative text . . . when incidental mention is made of items unrelated to the author's primary agenda" (*A Few Good Men*, 66).
28. nikāyaṃ kāyam ity uktam udaraṃ vihāram ucyate | vītarāgād bhavet yonau jarāyu jvalacīvaram ||; *Hevajra Tantra* II.iv.61 (Snellgrove, ed., vol. II, 70).
29. chos gos gsum (tricīvara); Tōh. 429 *Catuḥpīṭhākhyātamantraṃśa*, ch. 5, Sde Bka', Rgyud, vol. nga, f. 155a².
30. Stede and Rhys Davids, *Pali-English Dictionary*, s.v. *ticīvara*, "the 3 robes of a bhikkhu, consisting of: diguṇa sanghāṭi, ekacciya uttarāsanga, ekacciya antaravāsaka."

31. A prohibition against singing and dancing was one of the ten rules (*śikṣāpadas*), to which all monastics, novices, and fully-ordained alike, committed themselves. See, for example, Lamotte, *History*, 54.
32. Consider Kṛṣṇācāryapāda's *Yogaratnamālā* on HT II.iv.2: kasmāt saṃdeha prākṛta-gīta-nāṭyayor vipakṣa-rūpatvāt—"why does Vajragarbha have doubts [about the song and dance in the *caryāvrata*]? Because ordinary songs and dance are enemies [of proper monastic conduct];" likewise, Ratnākaraśānti's *Muktāvalī* glosses this as *akuśala*: prākṛtayor gīta-nāṭyayor akuśalatvāt sandehaḥ—"he has doubts because of the [ethical] unskillfulness of ordinary song and dance."
33. Tribe, "Mantranaya/Vajrayāna," 238–239: "Significantly the major figures in the transmission of the Caryā and Yoga Tantras to China in the eighth century . . . were all monks."
34. Nihom, "Identification," 494.
35. See Sankrityayan, "Origin of Vajrayana." Walpola Rahula similarly writes, "during the reign of Sena I (831–851 A.C.), . . . a member of the Vajraparvata sect in India came to Ceylon and spread Vājiriyavāda or Vajrayāna in the Island while residing at the Vīrāṅkura-ārāma in the Abhayagiri." (*History*, 109).
36. Sankrityayan, "Origin of Vajrayana," 119 [emphasis mine]. Compare *Nikáya Saṇgrahawa* (trans.), 18.
37. The *Nikāyasaṃgrahawa* describes this Tantric teacher in Sri Lanka as a "monk of the Vajraparvata Ordination Lineage" (*vajraparvvata-nikāyavāsīvū bhikṣu*). Thanks to Justin Henry for help with this text.
38. tato vikramapuraṃ gatvā sammatīyanikāya maitrīguptanāma bhikṣur babhūva; Lévi, "Un Nouveau Document," 423.
39. The Rāhulabhadra narrative is found in Bu ston, *Gsang 'dus bshad thabs*, ff. 28b[4]–29a[2].
40. For the narrative of Visukalpa, see chapter 3.
41. des kyang de'i don nyams su blangs pas bskyed rdzogs kyi don la brtan pa cung zad thob pa dang | mthar phyin par bya ba'i phyir | rab byung gi cha lugs sbas te | spyod pa la gshegs so|; *Gsang 'dus bshad thabs*, f. 29a[1].
42. Granoff, "Toleration," 301.
43. See Dupuche, *Abhinavagupta*, 16–17. See also Sanderson, "Purity and Power," and Padoux, *Vāc*, cited in Dupuche. That is, for example, David White (*Kiss of the Yoginī*) has entirely inverted the chronology of the Śaiva Tantras; this is possible largely because he uses much later (mid-second-millennium) sources to reconstruct what he believes to be the early (sixth–seventh century A.D.) traditions. The circularity of this should be apparent, albeit it is characteristic of a certain approach to the esoteric traditions, on which see Sanderson, "Śaiva Exegesis of Kashmir," 413–417.
44. Sanderson, "Śaiva Exegesis of Kashmir," 240–241.
45. Nattier, *A Few Good Men*, 78n11. This understanding gains further confirmation from M. Spiro's observations on twentieth-century Burmese usage. Concurring with La Vallée Poussin's observation that upāsakas are "member[s] of the third order, a tertiary," Spiro notes that "appropriately, therefore, the Burmese restrict the use of *upāsaka* to those who regularly observe the Sabbath" (Burmese *u.bouk nei.*; Pali *uposatha*); see Spiro, *Buddhism and Society*, 217.

46. Nattier, *A Few Good Men*, 76: "It is taken for granted [in the *Ugra*], first of all, that the lay bodhisattva will visit the monastery. . . . It is also assumed that he will have the opportunity to learn the specific specializations of the various monks within the monastery."
47. Nattier, *A Few Good Men*, 25n32.
48. Nattier, *A Few Good Men*, 25.
49. Li Rongxi, trans., *Great Tang Dynasty Record*, 266; cf. Beal, trans., *Buddhist Records*, 146–147.
50. Li Rongxi, trans., *Great Tang Dynasty Record*, 267.
51. Li Rongxi, trans., *Biography of the Tripiṭaka Master*, 126–128, cited in Skilling, "Buddhist Sealings," 680 and 684n18.
52. This passage may be found in Grags pa rgyal mtshan's "Reply to Questions Posed by Byang chub seng ge" (*Rnal 'byor byang chub seng ge'i dris lan*, ff. 209a4–209b2).

    R. Davidson is to be credited with drawing attention to this important passage, though the interpretation he advances—in which he presents Nāropā as a grotesque and vain figure—is based on some rather tendentious readings and inferences (*Indian Esoteric Buddhism*, 317–318). In Davidson's rendering, the regional ruler (*rgyal phran zhig*) appears as "some feudal prince." Nāropā is depicted as helplessly fat by interpreting *sku bongs che ba* (usually "tall") as "physically quite corpulent" and by inferring that he "needed assistance simply to walk up stairs" from the fact that he is carried on a palanquin (a common expression of respect). Davidson construes the *go la* Nāropā is eating—probably a sweet ball, like a modern *laḍḍu*—as betel leaf, which he then speculates would have stained his teeth and "given him the dramatic receding gums that afflict habitual users of that mild intoxicant." Davidson's further inference that "Nāropā preferred the company of important political personages over that of Buddhist monks, since a local prince's visit preempted the translator from actually speaking with the aging lay scholar," is likewise difficult to sustain, insofar as Nag tsho was in no way preempted, because (as the text says) Nag tsho was a nobody who arrived unannounced and was fortunate just to catch a glimpse of the celebrity teacher. This latter is all he wanted, because he indicates he was just trying "to get a glimpse of his face" (*zhal blta ba la*). Nag tsho actually expresses pleasure that he even got to see Nāropā, writing, "having gone to see him, I was very fortunate . . . ," (*de blta bar phyin pas nga bsod nams che bar byung ste*).
53. Royal teachers were given "marks of distinction" (*saṃmāna*) such as parasols, palanquins, fly whisks, and so forth, which pomp they were entitled to display when making public appearances; see Sanderson, "Religion and the State," 269.
54. Consider, for example, his *Sekoddeśaṭīkā*.
55. Th. Burrow, "A Translation of the Kharoṣṭhī documents" cited in von Hinüber, "Review of H. Bechert, *Der Buddhismus*," 86n36. I am grateful to Alexander von Rospatt for observing the importance of these texts in his work on Newar monasticism, see especially von Rospatt, "Transformation," 209n34.
56. bhāryāḥ sutā duhitaraś ca teṣu bhaviṣya gṛhisamānam |; *Rāṣṭrapālaparipṛcchā*, Finot, ed., 29. This example is also cited in von Hinüber, "Review of H. Bechert, *Der Buddhismus*," 83.

57. ardhe yad bhikṣavaḥ śikṣācārās tatrārpitās tayā | ardhe gārhasthyagarhyāś ca sa strīputrapaśustriyaḥ |; *Rājataraṅginī* III.12, 24; Stein's translation may be found in vol. I, 74.
58. See Skilling, "Buddhist Sealings," 679–680.
59. Much more careful work needs to be done on this question. There has been a tendency to assume that (because the Tantras are marginal) the Tantric communities were largely users of vernaculars. Some nondualist Tantras do contain vernacular portions, but it is not at all evident what this might mean for scholarly interpretation. The semiology of such code switching is not apparent in the current state of research.
60. Pollock, *Language of the Gods*, 104.
61. A similar point has occasionally been made by others. Friedhelm Hardy, for instance, also makes the observation that, because the literature is in Sanskrit and includes antinomian rituals that break social taboos, "it appears appropriate to locate [the social] position [of the tāntrika] somewhere above the tribals, peasants, artisans and villagers generally, with whom some of the features (like alcohol, meat, 'impurity') occur naturally. For only from the vista of 'middle class' (or better, of higher castes) certain practices could appear as 'taboo.'" See, F. Hardy, "The Esoteric Traditions," 651.
62. na yogaḥ pratibimbeṣu niṣiktādiṣu jāyate | bodhicittamahāyogayoginas tena devatāḥ || ātmā vai sarvabuddhatvaṃ sattvasauritvam eva ca | svādhidaivatayogena tasmād ātmaîva sādhayet ||; *Sarvabuddhasamāyoga Tantra*, cited in Lal, *Luptabauddhavacanasaṃgraha*, 83.
63. This is what *svadevatāyoga* means: emanating oneself in the form of a divinity.
64. *Hevajra Tantra* I.x.2: vasudhāṃ śodhayed yogī prathamaṃ devatātmakaḥ | . . . paścān maṇḍalam ālikhet ||.
65. *Saṃvarodaya Tantra*, chapter XXIII; 137–144; the description summarizes 137–142.
66. *Saṃvarodaya Tantra*, Chapter XIII; 113–119; the description summarizes 113–116.
67. That is, *oṃ svabhāvaśuddhāḥ sarvadharmāḥ svabhāvaśuddho 'ham*, and *oṃ śūnyatājñānavajrasvabhāvātmako 'ham*.
68. hṛdi madhyagataṃ vajraṃ bhāvayej jñānavajriṇaḥ | vajramaṇḍalamadhyasthaṃ vajramantrārthabhāvanā || . . . sarvamaṇḍalapārśveṣu sarvabuddhān niveśayet | pañcaraśmi-prabhedena sphārayan bodhim āpnute ||; GST XIII, vv. 29 and 33.
69. On this, see GST XII 51–57. In verse 57, I read *kāyair*, following PU.
70. Skilling, "Zombies," 314.
71. Skilling, *Mahāsūtras* II, 593. This scripture was considered important enough to have been entirely incorporated into the *Bhaiṣajyavastu* of the *Mūlasarvāstivāda Vinaya*; see Skilling, "Rakṣā Literature," 128–129.
72. iha bodhisattvaḥ tadrūpāṃ samādhivaśitāṃ pratilabhate yayā yāni mantrapadāni ītisaṃśamanāya sattvānām adhitiṣṭhanti; *Bodhisattvabhūmi*, Wogihara, ed., 272, cited in Braarvig, "*Dhāraṇī* and *Pratibhāna*," 26n14.
73. See Skilling, "Rakṣā Literature," 160; cf. *Śikṣāsamuccaya*, Vaidya, ed., 77–79.
74. These techniques may be found elucidated at GST XIII 69; GST XV 28–29; GST XV 103–105; GST XIII 72; and GST XV 109–110, respectively.

75. Sanderson, "Śaiva Exegesis," 290–291 [emphasis mine].
76. S. Collins, personal communication.
77. See discussion in chapter 5.
78. Davidson, *Indian Esoteric Buddhism*, 298.
79. Lincoln, *Authority*, 78.
80. Lincoln, *Discourse and the Construction*, 159.
81. Barthes, *Mythologies*, 41–42; he writes, "to instil into the Established Order the complacent portrayal of its drawbacks has nowadays become a paradoxical but incontrovertible means of exalting it. Here is the pattern in this new-style demonstration: take the established value which you want to restore or develop, and first lavishly display its . . . imperfection; then, at the last moment, save it *in spite of*, or rather *by* the heavy curse of its blemishes."
82. Davidson's interpretation is in this regard as well the precise inverse of my own; he takes the impact of Madhyamaka to have been an erosion of religious and ethical principles. See, *Indian Esoteric Buddhism*, 99–101.
83. Each of these is the subject of a chapter of Nāgārjuna's *Mūlamadhyamakakārikā*: nos. 8, 17, 13, 12, 16, 22, and 24, respectively.
84. See note 81 here.
85. Gluckman, *Rituals of Rebellion*, 6.
86. Gluckman, *Rituals of Rebellion*, 21.
87. These are exactly the problems that come up regularly in undergraduate courses on Buddhism; and they quite evidently troubled the tradition itself.
88. See discussion in chapter 3.
89. | de nas phyag na rdo rjes bcom ldan 'das kyi zhabs la gtugs ste | bcom ldan das la 'di skad ces gsol to | | sangs rgyas mtshan ma mi mnga' ste | | chos kyi sku la rnam par bzhugs | | mtshan med 'dus ma byas pa yi | | mtshungs pa med pa'i chos ston na | | dpa' bo chen po ci slad du | | mtshan mar bcad pa'i cho go 'di | | gsang sngags spyad pa bstan par mdzad |; MVT, sDe, bKa', vol. tha, f. 99b[3–4].
90. These issues were carried over into the discursive negotiations of China and Tibet as well. See, Gregory, *Sudden and Gradual*, and Ruegg, *Buddha-nature*.
91. Davidson, *Indian Esoteric Buddhism*, 322.
92. Note that, in the rite described in Davidson (*Indian Esoteric Buddhism*, 318–319; Tibetan text, 413n48), the intended practitioner is "one who has completed the collections of merit and gnosis" (*bsod nams ye shes tshogs rdzogs pa*). Given that perfecting these two is said to result in buddhahood, this would seem to be no slouch of a yogin.
93. Sanderson, "Religion and the State," 230.
94. Snellgrove, *Indo-Tibetan Buddhism* I, 170: "Despite these 'symbolic' interpretations, the actuality of these 'sacred sites and places' and the rites performed there links this class of tantric literature, at least in their origins, with fraternities of yogins who were very well acquainted with them. Moreover, similar fraternities of yogins have continued to exist in India and their practices, found as abhorrent by modern observers, correspond in very many details with those referred to in Buddhist tantras." ("Fraternities," of course, are well known to be reliable witnesses of their various exploits.)

95. Briggs, *Gorakhnāth*, 172–174.
96. Ward, *A View* I, 247–248.
97. Ward, *A View* I, lii.
98. Ward, *A View* I, 248.
99. Ward, *A View* II, 94n.
100. Ward, *A View* II, 94.
101. In fact, page 174 of Briggs' book is plagiarized verbatim from Aitkinson.
102. Aitkinson, *Himalayan Gazetteer* II, 866.
103. Aitkinson, *Himalayan Gazetteer* I, v.
104. "Urban legends are a specific class of legend, differentiated from 'ordinary' legends by their being provided and believed as accounts of actual incidents that befell or were witnessed by someone the teller almost knows (e.g., his sister's hairdresser's mechanic). These tales are told as true, local, and recent occurrences, and often contain names of places or entities located within the teller's neighborhood or surrounding region;" see http://www.snopes.com/info/glossary.asp (accessed June 1, 2010).
105. More recent examples can also be adduced. For instance, David White (*Kiss*, 120) reports that "David Knipe . . . participated in a Tantric *pañcamakāra* ritual in an underground crypt in Benares in the 1970s." White has this on the authority of "personal communication with David Knipe, Madison, Wisconsin, October 1992" (305n133). Presumably, then, Prof. Knipe has firsthand knowledge of these transgressive rites involving sex and meat. However, looking more closely, what exactly did Knipe witness? He "was made to meditate on a mandala composed of red and white flowers while the leader of the group performed sexual intercourse in an adjacent cell" (120). In short, in White's account Knipe actually witnessed nontransgressive, dualistic ritual, but was assured that there was transgression going on elsewhere, out of sight.
106. Wilson, "Sketch of the Religious Sects," 225–227. Note that Urban gives a somewhat misleading account of Wilson's position, citing him as lamenting that the "immoral and perverse practices . . . are becoming more and more prevalent." This does not jibe with my reading of Wilson. See Urban, *Tantra*, 51.
107. This is evident in the only contemporary ethnography of Indian Tantric communities that I am aware of. In a set of three articles published in *Folklore*, Bholanath Bhattacharya describes his encounters with Bengali Tantric practice, which largely comprise acrobatic sex and prostitution. Postures divorced from their informing context, much as in the contemporary practice of yoga. See B. Bhattacharya, "Some Aspects" I, II, and III; and compare, Singleton, *Yoga Body*.
108. Sanderson, "Vajrayāna," 92.
109. kahiṇu khu aviṇaṭṭhamūḷapāṭhaṃ [kutra nu khalv avinaṣṭamūlapāṭham]; *Mattavilāsaprahasana*, § 64.
110. Occam's razor is the principle of ontological parsimony in scientific work: *pluralitas non est ponenda sine necessitate*, or "plurality should not be posited without necessity." As the *Encyclopedia Britannica* notes, "The principle gives precedence to simplicity; of two competing theories, the simplest explanation of an entity is to be preferred.

The principle is also expressed 'Entities are not to be multiplied beyond necessity.'" See, "Ockham's razor," *Encyclopædia Britannica Online* <http://www.britannica.com/EBchecked/topic/424706/Ockhams-razor> (accessed June 4, 2010).

111. Gray, "Disclosing the Empty Secret," 439–441.
112. Jayabhadra is said to have been the third Tantric preceptor of Vikramaśīla. Cf. Tāranātha, *Chos 'byung*, f. 119b$^{4-5}$: "Jayabhadra . . . was a monk-scholar [*bhikṣu-paṇḍita] learned in all the scriptural collections of the Śrāvakas" (*rgyal ba bzang po . . . nyan thos kyi sde snod thams cad la mkhas par sbyang pa'i dge slong paṇḍita yin*).
113. See, for example, PU, 213, on ritual cunnilingus.
114. See Wedemeyer, "Antinomianism and Gradualism" and "Sex, Death, and 'Reform.'"
115. D. White, *Kiss of the Yoginī*, 219.
116. See note 43.
117. One might also consider the fact that David Snellgrove originally argued for the now thoroughly discredited view that the *Hevajra Tantra* was earlier than the *Guhyasamāja*, on the basis that "it refers directly to the circles of yogins, where all these works presumably originated" ("Notion of Divine Kingship," 216). Based upon a prior notion of how the Tantras developed, Snellgrove arranged the evidence to fit his model.
118. Paul Harrison ("Mediums," 116) has indicated twin dangers in Buddhist studies, writing, "danger lies on two sides, when studying literature like this, of either imposing one's own framework upon the material or of being sucked helplessly into its discourse. In Buddhist Studies, for some reason, it seems that the second of these two dangers, the loss of critical grip, is the more insidious."

CONCLUSION

1. Lincoln, *Theorizing Myth*, xii.
2. For an influential version of this thesis, see especially Hirakawa, "The Rise of Mahāyāna Buddhism."
3. Drewes, "Early Indian Mahāyāna I," 56.
4. Drewes, "Early Indian Mahāyāna I," 57.
5. This is the title of her study of the *Ugraparipṛcchā Mahāyāna Sūtra*. Paul Harrison ("Mediums and Messages," 129) has likewise noted that, "the Mahāyāna, far from being a revolt by the urban laity against monastic privilege and self-absorption in an attempt to bring salvation to the masses, was the work of hard-core ascetics."
6. Skilling, "Mahāyāna and Bodhisattva," 141.
7. These ten points are made in Skilling, "Mahāyāna and Bodhisattva," 145–147.
8. La Vallée Poussin, *Bouddhisme: études et Materiaux*, 6: "les Hindous bouddhistes étaient volontiers idolâtres, superstitieux ou métaphysiciens."
9. Veyne, *Writing History*, 12.
10. Veyne, *Writing History*, 13.

APPENDIX 1

1. Pad ma dkar po, *'Brug pa'i chos 'byung*, ff. $63a^5$–$64b^5$.
2. On the "Practice" (*caryā, spyod pa*), see chapter 5; on the three types of practices (with elaboration, etc.), see Wedemeyer, *Āryadeva's Lamp*, 112–120 and 277–331.

APPENDIX 2

1. The quatrain starting with this line through the beginning of the next quatrain ("Merely hearing 'quit . . .' ") is not found in the Tibetan translation (neither in Sde dge, Snar thang, Peking, Urga, or Stog). I have based my interpretation on that given in the *Abhayapaddhati* commentary.
2. Literally "on."
3. Skt (or, rather, Pkt) reads *viaya* (*viṣaya*); Tib suggests *vikalpa* (*rnam rtog*).

BIBLIOGRAPHY

INDIC SOURCES

Abhayapaddhati of Abhayākaragupta (*Buddhakapāla* commentary):

- See Dorje 2009.
- Tibetan translation by Ding ri chos grags (rev. Blo gros brtan pa), Sde dge Bstan 'gyur, rgyud 'grel, vol. ra, ff. 166b[1]–225b[2] (Tōh. 1654).

Abhidharmakośa and *-bhāṣya* of Vasubandhu: see Pradhan 1983.
Abhidharmasamuccaya of Asaṅga: see Pradhan 1950.
Abhisamayālaṃkārāloka of Haribhadra: see Vaidya 1960a.
Advayasiddhi of Śrī Lakṣmī: see Rinpoche 1987 and Shendge 1964.
Āmnāyamañjarī of Abhayākaragupta (*Saṃpuṭa* commentary):

- Tibetan translation by the author and Rtsa mi Sangs rgyas grags pa (rev. Chos kyi bzang po; rev. Blo gros brtan pa), Sde dge Bstan 'gyur, rgyud 'grel, vol. cha, ff. 1b[1]–316a[7] (Tōh. 1198).

Amoghapāśakalparāja: see Kimura, et al.
Amṛtakaṇikā of Raviśrījñāna: see Lal 1994.
Amṛtakaṇikodyotanibandha of Vibhūticandra: see Lal 1994.
Aṅguttara-Nikāya: see Hardy 1899.
Āryaprajñāpāramitānayaśatapañcāśatkaṭīkā of Jñānamitra:

- Tibetan translation in Sde dge Bstan 'gyur, Rgyud 'grel, vol. ju, ff. 272b[7]–294a[5] (Tōh. 2647); also, Snar thang Bstan 'gyur, Rgyud 'grel, vol. gu, ff. 278a[5]–304b[3] and Ganden "Golden" Bstan 'gyur manuscript, vol. gu, ff. 356a–389b[1].

Aṣṭasāhasrikāprajñāpāramitāsūtra: see Vaidya 1960a.
Atharvaveda Pariśiṣṭa 40: see Bisschop and Griffiths.
Bodhisattvabhūmi: see Dutt 1978.

Brahmayāmala Tantra:

- Unpublished manuscript in Nepal National Archives, NAK 3-370, NGMPP A42/2; palm leaf; Newari script; 1052 C.E.
- See also Hatley (chapters I, II, LV, LXXIII, and XCIX).

Buddhakapāla Mahāyoginī Tantra:

- Unpublished MS in Cambridge University Library Add. 1680.13.
- Tibetan translation by Gayādhara and Jo Zla ba'i 'od zer, Sde dge Bka' 'gyur, rgyud, vol. nga, ff. 143a[1]–167a[5] (Tōh. 424).

Cakrasaṃvara Tantra: see Pandey 2002.
Caṇḍamahāroṣaṇa Tantra:

- Unpublished MSS in Tokyo University Library, nos. 63 (New Catalogue; nr. 186 Old Cat.) and 64 (New; Old nr. 196).
- See also George (chapters I to VIII).
- Tibetan translation by Ratnaśri and Grags pa rgyal mtshan, Sde dge Bka' 'gyur, Rgyud, vol. da, ff. 304b[1]–343a[1] (Tōh. 431).

Caryāmelāpakapradīpa of Āryadeva: see Wedemeyer 2007.
Dīghanikāya: see Rhys Davids and Estlin Carpenter.
Gaṇapatihṛdaya: see Iwamoto 1937a.
Guhyasamāja Tantra: see Matsunaga 1978.
Guhyasiddhi of Padmavajra: see Rinpoche 1987.
Guṇāvatī of Ratnākaraśānti (*Mahāmāyā* commentary): see Rinpoche and Dwivedi 1992.
Herukābhidhāna/Laghusaṃvara: See *Cakrasaṃvara Tantra*.
Hevajra Tantra: see Snellgrove 1959.
Jataka (and *Jātaka Commentary*): see Fausbøll.
Jñānasiddhānta: see Soebadio.
Jñānavatī of Saraha (*Buddhakapāla* commentary):

- Tibetan translation by Gayādhara and Jo Zla ba'i 'od zer, Sde dge Bstan 'gyur, vol. ra, ff. 104b[1]–150a[2] (Tōh. 1652).

Kālacakratantra: see Upadhyaya 1986, 1994, and 1994.
Kālīkūlapañcaśataka: unpublished edition by M. Dyczkowski.
Kaulajñānanirnaya: see P. C. Bagchi 1934.
Kāvyālaṃkāra of Bhāmaha: see Sastry.
Kubjikāmata Tantra: see Goudriaan, et al.
Kulārṇava Tantra: see Tārānātha Vidyāratna.
Lalitavistara Sūtra: see Vaidya 1958.
Laṅkāvatāra Sūtra: see Vaidya 1963.
Mahākāla Tantra: see Stablein.
Mahāpratisarā: see Iwamoto 1938.
Mahāsāhasrapramardanī: see Iwamoto 1937b.
Mahāśītavatī Dhāraṇī: see Iwamoto 1937a.

Mahāvairocana Tantra:

- Tibetan translation by Śīlendrabodhi and Dpal brtsegs, Sde dge Bka' 'gyur, Rgyud, vol. tha, ff. 151b²–260a⁷ (Tōh. 494).

Mahāvastu: see S. Bagchi 1970a.
Mahāyāna-sūtrālaṅkāra of Asaṅga: see S. Bagchi 1970b.
Mañjuśrīmūlakalpa: see Sâstrî 1920–1925 and S. Bagchi 1964.
Mañjuśrīnāmasaṃgīti: see Davidson 1981.
Mañjuśriyamūlakalpa: see *Mañjuśrīmūlakalpa.*
Mattavilāsaprahasanam of Mahendra Vikrama Varma: see Lockwood and Bhat.
Milindapañha: see Trenckner.
Mṛgendra Tantra: see Bhatt 1962.
Muktāvalī of Ratnākaraśānti (*Hevajra* commentary): see Tripathi and Negi.
Nikāya Sangrahawa: see Wickremasinghe 1890.
Niṣpannayogāvalī of Abhayākaragupta: see Bhattacharyya 1972.
Niśvāsatattvasaṃhitā:

- Unpublished manucript in Nepal National Archives, NAK MS 1-227 (NGMPP reel no. A 41/14).

Pañcakrama of Ārya Nāgārjuna: see Mimaki and Tomabechi 1994.
Pāśupatasūtra: see Sastri 1940.
Picumata: see *Brahmayāmala.*
Prabodhacandrodaya of Kṛṣṇamiśra: see Pédraglio.
Pradīpoddyotana of Ārya Candrakīrti: see C. Chakravarti 1984.
Prajñāpāramitānayaśatapañcāśatkaṭīkā of Jñanamitra:

- See *Āryaprajñāpāramitānayaśatapañcāśatkaṭīkā.*

Prajñopāyaviniścayasiddhi of Anaṅgavajrapāda: see Rinpoche and Dwivedi 1987.
Pratyutpannabuddhasaṃmukhāvasthitasamādhisūtra: see Harrison 1978.
Rājataraṅgiṇī: see M. Stein.
Rāṣṭrapālaparipṛcchā: see Finot.
Rauravāgama: see Bhatt 1985.
Saddharmalaṅkāvatāra Sūtra: see *Laṅkāvatāra Sūtra.*
Saddharmapuṇḍarīka Sūtra: see Vaidya 1960b.
Saṃdhyāvyākaraṇa Tantra:

- Tibetan translation by Dharmaśrībhadra and Rin chen bzang po, Sde dge Bka' 'gyur, Rgyud, vol. ca, ff. 159a¹–207b⁷ (Tōh. 444).

Saṃkṣiptapratiṣṭhāvidhi Tantra:

- Tibetan translation by Kha che paṇ chen Jñānavajra and 'Bro Shes rab grags pa, Sde dge Bka' 'gyur, Rgyud, vol. ta, ff. 146b¹–150a⁷ (Tōh. 486).

Saṃpuṭodbhava Tantra:

- Unpublished manuscripts in Tokyo University Library, nos. 428 (new catalog; old no. 319) and 427 (new; old no. 324).

- See also Elder (chapters I–IV).
- Tibetan translation by Gayādhara and Śākya Ye shes, Sde dge Bka' 'gyur, Rgyud, vol. ga, ff. 73b¹–158b⁷ (Tōh. 381).

Saṃvarodaya Tantra: see Tsuda 1974 (chapters IIX, XIII, XVII–XIX, XXI, XXIII, XXVI, XXVIII, XXXI, and XXXIII).
Sarvadurgatipariśodhana Tantra: see Skorupski.
Sarvatathāgatatattvasaṃgraha: see Horiuchi.
Sekoddeśaṭīkā of Naḍapāda (Nāropā): see Sferra and Merzagora.
Siddhayogeśvarīmata: see Törzsök.
Śikṣāsamuccaya of Śāntideva: see Vaidya 1961.
Śūraṃgamasamādhi Sūtra:

- Tibetan translation by Śākyaprabha and Ratnarakṣita, Sde dge Bka' 'gyur, Mdo, vol. da, ff. 253b⁵–316b⁶ (Tōh. 132).

Svādhiṣṭhānaprabheda of Āryadeva: see Pandey 1990.
Tantrāloka of Abhinavagupta: see M.R. Shāstrī 1918–1938.
Tattvadaśaka of Advayavajra:

- See Shastri 1927.
- Tibetan translation by Phyag na and Mtshur (rev. Tshul khrims rgyal ba), Sde dge, Bstan 'gyur, Rgyud 'grel, vol. wi, ff. 112b⁷–113a⁶ (Tōh. 2236).

Udānavarga: see Bernhard.
Vajrapāṇyabhiṣeka Tantra:

- Tibetan translation by Śīlendrabodhi and Ye shes sde, Sde dge Bka' 'gyur, Rgyud, vol. da, ff. 1a¹–156b⁷ (Tōh. 496).

Vajrāralli Tantra:

- Tibetan translation by Gayādhara and Shākya ye shes, Sde dge Bka' 'gyur, Rgyud, vol. nga, ff. 171a¹–176a¹ (Tōh. 426).

Vajrasattvasādhana of Candrakīrti: see Hong and Tomabechi.
Vajrāvalī-nāma-maṇḍalopāyikā of Abhayākaragupta: MS facsimile in Chandra 1977.
Vajravidāraṇī: see Iwamoto 1937a.
**Vajrayānāntadvayanirākaraṇa* of Jñānaśrī:

- Tibetan translation (no translator given), Sde dge Bstan 'gyur, Rgyud 'grel, vol. tsu, ff. 115a⁷–120a².

Vimalakīrtinirdeśasūtra: see Study Group on Buddhist Sanskrit Literature 2006.
Vimalaprabhā of Mañjuśrī Yaśas (*Kālacakra* commentary): see Upadhyaya 1986, and Dwivedi and Bahulkar 1994a and 1994b.
Yājñavalkyasmṛti: see Ānandāśrama 1903–1904.
Yogaratnamālā (*Hevajra* commentary) of Kaṇha: see Snellgrove 1959.
Yoginīsaṃcāra Tantra: see Pandey 1998.
Yoginīsaṃcāratantranibandha of Tathāgatarakṣita: see Pandey 1998.

TIBETAN SOURCES

Bsod nams rtse mo. *Rgyud sde spyi'i rnam par gzhag pa* ["General Presentation of the Tantras"], in *The Complete Works of the Great Masters of the Sa skya Sect of the Tibetan Buddhism*, vol. II (Tokyo: The Toyo Bunko, 1968), 1–37.

Bu-ston. *Chos 'byung.* Zi ling: Krung go bod kyi shes rig dpe skrun khang, 1988.

——. *Gsang 'dus bshad thabs*, in *The Collected Works of Bu-ston*, vol. 9 (New Delhi: International Academy of Indian Culture, 1967), 1–106.

——. *Yo ga gru gzings*, in *The Collected Works of Bu-ston*, vol. 11 (New Delhi: International Academy of Indian Culture, 1968), 1–184.

Dpal ldan tshul khrims. *Chos 'byung kun gsal me long.* New Delhi: Bonpo Monastic Centre, 1971.

Dpa' bo Gtsug la phreng ba. *Chos 'byung mkhas pa'i dga' ston.* Two volumes. Varanasi: Vajra Vidya Institute, 2003.

'Gos Khug-pa Lhas-btsas. *Gsaṅ 'dus stoṅ thun.* New Delhi: Trayang, 1973.

'Gos Lo tsā ba Gzhon nu dpal. *The Blue Annals (Deb ther sngon po).* New Delhi: International Academy of Indian Culture, 1974.

Grags pa rgyal mtshan. *Rnal 'byor byang chub seng ge'i dris lan* ["Reply to Questions Posed by Yogin Byang chub seng ge"], in *The Complete Works of the Great Masters of the Sa skya Sect of the Tibetan Buddhism*, vol. III (Tokyo: The Toyo Bunko, 1968), 276–278.

——. *Dpal he ru ka'i byung tshul* ["Origins of Heruka"], in *The Complete Works of the Great Masters of the Sa skya Sect of the Tibetan Buddhism*, vol. III (Tokyo: The Toyo Bunko, 1968), 298–300.

Lde'u Jo sras. *Lde'u Chos 'byung.* Lhasa: Bod ljongs mi rigs dpe skrun khang, 1987.

Mkhan chen O ḍi ya na [O rgyan bsTan 'dzin rdo rje]. *Gsang sngags snga 'gyur bka' gter dang bcas pa'i chos 'byung bden tshig rdo rje'i glu dbyangs.* Clement Town: Ngagyur Nyingma College, 2006.

Mkhas pa Lde'u. *Rgya bod kyi chos 'byung rgyas pa.* Lhasa: Bod rang skyong ljong spyi tshogs tshan rig khang, 1987.

Ngor chen Kun dga' bzang po. *Rgyud kyi rgyal po dpal kye rdo rje'i byung tshul dang brgyud pa'i bla ma dam pa rnams kyi rnam par thar pa ngo mtshar rgya mtsho* ["Origins of the King of Tantras Glorious Hevajra and the Biographies of its Lineage Gurus, 'A Wondrous Ocean'"], in *The Complete Works of the Great Masters of the Sa skya Sect of the Tibetan Buddhism*, vol. IX (Tokyo: The Toyo Bunko, 1968), 278–284.

Nyang Nyi ma 'od zer. *Chos 'byung me tog snying po sbrang rtsi'i bcud.* [Lhasa:] Bod ljongs mi dmangs dpe skrun khang, 1988.

Pad ma dkar po, *'Brug pa'i chos 'byung*: see Chandra 1968.

Sa chen Kun dga' snying po. *Bde mchog nag po pa'i lugs kyi bla ma brgyud pa'i lo rgyus* ["Narrative of the Lineage of Mentors of the Śaṃvara Kṛṣṇapā Tradition"], in *The Complete Works of the Great Masters of the Sa skya Sect of the Tibetan Buddhism*, vol. I (Tokyo: The Toyo Bunko, 1968), 214–216.

Tāranātha, rJe btsun. *Dam pa'i chos rin po che 'phags pa'i yul du ji ltar dar ba'i tshul gsal bar ston pa dgos 'dod kun 'byung* [*Rgya gar chos 'byung*], in *Five Historical Works of Tāranātha* (Tezu, Arunachal Pradesh: Tibetan Nyingmapa Monastery, 1974), 1–261.

MODERN SOURCES

Ahmed, Syed Jamil. "Caryā Nṛtya of Nepal: When 'Becoming the Character' in Asian Performance in Nonduality in 'Quintessence of Void,'" *The Drama Review*, vol. 47, no. 3 (2003), 159–182.

Aitkinson, Edwin T. *Himalayan Gazetteer*. 1882–1886. New Delhi: Cosmo Publications, 1973.

Ali, Daud. *Courtly Culture and Political Life in Early Medieval India*. Cambridge: Cambridge University Press, 2004.

Ali, Daud, ed. *Invoking the Past: Uses of History in South Asia*. New Delhi: Oxford University Press, 1999.

Ānandāśramasthapaṇḍitaiḥ [Pandits resident at Ānandāśram], eds. *Yājñavalkyasmṛtiḥ*. Puṇyākhyapattana: Ānandāśramamudraṇālaya, 1903–1904.

Annual Bibliography of Indian Archæology for the Year 1933, vol. 8. Leyden: E. J. Brill, Ltd., 1935.

Apte, Vaman Shivaram. *The Practical Sanskrit-English Dictionary*. 1890. Delhi: Motilal Banarsidass, 1998.

Aris, Michael. *Views of Medieval Bhutan: The Diary and Drawings of Samuel Davis, 1783*. London: Serindia Publications, 1982.

Aristotle. "Poetics," in *The Basic Works of Aristotle*, Richard McKeon, ed. New York: Random House, 1941, 1455–1487.

Aufrecht, Th. *Catalogi Codicum Manuscriptorum Bibliothecae Bodleianae*. Oxonii: E Typographeo Clarendoniano, M.DCCC.LXIV. Oxford: Clarendon Press, 1864.

Austin, John L. *How to Do Things with Words*. Second edition. Cambridge: Harvard University Press, 1975.

Bachofen, Johann Jakob. *Myth, Religion, and Mother Right: Selected Writings of J. J. Bachofen*. Trans. Ralph Manheim. Bollingen Series LXXXIV. 1967. Princeton: Princeton University Press, 1973.

Bagchi, Prabodh Chandra. "Detailed Notices on Manuscripts," in *Studies in the Tantras* (Calcutta: University of Calcutta, 1939), 93–114.

——. ed. *Kaulajñāna-nirṇaya and some Minor Texts of Matsyendranātha* (Texts from Nepal, 1). Calcutta Sanskrit Series, no. III. Calcutta: Metropolitan Printing and Publishing House, Limited, 1934.

——. "On Foreign Element in the Tantra," *Indian Historical Quarterly*, vol. VII, no. 1 (March 1931), 1–16.

——. "On the Sādhanamālā," in *Studies in the Tantras*. Calcutta: University of Calcutta, 1939, 34–44.

——. "On Some Tāntrik texts studies in Ancient Kambuja II," *Indian Historical Quarterly* (March 1930), 97–107.

——. "The Sandhābhāṣā and Sandhāvacana," *Indian Historical Quarterly* (June 1930), 389–396.

——. "Some Technical Terms of the Tantra," in *Studies in the Tantras*, 61–73.

——. *Studies in the Tantras*. Calcutta: University of Calcutta, 1939.

Bagchi, S., ed. *Mahāvastu Avadāna*. Vol. I. Darbhanga: Mithila Institute, 1970a.

——, ed. *Mahāyāna-sūtrālaṅkāra of Asaṅga*. Darbhanga: Mithila Institute, 1970b.

——, ed. *Mahāyānasūtrasaṃgraha*, part II. Buddhist Sanskrit Texts, 18. Darbhanga: Mithila Institute, 1964.

Baldissera, Fabrizia. "The Satire of Tantric Figures in Some Works of Kṣemendra," in R. Torella, *Le parole e i marmi: studi in onore di Raniero Gnoli nel suo 70. compleanno* (Rome: Istituto Italiano per l'Africa e l'Oriente, 2001), 13–35.

Banerjee, Anil Chandra. "Hindus in Mediæval India," *Indian Culture*, vol. VII, no. 1 (JulSep 1940), 122–125.

Banerji, S.C. *Tantra in Bengal: A Study in its Origin, Development and Influence*. Calcutta: Naya Prokash, 1978.

Bareau, André. "Le Tantrisme," in A. Bareau, et al., *Les Religions de l'Inde III: Bouddhisme, Jaïnisme, Religions Archaïques*. Paris: Payot, 1966, 200–215.

Barth, Auguste. *The Religions of India*. Trsl. J. Wood. 1882. Chowkhamba Sanskrit Series, vol. XXV. Varanasi: Chowkhamba Sanskrit Series Office, 1963.

Barthes, Roland. "The Discourse of History," trans. Stephen Bann, in E. S. Shaffer, ed. *Comparative Criticism: A Yearbook 3*. Cambridge: Cambridge University Press, 1981, 3–20.

——. *The Eiffel Tower and Other Mythologies*. Trans. R. Howard. Berkeley, Los Angeles and London: University of California Press, 1979.

——. *Elements of Semiology*. Trans. Annette Lavers and Colin Smith. 1967. New York: Hill and Wang, 1973.

——. *Image-Music-Text*. Selected and translated by Stephen Heath. 1977. New York: Hill and Wang, 1978.

——. *Mythologies*. Trans. A. Lavers. New York: Hill and Wang, 1972.

Basham, Arthur Llewellen. "Notes on the Origins of Śāktism and Tantrism," in P. Jash, ed., *Religion and Society in Ancient India*. Calcutta: Roy & Chowdhury, 1984, 148–154.

——. *The Wonder that Was India*. 1954. New York: Grove Press, 1959.

Bautze-Picron, Claudine, with J. K. Bautze. *The Buddhist Murals of Pagan: Timeless Vistas of the Cosmos*. Bangkok: Orchid Press, 2003.

Beal, Samuel. *Buddhist Records of the Western World*. 1884. Delhi: Motilal Banarsidass, 1983.

Beane, Wendell Charles. *Myth, Cult and Symbols in Śākta Hinduism: A Study of the Indian Mother Goddess*. Leiden: E. J. Brill, 1977.

Bell, Catherine. *Ritual: Perspectives and Dimensions*. New York: Oxford University Press, 1997.

Bendall, Cecil, ed. *Subhāṣita-saṃgraha*. Louvain: J-B Istas, 1905.

Bentor, Yael. *Consecration of Images and Stūpas in Indo-Tibetan Tantric Buddhism*. Leiden and New York: Brill, 1996.

Bernhard, Franz, ed. *Udānavarga*. Band I. Sanskrittexte aus den Turfanfunden, X. Göttingen: Vandenhoeck & Ruprecht, 1965.

Bharati, Agehananda. *The Tantric Tradition*. Rev. edition. New York: Samuel Weiser, 1975.

Bhatt, N. R., ed., *Mataṅgapārameśvarāgama (Vidyāpāda)*. Publications de l'Institut Français d'Indologie, 56. Pondicherry: Institut Français d'Indologie, 1977.

——. *Mṛgendrāgama (Kriyāpāda et Caryāpāda) avec le commentaire de Bhaṭṭa-Nārāyaṇakaṇṭha*. Publications de l'Institut Français d'Indologie, 23. Pondichéry: Institut Français d'Indologie, 1962.

——, ed. *Rauravāgama*. Vol. I. Publications de l'Institut Français d'Indologie, 18. Pondichéry: Institut Français d'Indologie, 1985.

Bhattacharya, Bholanath. "Some Aspects of the Esoteric Cults of Consort Worship in Bengal: A Field Survey Report I," *Folklore*, vol. 18, no. 10 (Oct 1977), 310–324.

——. "Some Aspects of the Esoteric Cults of Consort Worship in Bengal: A Field Survey Report II," *Folklore*, vol. 18, no. 11 (Nov 1977), 359–365.

—— [as Bholanath Bhattacherjee]. "Some Aspects of the Esoteric Cults of Consort Worship in Bengal: A Field Survey Report III," *Folklore*, vol. 18, no. 12 (Dec 1977), 385–397.

Bhattacharya, Swapna. "The Ari Cult of Myanmar," in Gärtner, Uta, and Jens Lorenz, eds., *Tradition and Modernity in Myanmar*, vol. II. Münster: LIT, 1994, 251–271.

Bhattacharya, Tarapada. "Some Notes on the Mithuna in Indian Art," *Rupam*, no. 1 [sic] (Jan 1926), 22–24.

Bhattacharya, Vidusekhara. "Is it Caryācaryaviniścaya or Āścaryacaryācaya?" *Indian Historical Quarterly*, vol. VI, no. 1 (Mar 1930), 169–171.

Bhattacharyya, Benoytosh. "Buddhist Deities in Hindu Garb," in *Proceedings and Transactions of the Fifth Indian Oriental Conference*, vol. II. Lahore: University of Panjab, 1930, 1277–1298.

——, ed. *Guhyasamāja Tantra or Tathāgataguhyaka*. Baroda: Oriental Institute, 1931.

——. *The Indian Buddhist Iconography, mainly based on the Sādhanamālā and Cognate Tāntric Texts of Rituals*. London: Oxford University Press, 1924.

——. *The Indian Buddhist Iconography, mainly based on the Sādhanamālā and Cognate Tāntric Texts of Rituals*. 1958. Second edition, rev. and enlarged. Calcutta: Firma Mukhopadhyay, 1968.

——. *An Introduction to Buddhist Esoterism*. 1931. Delhi: Motilal Banarsidass, 1989.

——, ed. *Niṣpannayogāvalī of Mahāpaṇḍita Abhayākaragupta*. Gaekwad's Oriental Series, 109. 1949. Baroda: Oriental Institute, 1972.

——. "The Only Image of Cuṇḍa," in *Proceedings and Transactions of the Fifth Indian Oriental Conference*, vol. II. Lahore: University of Panjab, 1930, 1111–1113.

——. "Origin and Development of Vajrayāna," *Indian Historical Quarterly*, vol. III, no. 4 (Dec 1927), 733–746.

——. "A Peep into the Later Buddhism," *Annals of the Bhandarkar Oriental Research Institute, Poona*, vol. X, parts I–II (April 1929), 1–24.

——, ed. *Sādhanamālā*. 2 vols. (1925 and 1928). Second edition. Baroda: Oriental Institute, 1968.

——, ed. *Two Vajrayāna Works*. Baroda: Oriental Institute, 1929.

——[as Benoytosh Bhattacharya]. "Tāntrika Culture Among the Buddhists," in *Studies on the Tantras*. Calcutta: Ramakrishna Mission, 1989, 86–100.

Bisschop, Peter, and Arlo Griffiths, "The Pāśupata Observance (*Atharvavedapariśiṣṭa* 40)," *Indo-Iranian Journal*, vol. 46 (2003), 315–348.

Bloch, Marc. *The Historian's Craft*. Trans. Peter Putnam. New York: Alfred Knopf, 1959.

Boas, George. "Preface," in J. J. Bachofen, *Myth, Religion, and Mother Right*. Princeton: Princeton University Press, 1973, xi–xxiv.

Bolle, Kees W. *The Persistence of Religion: An Essay on Tantrism and Sri Aurobindo's Philosophy*. Studies in the History of Religions VIII. Leiden: Brill, 1971.

Bosch, F. D. K. "De Inscriptie op het Akṣobhya-beeld van Gondang Lor," *Tijdschrift voor Indische Taal-, Land- en Volkenkunde*, vol. LIX, no. 5 (1920), 498–528.

Bose, Atindra Nath. "The Five Hīnajātis," *Indian Culture*, vol. VII, no. 3 (Jan–Mar 1941), 287–303.

Boucher, Daniel. *Bodhisattvas of the Forest and the Formation of the Mahāyāna: A Study and Translation of the* Rāṣṭrapālaparipṛcchā-sūtra. Honolulu: University of Hawai'i Press, 2008.

Bourdieu, Pierre. *The Logic of Practice*. Trans. R. Nice. Stanford, CA: Stanford University Press, 1990.

Braarvig, Jens. "*Dhāraṇī* and *Pratibhāna*: Memory and Eloquence of the Bodhisattvas," *Journal of the International Association of Buddhist Studies*, vol. 8, no. 1 (1985), 17–29.

Breisach, Ernst. *Historiography: Ancient, Medieval, and Modern*. Second edition. Chicago and London: University of Chicago Press, 1994.

Briggs, George Weston. *Gorakhnāth and the Kānphaṭa Yogīs*. 1938. Delhi: Motilal Banarsidass, 1998.

Broido, Michael M. "Killing, Lying, Stealing, and Adultery: A Problem of Interpretation in the Tantras," in D. S. Lopez, Jr., ed., *Buddhist Hermeneutics*. Honolulu: University of Hawaii Press, 1988, 71–118.

Bronner, Yigal. *Extreme Poetry: The South Asian Movement of Simultaneous Narration*. New York: Columbia University Press, 2010.

Brunner, H., G. Oberhammer, and A. Padoux, eds. *Tāntrikābhidhānakośa I*. Beiträge zur Kultur- und Geistesgeschichte Asiens, 35. Wien: Verlag der Österreichischen Akademie der Wissenschaften, 2000.

——, eds. *Tāntrikābhidhānakośa II*. Beiträge zur Kultur- und Geistesgeschichte Asiens, 44. Wien: Verlag der Österreichischen Akademie der Wissenschaften, 2004.

Bühnemann, Gudrun. "Buddhist Deities and Mantras in the Hindu Tantras: I The *Tantrasārasaṃgraha* and the *Īśānaśivagurudevapaddhati*," *Indo-Iranian Journal*, vol. 42 (1999), 303–34.

——. "Buddhist Deities and Mantras in the Hindu Tantras: II The *Śrīvidyārṇavatantra* and the *Tantrasāra*," *Indo-Iranian Journal*, vol. 43 (2000), 27–48.

Bullen, J. B. *The Myth of the Renaissance in Nineteenth-Century Writing*. Oxford: Oxford University Press, 1994.

Burnouf, Eugène. *Introduction à l'Histoire du Buddhisme Indien*. Paris: Imprimerie Royale, 1844.

Canary, Robert H., and Henry Kozicki, eds. *The Writing of History: Literary Form and Historical Understanding*. Madison: The University of Wisconsin Press, 1978.

Carlstedt, Gunnar. *Studier i Kulārṇava-tantra*. Uppsala: Almqvist & Wiksell, 1974.

——. *Till Kulas Lov: Kulamāhātmyakathana ur Kulārṇava-tantra*. Uppsala: Almqvist & Wiksell, 1974.

Carrard, Philippe. *Poetics of the New History: French Historical Discourse from Braudel to Chartier*. Baltimore: The Johns Hopkins University Press, 1992.

Case, Shirley Jackson. "The Historical Study of Religion," *The Journal of Religion*, vol. I, no. 1 (1921), 1–17.

Certeau, Michel de. *The Writing of History*. Trans. Tom Conley. New York: Columbia University Press, 1988.

Chakravarti, Chintaharan. "Antiquity of Tāntricism," *Indian Historical Quarterly*, vol. VI, no. 1 (Mar 1930), 114–126.

——, ed. *Guhyasamājatantrapradīpoddyotanaṭīkāṣaṭkoṭivyākhyā*. Patna: K. P. Jayaswal Research Institute, 1984.

——. "A Note on the Age and Authorship of the Tantras," *Journal of the Asiatic Society of Bengal*, New Series, vol. XXIX (1933), 71–79.

——. *Tantras: Studies on their Religion and Literature*. Calcutta: Punthi Pustak, 1963.

Chandra, Lokesh. *Tibetan Chronicle of Padma-dkar-po*. New Delhi: International Academy of Indian Culture, 1968.

——. *Vajrāvalī: A Sanskrit Manuscript from Nepal Containing the Ritual and Delineation of Maṇḍalas*. New Delhi: International Academy of Indian Culture, 1977.

Chandra, Lokesh and David Snellgrove, eds. *Sarva-tathāgata-tattva-saṅgraha: facsimile reproduction of a tenth century Sanskrit manuscript from Nepal*. New Delhi: Sharada Rani, 1981.

Chartier, Roger. *On the Edge of the Cliff: History, Language, and Practices*. Trans. Lydia G. Cochrane. Baltimore and London: The Johns Hopkins University Press, 1997.

Chatterjee, Bijan Raj. *India and Java*. Second edition, in two parts. Calcutta: Greater India Society, 1933.

——. *Indian Cultural Influence in Cambodia*. Calcutta: University of Calcutta, 1928.

Chattopadyaya, Brajadulal. *The Making of Early Medieval India*. Delhi: Oxford University Press, 1994.

Ch'en, Kenneth. "Review of *An Introduction to Tantric Buddhism* by S. B. Dagupta," *Harvard Journal of Asiatic Studies*, vol. 15, no. 1/2 (June 1952), 197–201.

Choudhary, Radhakrishna. "Social Structure in Medieval Mithila (*c.* A.D. 1200–1600)," in in R. S. Sharma, ed., *Indian Society: Historical Probings in Memory of D. D. Kosambi* (New Delhi: People's Pub. House, 1974), 217–234.

Chutiwongs, Nandana. *The Iconography of Avalokiteśvara in Mainland South East Asia*. New Delhi: Indira Gandhi National Centre for the Arts, 2002.

Cicuzza, Claudio, ed. *The Laghutantraṭīkā by Vajrapāṇi: A Critical Edition of the Sanskrit Text*. Serie Orientale Roma, LXXXVI. Roma: Istituto Italiano per l'Africa e l'Oriente, 2001.

Clapp, J. E. *Random House Webster's Dictionary of the Law*. First edition. New York: Random House, 2000.

Clifford, James, and George E. Marcus, eds. *Writing Culture: The Poetics and Politics of Ethnography*. Berkeley, Los Angeles and London: University of California Press, 1986.

Cohen, Richard S. "Discontented Categories: Hīnayāna and Mahāyāna in Indian Buddhist History," *Journal of the American Academy of Religion*, vol. 63, no. 1 (Spring 1995), 1–25.

——. "Kinsmen of the Son: Śākyabhikṣus and the Institutionalization of the Bodhisattva Ideal," *History of Religions*, vol. 40, no. 1 (August 2000), 1–31.

——. "Nāga, Yakṣiṇī, Buddha: Local Deities and Local Buddhism at Ajanta," *History of Religions* vol. 37, no. 4 (May 1998), 360–400.

Collingwood, R. G. *The Idea of History*. 1946. London, Oxford, and New York: Oxford University Press, 1956.

Conze, Edward. *Buddhism: Its Essence and Development*. 1951. New York: Harper Torchbooks, 1975.

Cowell, E. B., and J. Eggeling. *Catalogue of Buddhist Sanskrit Manuscripts in the Possession of the Royal Asiatic Society (Hodgson Collection)*. Hertford, UK: Stephen Austin, 1876.

Croce, Benedetto. *History as the Story of Liberty*. Trans. Sylvia Sprigge. 1941. Lanham: University Press of America, 1970.

——. *Logic as the Science of the Pure Concept*. Trans. Douglas Ainslie. London: Macmillan and Co., 1917.

Cunningham, Alexander. *The Bhilsa Topes*. London: Smith, Elder and Co., 1854.

Dalton, Jacob P. "The Uses of the *Dgongs pa 'dus pa'i mdo* in the Development of the Rnying-ma School of Tibetan Buddhism." Doctoral dissertation, University of Michigan, 2002.

Dasgupta, Shashibhusan. *An Introduction to Tāntric Buddhism*. First edition. Calcutta: University of Calcutta, 1950.

——. *An Introduction to Tāntric Buddhism*. Third edition. Calcutta: University of Calcutta, 1974.

——. *Obscure Religious Cults*. 1946; third edition 1969. Calcutta: Firma KLM Private Limited, 1976.

——. "Vajra and Vajrasattva," *Indian Culture*, vol. VIII, no 1 (Jul-Sep 1941), 23–32.

Davidson, Ronald M. "Gsar ma Apocrypha: The Creation of Orthodoxy, Gray Texts, and the New Revelation," in H. Eimer and D. Germano, eds., *The Many Canons of Tibetan Buddhism* (Leiden: Brill, 2002), 203–224.

——. *Indian Esoteric Buddhism: A Social History of the Tantric Movement*. New York: Columbia University Press, 2002.

——. "An Introduction to the Standards of Scriptural Authenticity in Indian Buddhism," in R. Buswell, ed., *Chinese Buddhist Apocrypha* (Honolulu: University of Hawai'i Press, 1990), 291–325.

——, ed. and trans. "The Litany of Names of Mañjuśrī: Text and Translation of the *Mañjuśrīnāmasaṃgīti*," *Mélanges chinois et bouddhiques*, vol. XX. Bruxelles: Institut Belge des Hautes études Chinoises, 1981, 1–69.

——. "Masquerading as *Pramāṇa*: Esoteric Buddhism and Epistemological Nomenclature," in S. Katsura, ed., *Dharmakīrti's Thought and its Impact on Indian and Tibetan Philosophy* (Wien: Verlag der Österreichischen Akademie der Wissenschaften, 1999), 25–35.

——. "Reframing *Sahaja*: Genre, Representation, Ritual and Lineage," *Journal of Indian Philosophy*, vol. 30 (2002), 45–83.

——. *Tibetan Renaissance: Tantric Buddhism in the Rebirth of Tibetan Culture*. New York: Columbia University Press, 2005.

Davidson, Ronald M., and Charles D. Orzech. "Tantra," in R. Buswell, ed., *Encyclopedia of Buddhism*. New York: Macmillan, 2004, 820–826.

Davis, Kathleen. *Periodization and Sovereignty: How Ideas of Feudalism and Secularization Govern the Politics of Time* (Middle Ages). Philadelphia: University of Pennsylvania Press, 2008.

de Bary, William Theodore, ed. *The Buddhist Tradition in India, China and Japan*. New York: Vintage, 1969.

Doniger, Wendy. *The Hindus: An Alternative History*. New York: Penguin, 2009.

Dorje, Chog, ed. *Abhayapaddhati of Abhayākaragupta: Commentary on the Buddhakapālamahātantra*. Bibliotheca Indo-Tibetica Series, 68. Sarnath: Central Institute of Higher Tibetan Studies, 2009.

Drewes, David. "Early Indian Mahāyāna Buddhism I: Recent Scholarship," *Religion Compass*, vol. 4, no. 2 (2010), 55–65.

——. "Early Indian Mahāyāna Buddhism II: New Perspectives," *Religion Compass*, vol. 4, no. 2 (2010), 66–74.

Dreyfus, Georges B.J. *The Sound of Two Hands Clapping: The Education of a Tibetan Buddhist Monk*. Berkeley: University of California Press, 2003.

Dubuisson, Daniel. "Pourquoi et Comment Parle-t-on des Origines?" *Graphé* 4 (1995), 19–31.

——. *The Western Construction of Religion: Myths, Knowledge, and Ideology*. Translated by William Sayers. Baltimore and London: The Johns Hopkins University Press, 2003.

Dupuche, John R. *Abhinavagupta: The Kula Ritual as elaborated in Chapter 29 of the* Tantrāloka. 2003. Delhi: Motilal Banarsidass, 2006.

Durkheim, Emile. *The Elementary Forms of the Religious Life*. Trans. J. W. Swain. 1915. New York: Free Press, 1965.

Duroiselle, Chas. "The Arī of Burma and Tāntric Buddhism." *Annual Report of the Archaeological Survey of India*, 1915–1916. 79–93.

Dutt, Manmatha Nath. *Buddha, His Life, His Teachings, His Order* [*Together with the History of Buddhism*]. Calcutta: The Society for the Resuscitation of Indian Literature, 1901.

Dutt, Nalinaksha, ed. *Bodhisattvabhūmiḥ*. Patna: K.P. Jayaswal Institute, 1978.

Dwivedi, Vrajavallabh, and S. S. Bahulkar, eds. *Vimalaprabhāṭīkā of Kalkin Śr Puṇḍarīka on Śrīlaghukālacakratantrarāja by Śrīmañjuśrīyaśas*. Volumes two and three. Sarnath: Central Institute for Higher Tibetan Studies, 1994a and 1994b.

Eastman, Kenneth W. "The Eighteen Tantras of the Tattvasaṃgraha/Māyājāla," *Transactions of the International Conference of Orientalists in Japan*, No. XXVI (1981), 95–96.

——. "The Eighteen Tantras of the Vajraśekhara/Māyājāla," draft paper presented to the 26th International Conference of Orientalists in Japan, Tōkyo, May 8, 1981.

——. "Mahāyoga Texts at Tun-huang," *Bulletin of Institute of Buddhist Cultural Studies, Ryukoku University*, No. 22 (1983), 42–60.

Edkins, Joseph. *Chinese Buddhism: A Volume of Sketches, Historical, Descriptive, and Critical*. Second edition, revised. 1893. San Francisco: Chinese Materials Center, Inc., 1976.

Eitel, Ernest John. *Hand-book for the Student of Chinese Buddhism*. London: Trübner & Co., 1870.

——. *Hand-book for the Student of Chinese Buddhism*. Second edition. Hong Kong: Lane, Crawford & Co., 1888.

Elder, George R. "Problems of Language in Buddhist Tantra," *History of Religions*, vol. 15, no. 3 (1976), 231–250.

——. "The Saṃpuṭa Tantra: Edition and Translation, Chapters I–IV." Doctoral dissertation, Columbia University, 1978.

Eliade, Mircea. *Yoga: Immortality and Freedom*. Trans. Willard R. Trask. Bollingen Series LVI. Second edition. 1969. Princeton: Princeton University Press, 1990.

Eliot, Sir Charles. *Hinduism and Buddhism: An Historical Sketch.* 3 vols. London: Edward Arnold & Co., 1921.

English, Elizabeth. 2002. *Vajrayoginī: Her Visualizations, Rituals, and Forms.* Boston: Wisdom Publications.

Evans-Pritchard, E. E. *Theories of Primitive Religion.* Oxford: Oxford University Press, 1965.

Fabian, Johannes. *Time and the Other.* New York: Columbia University Press, 1983.

Farquhar, J. N. *An Outline of the Religious Literature of India.* London: Oxford University Press, 1920.

Farrow, G. W., and I. Menon, eds. and trans. *The Concealed Essence of the Hevajra Tantra.* Delhi: Motilal Banarsidass, 1992.

Faure, Bernard. *The Rhetoric of Immediacy: A Cultural Critique of Chan/Zen Buddhism.* Princeton: Princeton University Press, 1991.

Fausbøll, V., ed. *The Jātaka together with its Commentary.* Volume I. 1877. Oxford: Pali Text Society, 2000.

Fell, R. A. L. *Etruria and Rome.* Cambridge: Cambridge University Press, 1924.

Ferguson, James. *Tree and serpent worship: or, Illustrations of mythology and art in India in the first and fourth centuries after Christ. From the sculptures of the Buddhist topes at Sanchi and Amravati.* Second revised edition. London: W. H. Allen and Co., 1873.

Fernando, C. M., trans.; rev. and ed. by W. F. Gunawardhana. *The Nikáya Saṇgrahawa.* Colombo: H.C. Cottle, Government Printer, 1908.

Finot, Louis, ed. *Rāṣṭrapālaparipṛcchā: Sūtra du Mahāyāna.* Bibliotheca Buddhica 2. 1901. Tokyo: Meicho-Fukyū-Kai, 1977.

Flood, Gavin. *The Tantric Body: The Secret Tradition of Hindu Religion.* London: I. B. Tauris, 2006.

Freud, Sigmund. *Jokes and Their Relation to the Unconscious.* Translated by James Strachey. New York: Norton, 1960.

Fürer-Haimendorf, Christoph von. "Les Religions Archaïques," in A. Bareau, et al., *Les Religions de l'Inde III: Bouddhisme, Jaïnisme, Religions Archaïques.* Paris: Payot, 1966, 277–327.

Gadamer, Hans Georg. *Truth and Method.* Second revised Edition. New York: Crossroad, 1989.

Gangoly, Ordhendra C. "The Mithuna in Indian Art," *Rupam*, nos. 22+23 (Apr–Jul 1925), 54–61.

Garner, B. A., ed., *Black's Law Dictionary.* Eighth edition. St. Paul: Thomson West, 2004.

Geden, Alfred S. "Tantras," in J. Hastings, ed., *Encyclopedia of Religion and Ethics*, vol. XII (New York: Scribner's & Sons, 1908), 192–193.

Gellner, David N. "Hodgson's Blind Alley? On the So-Called Schools of Nepalese Buddhism," JIABS, vol. 12, no. 1 (1989), 7–19.

——. "Himalayan Conundrum? A Puzzling Absence in Ronald M. Davidson's Indian Esoteric Buddhism," *Journal of the International Association of Buddhist Studies*, vol. 27, no. 2 (2004), 411–417.

——. *Monk, Householder, and Tantric Priest: Newar Buddhism and its Hierarchy of Ritual.* 1992. Indian edition. Cambridge: Cambridge University Press, 1996.

George, Christopher S. *The Caṇḍamahāroṣaṇa Tantra: A Critical Edition and English Translation, Chapters I–VIII.* New Haven, CT: American Oriental Society, 1974.

Giebel, Rolf W. "The *Chin-kang-ting ching yü-ch'ieh shih-pa-hui chih-kuei*: An Annotated Translation. *Journal of Naritasan Institute for Buddhist Studies*, vol. 19 (1996), 107–201.

——., trans. *Two Esoteric Sutras: The Adamantine Pinnacle Sutra [and] The Susiddhiakara Sutra*. Berkeley: Numata Center for Buddhist Translation and Research, 2001.

Ginzburg, Carlo. *History, Rhetoric, and Proof*. The Menahem Stern Jerusalem Lectures. Hanover and London: University Press of New England, 1999.

Glasenapp, Helmuth von. *Der Buddhismus in Indien und im fernen Osten*. Berlin: Atlantis Verlag, 1936.

——. "Ein Buddhistischer Initiationsritus des Javanischen Mittelalters," in H. v.Glasenapp, *Ausgewählte Kleine Schriften*, ed. H. Bechert and V. Moeller (Wiesbaden: Franz Steiner Verlag, 1980), 450–461.

——. "Die Entstehung des Vajrayāna," *Zeitschrift der Deutschen Morgenländischen Gesellschaft*, vol. 90 (N.S. vol. 15) (1936), 546–572.

——. "A Jaina Tīrthaṅkara in a Buddhist Maṇḍala," *Jaina Siddhānta Bhāskara*, vol. III, no. 2 (Sep 1937), 47.

——. *Mystères Bouddhistes: Doctrines et Rites Secrets du 'Véhicule de Diamant.'* Paris: Payot, 1944.

Gluckman, Max. *Rituals of Rebellion in South-east Africa*. The Frazer Lecture, 1952. Manchester: Manchester University Press, 1954.

Gombrich, Richard. "Organized Bodhisattvas: A Blind Alley in Buddhist Historiography" in *Sūryacandrāya: Essays in Honour of Akira Yuyama on the Occasion of His 65th Birthday*. Swisttal-Odendorf: Indica et Tibetica Verlag, 1998. 43–56.

Gómez, Luis O. "Buddhism in India," in J. Kitagawa and M. Cummings, eds., *Buddhism and Asian History* (New York: Macmillan, 1989), 51–104.

Gonda, Jan. "Ascetics and Courtesans," *The Adyar Library Bulletin*, vol. XXV, parts 1–4 (1961), 78–102.

Goodall, Dominic, ed. and trans. *The Parākhyatantra: A Scripture of the Śaiva Siddhānta*. Collection Indologie, 98. Pondicherry: Institut Français de Pondichéry/école Française d'Extrême-Orient, 2004.

Gossman, Lionel. *Between History and Literature*. Cambridge: Harvard University Press, 1990.

Goudriaan, T., and J. A. Schoterman, eds. *The Kubjikāmatatantra: Kulālikāmnāya Version*. Leiden/New York/København/Köln: E.J. Brill, 1988.

Goudriaan, Teun, ed. *The Sanskrit Tradition and Tantrism*. Panels of the VIIth World Sanskrit Conference, vol. I. Leiden: Brill, 1990.

Granoff, Phyllis. "Maheśvara/Mahākāla: A Unique Buddhist Image from Kaśmīr," *Artibus Asiae*, vol. 41, no. 1 (1980), 64–82.

——. "My Rituals and My Gods: Ritual Exclusiveness in Medieval India," *Journal of Indian Philosophy* 29 (2001), 109–134.

——. "Other People's Rituals: Ritual Eclecticism in Early Medieval Indian Religious," *Journal of Indian Philosophy*, vol. 28 (2000), 399–424.

——. "Tolerance in the Tantras: Its Form and Function," *The Journal of Oriental Research, Madras*, vol. LVI–LXII (1986–92), 283–302.

Gray, David B. *The Cakrasamvara Tantra: The Discourse of Śrī Heruka*. New York: AIBS/CBS/THUS [Columbia Univ. Press], 2007.

——. "Disclosing the Empty Secret: Textuality and Embodiment in the Cakrasaṃvara Tantra," *Numen*, vol. 52 (2005), 417–444.

——. "Mandala of the Self: Embodiment, Practice, and Identity Construction in the Cakrasamvara Tradition," *Journal of Religious History*, vol. 30, no. 3 (Oct 2006), 294–310.

Gregory, Peter N., ed. *Sudden and Gradual: Approaches to Enlightenment in Chinese Thought*. Honolulu: University of Hawaii Press, 1987.

"Guhyasamāja-tantra." *Encyclopædia Britannica. Encyclopædia Britannica Online Academic Edition*. Encyclopædia Britannica, 2011. Web. 12 Sep. 2011. http://www.britannica.com.proxy.uchicago.edu/EBchecked/topic/248458/Guhyasamaja-tantra.

Gyatso, Janet. "Drawn from the Tibetan Treasury: The gTer ma Literature," in J. Cabezón and R. Jackson, eds. *Tibetan Literature* (Ithaca, Snow Lion Publications, 1996), 147–169.

——. "The Logic of Legitimation in the Tibetan Treasure Tradition," *History of Religions*, vol. 33, no. 2 (Nov 1993), 97–134.

——. "Signs, Memory and History: A Tantric Buddhist Theory of Scriptural Transmission," *Journal of International Association of Buddhist Studies*, vol. IX, no. 2, 7–35.

Handiqui, K. K. *Yaśastilaka and Indian Culture*. Jivaraja Jaina Granthamala, no. 2. Sholapur: Jaina Saṃskṛti Saṃrakshaka Sangha, 1968.

Handurukande, Ratna, ed. *Three Sanskrit Texts on Caitya Worship in relation to the Ahorātravrata*. Tokyo: International Institute for Buddhist Studies, 2000.

Hardy, E., ed. *Aṅguttara-Nikāya*. Part IV. London: Pali Text Society, 1899.

Hardy, Friedhelm. "The Esoteric Traditions and Antinomian Movements," in S. Sutherland, et al., eds., *The World's Religions*. Boston: G. K. Hall & Co, 1988, 649–659.

Harrison, Paul M. "Mediums and Messages: Reflections on the Production of Mahāyāna Sūtras," *The Eastern Buddhist*, vol. XXXV, nos 1 and 2 (2003), 115–151.

——, trans. *The Pratyutpanna Samādhi Sūtra translated by Lokakṣema*. BDK English Tripitaka 25-II. Berkeley: Numata Center for Buddhist Translation and Research, 1998.

——, trans. *The Samādhi of Direct Encounter with the Buddhas of the Present: An Annotated English Translation of the Tibetan Version of the Pratyutpanna-Buddha-Saṃmukhāvasthita-Samādhi-Sūtra*. Studia Philologica Buddhica Monograph Series, V. Tokyo: The International Institute for Buddhist Studies, 1990.

——. "Searching for the Origins of Mahāyāna: What Are We Looking For?" *The Eastern Buddhist*, vol. XXVIII, no. 1 (Spring 1995), 48–69.

——. *The Tibetan Text of the Pratyutpanna-buddha-saṃmukhāvasthita-sūtra*. Studia Philologica Buddhica monograph series I. Tokyo: The Reiyukai Library, 1978.

——. "Who Gets to Ride in the Great Vehicle? Self Image and Identity Among the Followers of the Early Mahayana." *Journal of the International Association of Buddhist Studies*, vol. 10, no. 1 (1987), 67–89.

Hatley, Shaman. "The *Brahmayāmalatantra* and Early Śaiva Cult of Yoginīs." Doctoral dissertation, University of Pennsylvania, 2007.

Hidas, Gergely. "Remarks on the Use of the Dhāraṇīs and Mantras of the Mahāpratisarā-Mahāvidyārājñī," C. Dezső, ed., *Indian Languages and Texts Through the Ages*. Delhi: Manohar, 2007, 185–207.

Hirakawa, Akira. "The Rise of Mahāyāna Buddhism and its Relationship to the Worship of Stupas," *Memoirs of the Research Department of the Toyo Bunko*, no. 22 (1963), 57–106.

Hjelmslev, Louis. "Udgiverens Forord," in Rasmus Rask, *Breve fra og til Rasmus Rask.* København: Ejnar Munksgaards Forlag, 1941.

Hodge, Stephen, trans. *The Mahā-vairocana-abhisaṃbodhi Tantra with Buddhaguhya's Commentary.* London: Routledge Curzon, 2003.

Hodgson, Brian Houghton. *Essays on the Languages, Literature and Religion of Nepal and Tibet.* London: Trübner & Co., 1874.

Hoffmann, Helmut. *The Religions of Tibet.* Trans. Edward Fitzgerald. London: George Allen & Unwin, Ltd., 1961.

Hong, Luo, and Toru Tomabechi, eds. *Candrakīrti's Vajrasattvaniṣpādanasūtra (Vajrasattvasādhana): Sanskrit and Tibetan Texts.* Sanskrit Texts from the Tibetan Autonomous Region, 6. Beijing–Vienna: China Tibetology Publishing House–Austrian Academy of Sciences Press, 2009.

Horiuchi, Janjin, ed. "The Revised and Romanized Text of an Esoteric Buddhist Sanskrit Scripture: 'Vajradhātu-Mahāmaṇḍala-Vidhi-Vistara' in SARVATATHĀGATA-TATTVA-SAṂGRAHA (I)," *Journal of Koyasan University* (高野山大学論叢), vol. III (March 1968), 35–118.

——, ed. "The Revised and Romanized Text of an Esoteric Buddhist Sanskrit Scripture: The Rest of 'Sarva-tathāgata-mahāyānābhisamayo nāma mahākalpa-rajaḥ' in *Sarvatathāgata-tattva-saṃgraha* (II)," *The Mikkyo Bunka* (密教文化), vol. 90 (Feb 1970), 85–74.

——, ed. "The Revised and Romanized Text of an Esoteric Buddhist Sanskrit Scripture: The Rest of 'Sarva-tathāgata-mahāyānābhisamayo nāma mahākalpa-rajaḥ' in *Sarvatathāgata-tattva-saṃgraha* (the rest of Part II)," *The Mikkyo Bunka* (密教文化), vol. 91 (Jul 1970), 96–72.

——, ed. "The Revised and Romanized Text of an Esoteric Buddhist Sanskrit Scripture: The Rest of 'Vajra-samayo nāma Mahā-kalpaḥ' in *Sarvatathāgata-tattva-saṃgraha* (the rest of Part III)," *The Mikkyo Bunka* (密教文化), vol. 97 (Dec 1971), 96–43.

——, ed. "The Revised and Romanized Text of an Esoteric Buddhist Sanskrit Scripture: 'Trailokacakra-mahāmaṇḍala-vidhivistara' in *Sarvatathāgata-tattva-saṃgraha* (the rest of Part III)," *The Mikkyo Bunka* (密教文化), vol. 90 (Mar 1972), 104–165.

——, ed. "The Revised and Romanized Text of an Esoteric Buddhist Sanskrit Scripture: The Rest of 'Sarva-tathāgata-mahāyānābhisamayo nāma mahākalpa-rajaḥ' in *Sarvatathāgata-tattva-saṃgraha* (the rest of Part IV)," *The Mikkyo Bunka* (密教文化), vol. 103 (Jul 1973), 96–52.

——, ed. "The Revised and Romanized Text of an Esoteric Buddhist Sanskrit Scripture: The Rest of 'Sarva-vajra-kula-vajra, dharma, karmamaṇḍala-vidhi-vistara' in *Sarvatathāgata-tattva-saṃgraha* (the rest of Part IV)," *The Mikkyo Bunka* (密教文化), vol. 104 (Dec 1973), 76–67.

I., J. "Gothic Architecture," *Notes and Queries*, no. 9 (Dec 29, 1849), 134.

Ibn Khaldûn, *The Muqaddimah: an Introduction to History.* Trans. Franz Rosenthal. Princeton: Princeton University Press, 1969.

Inden, Ronald. *Imagining India.* Oxford: Blackwell, 1990.

Iwamoto, Yutaka, ed. *Kleinere Dhāraṇī Texte.* Beiträge zur Indologie, Heft 2. Kyoto: Iwamoto Yutaka, 1937a.

——, ed. *Mahāpratisarā* (Pañcarakṣā II). Beiträge zur Indologie, Heft 3. Kyoto: Iwamoto Yutaka, 1938.

——, ed. *Mahāsāhasrapramardanī* (Pañcarakṣā I). Beiträge zur Indologie, Heft 1. Kyoto: Iwamoto Yutaka, 1937b.

Jackson, Roger R. "Ambiguous Sexuality: Imagery and Interpretation in Tantric Buddhism," *Religion*, vol. 22 (1992), 85–100.

——. "Buddha as Pramāṇabhūta: Epithets and Arguments in the Buddhist 'Logical" Tradition," *Journal of Indian Philosophy*, vol. 16, no. 4 (Dec 1988), 335–365.

Jamspal, L., et al., trans. *The Universal Vehicle Discourse Literature (Mahāyānasūtrālaṃkāra) with its Commentary (Bhāṣya)*. New York: AIBS [Columbia University Press], 2004.

Jha, D. N. "Temples as Landed Magnates in Early Medieval South India (*c.* A.D. 700–1300)," in R. S. Sharma, ed., *Indian Society: Historical Probings in Memory of D.D. Kosambi* (New Delhi: People's Pub. House, 1974), 202–216.

Jha, Vivekanand. "From Tribe to Untouchable: The Case of Niṣādas," in R.S. Sharma, ed., *Indian Society: Historical Probings in Memory of D.D. Kosambi* (New Delhi: People's Pub. House, 1974), 67–84.

Joshi, Lal Mani. *Discerning the Buddha: A Study of Buddhism and of the Brahmanical Hindu Attitude to It*. New Delhi: Munshiram Manoharlal, 1983.

——. *Studies in the Buddhistic Culture of India during the Seventh and Eighth Centuries A.D.* Second edition. 1977. Delhi: Motilal Banarsidass, 1987.

Joshi, M. C. "Historical and Iconographic Aspects of Śākta Tantrism," in Harper and Brown, eds., *The Roots of Tantra*. Albany: State University of New York Press, 2002, 39–55.

Kalamandapa, ed. *Buddhist Ritual Dance*. Kathmandu: Kala Mandapa, 1986.

Kane, Pandurang Vaman. *History of Dharmaśāstra*. Poona: Bhandarkar Oriental Research Institute, 1930–1962.

Kapstein, Matthew. "King Kuñji's Banquet," in D.G. White, *Tantra in Practice* (Princeton, NJ: Princeton University Press, 2000), 52–71.

——. "The Purificatory Gem and its Cleansing," in *The Tibetan Assimilation of Buddhism* (New York: Oxford, 2000), 121–137.

——. "Scholastic Buddhism and the Mantrayāna," in *Reason's Traces: Identity and Interpretation in Indian and Tibetan Buddhist Thought* (Boston: Wisdom Publications, 2001), 233–255.

——. *The Tibetan Assimilation of Buddhism: Conversion, Contestation, and Memory*. New York and Oxford: Oxford University Press, 2000.

——. "Weaving the World: The Ritual Art of the *Paṭa* in Pāla Buddhism and its Legacy in Tibet," *History of Religions*, vol. 34, no. 3 (Feb 1995), 241–262.

Karmay, Samten. "King Tsa/Dza and Vajrayāna," *Mélanges Chinois et Bouddhiques*, vol. XX (Bruxelles: Institut Belge des Hautes études Chinoises, 1981), 192–211.

Kern, H. "De Sanskrit-inscriptie van het Mahākṣobhya-beeld te Simpang," in H. Kern, *Verspreide Geschriften*, vol. VII, ('S-Gravenhage: Martinus Nijhoff, 1917), 187–197.

——. trans. *Saddharmapuṇḍarīka or The Lotus of the True Law*. Sacred Books of the East, 21. 1884. New York: Dover, 1963.

Kimura, Yakayasu, Ōtsuka Nobuo, and Sugiki Tsunehiko. "Transcribed Sanskrit Text of the Amoghapāśakalparāja Part I," *Annual of the Institute for Comprehensive Studies of Buddhism, Taisho University* (大正大学綜合佛教研究所年報), No. 20 (March 1998), 304–251 (1–54).

——. "Transcribed Sanskrit Text of the Amoghapāśakalparāja Part II," *Annual of the Institute for Comprehensive Studies of Buddhism, Taisho University* (大正大学綜合佛教研究所年報), No. 21 (March 1999), 154–107 (81–128).

——. "Transcribed Sanskrit Text of the Amoghapāśakalparāja Part III," *Annual of the Institute for Comprehensive Studies of Buddhism, Taisho University* (大正大学綜合佛教研究所年報), No. 22 (March 2000), 372–309 (1–64).

——. "Transcribed Sanskrit Text of the Amoghapāśakalparāja Part IV," *Annual of the Institute for Comprehensive Studies of Buddhism, Taisho University* (大正大学綜合佛教研究所年報), No. 23 (March 2001), 406–331 (1–76).

——. "Transcribed Sanskrit Text of the Amoghapāśakalparāja Part V," *Annual of the Institute for Comprehensive Studies of Buddhism, Taisho University* (大正大学綜合佛教研究所年報), No. 26 (March 2004), (120–183).

King, Richard. *Orientalism and Religion: Postcolonial Theory, India and the "Mystic East."* 1999. London and New York: Routledge, 2003.

Kiss, Csaba. "Notes on the *Matsyendrasaṃhitā*," in Csaba Dezső, ed., *Indian Languages and Texts Through the Ages*. New Delhi: Manohar, 2007, 147–184.

Kopf, David. "A Historiographical Essay on the Idea of Kali," in T. K. Stewart, ed., *Shaping Bengali Worlds, Public and Private*. East Lansing: Asian Studies Center MSU, 1989, 112–127.

Köppen, Carl Friedrich. *Die Religion des Buddha*. Vol. 1: Die Religion des Buddha und ihre Entstehung. Berlin: Ferdinand Schneider, 1857.

——. *Die Religion des Buddha*. Vol. 2: Die Lamaische Hierarchie und Kirche. Berlin: Ferdinand Schneider, 1859.

Kramrisch, Stella. "Pāla and Sena Sculpture," *Rupam*, no. 40 (Oct. 1929), 107–126.

Krishna Iyer, L. A., and L. K. Bala Ratnam. *Anthropology in India*. Bombay: Bharatiya Vidya Bhavan, 1961.

Kuijp, Leonard W.J. van der. "Dating the Two Lde'u Chronicles of Buddhism in India and Tibet," *Asiatische Studien/études Asiatiques*, vol. XLVI, no. 1 (1992), 468–491.

——. "*Nāgabodhi/Nāgabuddhi: Notes on the Guhyasamāja Literature," in B. Kellner, H. Krasser, H. Lasic, M.T. Much, and H. Taucher, eds., *Pramāṇakīrtiḥ: Papers dedicated to Ernst Steinkellner on the Occasion of his 70th Birthday*, vol. 2 (Vienna: Arbeitskreis für Tibetische und Buddhistische Studien Universität Wien, 2007), 1001–1022.

——. "On the Authorship and Date of the Ecclesiastical Chronicle *Chos 'byung rin po che'i gter mdzod bstan pa'i gsal bar byed pa'i nyi 'od*," in Dieter Schuh, Petra Maurer, and Peter Schwieger, eds., *Tibetstudien: Festschrift für Dieter Schuh zum 65. Geburtstag*. Bonn: Bier'sche Verlagsanstalt, 2007, 127–148.

Kværne, Per. *An Anthology of Buddhist Tantric Songs: A Study of the Caryāgīti*. 1977. Bangkok: White Orchid Press, 1986.

——. "On the Concept of Sahaja in Indian Buddhist Tantric Literature," *Temenos: Studies in Comparative Religion*, vol. 11–12 (1975–76), 88–135.

——. "Review of Alex Wayman, *Yoga of the Guhyasamājatantra*," *Indo-Iranian Journal*, vol. 22, no. 3 (July 1980), 242–247.

Lal, Banarsi, ed. *Āryamañjuśrīnāmasaṃgīti with Amṛtakaṇikā-ṭippaṇī by Bhikṣu Raviśrījñāna and Amṛtakaṇikodyota-nibandha of Vibhūticandra*. Bibliotheca Indo-Tibetica, XXX. Sarnath: Central Institute for Higher Tibetan Studies, 1994.

——, ed. *Luptabauddhavacanasaṃgrahaḥ*. Part 2. Rare Buddhist Texts Series, 25. Sarnath: Central Institute for Higher Tibetan Studies, 2001.

Lamotte, étienne. "The Assessment of Textual Interpretation in Buddhism," *Buddhist Studies Review*, vol. II, no. 1 (1985), 4–24.

——. *History of Indian Buddhism: From the Origins to the Śaka Era*. Trans. Sara Webb-Boin. Louvain-La-Neuve: Institut Orientaliste, 1988.

——. "La Légende du Bouddha," *Revue de l'Histoire des Religions*, vol. 134 (1948), 37–71.

——. *Śūraṃgamasamādhisūtra: The Concentration of Heroic Progess*. Trans. S. Boin-Webb. Richmond: Curzon Press, 1998.

Larsson, Stefan. "The Birth of a Heruka: How Sangs rgyas rgyal mtshan became gTsang smyon Heruka: A Study of a Mad Yogin" Doctoral dissertation, Stockholm University, 2009.

La Vallée Poussin, Louis de. *Bouddhisme: études et Materiaux: Adikarmapradipa: Bodhicaryavataratika*. London: Luzac, 1898.

——. *Bouddhisme: Opinions sur l'Histoire de la Dogmatique*. 5th Edition. Paris: Gabriel Beauchesne, 1925.

——. "Notes de bibliographie bouddhique." *Mélanges chinois et bouddhiques*, vol. III (1934–35), 397–405.

——. "Tāntrism (Buddhist)," in James Hastings, ed., *Encyclopedia of Religion and Ethics*, vol. XII (New York: Scribner's & Sons, 1908), 193–197.

Law, Bimala Churn. *Tribes in Ancient India*. Bhandarkar Oriental Series, no. 4. Poona: Bhandarkar Oriental Research Institute, 1943.

Leauchli, Samuel. *The Language of Faith: An Introduction to the Semantic Dilemma of the Early Church*. New York: Abington Press, 1962.

Lessing, F. D., and Alex Wayman, eds. and trans. *Introduction to the Buddhist Tantric Systems*. Second edition. Delhi: Motilal Banarsidass, 1980.

Lévi, Sylvain. "Un nouveau document sur le bouddhisme de basse epoque dans l'Inde," *Bulletin of the School of Oriental and African Studies, University of London*, vol. 6, no. 2 (May 1931), 417–429.

——. *Le Népal: étude Historique d'un Royaume Hindou*. 3 volumes. Paris: Ernest Leroux, 1905–1908.

Li Rongxi, trans. *The Great Tang Dynasty Record of the Western Regions*. BDK English Tripiṭaka, 79. Berkeley: Numata Center for Buddhist Translation and Research, 1996.

Lin Li-kouang. "Puṇyodaya (Na-T'i), Un Propagateur du Tantrisme en Chine et au Cambodge à l'époque de Hiuan-tsang," *Journal Asiatique*, vol. CCXXVII (Jul–Sep 1935), 83–100.

Lincoln, Bruce. *Authority: Construction and Corrosion*. Chicago: University of Chicago Press, 1994.

——. *Discourse and the Construction of Society: Comparative Studies of Myth, Ritual, and Classification*. New York: Oxford University Press, 1989.

——. "How to Read a Religious Text: Reflections on Some Passages of the Chāndogya Upaniṣad," *History of Religions*, vol. 46, no. 2 (Nov 2006), 127–139.

——. *Theorizing Myth: Narrative, Ideology, and Scholarship*. Chicago and London: University of Chicago Press, 1999.

Lorenzen, David N. *The Kāpālikas and Kālamukhas: Two Lost Śaivite Sects*. Second edition. Delhi: Motilal Banarsidass, 1991.

Lutgendorf, Philip. "Dining Out at Lake Pampa: The Shabari Episode in Multiple Ramayanas," in P. Richman, ed., *Questioning Ramayanas: A South Asian Tradition*. New Delhi: Oxford University Press, 2000, 119–136.

Lyon, Bruce. *The Middle Ages in Recent Historical Thought: Selected Topics*. Second edition. Washington: American Historical Association, 1965.

Macdonald, Ariane. *Le Maṇḍala du Mañjuśrīmūlakalpa*. Paris: Adrien-Maisonneuve, 1962.

Mahendra Vikrama Varma, King of Kanchi. *The Farce of the Pious Courtesan (Bhagavad-Ajjuka Prahasanam) and A Farce of Drunken Sport (Matta-vilāsa Prahasanam)*. Ed. and trans. by Michael Lockwood and A. Vishnu Bhat. Madras: Tambaram Research Associates, 1991.

Marrou, Henri Irénée. *The Meaning of History*. Trans. Robert J. Olsen. Baltimore: Helicon, 1966.

Martin, Dan, in collaboration with Yael Bentor. *Tibetan Histories: A Bibliography of Tibetan-Language Historical Works*. London: Serindia Publications, 1997.

Masefield, Peter. *Divine Revelation in Pali Buddhism*. 1986. New York: Routledge, 2008.

Masuzawa, Tomoko. *The Invention of World Religions Or, How European Universalism Was Preserved in the Language of Pluralism*. Chicago: University of Chicago Press, 2005.

Matsunaga, Yūkei. "A Doubt to the Authority of the Guhyasamāja-ākhyāna-Tantras," *Journal of Indian and Buddhist Studies*, vol. XII.2 (1964), 16–25.

——, ed. *The Guhyasamāja Tantra*. Osaka: Yoho Shuppan, 1978.

——. "Indian Esoteric Buddhism as Studied in Japan," in Y. Matsunaga, ed., *Studies of Esoteric Buddhism and Tantrism*. Koyasan: Koyasan University, 1965, 229–242.

——. "Some Problems of the Guhyasamāja-Tantra," in Chandra, Lokesh, and Perala Ratnam, eds., *Studies in Indo-Asian Art and Culture*, Vol. 5. New Delhi: International Institute for Indian Culture, 1977.

——, ed. *Studies of Esoteric Buddhism and Tantrism in Commemoration of the 1,150th Anniversary of the Founding of Koyasan* [密教学密教史論文集 / 高野山大学編]. Kōya: Kōyasan Daigaku, 1965.

Mayer, Robert. "Caskets of Treasures and Visions of Buddhas: Indic Antecedents of the Tibetan gTer-ma Tradition," in P. Connolly and S. Hamilton, eds., *Indian Insights: Buddhism, Brahmanism and Bhakti*. London: Luzac, 1997, 137–151.

——. "The Importance of the Underworlds: Asuras' Caves in Buddhism, and Some Other Themes in Early Buddhist Tantras Reminiscent of the Later Padmasambhava Legends," *Journal of the International Association of Tibetan Studies*, no. 3 (Dec 2007), 1–31.

——. "Scriptural Revelation in India and Tibet: Indian Precursors of the gTer-ma Tradition," in P. Kværne, ed., *Tibetan Studies* (Oslo: The Institute for Comparative Research in Human Culture, 1994), 533–544.

McCloskey, Deirdre [Donald] N. *The Rhetoric of Economics*. Madison: University of Wisconsin Press, 1985. [also second edition]

Meisezahl, R. O. "Amoghapāśa: Some Nepalese Representations and Their Vajrayānic Aspects," *Monumenta Serica*, vol. 26 (1967), 455–497.

——. "The *Amoghapāśahṛdaya-dhāraṇī*: The Early Sanskrit Manuscript of the Reiunji Critically Edited and Translated." *Monumenta Nipponica* 17:1/4 (1962), 265–328.

——. *Geist und Ikonographie des Vajrayāna-Buddhismus: Hommage à Marie-Thérèse de Mallmann*. Beiträge zur Zentralasienforschung, 2. Sankt Augustin: VGH Wissenschaftsverlag, 1980.

Mimaki, Katsumi, and Toru Tomabechi. *Pañcakrama*. Tokyo: Center for East Asian Cultural Studies for Unesco, 1994.

Mink, Louis O. *Historical Understanding*. Brian Fay, Eugene O. Golob, and Richard T. Vann, eds. Ithaca and London: Cornell University Press, 1987.

Mitra, Rājendralāl. [1882] 1971. *Sanskrit Buddhist Literature of Nepal*. Calcutta: Sanskrit Pustak Bhandar.

Modak, B. R. "The Pāśupata-vrata," *Journal of the Karnatak University, Humanities*, vol. 11 (1967), 7–10.

Moens, J. L. "Het Buddhisme op Java en Sumatra in zijn laatste Bloeiperiode," *Tijdschrift voor Taal-, Land-, en Volkenkunde*, vol. LXIV (1924), 521–579.

Momigliano, Arnaldo. "The rhetoric of history and the history of rhetoric: On Hayden White's tropes," in E. S. Shaffer, ed. *Comparative Criticism: A Yearbook 3*. Cambridge: Cambridge University Press, 1981, 259–268.

Monier-Williams, Monier. *Buddhism, in its connexion with Brāhmanism and Hindūism, and in Contrast with Christianity*. London: John Murray, 1889.

——. *A Sanskrit-English Dictionary Etymologically and Philologically Arranged*. 1899. Delhi: Motilal Banarsidass, 1990.

Montell, Gösta. *The Chinese Lama Temple: Potala of Jehol*. Chicago: A Century of Progress Exposition, 1932.

Mullin, Glenn, ed. and trans. *Tsongkhapa's Six Yogas of Naropa*. Ithaca: Snow Lion Publications, 1996.

Munz, Peter. *The Concept of the Middle Ages as a Sociological Category*. Wellington: The Victoria University of Wellington, 1969.

Mus, Paul. "Barabuḍur; les origines du Stūpa et la transmigration; essai d'archéologie religieuse comparée," *Bulletin de l'école Française d'extrême Orient*, vol. XXXIII, no. 2 (1933), 577–980.

——. *La Lumière sur les Six Voies: Tableau de la transmigration bouddhique d'après des sources sanskrites, pāli, tibétaines et chinoises en majeure partie inédités*. Université de Paris, Travaux et Mémoires de l'Insitut d'Ethnologie, XXXV. Paris: Institut d'Ethnologie, 1939.

Nakamura, Hajime. *A Critical Survey of Tibetology and Esoteric Buddhism chiefly based on Japanese Studies*. Tokyo: The Institute of Tibetan Studies, Faculty of Letters, University of Tokyo, 1965.

Nambiar, Sita K. *Prabodhacandrodaya of Kṛṣṇamiśra*. Second edition. Delhi: Motilal Banarsidass, 1998.

Nance, Richard. "Indian Buddhist Preachers Inside and Outside the Sūtras," *Religion Compass*, vol. 2, no. 2 (2008), 134–159.

Nattier, Jan. *A Few Good Men: The Bodhisattva Path according to the Inquiry of Ugra (Ugraparipṛcchā)*. Honolulu: University of Hawai'i Press, 2005.

——. *Once Upon a Future Time: Studies in a Buddhist Prophecy of Decline*. [n.p.]: Asian Humanities Press, 1991.

Newman, John Ronald. "A Brief History of the Kalachakra," in Geshe Lhundup Sopa, et al., *The Wheel of Time: The Kalachakra in Context*. Ithaca: Snow Lion, 1985, 51–90.

——. "The Outer Wheel of Time: Vajrayāna Buddhist Cosmology in the Kālacakra Tantra." Doctoral dissertation, University of Wisconsin-Madison, 1987.

Nietzsche, Friedrich. "On Truth and Lies in a Nonmoral Sense," in *Philosophy and Truth: Selections from Nietzsche's Notebooks of the Early 1870's*, ed. and trans. Daniel Breazeale (New Jersey and London: Humanities Press International, 1979), 79–97.

Nihom, Max. "The Identification and Original Site of a Cult Statue on East Java: The Jaka Dolog," *Journal of the American Oriental Society*, vol. 106, no. 3 (Jul–Sep 1986), 485–499 and 501.

——. "On Attracting Women and Tantric Initiation: Tilottamā and *Hevajratantra* II, v. 38–47 and I, vii. 8–9," *Bulletin of the School of Oriental and African Studies, University of London*, vol. 58, no. 3 (1995), 521–531.

——. "Studies in the Buddhist Tantra." Doctoral dissertation, Leiden, 1982.

Norman, K. R. *Pāli Literature: including the canonical literature in Prakrit and Sanskrit of all the Hīnayāna schools of Buddhism*. History of Indian Literature, vol. 7, fasc. 2. Wiesbaden: Otto Harrassowitz, 1983.

Olivelle, Patrick. "When Texts Conceal: Why Vedic Recitation in Forbidden at Certain Times and Places," *Journal of the American Oriental Society*, vol. 126, no. 3 (2006), 305–322.

Orzech, Charles D. "The 'Great Teaching of Yoga,' the Chinese Appropriation of the Tantras, and the Question of Esoteric Buddhism," *Journal of Chinese Religions*, vol. 34 (2006), 29–78.

——. "The Legend of the Iron Stūpa," in D.S. Lopez, Jr., ed., *Buddhism in Practice*. Princeton: Princeton University Press, 1995, 314–317.

——. *Politics and Transcendent Wisdom: The* Scripture for Humane Kings *in the Creation of Chinese Buddhism*. University Park: Pennsylvania State University Press, 1998.

Padoux, André. "Le Tantrisme," in L. Silburn et al., eds., *Le Bouddhisme*. Paris: Fayard, 1977, 293–328.

Paidipaty, Poornima. "Tribal Nation: Politics and the Making of Modern Anthropology in India." Doctoral dissertation, Columbia University, 2009.

Pandey, Janardan Shastri. "Durlabha Grantha Paricaya," *Dhīḥ*, vol 10 (1990), 3–25.

——, ed. *Śrīherukābhidhānam / Cakrasaṃvaratantram with the Vivṛti Commentary of Bhavabhaṭṭa*. 2 vols. Rare Buddhist Texts Series, 26. Sarnath: Central Institute of Higher Tibetan Studies, 2002.

——, ed. *Yoginīśañcāratantram with Nibandha of Tathāgatarakṣita and Upadeśānusāriṇīvyākhyā of Alakalakaśa*. Rare Buddhist Texts Series, 21. Sarnath: Central Institute for Higher Tibetan Studies, 1998.

Patel, Prabhubhai. "Cittaviśuddhiprakaraṇam of Āryadeva," *Indian Historical Quarterly*, vol. IX (1933), 705–721.

——, ed. *Cittaviśuddhiprakaraṇa of Āryadeva: Sanskrit and Tibetan Texts*. Viśva-Bharati Studies, No. 8. [Santiniketan:] Visva-Bharati, 1949.

Pathak, Suniti Kumar. "A Dharani-Mantra in the Vinayavastu," *Bulletin of Tibetology*, vol. 25, no. 2 (new series), 31–39.

Pédraglio, Armelle. *Le Prabodhacandrodaya de Kṛṣṇamiśra: un drame allégorique sanskrit*. Paris: Institut de civilisation indienne, 1974.

Pollock, Sheldon. "Future Philology? The Fate of a Soft Science in a Hard World," *Critical Inquiry* 35 (Summer 2009), 931–961.

——. *The Language of the Gods in the World of Men: Sanskrit, Culture, and Power in Premodern India*. Berkeley: University of California Press, 2006.

——. "The Theory of Practice and the Practice of Theory in Indian Intellectual History," *Journal of the American Oriental Society*, vol. 105 (1985), 499–519.

Popkin, Richard H. *The History of Skepticism from Erasmus to Spinoza*. Berkeley: University of California Press, 1979.

Pott, P. H. *Yoga and Yantra: Their Interrelation and their Significance for Indian Archaeology*. Trans. Rodney Needham. Koninklijk Instituut voor Taal-, Land- en Volkenkunde, Translations Series, 8. The Hague: Martinus Nijhoff, 1966.

Pradhan, P., ed. *Abhidharmakośa of Vasubandhu with the Commentary*. Bhoṭadeśīya-Saṃskrta-granthamālā, 23. Patna: K.P. Jayaswal Research Institute, 1983.

——. *Abhidharmasamuccaya*. Santiniketan: Visva-bharati, 1950.

Prebish, Charles. *Buddhist Monastic Discipline: The Sanskrit Prātimokṣa Sūtras of the Mahāsaṃghikas and Mūlasarvāstivādins*. University Park and London: The Pennsylvania State University Press, 1975.

Preus, J. Samuel. *Explaining Religion: Criticism and Theory from Bodin to Freud*. New Haven: Yale University Press, 1987.

Przyluski, Jean. "Heruka-Śambhara," *Polski Biuletyn Orientalistyczny* (*The Polish Bulletin of Oriental Studies*), vol. I (1937), 42–45.

——. "Le Bouddhisme Tantrique à Bali, d'après une publication récente," *Journal Asiatique*, Tome CCXVIII (1931), 159–167.

——. "Les Vidyārāja: Contribution à l'Histoire de la Magie dans les sectes Mahāyānistes," *Bulletin de l'école Française de l'Extrême Orient*, vol. XX (1923), 301–318.

Rahula, Walpola. *History of Buddhism in Ceylon: The Anurādhapura Period (3rd Century BC–10th Century AC)*. Second edition. Colombo: M. D. Gunasena & Co., Ltd., 1966.

Rastogi, Navjivan. *The Krama Tantricism of Kashmir: Historical and General Sources*, vol. 1. 1979. Delhi: Motilal Banarsidass, 1996.

Ray, Nihar-Ranjan. *Sanskrit Buddhism in Burma*. Amsterdam: H. J. Paris, 1936.

Ray, Reginald. "Reading the Vajrayāna in Context: A Reassessment of Bengal Blackie," *Buddhist-Christian Studies*, vol. 5 (1985), 173–189.

——. "Understanding Tantric Buddhism: Some Questions of Method," *Journal of Asian Studies*, vol. XXXIV, no. 1 (Nov 1974), 169–175.

Renou, Louis. "Préface" to Ryūjun Tajima, *Les Deux Grands Maṇḍalas et la Doctrine de l'Esoterisme Shingon.* Tokyo: Maison franco-japonaise, 1959, i–iv.

Rhys Davids, T. W. *Buddhism: Being a Sketch of the Life and Teachings of Gautama, the Buddha.* Revised edition. London: Society for Promoting Christian Knowledge, 1894.

——. *Buddhist India.* 1903. Delhi: Motilal Banarsidass, 1993.

Rhys Davids, T. W., and J. Estlin Carpenter, eds. *The Dīgha Nikāya.* Vol. II. London: Pali Text Society, 1903.

Rigney, Ann. *The Rhetoric of Historical Representation: Three Narrative Histories of the French Revolution.* Cambridge: Cambridge University Press, 1990.

Rinpoche, S., and Vrajvallabh Dwivedi, eds. *Guhyādi-aṣṭasiddhi-saṅgraha.* Rare Buddhist Texts Series, 1. Sarnath: Central Institute of Higher Tibetan Studies, 1987.

——, eds. *Kṛṣṇayamāritantram with Ratnāvalīpañjikā of Kumāracandra.* Rare Buddhist Texts Series, 9. Sarnath: Central Institute of Higher Tibetan Studies, 1992.

——, eds. *Mahāmāyātantram with Guṇavatī by Ratnākaraśānti.* Rare Buddhist Texts Series, 10. Sarnath: Central Institute of Higher Tibetan Studies, 1992.

——. *Vasantatilakā of Caryāvratī Śrīkṛṣṇācārya with Commentary Rahasyadīpikā by Vanaratna.* Sarnath: Central Institute for Higher Tibetan Studies, 1990.

Robinson, Fred C. "Medieval, the Middle Ages," *Speculum*, vol. 59, no. 4 (1984), 745–756.

Robinson, Richard H. *The Buddhist Religion: A Historical Introduction.* First edition. Belmont: Dickenson, 1970.

Robinson, Richard H., and Willard L. Johnson. *The Buddhist Religion: A Historical Introduction.* Second edition. Encino: Dickenson, 1977.

Robinson, Richard H., Willard L. Johnson, and Thanissaro Bhikkhu (Geoffrey DeGraff). *The Buddhist Religion: A Historical Introduction.* Fifth edition. Belmont: Wadsworth/ Thomson, 2005.

Robinson, Richard H., and Willard L. Johnson, with Kathryn Tsai and Shinzen Young. *The Buddhist Religion: A Historical Introduction.* Third edition. Belmont: Wadsworth, 1982.

Robinson, Richard H., and Willard L. Johnson, assisted by Sandra A. Wawrytko and Thanissaro Bhikkhu (Geoffrey DeGraff). *The Buddhist Religion: A Historical Introduction.* Fourth edition. Belmont: Wadsworth, 1997.

Rodrigues, Hillary. *Introducing Hinduism.* New York and London: Routledge, 2006.

Rousseau, Jean-Jacques. "On the Social Contract," in *The Basic Political Writings*, (Indianapolis: Hackett, 1987), 141–227.

Roy, Satindra Narayan. "The Witches of Orissa," *Journal of the Anthropological Society of Bombay*, XIV (1927), 185–200.

Ruegg, David Seyfort. 1989. "Allusiveness and Obliqueness in Buddhist Texts: *Saṃdhā*, *Saṃdhi*, *Saṃdhyā* and *Abhisaṃdhi*." In *Dialectes dans les Littératures Indo-Aryennes*, 295–328. Ed. by C. Caillat. Paris: Institut de Civilisation Indienne.

——. *Buddha-nature, Mind and the Problem of Gradualism in Comparative Perspective: On the Transmission and Reception of Buddhism in India and Tibet.* 1989. New Delhi: Heritage Publishers, 1992.

——. "A Note on the Relationship between Buddhist and 'Hindu' Divinities in Buddhist Literature and Iconology: The *Laukika/Lokkotara* Contrast and the Notion of an Indian

'Religious Substratum,'" in R. Torella, ed., *Le parole e i marmi: studi in onore di Raniero Gnoli nel suo 70. compleanno*, (Rome: Istituto Italiano per l'Africa e l'Oriente, 2001), 735–742.

——. "Problems in the Transmission of Vajrayāna Buddhism in the Western Himalaya about the Year 1000," *Acta Indologica* VI (1984), 369–381.

——. "Sur les rapports entre le Bouddhisme et le 'substrat religieux' Indien et Tibétain," Journal Asiatique, vol. CCLII, no. 1 (1964), 77–95.

——. *The Symbiosis of Buddhism with Brahmanism/Hinduism in South Asia and of Buddhism with 'Local Cults' in Tibet and the Himalayan Region*. Beiträge zur Kultur- und Geistesgeschichte Asiens, 58. Vienna: Verlag der Österreischischen Akademie der Wissenschaften, 2008.

Sachau, Edward C. *Alberuni's India*. 2 vols. London: Kegan Paul, Trench, Trubner & Co. Ltd, 1910.

Said, Edward W. *Orientalism*. New York: Pantheon Books, 1978.

——. *The World, The Text, and the Critic*. Cambridge, MA: Harvard University Press, 1983.

Samuel, Geoffrey. *Civilized Shamans: Buddhism in Tibetan Societies*. Washington, DC: Smithsonian Institution Press, 1993.

——. *The Origins of Yoga and Tantra: Indic Religions to the Thirteenth Century*. Cambridge: Cambridge University Press, 2008.

——. *Tantric Revisionings: New Understandings of Tibetan Buddhism and Indian Religion*. Delhi: Motilal Banarsidass, 2005.

Sanderson, Alexis. "A Commentary on the Opening Verses of the *Tantrasāra* of Abhinavagupta," S. Das and E. Fürlinger, eds., *Sāmarasya: Studies in Indian Arts, Philosophy, and Interreligious Dialogue in Honour of Bettina Bäumer*. New Delhi: D.K. Printworld (P) Ltd., 2005, 89–148.

——. "History through Textual Criticism in the Study of Saivism, the Pancaratra and the Buddhist Yoginitantras," in François Grimal, ed., *Les Sources et le Temps*. Pondicherry: Institute Français de Pondichéry, 2001, 1–62.

——. "The Lākulas: New Evidence of a System Intermediate between Pāñcārthika Pāśupatism and Āgamic Śaivism," *Indian Philosophical Annual* 24 (2006), 143–217.

——. "Purity and Power among the Brahmans of Kashmir," in M. Carrithers, et al., *The Category of the Person: Anthropology, philosophy, history*. Cambridge: Cambridge University Press, 1985, 190–216.

——. "Religion and the State: Śaiva Officiants in the Territory of the King's Brahmanical Chaplain," *Indo-Iranian Journal*, vol. 47 (2004), 229–300.

——. "Śaivism and the Tantric Traditions," in S. Sutherland, et al., eds., *The World's Religions*. Boston, MA: G. K. Hall & Co, 1988, 660–704.

——. "The Śaiva Age: The Rise and Dominance of Śaivism during the Early Medieval Period," in S. Einoo, ed., *Genesis and Development of Tantrism*. Tokyo: Institute of Oriental Culture, University of Tokyo, 2009, 41–349.

——. "The Śaiva Exegesis of Kashmir," in D. Goodall and A. Padoux, eds., *Mélanges tantriques à la mémoire d'Hélène Brunner/Tantric Studies in Memory of Hélène Brunner*. Pondicherry: Institut Français de Pondichéry/école Française d'Extrême Orient, 2007, 231–442.

——. "The Śaiva Religion among the Khmers, Part I," *Bulletin de l'école française d'Extrême-Orient*, vol. 90–91 (2003–2004), 349–462.

——. "Vajrayāna: Origin and Function" in *Buddhism into the Year 2000: International Conference Proceedings*. Bangkok and Los Angeles, Dhammakaya Foundation, 1994, 87–102.

Sanford, James H. "The Abominable Tachikawa Skull Ritual," *Monumenta Nipponica* 46:1 (Spr 1991), 1–20.

Sankrityayan, Rahul. "The Origin of Vajrayana and Its Eighty-four Mystics," in *Selected Essays of Rahul Sankrityayan*. New Delhi: People's Publishing House, 1984, 114–130.

——. "Recherches Bouddhiques," *Journal Asiatique*, vol. CCXXV, no. 2 (Oct–Dec 1934), 195–230.

——. "The Rise and Fall of Buddhism in India," in *Selected Essays of Rahul Sankrityayan*. New Delhi: People's Publishing House, 1984, 179–195.

——. *Selected Essays of Rahul Sankrityayan*. New Delhi: People's Publishing House, 1984.

Sanyal, Niradbandhu. "A Buddhist Inscription from Bodh-Gaya of the Reign of Jayaccandradeva," *The Indian Historical Quarterly*, vol. V, no. 1 (March 1929), 14–30.

Sapir, Edward. "The Status of Linguistics as a Science," *Language*, vol. 5, no 4 (Dec 1929), 207–214.

Sastri, R. Ananthakrishna. *Pāsupata sūtras with Panchārthabhāshya of Kaundinya*. Trivandrum: Oriental Manuscripts Library of the University of Travancore, 1940.

Sâstrî, T. Gaṇapati, ed. *Āryamañjuśrīmūlakalpa*. Trivandrum Sanskrit Series, vols. LXX, LXXVI, and LXXXIV. Trivandrum: Superintendent Government Press, 1920–1925.

Sastry, P. V. Naganatha, ed. and trans. *Kāvyālaṃkāra of Bhāmaha*. Delhi: Motilal Banarsidass, 1970.

Saunders, E. Dale. "A Note on Śakti and Dhyānibuddha," *History of Religions*, vol. I, no. 2 (Winter 1962), 300–306.

Saussure, Ferdinand de. *Cours de Linguistique Générale*. Fourth edition. Paris: Payot, 1949.

——. *Course in General Linguistics*. Trans. R. Harris. 1983. Chicago: Open Court, 1997.

Scharf, Robert H. "Buddhist Modernism and the Rhetoric of Meditative Experience." *Numen*, vol. 42 (1995), 228–283.

——. "On Esoteric Buddhism in China," in Robert H. Scharf, *Coming to Terms with Chinese Buddhism: A Reading of the* Treasure Store Treatise. Honolulu: University of Hawai'i Press, 2002, 263–278.

Schiefner, Anton, trans. *Târanâtha's Geschichte des Buddhismus in Indien*. St. Petersburg: Commissionäre der Kaiserlichen Akademie der Wissenschaften, 1869.

Schopen, Gregory. "Archaeology and Protestant Presuppositions in the Study of Indian Buddhism," in G. Schopen, *Bones, Stones, and Buddhist Monks*. Honolulu: University of Hawai'i Press, 1997, 1–22.

——. "On Monks, Nuns, and 'Vulgar' Practices: The Introduction of the Image Cult into Indian Buddhism," in G. Schopen, *Bones, Stones, and Buddhist Monks*. Honolulu: University of Hawai'i Press, 1997, 238–257.

Schoterman, J. A., ed. and trans. *The Ṣaṭsāhasra Saṃhitā: Chapters 1-5*. Orientalia Rheno-Traiectina, 7. Leiden: Brill, 1982.

Schader, F. Otto. *Introduction to the Pāñcarātra and the Ahirbudhnya Saṃhita*. Second edition. Madras: Adyar Library, 1973.

Sferra, Francesco. "The *Laud of the Chosen Deity*, the First Chapter of the *Hevajratantrapiṇḍārthaṭīkā* by Vajragarbha," in S. Einoo, ed., *Genesis and Development of Tantrism*. Tokyo: Insitute of Oriental Culture, Univ. of Tokyo, 2009, 435–468.

——. *The* Ṣaḍaṅgayoga *by Anupamarakṣita with Raviśrījñāna's* Guṇabharaṇīnāmaṣaḍaṅ gayogaṭippaṇī. Serie Orientale Roma, LXXXV. Roma: Istituto Italiano per l'Africa e l'Oriente, 2000.

——. "Some Considerations on the Relationship Between Hindu and Buddhist Tantras," in G. Verardi and S. Vita, eds. *Buddhist Asia 1: Papers from the First Conference of Buddhist Studies Held in Naples in May 2001*. Kyoto: Italian School of East Asian Studies, 2003, 57–84.

Sferra, Francesco, and Stefania Merzagora, eds. *The Sekoddeśaṭīkā by Nāropā (Paramārthasaṃgraha)*. Serie Orientale Roma, XCIX. Roma: Istituto Italiano per l'Africa e l'Oriente, 2006.

Shafer, Robert. *Ethnography of Ancient India*. Wiesbaden: Otto Harrassowitz, 1954.

Sharma, R. S. *Early Medieval Indian Society: A Study in Feudalism*. Hyderabad: Orient Longman, 2001.

——. "Material Milieu of Tantricism," in R.S. Sharma, ed., *Indian Society: Historical Probings in Memory of D. D. Kosambi* (New Delhi: People's Pub. House, 1974), 175–189.

Sharpe, Eric. *Comparative Religion: A History*. Second edition. 1986. London: Duckworth, 2003.

Shastri, Haraprasad, ed. *Advayavajrasaṃgraha*. Baroda: Oriental Institue, 1927.

——. The discovery of a work by Āryadeva in Sanskrit," *Journal of the Asiatic Society of Bengal*, vol. 67, pt. 1 (1898), 175–184.

Shāstri, Mahāmahopādhyāya Haraprasād. *A Descriptive Catalogue of the Sanscrit Manuscripts in the Government Collection under the Care of the Asiatic Society of Bengal*, vol. I (Buddhist Manuscripts). Calcutta: Asiatic Society of Bengal, 1917.

——. "Introduction" in N. N. Vasu, *The Modern Buddhism and its Followers in Orissa*. Calcutta: N. N.Vasu, 1911.

Shāstrī, Mahāmahopādhyāya Paṇḍit Mukund Rām. *The Tantrāloka of Abhinava Gupta with Commentary by Rājānaka Jayaratha*. Twelve volumes. Kashmir Series of Texts and Studies, vols. XXIII, XXVIII, XXX, XXXVI, XXXV, XXIX, XLI, XLVII. LIX, LII, LVII, LVIII. Allahabad: The Indian Press, 1918–1938.

Shaw, Miranda. *Passionate Enlightenment: Women in Tantric Buddhism*. Princeton: Princeton University Press, 1994.

Shen, Weirong. "Magic Power, Sorcery and Evil Spirit: The Image of Tibetan Monks in Chinese Literature during the Yuan Dynasty," in C. Cüppers, ed., *The Relationship Between Religion and State (chos srid zung 'brel) in Traditional Tibet* (Lumbini: LIRI, 2004), 189–228.

Shendge, Malati J., ed. *Advayasiddhi*. Baroda: Oriental Institute, 1964.

Shrestha, Rajendra. *Buddhist Ritual Dance*. Kathmandu: Kalamandapa, 1986.

Siegel, Lee A. "Bengal Blackie and the Sacred Slut: A Sahajayāna Buddhist Song," *Buddhist-Christian Studies*, vol. 1 (1981), 51–58.

——. "Bengal Blackie Rides Again," *Buddhist-Christian Studies*, vol. 5 (1985), 191–192.

Silburn, Lilian, et al., eds. *Le Bouddhisme*. Paris: Fayard, 1977.

Silk, Jonathan. "A Bibliography on Ancient Indian Slavery" *Studien zur Indologie und Iranistik* 16 (1992), 277–285.

Simpson, John, and Edmund Weiner, eds. *The Oxford English Dictionary*. Second Edition. Oxford: Clarendon Press, 1989.

Singh, K. Suresh. "A Study in State-formation Among Tribal Communities," in R. S. Sharma, ed., *Indian Society: Historical Probings in Memory of D. D. Kosambi* (New Delhi: People's Publishing House, 1974), 317–336.

Singleton, Mark. *Yoga Body: The Origins of Modern Posture Practice*. New York: Oxford University Press, 2010.

Sircar, D. C., ed. *The Śakti Cult and Tārā*. Centre of Advanced Study in Ancient Indian History and Culture, University of Calcutta, Lectures and Seminars, no. II-B (Seminars). Calcutta: University of Calcutta, 1967.

Skalník, P. "Tribe as Colonial Category," in Emile Boonzaier and John Sharp, eds., *South African Keywords: The Uses and Abuses of Political Concepts*. Cape Town and Johannesburg: David Philip, 1988, 68–78.

Skilling, Peter. "'Buddhist Sealings': Reflections on Terminology, Motivation, Donors' Status, School-Affiliation, and Print-Technology," in Catherine Jarrige and Vincent Lefèvre, eds. *South Asian Archaeology 2001. Vol. II, Historical Archaeology and Art History*. Paris: éditions Recherches sur les Civilisations, 2005, 677–685.

——. "*Dharma, Dhāraṇī, Abhidharma, Avadāna*: What was taught in Trayastriṃśa?," *Annual Report of the International Research Institute for Advanced Buddhology at Soka University*, vol. CI (March 2008), 37–60.

——. *Mahāsūtras: Great Discourses of the Buddha*. Volume II. Oxford: Pali Text Society, 1997.

——. "Mahāyāna and Bodhisattva: An essay towards historical understanding," in P. Limpanusorn, ed., *Phothisatawa barami kap sangkom thai nai sahatsawat mai* [*Bodhisattvaparami and Thai Society in the New Millennium*]. Bangkok: Thammasat University Press, 2547 [2004], 139–156.

——. "The Rakṣā Literature of the Śrāvakayāna," *Journal of the Pali Text Society*, vol. XVI (1992), 109–182.

——. "Review of Paul Harrison, *The Samādhi of Direct Encounter with the Buddhas of the Present*," *Journal of the Siam Society*, vol. 79, part 2 (1991), 152–156.

——. "Zombies and Half-Zombies: Mahāsūtras and Other Protective Measures," *Journal of the Pali Text Society*, vol. XXIX (2007), 313–330.

Skorupski, Tadeusz, ed. and trans. *The Sarvadurgatipariśodhana Tantra: Elimination of All Evil Destinies*. Delhi: Motilal Banarsidass, 1983.

Smith, Jonathan Z. *Drudgery Divine: On the Comparison of Christianity and the Religions of Antiquity*. Chicago and London: University of Chicago Press, 1992.

——. *Imagining Religion: From Babylon to Jonestown*. Chicago: University of Chicago Press, 1982.

——. *Relating Religion: Essays in the Study of Religion*. Chicago: University of Chicago Press, 2004.

Smith, Vincent A. *The Early History of India: From 600 B.C. to the Muhammadan Conquest including the Invasion of Alexander the Great*. Oxford: Clarendon Press, 1904.

Snellgrove, David L. "Categories of the Buddhist Tantras," in *orientalia Iosephi Tucci Memoriae Dicata*, ed. g. gnoli and l. lanciotti, Serie orientale Roma 56, no. 3, 1353–1384.

——. "The Notion of Divine Kingship in Tantric Buddhism," *Studies in the History of Religion*, vol. 4 (1959): 204–218.

——, ed. *The Hevajra Tantra: A Critical Study*. 2 vols. Oxford: Oxford University Press, 1959.

——. *Indo-Tibetan Buddhism*. 2 volumes. Boston: Shambhala Publications, 1987.

——. "Introduction," in Lokesh Chandra and David Snellgrove, eds., *Sarva-tathāgata-tattva-saṅgraha*. New Delhi: Sharada Rani, 1981.

——. "Review of S. B. Dasgupta, Introduction to Tantric Buddhism," *Bulletin of the School of Oriental and African Studies*, vol. XVI, no. 1 (1954), 178–179.

Snellgrove, David, and Hugh Richardson. *A Cultural History of Tibet*. 1968. Boston: Shambhala, 1995.

Soebadio, Haryati, ed. and trans. *Jñānasiddhānta*. The Hague: Martinus Nijhoff, 1971.

Spiro, Melford. *Buddhism and Society: A Great Tradition and its Burmese Vicissitudes*. New York, Evanston, and London: Harper & Row, 1970.

Srinivasan, Doris. "Unhinging Śiva from the Indus Civilization," *Journal of the Royal Asiatic Society*, New Series, vol. 116, no. 1 (1984), 77–89.

Stein, Burton. *A History of India*. 1998. New Delhi: Oxford University Press, 2003.

Stein, Marc Aurel, ed. and trans. *Kalhaṇa's Rājataraṅgiṇī: Chronicle of the Kings of Kashmir*. Three volumes. 1900 (vols I and II) and 1892 (vol. III). Delhi: Motilal Banarsidass, 1989 and 1988.

Steinkellner, Ernst. 1978. "Remarks on Tantristic Hermeneutics." In *Proceedings of the 1976 Csoma de Kőrös Memorial Symposium*, 445–458. L. Ligeti, ed. Budapest: Akadémiai Kiadó.

Strachan, Paul. *Imperial Pagan: Art and Architecture of Burma*. Honolulu: University of Hawaii Press, 1990.

Streuver, Nancy S. *The Language of History in the Renaissance: Rhetoric and Historical Consciousness in Florentine Humanism*. Princeton, NJ: Princeton University Press, 1970.

Strickmann, Michel. "The *Consecration Sūtra*: A Buddhist Book of Spells," in R. E. Buswell, ed., (Honolulu: University of Hawaii Press, 1990), 75–118.

——. *Mantras et Mandarins: Le bouddhisme tantrique en Chine*. Bibliothèque des Sciences Humaines. Paris: Gallimard, 1996.

——. "The Seal of the Jungle Woman," *Asia Major*, third series, vol. VIII, part 2 (1995), 147–153.

Study Group in Buddhist Sanskrit Literature, The Institute for Comprehensive Studies of Buddhism, Taisho University. *Vimalakīrtinirdeśa: A Sanskrit Edition Based upon the Manuscript Newly Found at the Potala Palace*. Tokyo: Taisho University Press, 2006.

Szántó, Péter-Dániel. "Antiquarian Enquiries into the Initiation Manuals of the Catuṣpīṭha," *Newsletter of the NGMCP*, no. 6 (Spring-Summer 2008), 2–12.

Tajima, Ryūjun. *Les Deux Grands Maṇḍalas et la Doctrine de l'Esoterisme Shingon*. Tokyo: Maison franco-japonaise, 1959.

Takasaki, Jikido. "Sources for the *Laṅkāvatāra* and its position in Mahāyāna Buddhism," in L. A. Hercus, et al., eds., Indological and Buddhist Studies: Volume in Honour of Professor J.W. de Jong on his Sixtieth Birthday. Canberra: Faculty of Asian Studies, 1982, 545–568.

Takubo, Shūyo, ed. *Ārya-mahā-māyūrī Vidyā-rājñī*. Tokyo: Tokyo Sankibo, 1972.

Tanemura, Ryugen. "Justification for and Classification of the Post-initiatory Caryā in Later Indian Tantric Buddhism," *International Journal of South Asian Studies*, vol. 1 (2008), 53–75.

——. "Superiority of Vajrayāna — Part II: Superiority of the Tantric Practice Taught in the **Vajrayānāntadvayanirākaraṇa (rDo rje theg pa'i mtha' gnyis sel ba)*," in S. Einoo, ed., *Genesis and Development of Tantrism*. Tokyo: Institute of Oriental Culture, University of Tokyo, 2009, 487–514.

Tārānātha Vidyāratna, ed. *Kulārṇava Tantra*. 1965. Delhi: Motilal Banarsidass, 2000.

Tatz, Mark. "The Life of the Siddha-philosopher Maitrīgupta," *Journal of the American Oriental Society*, vol. 107, no. 4 (1987), 695–711.

——. "Maitrīpa and Atiśa," in H. Uebach and J.L. Panglung, eds., *Tibetan Studies: Proceedings of the 4th Seminar of the International Association for Tibetan Studies* (Munich: Bayerische Akademie der Wissenschaften, 1988), 473–481.

Thomas, Edward J. *The History of Buddhist Thought*. 1933. New York: Barnes and Noble, 1951.

Thurman, Robert A. F. "Vajra Hermeneutics." In D. S. Lopez, Jr., ed., *Buddhist Hermeneutics*. Honolulu: University of Hawaii Press, 1988, 119–148.

Törzsök, Judit. "The Doctrine of Magic Female Spirits: A Critical Edition of Selected Chapters of the *Siddhayogeśvarīmata(tantra)* with Annotated Translation and Analysis." Doctoral dissertation, Merton College, Oxford University, 1999.

Trenckner, V., ed. *The Milindapañho: being Dialogues between King Milinda and the Buddhist Sage Nāgasena*. 1880. Oxford: The Pali Text Society, 1997.

Tribe, Anthony. "Mantranaya/Vajrayāna—Tantric Buddhism in India," in P. Williams with A. Tribe, *Buddhist Thought: A Complete Introduction to the Indian Tradition*. London: Routledge, 2000, 192–244.

Tripathi, Ram Shankar, and Thakur Sain Negi, eds. *Hevajratantram with Muktāvalī Pañjikā of Mahāpaṇḍitācārya Ratnākaraśānti*. Sarnath: Central Institute of Higher Tibetan Studies, 2001 (B.E. 2545).

Tsuda, Shiníchi. "A Critical Tantrism," *Memoirs of the Research Department of the Toyo Bunko*, vol. 36 (1978), 167–231.

——. "The Cult of Śmaśāna, the Realities of Tantrism," in T. Goudriaan, ed., *The Sanskrit Tradition and Tantrism*. Leiden: Brill, 1990, 96–108.

——. "The Original Formation and Performance of the 'Secret Assembly' (*guhyasamāja*), an Integration of the *Guhyasamāja-tantra* into the History of Tantric Buddhism in India," *Journal of the International College of Advanced Buddhist Studies* (1999), 103–146.

——. *The Saṃvarodaya-Tantra: Selected Chapters*. Tokyo: Hokuseido Press, 1974.

——. "*Vajrayoṣidbhageṣu Vijahāra*: Historical Survey from the Beginnings to the Culmination of Tantric Buddhism," in L. A. Hercus, et al., eds., *Indological and Buddhist Studies, Volume in Honour of Professor J.W. de Jong on his Sixtieth Birthday*. Canberra: Faculty of Asian Studies, 1982, 595–616.

Tucci, Giuseppe. "Animadversiones Indicae," *Journal of the Asiatic Society of Bengal*, vol. 26 (1930), 125–160.

——. "Some Glosses upon the Guhyasamāja," in *Mélanges chinois et bouddhiques*, vol. III. Bruxelles: l'Institut Belge des Hautes études Chinoises, 1935, 339–353.

——. *Tibetan Painted Scrolls*. Three vols. Rome: La Libreria della Stata, 1949.

Tuck, Andrew P. *Comparative Philosophy and the Philosophy of Scholarship: On the Western Interpretation of Nāgārjuna*. New York: Oxford University Press, 1991.

Tylor, Edward B. *Primitive Culture: Researches into the Development of Mythology, Philosophy, Religion, Language, Art, and Custom*. Sixth edition. Two vols. London: John Murray, 1929.

Upadhyaya, Jagannatha, ed. *Vimalaprabhāṭīkā of Kalki Śrī Puṇḍarīka on Śrī Laghukālacakratantrarāja by Śrī Mañjuśrīyaśa*. Volume one. Sarnath: Central Institute for Higher Tibetan Studies, 1986.

Urban, Hugh B. "The Extreme Orient: The Construction of 'Tantrism' as a Category in the Orientalist Imagination," *Religion*, vol. 29 (1999), 123–146.

——. *Tantra: Sex, Secrecy, Politics and Power in the Study of Religion*. Berkeley: Univ. of California Press, 2003.

Vaidya, P. L., ed. *Aṣṭāsāhasrikā Prajñāpāramitā with Haribhadra's Commentary Called Āloka*. Darbhanga: Mithila Institute, 1960a.

——. *Lalitavistara*. Buddhist Sanskrit Texts, 1. Darbhanga: Mithila Institute, 1958.

——. "Mañjuśrīmūlakalpa," in *Mahāyānasūtrasaṃgraha*, part II. Darbhanga: The Mithila Institute, 1964.

——. *Saddharmapuṇḍarīkasūtra*. Buddhist Sanskrit Texts, 6. Darbhanga: Mithila Institute, 1960b.

——, ed. *Saddharmalaṅkāvatārasūtram*. Darbhanga: Mithila Institute, 1963.

—— ed. *Śikṣāsamuccaya of Śāntideva*. Darbhanga: Mithila Institute, 1961.

Van Gulik, Robert H. *Hayagrīva: The Mantrayānic Aspect of Horse-cult in China and Japan*. Internationales Archiv für Ethnographie, Supplement zu Band XXXIII. Leiden: Brill, 1935.

Vassilief, V. P. *Le Bouddisme: Ses dogmes, son histoire et sa littérature*. Première Partie: Aperçu Général. Translated from the Russian by G. A. La Comme. Paris: Auguste Durand, 1865.

Vasu, Nagendra Nath. *The Modern Buddhism and its Followers in Orissa*. Calcutta: N. N.Vasu, 1911.

Veyne, Paul. *Comment on écrit l'histoire: essai d'épistémologie*. Univers historique. Paris: éditions de Seuil, 1971.

——. *Did the Greeks Believe in Their Myths?: An Essay on the Constitutive Imagination*. Trans. Paula Wissing. Chicago: University of Chicago Press, 1983.

——. *Writing History: Essay on Epistemology*. Trans. Mina Moore-Rinvolucri. Middletown, CT: Wesleyan University Press, 1984.

Vico, Giambattista. *The New Science of Giambattista Vico*. Trans. Thomas Goddard Bergin and Max Harold Fisch. Ithaca, NY: Cornell University Press, 1948.

Von Hinüber, Oskar. "Review of H. Bechert, *Der Buddhismus I*," *Indo-Iranian Journal* 45 (2002), 77–86.

von Rospatt, Alexander. "The Transformation of the Monastic Ordination (*pravrajyā*) into a Rite of Passage in Newar Buddhism," in J. Gengnagel, U. Hüsken, and S. Raman, eds., *Words and Deeds: Hindu and Buddhist Rituals in South Asia* (Wiesbaden: Harrassowitz Verlag, 2005), 199–234.

Vostrikov, A. I. *Tibetan Historical Literature*. Trans. Harish Chandra Gupta. London: RoutledgeCurzon, 1994.

Wach, Joachim. *Introduction to the History of Religions*. J. M. Kitagawa and G. D. Alles, with K.W. Luckert, eds. New York: Macmillan, 1988.

Waddell, L. Austine. *The Buddhism of Tibet or Lamaism with its Mystic Cults, Symbolism and Mythology, and its Relation to Indian Buddhism*. 1899. New Delhi: Asian Educational Services, 1991.

Wallis, Glenn. *Mediating the Power of Buddhas: Ritual in the* Mañjuśrīmūlakalpa. Albany: State University of New York Press, 2002.

Walters, Jonathan S. "Mahāyāna Theravāda and the Origins of the Mahāvihāra," *Sri Lanka Journal of the Humanities*, vol 23, no. 1–2 (1997), 100–119.

Ward, William. *A View of the History, Literature, and Religion of the Hindoos*. 2 vols. London: Black, Parbury, and Allen, 1817.

Warder, A. K. 1970. *Indian Buddhism*. Delhi: Motilal Banarsidass, 2004.

Watanabe, Kaikioku. "Studien über die Mahāmāyūrī," in K. Watanabe, *Kogetsu zenshū: Watanabe Kaigyoku ibunshū* (壼月全集: 渡辺海旭遺文集). Tōkyō: Kogetsu Zenshū Kankōkai, Shōwa 8 [1933].

Waterhouse, David M., ed. *The Origins of Himalayan Studies: Brian Houghton Hodgson in Nepal and Darjeeling, 1820–1858*. Royal Asiatic Society Books. London: RoutledgeCurzon, 2004.

Watt, Paul. "Tantric Buddhism in China," in Takeuchi Yoshinori, ed., *Buddhist Spirituality: Indian, Southeast Asian, Tibetan, and Early Chinese*. Delhi: Motilal Banarsidass, 1995, 397–404.

Wayman, Alex. *The Buddhist Tantras: Light on Indo-Tibetan Esotericism*. 1973. Delhi: Motilal Banarsidass, 1993.

——. "Esoteric Buddhism," in J. Kitagawa and M. Cummings, eds., *Buddhism and Asian History* (New York: Macmillan, 1989), 241–256.

——. "*Guhyasamājatantra*: Reflections on the Word and its Meaning," *Transactions of the International Conference of Orientalists in Japan*, no. XV (1970), 34–44.

——. "Observations on the History and Influence of the Buddhist Tantra in India and Tibet," in A. K. Narain, ed., *Studies in History of Buddhism*. Delhi: B. R. Pub. Corp., 1980, 359–363.

——. *Yoga of the Guhyasamājatantra: The Arcane Lore of Forty Verses*. 1977. Delhi: Motilal Banarsidass, 1991.

Wayman, Alex, and R. Tajima. *The Enlightenment of Vairocana*. 1992. Delhi: Motilal Banarsidass, 1998.

Weber, Max. *The Protestant Ethic and the Spirit of Capitalism*. Trans. Talcott Parsons. 1958. New York: Charles Scribner's Sons, 1976.

Wedemeyer, Christian K. "Antinomianism and Gradualism: The Contextualization of the Practices of Sensual Enjoyment (*caryā*) in the Guhyasamāja Ārya Tradition." *The Indian International Journal of Buddhist Studies*. New Series, no. 3 (2002), 181–195.

——. *Āryadeva's* Lamp that Integrates the Practices (Caryāmelāpakapradīpa): *The Gradual Path of Vajrayāna Buddhism according to the Esoteric Community Noble Tradition*. New York: AIBS/Columbia University Press, 2007.

——. "Beef, Dog and Other Mythologies: Connotative Semiotics in Mahāyoga Tantra Scripture and Ritual," *Journal of the American Academy of Religion*, vol. 75, no. 2 (June 2007), 383–417.

——. "Locating Tantric Antinomianism: An Essay Toward an Intellectual History of the 'Practices/Practice Observance' (*caryā/caryāvrata*)," *Journal of the International Association of Buddhist Studies*, vol. 34 (forthcoming).

——. "Pseudepigrapha in the Tibetan Buddhist 'Canonical Collections': The Case of the *Caryāmelāpakapradīpa Commentary* Attributed to Śākyamitra," *Journal of the International Association for Tibetan Studies*, no. 5 (December 2009), 1–31.

——. "Review of Ronald M. Davidson, *Indian Esoteric Buddhism*," *History of Religions*, vol. 45, no. 4 (May 2006), 373–376.

——. "Sex, Death, and 'Reform' in Eleventh-century Tibetan Buddhist Esoterism: 'Gos Khug pa Lhas btsas, *spyod pa (caryā)*, and *mngon par spyod pa (abhicāra)*," in Todd Lewis and Bruce Owens, eds., *Sucāruvādadeśika: A Festschrift Honoring Prof. Theodore Riccardi, Jr.* (forthcoming)

——. "Tantalising Traces of the Labours of the Lotsāwas: Alternative Translations of Sanskrit Sources in the Writings of Rje Tsong kha pa," in R. M. Davidson and Chr. K. Wedemeyer, eds., *Tibetan Buddhist Literature and Praxis: Studies in its Formative Period, 900–1400.* Leiden and Boston: E.J. Brill, 2006, 149–182.

——. "Tropes, Typologies and Turnarounds: A Brief Genealogy of the Historiography of Tantric Buddhism," *History of Religions*, vol. (Feb 2001), 223–259.

White, David G. *Kiss of the Yoginī: "Tantric Sex" in its South Asian Contexts.* Chicago: University of Chicago Press, 2003.

White, Hayden. *The Content of the Form: Narrative Discourse and Historical Representation.* Baltimore and London: The Johns Hopkins University Press, 1987.

——. *Metahistory: The Historical Imagination in Nineteenth-century Europe.* 1974. Baltimore and London: The Johns Hopkins University Press, 1990.

——. *Tropics of Discourse: Essays in Cultural Criticism.* 1978. Baltimore and London: The Johns Hopkins University Press, 1985.

——. "The Value of Narrativity in the Representation of Reality," *Critical Inquiry*, vol. 7, no. 1 (Autumn 1980), 5–27.

Whorf, Benjamin Lee. "The Relation of Habitual Thought and Behavior to Language," In S. I. Hayakawa, ed., *Language, Meaning, and Maturity: Selections from Etc. a Review of General Semantics, 1943–1953.* New York: Harper, 1954, 197–215.

Wickremasinghe, Don M. de Zilva, ed. *Nikāya Sangrahawa or Śāsanāwatāraya: A History of Buddhism in India and Ceylon by Dewarakṣhita Dharmakīrti Mahāthera.* Colombo: H.C. Cottle, Acting Government Printer, 1890.

Wild, S. E., ed., *Webster's New World Law Dictionary* Hoboken, NJ: Wiley, 2006.

Williams, Monier. *Buddhism, in Its Connexion with Brāhmanism and Hindūism, and in Its Contrast with Christianity.* London: John Murray, 1889.

Williams, Paul, with Anthony Tribe. *Buddhist Thought: A Complete Introduction to the Indian Tradition.* London and New York: Routledge, 2000.

Williams, Raymond. *Keywords: A Vocabulary of Culture and Society.* Revised edition. New York: Oxford University Press, 1983.

——. *Marxism and Literature.* Oxford and New York: Oxford University Press, 1977.

Wilson, Horace Hayman. "Sketch of the Religious Sects of the Hindus, *Asiatic Researches*, vol. 17, 169–313.

——. "Notice of Three Tracts received from Nepal," *Asiatic Researches*, vol. XVI (1828), 450–478.

Wink, André. *Al-Hind: The Making of the Indo-Islamic World*, volume I: Early Medieval India and the Expansion of Islam. Leiden: Brill, 1990.

Winternitz, Maurice. "Notes on the Guhyasamāja-Tantra and the Age of the Tantras," *Indian Historical Quarterly*, vol. IX, no. 1 (March 1933), 1–10.

——. "Some Important Sanskrit Publications," *Indian Culture*, vol. IV, no. 2 (Oct 1937), 258–262.

Wulff, K. *Sang Hyang Kamahāyānan Mantrānaya: Ansprache bei der weihe buddhistischer Mönche aus dem Altjavanischen übersetzt und sprachlich erlaütert*. Det Kgl. Danske Videnskabernes Selskab, Historisk-filologiske Meddelser, XXI, 4. København: Levin & Munksgaard, 1935.

Yamada, Ryūjō. *Bongo butten no shobunken* (梵語仏典の諸文献). Kyōto: Heirakuji Shoten, 1959.

Yamaguchi, Zuiho, ed. *Catalogue of the Toyo Bunko Collection of Tibetan Works on History*. Classified Catalogue of the Toyo Bunko Collection of Tibetan Works, vol. 1. Tokyo: The Toyo Bunko, 1970.

Zhang, Yisun. *Bod rGya Tshig mDzod Chen Mo* [*The Great Tibetan-Chinese Dictionary*]. Three volumes. Lhasa: Mi Rigs dPe sKrun Khang, 1984.

Zürcher, Erik. *The Buddhist Conquest of China: The Spread and Adaptation of Buddhism in Early Medieval China*. Sinica Leidensia, XI. Leiden: Brill, 1959.

Zysk, Kenneth G. *Asceticism and Healing in Ancient India: Medicine in the Buddhist Monastery*. 1991. Corrected edition. Delhi: Motilal Banarsidass, 1998.

INDEX

Abhayadatta, 175
Abhayākaragupta, 250n58
Abhayapaddhati (Abhayākaragupta), 245n14, 250n58
Abhidharma, 73–74, 88, 226nn26, 32, 228n51, 231n88
Abhidharmakośabhāṣya (Vasubandhu), 150
Abhidharmasamuccaya (Asaṅga), 150
Abhinavagupta, 166, 198
abhiṣeka (initiation), 9, 171–172, 184–185, 212n21, 248n40, 249n48, 258n130
actual observance question, 192–199; and contemporary practice, 195, 264n107; homeopathic approach, 243n82; and literal vs. figurative interpretations, 131–132; and monastic domestication model, 197–198, 265nn112, 117; scholarly approaches to, 193–195, 198–199, 263–264n94, 110, 265n118; and tribal origin theory, 196–197; and urban legends, 194, 264n104
Advayavajra, 170, 174
advertising, 123, 189
Aitareya Brāhmaṇa, 215n42
Aitkinson, Edwin, 193–194
Alaṃkakalāśa, 91
ambrosia. *See* five ambrosias/five meats
Amoghapāśa Mahākalparāja, 79–80

Amoghavajra, 91–92
anadhyāya, state of, 146, 147
Ānandagarbha, 91
Anaṅgavajrapāda, 247n29
antinomianism. *See caryāvrata*; transgression in Tantric Buddhism
Apabhraṃśa, 184
Aparārka, 252n70, 253n85
Aristotle, 38, 39, 58, 218nn5, 7
Āryadeva, 152, 191, 238–239n44, 249–250n48, 257n128
Asaṅga, 135, 150, 186
Aṭavīla, 175
Atharvaveda, 213n4
Atharvaveda Pariśiṣṭa, 157
Austin, J. L., 3, 211n4

Bachofen, J. J., 54–55, 57, 217n70, 220n48, 221n64
Bakhtin, Mikhail, 188
Bareau, André, 21
Barth, Auguste, 220n39, 244n85
Barthes, Roland, 5, 7, 106–107, 113, 114–116, 122–123, 124, 130, 189, 211n9, 212n15, 237n29, 263n81
Basham, A. L., 43, 214n23
Bell, Catherine, 241n61
Bendall, Cecil, 45, 120
Bentor, Yael, 117

Bergson, Henri, 211*n*3
Bhāmaha, 241*n*65
Bhattacharya, Bholanath, 264*n*107
Bhattacharyya, Benoytosh, 18, 19, 68, 108, 109, 219*n*28, 242*n*69
Bhavabhaṭṭa, 197, 246*n*18
Bhāvanākrama (Kamalaśīla), 191
binaries. *See* dualism
Bloch, Marc, 5, 33, 218*n*75
Boas, Franz, 221*n*64
Bodhicaryāvatāra (Śāntideva), 135
Bodhisattvabhūmi, 135
Bourdieu, Pierre, 106, 131, 237*n*29
Brahmayāmala, 166. *See also Picumata/Brahmayāmala*
Briggs, George, 193
Broido, Michael, 110
Bsod nams rtse mo, 88–90, 232*nn*90, 93
Buddha, The. *See* Śākyamuni Buddha; Śākyamuni Buddha as source of scripture
Buddhakapāla commentary. *See Abhayapaddhati*; *Gnostic Commentary on the Buddhakapāla*
Buddhakapāla Tantra, 138, 140, 150, 209–210
buddhas: epistemic function of, 97; historical, 68, 77. *See also* cosmic/multiple buddhas; Maitreya; Śākyamuni Buddha; Śākyamuni Buddha as source of scripture; Vajradhara
Buddhist epistemology, 97, 234*n*133; tensions in, 190–191, 263*nn*87, 90
The Buddhist Religion (Robinson), 58, 221*nn*68, 69
Bullen, J. B., 221*n*74, 243*n*77
Burnouf, Eugène, 22, 108, 223*n*108, 225*n*15
Bu ston Rin chen grub, 91

Cakrasaṃvara Tantra, 89, 197, 232*n*90
Caṇḍamahāroṣaṇa Tantra, 138, 150, 250*n*55
Candrakīrti: on literal vs. figurative interpretations, 105, 110, 111, 126; on self-creation rite, 117, 237*n*32, 238*n*34; and social strictures, 239*n*44. *See also Pradīpoddyotana*
carnivalesque, 188
Carrard, Philippe, 37
caryā dance (*caryānṛtya*), 257–258*n*130
caryāgīti (Caryā Songs), 168
Caryāmelāpakapradīpa (Āryadeva), 152, 191, 238–239*n*44, 249–250*n*48, 257*n*128
caryānṛtya (caryā dance), 257–258*n*130
Caryā Songs (caryāgīti), 168
caryāvrata, 133–151; *Buddhakapāla Tantra* on, 138, 140, 150, 209–210; on dress/accoutrements of practice, 140, 141, 246*n*16; and dualistic esoteric Buddhism, 145, 152, 160, 252*n*73; duration of practice, 152, 153, 251*nn*60, 61; as elite practice, 136, 152, 168, 250*n*58, 258*n*30; frequent usage of, 135–136, 245*n*12; intentional transgression in, 144–145, 146–148, 246–247*nn*21–24; and Kṛṣṇācārya, 150, 250*n*56; and Nepalese caryā dance, 257–258*n*130; nondual gnosis as goal of, 145–146, 160–161, 162, 247*n*29, 248*n*36; prerequisites for, 149–150, 151, 152, 249–250*n*48; on prescribed behaviors, 140, 142, 147–148; on proscribed behaviors, 140, 143, 144, 246*n*20; scholarly misunderstanding of, 134–135, 168, 244–245*nn*4, 7; on sites of practice, 138, 139, 140, 147, 248*nn*39, 40, 251*n*59; and temporary marginality, 258*n*9; as term of art, 136, 137, 168, 245*nn*12, 13; as "The Practice," 168, 169, 171, 173, 258*n*130; in Tibetan Buddhism, 148, 149, 249–250*nn*46–48. *See also caryāvrata* in Śaiva tradition
caryāvrata in Śaiva tradition, 136–137, 154–167; and Brahman murder, 155–156, 252*nn*70, 71, 256*n*111;

dualistic forms, 156, 157, 158, 159; and *Guhyasamāja Tantra*, 160–163; and Krama tradition, 94, 166–167, 257nn123, 128; and Lākula practices, 157–158, 253–254nn81–83, 85, 86; and later traditions, 168, 169, 247n27, 257n120; mimetic function of, 165–166; and nondual gnosis, 160–161, 162, 164, 166–167, 256n116, 257nn123, 124; and Pāśupata *vrata*, 156–157, 253n84; and *Picumata/Brahmayāmala*, 154–155, 158–159, 245n12; and *poṣadha*, 156, 252n75; and re-coding, 167, 257n129; and Śaiva origin theory of Tantric Buddhism, 154–155, 251nn64–66, 252n67; and shared zeitgeist, 155, 163–164, 252nn68, 69, 256nn104, 109–111; and *Siddhayogeśvarīmata*, 159, 248n40, 255nn90, 95; and *Tantrasadbhāva/ Kubjikāmata Tantra*, 159, 165–166, 255nn92, 93, 95, 257n120; as term of art, 159, 245n12, 255n95; and *Viṇāśikha Tantra*, 160, 255n96

Catuṣpīṭha, 83–84, 86, 87, 98, 250n54
Catuṣpīṭhākhyāta-mantrāṃśa, 150, 178, 250n54
Chakravarty, Cintaharan, 21–22
Ch'an Buddhism, 233n114
Chanting the Names of Mañjuśrī (Mañjuśrīnāmasaṃgīti), 80, 87, 228n59
Chinese Buddhism: sudden-gradual debate in, 263n90; traditional historiography, 91–93, 233nn103, 104, 108, 110, 112
classical history, 47–48, 99–101, 219nn33, 35, 221n65
Collingwood, R. G., 8, 44
Collins, Steven, 187
commentaries on Tantric scriptures, 109, 111, 126, 236–237nn16, 23, 24. *See also Abhayapaddhati; Explanation of the Intention; Gnostic Commentary on the Buddhakapāla; Guṇāvatī Commentary; Pradīpoddyotana; Vimalaprabhā Commentary; Yoginīsaṃcāratantranibandha*
communion (*yuganaddha*), 121–122. *See also* five stages; Noble Tradition of the Esoteric Community; nondual gnosis as goal of transgression
conceptuality (*vikalpa*), transcendence of, 129, 145–146, 160, 161, 164, 166, 167. *See also* dualism; nondual gnosis as goal of transgression
Concise Consecration Ritual Tantra (Saṃkṣiptapratiṣṭhāvidhi Tantra), 78, 228n50
connotative semiotics, 106–107, 113–116, 237n29; arbitrary signifiers in, 125, 241nn62, 63; on historiography, 130, 243n77; occluded intention in, 122–123, 240n58, 241n61; unselfconscious employment of, 241n66
consecration (*pratiṣṭhā*) rituals, 78, 191, 227n48, 228n50
Consecration Sūtra (Kuan-ting ching), 92, 233n110
constitutive imagination, 69, 224n11
contemporary "primitive" cultures, 21–22, 24–25, 52, 215n36
Conze, Edward, 52–53, 220n55
cosmic buddhas. *See* cosmic/multiple buddhas
cosmic/multiple buddhas: in Śrāvaka Buddhist historiography, 74; in traditional esoteric Buddhist historiography, 79, 80, 81–82, 96; in traditional Mahāyāna historiography, 76, 77, 78, 226nn35, 36, 227–228nn38, 49; in traditional Tibetan historiography, 89, 93, 232n90, 233n119
Croce, Benedetto, 42
Cunningham, Alexander, 48

Dalton, Jacob, 232nn96, 97
Dāmodara, 174, 179–180
Dasgupta, Shashibhusan, 18, 52

Davidson, Ronald, 18, 22, 25, 29–30, 50, 63, 64, 66, 108, 109, 111, 132, 168, 173–174, 188, 213n4, 214–215n32, 222n92, 223nn96, 97, 225n12, 229nn69, 70, 230nn76, 77, 231n85, 236n23, 242n68, 245n11, 261n52, 263nn82, 92

de Bary, William Theodore, 43

decline narratives, 43–50; Buddhism overview, 45–47; and classical history, 47–48, 219nn33, 35; and Enlightenment history, 48–49, 220nn38, 39; and "natural life," 46, 219n28; organic development metaphor, 43–45, 219n24; and sexual behavior, 47–48, 49–50, 220n36; Weber on, 220n42. *See also* degenerate monks origin theory

defamiliarization, 69

degenerate monks origin theory, 19–20, 23–24, 108, 214–215nn29, 32. *See also* decline narratives

de Saussure, Ferdinand, 113, 125, 212n15

Dhammapada, 112, 236n20. *See also* *Udānavarga*

Dharmasaṃgīti Scripture, 77

Dīgha Nikāya, 73, 225n23

direct-encounter revelation narratives: in traditional Chinese Buddhist historiography, 92; in traditional esoteric Buddhist historiography, 79, 86, 98, 99; in traditional Mahāyāna historiography, 76–77, 78; in traditional Śaiva historiography, 93–94

"Dispelling the Two Extreme [Views] with Regard to the Adamantine Way" (Jñānaśrī), 148

Drewes, David, 226nn31, 33

Dreyfus, Georges, 69, 224n8

dualism: and classical history, 221n65; in medieval narratives, 61–62; in primordial origin narratives, 51, 55–57. *See also* conceptuality; dualistic esoteric Buddhism; nondual gnosis as goal of transgression; pure/impure dualism

dualistic esoteric Buddhism, 10, 126; and *caryāvrata*, 145, 152, 160, 252n73; cultural continuities with transgressive Tantra, 172–173, 184–187, 202; mimesis in, 165–166, 184, 262n63; transgressive knowledge of, 131, 175–177, 184, 204, 259n19

Dubuisson, Daniel, 33, 34

Durkheim, Emile, 18

Eastman, Kenneth W., 229n70, 230nn76, 77

Elder, George, 51–52

Eliade, Mircea, 53–54, 57–58

Enlightenment history, 48–49, 57, 220nn38, 39

Enquiry of Ugra (Ugraparipṛcchā), 181

Esoteric Accomplishment. *See* Guhyasiddhi

esoteric Buddhism, 9–10, 212n21. *See also* dualistic esoteric Buddhism; traditional esoteric Buddhist historiography

Esoteric Community Tantra. *See* *Guhyasamāja Tantra*

Evans, Richard, 66

Evans-Pritchard, E. E., 17, 213n4, 214n29, 244n1

Explanation of the Intention (Sandhyāvyākaraṇa), 236n19

Fabian, Johannes, 52
Farrow, G. W., 246n20
Fell, R. A. L., 47
Fergusson, James, 65–66, 67
Feuerbach, L., 17
five ambrosias/five meats, 106, 118–121, 125, 145, 235–236n4, 238–240n44, 47–52, 243n82. *See also* transgression in Tantric Buddhism

five stages (*pañcakrama*), 122, 149, 249n48
Five Stages (Pañcakrama) (Nāgārjuna), 122
Foucault, Michel, 101
Freud, Sigmund, 240n58
Frye, Northrop, 40

funereal imagery: in *caryāvrata*, 138, 140, 147; and eating/offering, 239n50; in *Guhyasamāja Tantra*, 163; and Indian social strictures, 239n44; and monasticism, 179, 180; and nonhuman protection, 256n103; in Śaivism, 155, 158, 164–165, 167, 254n86; in *Siddhayogeśvarīmata*, 159; in *Tantrasadbhāva*, 159. *See also* pure/impure dualism

gaṇa-cakra (host circle) ritual, 192, 193–195, 263n92
Gaṇapatihṛdaya, 79
Garland of Practices (Sādhanamālā), 176
Geden, A., 217n60
gender, 53
General Presentation of the Tantras (Rgyud sde spyi rnam) (Bsod nams rtse mo), 88–90, 232n90
Gibbon, Edward, 49
Gluckman, Max, 13, 190
gnosis. *See* nondual gnosis as goal of transgression
Gnostic Commentary on the Buddhakapāla (Saraha), 250n58
Gombrich, Richard, 225n21
Gómez, Luis O., 224n1
Goodall, Dominic, 248n39, 250n55
Goudriaan, Teun, 255n96
Grags pa rgyal mtshan, 93
Granoff, Phyllis, 96, 97, 163, 234n135, 252n68
Gray, David, 232n90, 246n18
Guhyasamāja Tantra (GST): on *caryāvrata*, 138, 152, 160–163; explanatory tantra of, 236n19; on five ambrosias/five meats, 106, 119, 235–236n4; importance of, 235n3; literal vs. figurative interpretations, 2, 111; nondual gnosis in, 127, 128–130, 145, 241–242n67; revelation narratives, 89–90, 92, 232n93; transgression as interpretive quandary in, 2; and transgressive-nontransgressive cultural continuities, 185–186; and transgressive professionalism, 184; and tribal origin theory, 29–30. *See also* transgression in Tantric Buddhism
Guhyasiddhi (Padmavajra), 26, 149, 163, 251n59
Guṇāvatī Commentary (Ratnākaraśānti), 144
Gyatso, Janet, 225n12

Harappan civilization, 22, 24, 214n23, 215n34
Hardy, Friedhelm, 262n61
Harrison, Jane, 32
Harrison, Paul, 32–33, 73, 76, 217n69, 225n12, 227nn38, 39, 233n110, 265n5, 265n118
heavenly/other-worldly revelation narratives: in traditional Indian esoteric Buddhist historiography, 80, 83–87, 228n55, 229n67; in traditional Mahāyāna historiography, 78, 79; in traditional Śaiva historiography, 94; in traditional Śrāvaka Buddhist historiography, 74, 75, 226n28; in traditional Tibetan historiography, 90, 91
Hegel, G. W. F., 45
Herukābhidhāna/Laghusaṃvara Tantra, 138, 140, 251n64
Hevajra Tantra, 109–110, 138, 140, 142, 178, 236nn18, 19
Hīnayāna, 45, 66, 202
historical buddhas, 68, 77. *See also* Śākyamuni Buddha; Śākyamuni Buddha as source of scripture
historiography: and connotative semiotics, 130, 243n77; and constitutive imagination, 69, 224n11; context issues, 40–41, 69, 211n5; interpretation in, 5–6, 35–36, 101, 102, 211n9, 235n152; organic development metaphor, 43–45, 219n24. *See also* narrative historiography; origin theories of Tantric Buddhism; scholarly distortions; traditional historiography

history of religions, 32, 37, 67, 69
Hjelmslev, Louis, 113
Hoffman, Helmut, 59
host circle (*gaṇa-cakra*) ritual, 192, 193–195, 263n92
human sciences, 8–9, 18, 32–34, 37
Hume, David, 200
Hunter, Robert, 200

Ibn Khaldûn, 44
ideology in historiography, 41–42, 66–67, 70, 219nn13, 16
impurity. *See* pure/impure dualism
Inden, Ronald, 6
Indian social strictures, 119–120, 238–239nn38–40, 44, 45
indigenous historiography. *See* traditional historiography
Indrabhūti, 84–85, 207–208
initiation (*abhiṣeka*), 9, 171–172, 184–185, 212n21, 248n40, 249n48, 258n130
institutional esoterism, 171–172
intention, 122–123
isogesis, 8, 212n17

Jainism, 31, 180, 196
Japanese traditional Buddhist historiography, 93
Jayabhadra, 197, 265n112
Jayadrathayāmala, 166, 257n122
Jayasena, 182, 183
jñāna (gnosis). *See* nondual gnosis as goal of transgression
Jñānamitra, 84–86, 90, 91. *See also* *Prajñāpāramitānaya-pañcaśatikā*
Jñānavatī commentary (Saraha). *See Gnostic Commentary on the Buddhakapāla*
Joshi, M. C., 221n59, 224nn1, 2
jugupsa (revulsion). *See* five ambrosias/ five meats; transgression in Tantric Buddhism
Jvālāmālinīkalpa, 180

Kālacakra Tantra, 86–87, 100, 144, 224n2, 231n82, 243n82, 246n23
Kālikākramapañcaśikā, 94
Kamalaśīla, 191
kapāla. *See* funereal imagery; skulls
Kapstein, Matthew, 97–98, 225n12, 229n72, 259n14
Kaula tradition, 180, 198
Kauṇḍinya, 157
Kāvyālaṃkāra (Bhāmaha), 241n65
Kĕrtanagara, 179
King, Richard, 64
Knipe, David, 264n105
Kōbō Daishi, 93
Krama tradition, 94, 166–167, 257nn123, 128
Kramrisch, Stella, 20
Kṛṣṇācārya, 150, 250n56
Kṛṣṇayamāri Tantra, 29–30
Kubjikāmata Tantra, 159, 165, 166, 255nn95, 96
Kula traditions, 180
Kværne, Per, 43

Laghusaṃvara Tantra. *See Herukābhidhāna/ Laghusaṃvara Tantra*
Lākula practices, 157–158, 253–254nn81–83, 85, 86
Lalitavistara, 246–247n24
Lamotte, Etienne, 73, 225–226n25
language in Tantric communities, 184, 262n59
Laṅkāvatāra Sūtra, 164, 191
La Vallée Poussin, L. de, 18, 22, 30, 43, 46, 181, 203–204, 222n86, 251n63, 260n45
Law, B. C., 215nn39, 45
Lévi, Sylvain, 88, 231n87
Lincoln, Bruce, 35, 70, 189
lineages, 92–93, 233n114
Livy, 100
Lorenzen, David N., 154, 163, 165, 257n124
Lotus Sūtra (*Saddharmapuṇḍarīka Sūtra*), 76, 226n36
Lutgendorf, P., 216n49

Mahākāla Tantra, 138
Mahāpratisarā, 178
Mahāśītavatī Dhāraṇī, 80
Mahāvairocana Tantra (MVT): on *caryāvrata*, 152, 161, 251n61, 252n77, 255n100; revelation narratives, 81, 92, 93, 229n63, 234n131; and transgressive knowledge of mainstream forms, 176; *vidyāvrata* in, 161, 255n100
Mahāvastu, 135
Mahāyāna Buddhism: in decline narratives, 45–46; re-visioning of, 202–205. *See also* traditional Mahāyāna historiography
Mahāyānasaṃgraha, 112
Mahāyānasūtrālaṃkāra (Asaṅga), 135
Maitreya (future buddha), 72, 87, 234n134
Mānava Śrautasūtra, 215n42
Mañjuśrīmūlakalpa (MMK), 68, 77–78, 97, 126, 147, 224n3, 234n135
Mañjuśrīnāmasaṃgīti (Chanting the Names of Mañjuśrī), 80, 87, 228n59
Mañjuśriyamūlakalpa, 224n3. *See also* *Mañjuśrīmūlakalpa*
Mantranaya (Method of Mantra), 79, 180, 247n27. *See also* esoteric Buddhism
marginality, 173–175, 187–188, 258nn6, 9. *See also* tribal origin theory
Marshall, John, 214n23
Masefield, Peter, 244n4
Mataṅgapārameśvarāgama, 27–28, 156, 174
matriarchy, 54–55, 57, 217n70, 220n48, 221n64
Mattavilāsaprahasana, 23, 196, 214–215n32
Mayer, Robert, 225n12
medieval narratives, 58–66, 222n87; and chronological inconsistency, 59–61; dualism in, 61–62; and European analogies, 59, 61, 63, 65–66, 221nn74, 79, 222–223nn89, 92, 94; negative character of, 62–66, 222n86, 223nn95, 108; popularity of, 58–59, 221n69; relational nature of, 61, 221–222n81

meditation practices, 76–77. *See also* ritual practice
Meisezahl, R. O., 21
Menon, I., 246n20
metalanguage, 113–114
methodology. *See* connotative semiotics; historiography; history of religions; human sciences; semiology; structural analysis
Milindapañhā, 256n103
mimetic excess, 212n18
Mink, Louis, 39
Mitchell, Margaret, 221n65
Mitra, Rajendralal, 2, 36, 108, 201
Mkhas pa Lde'u, 231n88
Momigliano, Arnaldo, 235n152
monasticism: and decline narratives, 48, 50; degenerate monks origin theory, 19–20, 23–24, 108, 214–215nn29, 32; domestication model, 132, 197–198, 265nn112, 117; and social context of Tantric Buddhism, 177–181, 203, 204, 259nn24, 27, 260nn31–33, 35, 37
Monier-Williams, Monier, 46, 58–59, 108, 219nn27, 28
Mother Right: An Investigation of Matriarchy in the Ancient World in Its Religious and Juridical Character (Bachofen), 54
Mṛgendra Tantra, 156
Mūlamadhyamakakārikā (Nāgārjuna), 248n36
Mūlasarvāstivāda Vinaya, 178
Müller, Max, 215n36
Munidatta, 132. *See also* Caryā Songs
Munz, Peter, 221–222n81
mythic speech. *See* connotative semiotics

Naḍapāda (Nāropā, Nāropāda), 179–180, 182–183, 261n52
Nāgārjuna: on nondual gnosis, 122, 248n36; and revelation narratives, 84, 86; on self-creation rite, 117, 237n32, 238n33; and transgression as reinforcement of mainstream, 189, 263n83; and Triśaraṇa, 174, 258n6

Nāmasaṃgīti, 87
Nāradasmṛti, 98–99
Nārāyaṇakaṇṭha, Bhaṭṭa, 156
Nāropāda, 179–180
Nāropā (Naḍapāda), 179–180, 182–183, 261n52
narrative historiography, 37–67; ideology in, 41–42, 66–67, 219nn13, 16; imaginative element in, 38–40, 218nn3, 4–5, 7; importance of, 37–38; and narrative forms, 40–41; triumph tropes, 50. *See also* decline narratives; medieval narratives; primordial origin narratives; traditional historiography
Nattier, Jan, 177, 181, 203, 259n27, 261n46, 265n5
Nietzsche, Friedrich, 6
Nikāya-saṃgrahawa, 179, 260n37
Niśvāsatattvasaṃhitā, 157–158, 163, 253–254nn81–86
Noble Tradition of the Esoteric Community (gsang 'dus 'phags lugs), 149, 240n53, 249n48
non-Buddhist origin theories: Śaiva origin theory, 22–23, 30–31, 154–155, 251nn63–66, 252n67; Scythian origin theory, 30, 217n61; Veda origin theory, 213n4
nondual gnosis, and *caryāvrata* in Śaiva tradition, 160–161, 162, 164, 166–167, 256n116, 257nn123, 124
nondual gnosis as goal of transgression, 126, 201; and astrology, 241n64; in *caryāvrata*, 145–146, 160–161, 162, 247n29, 248n36; and *caryāvrata* in Śaiva tradition, 164, 166–167, 256n116, 257nn123, 124; and nonhuman protection, 162, 256n103; in self-creation rite, 121–122, 124–125; in Tantric scripture, 127–130, 242nn72, 73; and transgressive knowledge of mainstream forms, 131, 176
nondualism: mimetic, 165–166; as nonconceptuality, 129, 145–146, 160, 161, 164, 166, 167; of physical sensations, 256n119. *See also* nondual gnosis as goal of transgression
nontransgressive esoteric Buddhism. *See* dualistic esoteric Buddhism

Occam's razor, 197, 264–265n110
Oḍḍiyāna, 83–84, 88–89, 90, 91, 94, 207–208, 229n67
O'Dwyer, Michael, 216n45
omnipresent buddhas. *See* cosmic/multiple buddhas
organic development metaphor, 43–45, 219n24
Orientalism, 4
origin theories of Tantric Buddhism, 18–36; amalgamated theories, 31–32; degenerate monks theory, 19–20, 23–24, 108, 214–215nn29, 32; normative nature of, 31, 33–34, 218n76; political theory, 213n4; popularity of, 18, 23, 32–33, 217–218nn69, 70, 75; popularization theory, 213n4; reductive nature of, 35–36; Śaiva theory, 22–23, 30–31, 154–155, 251nn63–66, 252n67; Scythian theory, 30, 217n61; Veda theory, 213n4. *See also* tribal origin theory
Orzech, Charles D., 223n97

Padmavajra, 26, 149, 163, 251n59
Paidipaty, Poornima, 215n37
Pāñcarātra-prāmāṇya, 101
Pāśupatasūtra, 157, 253n79
Pāśupata *vrata*, 156–157, 253nn79, 84
patronage, 35, 191–192
Pausanias, 100
Perfection of Wisdom (*prajñāpāramitā*) literature, 110, 189
performative, 211n4, 241n61
Picumata/Brahmayāmala, 154–155, 158–159, 166, 245n12
pledge substances (*samaya*), 145, 238–239nn44, 48. *See also* five

ambrosias/five meats; transgression in Tantric Buddhism
political origin theory, 213n4
Pollock, Sheldon, 98, 102
popularization origin theory, 213n4
poṣadha, 144, 156, 246–247n24, 252n75
Prabodhacandrodaya, 23
Practice, The. See caryāvrata
practice observance. See caryāvrata; ritual practice
practitioner/divine dualism, 10
Pradīpoddyotana (Candrakīrti), 29–30, 105, 110, 111, 236n16, 241–242n67, 249n48
Prajñāpāramitānaya-pañcaśatikā (Jñāmitra), 84–86, 229nn69, 70, 72, 230nn76, 77
prajñāpāramitā (Perfection of Wisdom) literature, 110, 189
Prajñopāyaviniścayasiddhi (Anaṅgavajrapāda), 247n29
Pratyutpannabuddha-saṃmukhāvasthita-samādhi-sūtra (Scripture of the Samādhi of Face-to-Face Confrontation with the Buddhas of the Present), 76–77, 78, 227nn38, 39, 228n51
primitive origin theory. See tribal origin theory
primordial origin narratives, 51–58; and Bachofen, 54–55, 57, 220n48, 221n64; dualism in, 51, 55–57; and social class, 52, 220nn47, 48; Tucci on, 51, 220n45; and valorization of primitive, 57–58. See also tribal origin theory
pure/impure dualism, 10, 121–122, 126, 130–131, 132, 152, 241n64, 244n85. See also dualistic esoteric Buddhism; nondual gnosis as goal of transgression

Rahula, Walpola, 260n35
Rāmāyana (Valmiki), 216n49
Ratnākaraśānti, 144
Rauravasūtrasaṃgraha, 94

revelation narratives. See traditional historiography
revulsion (jugupsa). See five ambrosias/five meats; transgression in Tantric Buddhism
rhetoric, 7, 8, 40, 69, 105–106, 212n15
Rhys Davids, T. W., 49, 108
ritual practice, 118–125; and arbitrary signifiers, 125, 241n63; eating/offering in, 120–121, 239–240nn47–52; host circle (gaṇa-cakra) ritual, 192, 193–195, 263n92; and Indian social strictures, 119–120, 238–239nn37–39, 43, 44; occluded intention in, 123–125, 240n58, 241n61; sādhana (self-creation) rite, 117–125, 185, 237–238nn32–6; scholarly neglect of, 126–127; and traditional esoteric Buddhist historiography, 95; and traditional Mahāyāna historiography, 77–78, 227–228nn48, 49, 50. See also caryāvrata
rituals of rebellion, 13, 188–191, 204
Robinson, Fred C., 61, 62, 222n86, 223n95
Robinson, Richard, 58, 221n68
Rodrigues, H., 31–32, 217n67
Romantic historiography, 57
Rousseau, Jean-Jacque, 44, 219n24
Ruegg, David Seyfort, 164, 252n68, 256n110

Śabareśvara, 174, 175, 179
Saddharmapuṇḍarīka Sūtra (Lotus Sūtra), 76, 226n36
sādhana (self-creation) rite, 117–125, 185, 237–238nn32–6
Said, Edward, 4, 211n7
Śaiva-Buddhist interactions, 31, 136–138, 154–155, 251n63; re-coding as essential element of, 257n129; Śaiva origin theory of Tantric Buddhism, 22–23, 30–31, 154–155, 251nn63–66, 252n68. See also caryāvrata in Śaiva tradition

Śaivism: dualistic, 147–148, 156, 157, 158, 159, 248n40; social context of, 175, 180–181, 187, 260n43; traditional historiography, 93–94, 96–97. *See also* Śaiva-Buddhist interactions

Śāktism, 20, 28–29, 46

Śākyamuni Buddha: and decline narratives, 45; mediated forms of, 72. *See also* historical buddhas; Śākyamuni Buddha as source of scripture

Śākyamuni Buddha as source of scripture: after-death teaching, 228n53; decentering of, 75–76, 81–82, 226nn33, 35, 229n63; and enlightenment of Śākyamuni, 81–82, 229n63; as limited in time, 71–72; scholarly approaches to, 72, 225n21; in Tantric Buddhism, 68, 224n2; in traditional esoteric Buddhist historiography, 79–80, 86, 228n53; in traditional Tibetan historiography, 88–89, 231n88. *See also* heavenly/other-worldly revelation narratives

Samādhi of Face-to-Face Confrontation with the Buddhas of the Present (Pratyutpannabuddha-saṃmukhāvasthita-samādhi-sūtra), 76–77, 78, 227nn38, 39, 228n51

samāpatti, 150

sāmārthya, 150

samaya. *See* pledge substances

Saṃkṣiptapratiṣṭhāvidhi Tantra (Concise Consecration Ritual Tantra), 78, 228n50

Saṃpuṭodbhava Tantra, 1–2, 138, 145–146, 247–248n34

Samuel, Geoffrey, 18, 22, 25

Saṃvarodaya Tantra, 134, 138, 185

Saṃvartasmṛti, 253n85

Saṃyutta Nikāya, 73

Sanderson, Alexis, 23, 26, 31, 94, 154, 158, 163, 164, 175, 180–181, 187, 192, 196, 222–223n94, 229n67, 247n27, 251nn64–66, 252n67, 253–254n86, 255n96, 256n111, 257nn123, 129

Sankrityayan, Rahul, 179

Śāntideva, 135

Saraha, 250n58

Sarvabuddhasamāyoga (Union of All Buddhas), 184

Sarvadurgatipariśodhana Tantra, 83

Sarvatathāgatatattvasaṃgraha (STTS), 82, 91, 92, 179

Sautrāntika, 226n26

scholarly approaches to Tantric Buddhism: actual observance question, 193–195, 198–199, 263–264n94, 110, 265n118; context issues, 2–3; critical self-consciousness, 8–9, 212nn18, 19; isogesis, 8, 212n17; literal vs. figurative interpretations, 106–112, 126, 131–132, 236–237nn5, 11, 16, 18–20, 23, 24, 243n82; projecting into the past, 215n36; and rhetoric, 7, 8, 40, 69, 212n15. *See also* historiography; scholarly distortions; semiology; structural analysis

scholarly distortions: and *caryāvrata*, 134–135, 168, 244–245nn4, 7; and evidence, 102, 235n152; and ideology, 66–67, 219n16; and origin theories, 35–36; semiological errors, 26–30, 216nn49, 51, 57, 217n59; solipsism, 4–5, 30, 101, 211n7, 21760

Scripture Collecting the Intention (Mdo dgongs 'dus), 90, 232nn96, 97

Scythian origin theory, 30, 217n61

self-creation (*sādhana*) rite, 117–125, 185, 237–238nn32–6

semiology, 3, 6–7, 9, 101–102, 201, 211nn4, 5; as evidence-based, 205–206; on historiography, 130, 243n77; and rhetoric, 7, 105–106, 212n15. *See also* connotative semiotics; structural analysis

sequestered scriptures: in traditional Chinese Buddhist historiography, 92, 233nn108, 110, 112; in traditional esoteric Buddhist historiography,

79, 83, 86, 92, 96; in traditional
Mahāyāna historiography, 77, 227n44;
in traditional Śaiva historiography, 94;
in traditional Tibetan historiography,
89–90, 91, 233nn101, 102
sexual behavior: in caryāvrata, 140, 160,
161, 162–163, 246nn18, 20, 247n29;
and decline narratives, 47–48, 49–50,
220n36; and degenerate monks origin
theory, 24; and monasticism, 179
Sferra, Francesco, 252n68
Shamsher Manuscript, 88, 174, 179–180,
231nn85, 87
Sharma, R. S., 27, 222n89
Sharpe, Eric, 32
Shastri, H. P., 217n61
Shaw, Miranda, 22, 50
Shingon Buddhism, 93
Shklovsky, Victor, 69
siddha esoterism, 171, 172
Siddhayogeśvarīmata, 159, 248n40,
255nn90, 95
Śikṣāmuccaya (Śāntideva), 135, 227n44
Silk, Jonathan, 61
Śiva Sūtra, 93–95
Skilling, Peter, 73, 95, 186, 203, 225n23
skulls (kapāla), 140, 158. See also funereal
imagery
Smith, J. Z., 224n7
Snellgrove, David, 18, 22, 108–109, 193,
224n1, 246n20, 263n94
social context of Tantric Buddhism,
170–199; monasticism, 177–181, 203,
204, 259nn24, 27, 260nn31–33, 35, 37;
patronage, 191–192; professionalism,
181–184, 261nn52, 53; subgroup theory,
171–172; temporary marginality, 173–
175, 187–188, 258nn6, 9; transgression
as reinforcement of mainstream, 188–
192, 204, 263nn81–83; transgressive-
nontransgressive cultural continuities,
172–173, 184–187, 202. See also actual
observance question
Spiro, M., 260n45

Śrautasūtras, 215n42
Śrāvaka Buddhism: and decline
narratives, 45; historiography,
71–74, 225–226nn20, 21, 25, 28; and
Mahāyāna Buddhism, 202–203;
transgression in, 112, 236n20
Śrīcakrasaṃvarapañjikā Śūramanojñā
(Bhavyakīrti), 232n90
Śrīdharānanda, Sādhuputrapaṇḍita, 87
Srinivasan, Doris, 214n23
Stories of the Eighty-four Siddhas
(Abhayadatta), 175, 259n14
Strickmann, Michel, 212n21, 222n86,
233n110
structural analysis, 6–9, 101–102,
200–202; and connotative semiotics,
113–116, 243n77; and narrative
historiography, 37–42, 66–67; and
social context of Tantric Buddhism,
198; and traditional historiography,
95–96. See also semiology
Subhāṣitasaṃgraha, 120
Śūraṃgamasamādhi Scripture, 76
Susiddhikara, 177–178
Sūtra-melāpaka (Nāgārjuna), 237n32
svādhidaivatāyoga, 184, 262n63
Szántó, Péter-Dániel, 250n54, 251n64

Tanemura, Ryugen, 154–155, 162, 245n11,
245n13, 249–250n48, 251n66
Tantrasadbhāva, 159, 165–166, 257n120
Tantric Age, 155, 252n69
Tantric Buddhism, defined, 9–10
Tathāgatarakṣita, 245n12
Tatz, Mark, 231n85, 259n14
Taussig, Michael, 212n18
terms of art, 134, 136, 137, 159, 244nn2, 4,
245nn12, 13, 255n95
Theravāda Buddhism: and decline
narratives, 45; transgression in, 112,
236n20
Theravāda canon, 73, 225n22
Thomas, Edward J., 20, 220n36
Thurman, Robert, 110

Tibetan Buddhism: *caryāvrata* in, 148, 149, 249–250nn46–48; sudden-gradual debate in, 263n90; traditional historiography, 88–91, 231n88, 232nn90, 92, 93, 96, 97, 233nn, 101, 102, 119
traditional esoteric Buddhist historiography, 79–95; *Amoghapāśa Mahākalparāja*, 79–80; *Catuṣpīṭha*, 83–84, 86, 87, 98; *Chanting the Names of Mañjuśrī*, 80, 87, 228n59; Chinese, 91–93, 233nn103, 104, 108, 110, 112; and classical history, 99–101; and consensus building, 97–98, 99, 235n141; *Gaṇapatihṛdaya*, 79; Japanese, 93; *Kālacakra Tantra*, 86–87, 231n82; *Mahāsītavatī Dhāraṇī*, 80; *Mahāvairocana Tantra*, 81, 229n63; *Prajñāpāramitānayapañcaśatikā*, 84–86, 229nn69, 70, 72, 230nn76, 77; and primordial nature of truth, 96–97, 98, 99, 234n131; redaction process in, 83–84, 86–87, 98–99; revelation types in, 79, 95–96, 228n53; and ritual practice, 95; *Sarvadurgatipariśodhana Tantra*, 83; *Sarvatathāgatatattvasaṃgraha*, 82; Shamsher Manuscript, 88, 231nn85, 87; Tibetan, 88–91, 231n88, 232nn90, 92, 93, 96, 97, 233nn, 101, 102, 119; and traditional Śaiva historiography, 93–94, 96–97; *vajravidāraṇī*, 81
traditional historiography, 68–74; importance of, 69, 224nn7, 8, 225n13; recent attention to, 225n12; scholarly neglect of, 68, 70, 224n1; sources for, 71, 225n15; Śrāvaka Buddhist, 71–74, 225–226nn20, 21, 25, 28. *See also* Śākyamuni Buddha as source of scripture; traditional esoteric Buddhist historiography; traditional Mahāyāna historiography
traditional Mahāyāna historiography, 74–79; and Abhidharma, 226n32, 228n51; cosmic/multiple buddhas in, 76, 77, 78, 226nn35, 36, 227–228nn38, 49; decentering of Śākyamuni Buddha

in, 75–76, 226nn33, 35; influence on Tantric Buddhist historiography, 71, 225n16; objections to, 228n51; and ritual practice, 77–78, 227–228nn48, 49, 50; and scriptural efflorescence, 74–75, 226n31; sequestered scriptures in, 77, 227n44
transgression in Tantric Buddhism, 10, 105–132; and arbitrary signifiers, 125, 241n63; as bad speech (*durbhāṣita*), 128; and connotative semiotics, 106–107, 113–116, 237n29; and eating/offering, 120–121, 239–240nn47–52; as elite practice, 136, 152, 168, 201–202, 250n58, 258n30; as evidence of social opposition, 127, 242n69; and Indian social strictures, 119–120, 238–239nn38–40, 44, 45; intentional nature of, 120, 128, 144–145, 146–148, 246–247nn21–24; as interpretive quandary, 1–2, 6, 105, 201, 211n3; and knowledge of mainstream forms, 131, 175–177, 184, 204, 259n19; and later traditions, 145, 247n27; and lay authorship theory, 107, 236n5; literal vs. figurative interpretations, 106–112, 126, 131–132, 236–237nn5, 11, 16, 18–20, 23, 24, 243n82; and literary conventions, 126, 241n65; and occluded intention, 122–125, 240n58, 241n61; and origin theories, 20, 24, 35; and pure/impure dualism, 130–131, 132, 244n85; as reinforcement of mainstream, 188–192, 263nn81–83; *sādhana* (self-creation) rite, 117–125, 185, 237–238nn32–6; as sanction for deviant practices, 127, 242n68; semantic issues, 244n1; sources for, 106, 235–236nn3, 4; and terms of art, 134, 244n2. *See also caryāvrata*; nondual gnosis as goal of transgression; social context of Tantric Buddhism
Trayastriṃśa, 74, 75, 83, 226n28. *See also* heavenly/other-worldly revelation narratives

tribal origin theory, 24–30; and actual observance question, 196–197; and contemporary "primitive" cultures, 21–22, 24–25, 215n36; and Harappan civilization, 22, 24, 214n23, 215n34; and historiographical solipsism, 30, 217n60; and literal interpretation, 126; and nature/existence of tribes, 25, 215–216nn37, 39, 42, 45; and ritually impure women, 28–29; and Śāktism, 20, 28–29; and semiological errors, 27–30, 216nn49, 51, 57, 217n59; and temporary marginality, 173–175. See also primordial origin narratives
Tribe, Anthony, 109–110, 224n1
Trika tradition, 166, 167, 257n128
Tripiṭaka, 73
Triśaraṇa, 174, 258n6
triumph tropes, 50
Tsongkhapa, 249n47
Tsuda, Shinīchi, 53, 239n45
Tubb, Gary, 247–248n34
Tucci, Giuseppe, 51, 100, 220n45, 225n16, 231n85
Tuck, Andrew, 212n17
Tylor, Edward B., 220n48

Udānavarga, 112, 236n20. See also Dhammapada
Union of All Buddhas (Sarvabuddhasamāyoga), 184
upāsaka, 181–182, 260n45, 261n46
Urban, Hugh B., 212n18
urban legends, 194, 264n104
ūṣman, 150

Vaiśālīpraveśa, 186, 262n71
Vajradhara, 83–84, 117, 127–129
Vajrāralli Tantra, 138
Vajrasattva-sādhana (Candrakīrti), 237n32
vajravidāraṇī, 81
Vajrayāna (Adamantine Way), 247n27
Van Gulik, Robert H., 21
Vasubandhu, 150

Vātūlanāthasūtra, 94
Veda origin theory, 213n4
Veyne, Paul, 17, 99–100, 101, 205, 218n76, 224n11
Vico, Giambattista, 33, 44, 47
Vidyānanda, 94, 175
vidyāvrata, 136, 159, 160, 161–162, 255nn95, 100. See also caryāvrata
Vimalakīrtinirdeśasūtra, 226n35
Vimalaprabhā Commentary, 86–87, 243n82, 246n23
Viṇāśikha Tantra, 160, 255n96
viśuddhi (purity). See pure/impure dualism
Von Fürer-Haimendorf, C., 25, 215n36
von Glasenapp, H., 18
vratacaryā. See caryāvrata

Waddell, L. Austine, 220n38, 242n68
Walters, Jonathan, 225n20
Ward, William, 193, 195
Warder, A. K., 109, 224n1
Wayman, Alex, 23–24, 42, 219n16, 224n1, 233n117
Weber, Max, 220n42
White, David, 198, 260n43, 264n105
White, Hayden, 35, 38, 39–40, 41, 45, 66, 235n152
Williams, Paul, 224n1
Wilson, Horace Hayman, 22, 194–195
Wink, André, 63, 222n89
Wynne, Alexander, 225n21

Xuanzang, 119, 182

Yājñavalkyasmṛti, 155
Yoginīsaṃcāra Tantra, 138, 251n64
Yoginīsaṃcāratantranibandha (Tathāgatarakṣita), 245n12
yuganaddha (communion). See nondual gnosis

Zhao Qian, 92–93
Zimmer, Heinrich, 220n45

GPSR Authorized Representative: Easy Access System Europe, Mustamäe tee 50, 10621 Tallinn, Estonia, gpsr.requests@easproject.com

www.ingramcontent.com/pod-product-compliance
Lightning Source LLC
Chambersburg PA
CBHW071234290426
44108CB00013B/1413
* 9 7 8 0 2 3 1 1 6 2 4 1 8 *